THE DISASTER RECOVERY HANDBOOK

A Step-by-Step Plan to
Ensure Business Continuity
and Protect Vital Operations,
Facilities, and Assets

MICHAEL WALLACE and LAWRENCE WEBBER

AMACOM

American Management Association

New York | Atlanta | Brussels | Chicago | Mexico City | San Francisco
Shanghai | Tokyo | Toronto | Washington, D.C.

Special discounts on bulk quantities of AMACOM books are available to corporations, professional associations, and other organizations. For details, contact Special Sales Department, AMACOM, a division of American Management Association, 1601 Broadway, New York, NY 10019.
Tel.: 212-903-8316. Fax: 212-903-8083.
Web site: www.amacombooks.org

This publication is designed to provide accurate and authoritative information in regard to the subject matter covered. It is sold with the understanding that the publisher is not engaged in rendering legal, accounting, or other professional service. If legal advice or other expert assistance is required, the services of a competent professional person should be sought.

Library of Congress Cataloging-in-Publication Data

Wallace, Michael
The disaster recovery handbook : a step-by-step plan to ensure business
  continuity and protect vital operations, facilities, and assets /
  Michael Wallace and Lawrence Webber.
     p.   cm.
     Includes index.
     ISBN-10: 0-8144-7240-0
     ISBN-13: 978-0-8144-7240-8
1. Emergency management—Handbooks, manuals, etc.   2. Crisis
management—Handbooks, manuals, etc.   3. Computer security—Handbooks,
manuals, etc.   4. Data protection—Handbooks, manuals, etc.   5. Data
recovery (Computer science)—Planning—Handbooks, manuals, etc.   6.
Business planning—Handbooks, manuals, etc.   I. Webber, Lawrence, 1954–
II. Title.

  HD49.W36   2004
  658.4'77—dc22

                                                                2004003905

Printing number

10   9   8   7

DEDICATION/ACKNOWLEDGMENTS

Michael would like to dedicate this book to his lovely wife Tami, whose faith and support made this book possible. Michael would also like to make a dedication to his mentor and former teacher George Jenkins. George has been a great teacher and a good friend.

Our special thanks to John Hiatt, who helped us start this project, and to Marilyn Allen, who never gave up on us. Thanks to Christina McLaughlin who helped us to make this a better book.

Thanks also to Chuck Carlos, Mike James, Gregory Pinchbeck, Dan Holt, Tim McDaniel and Michael Noel for providing insight into disaster recovery planning from their unique points of view. Tim provided much of the material in Chapter 19—Health and Safety.

CONTENTS

PART 1 THE PLAN

This section shows you how to get started with the nuts and bolts
of developing your disaster recovery plan.

CHAPTER 1 Getting Started: Overview of the Project   3

Some companies live and breathe proper project planning and
the methodical construction of business processes. A team made
up of the right people using proper project management processes
will help ensure the success of your disaster recovery project.

CHAPTER 2 Risk Assessment: Understanding What Can Go Wrong   29

A risk assessment is the key to your disaster plan. It identifies
what risks you need to address. It breaks your risks into five
layers ranging from natural disasters down to a crisis at your desk.

CHAPTER 3 Build an Interim Plan: Don't Just Sit There, Do Something   69

Some projects are like a bad lunch—they never seem to go away.
What can I do until the plan is completed? This chapter identifies
actions that you can do *today* to assemble a useful interim plan
to provide some initial protection. Everything you do here is
needed in the final document. If you read no other chapter, at
least read this one.

In the event of a disaster, there must be a single place where
people can call to report problems and find out what is going on.
We will describe the sort of things required in an emergency
operations center (sometimes called a "war room"), and how it
might run.

Here is where we lay a bit more groundwork for the plan. We
establish a standard format for the documents and explain what
needs to be included—and excluded—from a plan.

A plan is a wonderful thing but until it is tested and debugged,
it should not be relied upon. Testing can be formally done or can
be incorporated with other maintenance activities. In either case,
the results of using a plan should be recorded. Testing a plan is an
excellent way to familiarize your team with your plan and to gain
their ideas on improving it.

This section discusses the various assets most firms have to
protect and tells you what you need to know to make sure they're
covered in your disaster recovery plan.

It is hard to imagine work without electricity. We use it constantly at
home (if for nothing else but to keep the clocks on time). We use
it all day at work. We have all also experienced the effects of a power
outage. What should our workers be doing if the lights go out?

Few companies can quickly walk or drive to their customers' or
suppliers' sites. Telecommunications makes coordination between
companies quick and easy. It provides a medium for fax messages
and also provides the data communications lines. How long can
your company run without it?

CHAPTER 9 **Vital Records Recovery: Covering Your Assets**   **183**

There are many documents essential to your company's operations, such as invoices, checks, software licenses, receipts, and on and on. Some of these documents you must safeguard to meet legal and regulatory requirements. What if, what if, what if . . .

CHAPTER 10 **Data: Your Most Irreplaceable Asset**   **211**

Data is one asset that cannot be easily replaced. No one else has the same data you do. What are the unique issues encountered when planning for data processing recovery?

CHAPTER 11 **Networks: The Ties That Bind**   **223**

Years ago, we used overnight batch programs to generate mounds of paper. Today we view our data in real time. We check inventory levels, the status of customer orders and many things we take for granted. This is all made possible by a very complex system called a data network. Lose this and it's back to piles of last night's reports for answers!

CHAPTER 12 **End-User PCs: The Weakest Link**   **237**

The personal in personal computers means that many people can develop tools to make their job easier. Along with these tools is data. Lots of company data. If it is useful, then it needs to be backed up. PCs are also a source of virus attacks on your company.

CHAPTER 13 **Customers: Other People to Worry About**   **251**

Customers have their own problems. In a time of lean inventories, they cannot tolerate a very long delay in getting their materials or their own efforts will enter a crisis. So if they hear that you have had a disaster, might they shift their orders to someone else? This is even more of a problem if the fire was in your offices and you have a warehouse full of goods that need to be sold.

CHAPTER 14 **Suppliers: Collateral Damage**   **259**

Suppliers extend credit to you in the form of goods. Their terms may be 30, 45 or 60 days. If they hear of a disaster, they may fear that your company will become insolvent and cease all shipments to you. They need to know the facts. You need to tell all of them.

Few of us question the importance of having insurance, yet too often businesses fail to consider a *Business Continuity Plan* as invaluable protection against disasters.

If you have delayed starting your business continuity plan because you think it will be too complicated, too costly, or too time consuming—or because you simply aren't sure where to begin, *The Disaster Recovery Handbook* will provide the resources you need to get your plan up and running. Everyone, regardless of experience, can benefit from the authors' insights and common sense tips in creating and updating viable business continuity plans.

Down to earth, easy to read, and wonderfully (even surprisingly) interesting, this comprehensive "how-to" manual guides you step by step. The authors' sequential and logical approach takes what can be a daunting challenge and breaks it down into manageable pieces.

Michael Wallace and Lawrence Webber's combined expertise pulses from the pages, as their relevant, real-life examples clarify the subject matter and bring home the topics to us. As you progress through the book, you'll find your questions have already been anticipated and answered. Loaded with examples, references, statistics, and guidelines, the text addresses every detail.

Through our business, Fireproof Records Center, which specializes in information management, business continuity and disaster recovery, we have had the good fortune to have met and worked with Michael Wallace. He has been a keynote speaker at numerous seminars we sponsor, and we refer clients to him on a regular basis. We asked Michael what prompted his collaborative work with Lawrence Webber. He told us their search for reference material turned up significant information aimed primarily at people working in information technology—but nothing that covered *all of the business processes for small and medium sized companies.* So they joined forces to fill that need by sharing knowledge and insight gained from their unique and considerable experiences.

At Fireproof, we think companies can never be too prepared—especially when it comes to business continuity. We are pleased that such a valuable tool has been developed by these highly qualified authors. If you can add but one reference to your corporate library, it should be this handbook.

Michael James
CEO
Fireproof Records Center

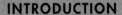

INTRODUCTION

THE DISASTER RECOVERY HANDBOOK: *A Step-by-Step Plan to Ensure Business Continuity and Protect Vital Operations, Facilities, and Assets,* is designed to provide proven processes and techniques to help you develop a disaster recovery plan to protect your business in the event of a disaster. A disaster can mean anything from the loss of a critical machine to a natural disaster destroying your entire facility. Anything that can cause a disruption in the normal operation of your business can be a disaster. Without careful planning, most organizations do not survive a major interruption in the operation of their business.

Business Continuity Plans are really nothing new to your life. They are grounded on basic actions you take on a daily basis. In fact, these actions are considered so normal that you probably don't even think about why you do them. These actions fall into three general classes: mitigation, avoidance, and transference.

> **MITIGATION** is something you do to reduce the likelihood of occurrence or the amount of damage caused by an event that you could not avoid.

> **AVOIDANCE** is something you do to steer clear of an event.

> **TRANSFERENCE** is to shift your risk of an uncontrolled event to a third party.

For example, if you owned a grocery store, you could mitigate the slowdown in business due to a snowstorm by buying your own snowplow to clear your parking lot. You avoid all damage from a snowstorm by moving your business to the Bahamas. You can transfer the risk of financial loss from your roof collapsing from too much snow by purchasing insurance.

You practice risk avoidance, mitigation, and transference in your daily life. For example, take the car you drive. It has a spare tire and a car jack in it to mitigate the amount of time lost and cost due to a flat tire. Instead of the expense and time involved in calling a tow truck, you can change the tire yourself and return to the road for a drive to the repair shop. If you did not believe there was a possibility of a flat tire, you would have long ago removed the spare and jack from your car to save weight and get better gas mileage. Therefore, you believe that you cannot avoid a flat tire, but have devised a way to reduce its inconvenience.

Throughout this book, we will frequently use the term Business Continuity Planning. In recent years, variations on this theme have included Business Recovery Planning and Disaster Recovery Planning. Strictly speaking, in the recovery business jargon, we will be detailing a Business Continuity Plan because it will handle any disruption to the normal operation of your business. We occasionally use the term *disaster* because, in data processing or business recovery planning, it is the more common term. We also use it because our plan will encompass everything from large natural events to smaller day-to-day inconveniences. The terms we will use and their meanings include these:

➤ **Disaster Recovery Planning (DRP).** The actions you would take to recover from a disaster. Includes the planning steps to avoid risks, to mitigate them, or to shift the risk to someone else through insurance or other means. DRP is applicable to all aspects of a business but usually used in the context of data processing operations.

➤ **Business Recovery Planning (BRP).** Takes Disaster Recovery Planning one step further and includes efforts by the rest of the company's operations including customer and supplier relations to recover from the problem.

➤ **Business Continuity Planning (BCP).** These are plans that allow your business to function at possibly a reduced level during and immediately after an emergency.

The goal of this book is to show you a systematic approach to analyzing your business situation and building written procedures for avoiding problems or reducing the damage should they occur. These concepts apply equally to offices, factories, hospitals, hotels, transportation companies, and even your home. As we progress, you will see how in many areas you already practice disaster planning but never tied it all together into one big picture.

Many firms have what we call the "resident expert." This is the person everyone turns to when problems occur. Usually through sheer longevity in their current position, this person has amassed a wealth of information (but poorly documented) on how things really work. A good start to a business recovery plan is to simply document what this person has in their head and in notes scattered within their files.

A common misconception of disaster planning is that we are out to build a know-all book of what to do when the great flood hits again. That is not our goal. Your final disaster plan will consist of a series of smaller plans to address specific issues (such as a loss of cooling in your telephone switch room). Additionally, there will be a section on natural hazards and how they will be dealt with. Some of these specific plans may only be a few pages. In the telephone room air conditioning example, we are not going to write a manual on repairing cooling systems. The plan should explain what to check before calling the technician and actions you might take to cool the room until the technician arrives. The plan documents who the contracted technician is, how to contact them, what sort of service agreement you have with them, etc.

DO I REALLY NEED TO DO THIS?

Disasters happen much more often than people realize. The big things that end up on the evening news are not frequent, but there are a multitude of smaller disasters that can do just as much damage. Things like computers failing, water leaking on paper files, a labor problem causing equipment to mysteriously malfunction, etc. It not a question of *if* something will happen, but *when* it will happen. Unless you can answer yes to all the following questions, you need this manual to help you develop your plan to survive a disaster:

1. Do you know how long your Uninterruptible Power Supply (UPS) will power your equipment if the electrical grid fails? Do you know which equipment can be shut down first?

2. Do you know where you can get critical supplies if your primary supplier has a problem?

3. Do you know the location of all your software licenses?

4. Do you have a plan to contact customers to make sure they don't immediately go to competitors if they hear you've had a disaster?

5. Have you tested your backups to ensure you can restore critical data? What about any custom applications? Is your backup software up to date?

6. Do our employees know who to call if they see on the news that your building had a fire?

7. Do you know what to do if a backhoe cuts your telecommunications cables?

8. Is your virus protection up to date?

9. Can you name the location of your warranty information, registration codes, and CD keys for all your hardware and software?

10. Do you have a plan for using alternative equipment until you can restore or replace your production equipment?

These issues and more are covered in this manual. Although you can't always prevent a disaster, you can have a plan in place to ensure that it doesn't put you out of business.

According to several recent surveys, almost 50% of all businesses that suffer from a disaster and do not have a disaster recovery plan in place never reopen for business.

WHAT THIS MANUAL WILL DO FOR YOU

No two organizations are alike, but many share some basic elements such as facilities, important documents, computer systems, and personnel. This manual defines the common threads that link all business operations, providing for a variety of situations—not as a "one size fits all" model, but instead as an updated guide and decision-making reference that can help you devise a disaster recovery program tailored to the needs of your organization.

The Health Insurance Portability and Accountability Act of 1996 requires any organization that processes health record information to have a documented disaster recovery plan. This includes hospitals, nursing homes, medical centers, doctor's offices, pharmacies, and medical laboratories.

ORGANIZED FOR QUICK ACCESS

For fingertip access to the information you need on disaster recovery planning, this ready-reference desk-side manual is organized to help you find what you need quickly and easily. You or your staff can use the book itself as a model or a template to create similar documents for your own organization.

The book consists of three major parts. Part 1: The Plan, details the steps you need to take to develop your plan; Part 2: The Assets, describes the various assets that drive your business and the steps you should take to protect them; Part 3: Preventing Disaster, gives you the information you need to help mitigate threats to your organization.

"Simplicity is the ultimate design." Often, a dearth of forms is included in disaster recovery handbooks, but this manual provides a multitude of forms that can jump-start your disaster recovery planning process. All the forms discussed in the book are included on the CD-ROM, so that you can quickly and easily put them to use. As an operation grows in complexity, the challenge to keep it running smoothly grows, and thus the need for a formal system of operations becomes a necessity. A disaster recovery plan can greatly improve your understanding of how the organization really works. Organizations that have a formal disaster recovery manual in place are noticeably more efficient.

To build our plan, we will repeatedly ask the following questions:

➤ What are my critical assets?

➤ What are the risks to these assets?

➤ How can I reduce the likelihood of a threat occurring?

➤ How can I minimize the damage if it is unavoidable?

➤ What does the team do when it happens?

➤ Where can I find information on this to develop my plan?

ADDED STRATEGIC VALUE

The real benefit of a Business Continuity Plan is how it forces you to look at the weaknesses in your business tools and processes and to strengthen them before a tragedy occurs. The analysis required in developing your plan will help you to better understand your business, and it almost invariably uncovers inefficient or unnecessary activities within the organization. A well-designed plan can also increase your competitive edge as part of the overall value chain. Many companies have reduced their in-house inventories and therefore require reliable suppliers to keep their own operations running. The more reliable your operation is, the higher your delivery credibility will be. This may be a distinct advantage over your competition; or they may already be at that level and you need to raise your delivery credibility just to stay in business. (This implies you should also check out the Business Continuity Plans of your key suppliers—especially if they deliver to you "just-in-time").

The Disaster Recovery Handbook: A Step-by-Step Plan to Ensure Business Continuity and Protect Vital Operations, Facilities, and Assets is a compilation of disaster recovery processes—the best practices within the industry—in current use. This manual is a process development tool that any seasoned business manager, working in a large or small organization, will find useful.

SAVING YOU TIME

To make the manual even more valuable, a CD-ROM is included, containing the manual's forms and text. Use the included forms as a starting point for developing your own, by importing it into a word processor on a PC. Of course, you can also make needed changes and post the forms on a local area network or even on a company intranet site.

In addition to this book, there is a wide range of help available for building your plan. Help is available from local and federal governments, from emergency agencies, from trade organizations, and on and on. Appendix A will give you a start in finding resources in your area.

Whatever format you use to publish your plan, a well-designed disaster recovery plan will help ensure that your business is prepared to deal with whatever may happen in the uncertain world in which we live.

Out of the blue? We all shared in the tragedy of New York City on September 11, 2001. Yet while many dedicated rescue workers were struggling to save those people that they could, the Business Continuity Plans for the companies affected immediately kicked into high gear. The disaster not only involved the World Trade Center, but many of the surrounding office buildings were also severely damaged. Traffic to that part of the city was cut off. Even if your business was several blocks away, the confusion and rushing of rescue equipment severely interrupted your workflow.

Were you affected by this attack? Would your company have survived if it was in one of these buildings?

PART ONE
THE PLAN

CHAPTER 1

GETTING STARTED
Overview of the Project

Nothing is impossible for the man
who doesn't have to do it himself.
—A.H. Weiler

INTRODUCTION

Building a business continuity plan is much like any other business project. A formal project management process is necessary to coordinate the various players and company disciplines required to successfully deliver the desired results of the project. This chapter is a review of the process you should follow to successfully build your project plan. It will give you a high-level roadmap of what you should expect as you prepare to lead a business continuity project. A sample project plan is included on the CD-ROM accompanying this book. Adapt this chapter and the project plan to fit your business goals, company timeline, and the scope of your project.

Most projects tend to run in a well-defined sequence. For example, to build a new house, first you clear the land, then build the foundation, then build a floor, etc. Many things cannot begin before the previous step has been completed. A business continuity plan project is a bit different; in its early stages most actions logically follow each other, but once the basic elements are in place, the project bursts out into parallel tracks as each department documents their own areas. How you proceed in your company is of course determined by your corporate culture, the resources you have to work with to complete the process, and the level of visible support from the project's sponsor. Most business continuity projects follow these steps:

1. An executive within the organization decides that a business continuity plan is needed. This might be due to an auditor's report or the result of a business disruption that was more painful than it would have been if a plan had been in place. Or it could be that an alert employee realized that a good plan did not exist and brought this to the executive's attention. This executive normally becomes the *sponsor* for the project.

2. The first (and most important step) that the sponsor takes is to select someone to lead the project. This person is most often called the *Contingency Planning Coordinator* and is responsible for the successful completion of the project.

3. The project sponsor and the Contingency Planning Coordinator meet to clearly define the scope of the project, the project timeline, and expectations. The Contingency Planning Coordinator must be comfortable that the resources available are adequate to meet all the objectives of the project.

4. The Contingency Planning Coordinator selects the team that will work together to complete the project. Both technical and political considerations are important in selecting a team that can successfully develop a workable business continuity plan.

5. The Contingency Planning Coordinator together with the team now develops the project plan to be used in managing the project. Tasks are identified and assigned, task durations calculated, and activities are sequenced as the project plans are developed.

6. The project plans are executed. The Contingency Planning Coordinator oversees the project as the plan unfolds; keeping everyone focused on completing their tasks, and ensuring that milestones are met and that important stakeholders are kept informed as to the project's progress. It is here where the actual continuity plans for the organization are created.

7. Once the business continuity plans have been developed and tested, the Contingency Planning Coordinator closes the project by making sure that everything was documented properly and handing the project results over to the individual(s) responsible for keeping the plan up to date. Each affected department will normally have someone responsible for keeping their portion of the plan current. A report is also generated for the sponsor recapping the project and documenting lessons learned.

In many organizations, the job of Business Continuity Plan Project Manager is not taken as seriously as it should be. Management in these organizations only wants you to write *something,* anything to make the auditors go away. That's OK because as you build the plan, and as they begin to see the benefits, their interest and support will grow. If your management wants you to build a superficial plan, then don't stop until you have at least finished Chapter 3. It won't take you very long, and they'll think you've written a super plan.

A project plan organizes the team to focus their skills on specific actions to get the job done. This respects their time and brings the project to a prompt but successful solution.

INITIATING THE PROJECT

Every project starts with a *sponsor.* A sponsor should be a person with enough organizational influence to give the project credibility, financing, and strategic direction. They should also be in a position to ensure the willing cooperation of other departments and to ensure that the project is adequately funded. Building a business continuity plan in many cases involves changing people's attitudes and some of their tried-and-true business processes. Business continuity planning is a logical step toward mistake-proofing a business. So, to suppress the reluctance to change or even participate in the project, it is important for the sponsor to be of sufficient stature as to overcome objections before they are raised.

Ideally, the sponsor is the company's CEO, or the Vice President in charge of the local facility. However, sometimes it is a department manager who realizes that something must be done. Whoever assumes this role, they must remain involved with the project throughout its lifetime. *As the sponsor's interest fades, so will the interest of your team.* Find out why they want to sponsor the project. It will tell you how much support to expect.

In some cases, the sponsor honestly believes the project is a good idea and is personally interested in seeing it is completed. In other cases, they were required to start this project due to an auditor's citation of a poor business practice. In this situation, they may only want the minimum recovery plan to satisfy the audit citation. Spend some time early in the project digging out what is motivating them to support this project. By understanding what motivates the sponsor, you can gauge how much time and money will be available to you. It is also possible for you to educate the sponsor on the many advantages in having a well-written company-wide plan.

The sponsor's first task is the selection of the Project Manager, usually called the *Contingency Planning Coordinator.* In most companies, the cynics say that if you raised the issue, then the job is yours! This isn't a bad way to assign projects because only the people who believe in something would raise the issues. Still, the selection of the right Contingency Planning Coordinator will help make this project a success and the wrong one will make success much more difficult to attain.

The sponsor has the additional duties of approving the plan's objectives, scope, and assumptions. The sponsor must also obtain approval for funding.

THE CONTINGENCY PLANNING COORDINATOR

The selection of the person to spearhead this project is the single most important part of building a plan. The Contingency Planning Coordinator should be someone who can gain the willing cooperation of the team members and their supervisors. To help ensure the support of everyone in the organization, the Contingency Planning Coordinator should be publicly assigned to this task with the sponsor's unqualified support. This is essential to overcome internal politics and to let everyone know that their assistance is important and required. As the project moves forward, regular public displays of support are required if the project is to result in a complete and usable plan. Form 1-1 on the CD-ROM is an example letter appointing the Contingency Planning Coordinator.

Some sponsors begin a business continuity project by hiring an outside consultant to build the plan. This can be a good way to get the project started and to mentor someone in the organization to assume the Contingency Planning Coordinator position. Generally speaking, it takes more effort and expertise to organize and develop the plan than it does to administer it. As the plan is built, the consultant can teach the Contingency Planning Coordinator the ropes.

Understand that even though the consultant is guiding the project, the consultant should not assume the role of Contingency Planning Coordinator. Every company, every facility, every computer site is unique. The actions necessary to promptly restore service are the result of the key people at each site writing down what to do and how to do it. Outside consultants can provide considerable insight into the basic services (electrical, telephone, water, data processing) but lack in-depth experience at your company. They don't know your business processes. They don't understand the pulse of your business and what its key elements are.

Building a solid plan will take a lot of time. An experienced consultant working with an internal Contingency Planning Coordinator can help move the project along quicker. The Contingency Planning Coordinator is also the logical candidate to become the plan's ongoing administrator once the initial project is completed. This person will be responsible for keeping the plan relevant and current. Writing a plan and then filing it away is a waste of money. Whoever builds the plan will be intimately familiar with it. They can easily continue responsibility for maintaining it and teaching others how to keep their portion of it current. Using an outside consultant as a Contingency Planning Coordinator raises the possibility that no one has internal ownership to ensure it is updated and tested periodically. The plan must be kept up to date if it is to be useful when it is needed most.

As the plan administrator, the Contingency Planning Coordinator will ensure that as new equipment enters the building, as new products are rolled out, as new business processes are implemented, they are reflected in the Business Continuity Plan. The Contingency Planning Coordinator also schedules and evaluates the ongoing testing of the plan by department, or by a specific threat, such as the loss of electrical power, to ensure it works. Once the plan is written, the Contingency Planning Coordinator's role will evolve into ensuring the plan is an integral part of the company's ongoing operations. No new company process or piece of equipment should begin operation until the mitigation and recovery plans have been tested and approved.

SCOPE OF THE PROJECT

One of the first tasks the Contingency Planning Coordinator must perform is to come to an agreement with the project sponsor as to the scope of the project. The scope of the project defines its boundaries. It identifies what is included in the project and what is not. If the project is too vast, it will probably fail. If it is too small, then it would be best assigned to a single person like any other office detail. The scope of the project must be given a lot of thought. If in doubt, start with a narrow focus on a specific department or function to demonstrate the plan's value and build up from there. One guideline suggested is any event that would cost (in lost wages, sales, etc.) more than 5% of your quarterly revenues merits its own plan. So if a temporary outage of a critical machine stops the entire factory, then it needs a plan. If the same machine stoppage means that three extra workers must drill holes with hand tools until the machine is repaired, then it probably does not need a plan.

A good way to approach the plan is to address areas that everyone uses, such as security, data processing, electrical, etc. Don't try to tackle too much, too fast. Start with building services, then security and safety, then data processing, etc. In this way, if the project is killed, you still have some useful documents.

If your recovery plans will encompass many sites, or a large complex, then start with a pilot project for a single building, a business function, or even for your Data Processing department. This will build your team's expertise and confidence, resulting in a very useful document, and demonstrate real value to top management. The scope of the project will drive the resource requirements for the project in terms of how many people it will involve, how long it will take, and the budget required to complete it.

The project scope must be a written statement. Here are three examples with gradually narrowing requirements. As you read these scope statements, imagine what sort of implied tasks these statements carry (or as they say, "The devil is in the details!"). Follow up on the scope statement by clarifying the timelines, criteria for success, and overall expectations for this project. Otherwise, you would be digging up information and writing forever.

Example #1

If you were in a factory's Data Processing department, your scope statement might be:

"Develop, implement and provide ongoing testing for a Business Continuity Plan for the factory's automated systems to include the computer rooms, the internal and external telephone system, the shop floor control systems, and data connections to both internal and external sites. This plan will provide specific action steps to be taken up to and including emergency replacement of the entire computer and telecommunications rooms."

Note that this statement does not include the factory machines (drill presses, mills, conveyors, etc.) or the front offices. It is focused on the telephone system and the internal data processing processes.

Example #2

If you were the Director for Building Security, your scope might be:

"Write an emergency contingency plan to address the possibility of fire, personal injury, toxic material spill, and structural collapse. Include escalation procedures, emergency telephone numbers, employee education, and specific emergency actions. Make recommendations concerning potential mitigation actions to take before a disaster strikes. Ensure the plan conforms to all legal, regulatory, and insurance requirements."

The project scope described in this statement does not include flood controls, security actions, etc. Although some security tasks may be implied, very little is called for.

Example #3

An even narrower approach might be:

"Document all the payroll procedures and recovery processes to ensure that paychecks are always on time and that the automated vacation balance tracking system is available even during an electrical outage."

Note that this scope statement does not include time clocks, exception reporting, or interfaces with your accounting system.

Most people do not have any idea of what a disaster plan would look like. They imagine some large book just sitting on the shelf. In this situation, you could demonstrate the usefulness of the plan by building it a piece at a time. You might build the part that covers the core utilities for a facility (electricity, gas, telecommunications, water, and heating and air conditioning). As you review with the sponsor how these essential services will be recovered after a disaster, the sponsor will begin to see the usefulness of your work. If your company has multiple sites, it might work better for you to build the plan one site at a time.

Timelines, Major Milestones, and Expectations

The output of a scope statement is to build a list of goals for the project. These are specific results against which the success of the project will be judged. Detail any expectations as to a completion date or major milestone dates. If this project is in response to an internal audit item, then the due date might be when the auditor is scheduled to return. If the Board of Directors required this to be done, then progress reports might be due at every directors meeting. Ensure all key dates are identified and explain why they were selected.

The term "expectations" can also be described as the criteria for success. Be clear in what you are asking for. A business continuity plan should only include critical processes. A critical process is usually defined as a process whose interruption would cause a material financial and operational impact over some period of time that you define (5% or greater of quarterly revenues is standard). You can't plan for what to do down to the front door being stuck open. That level of detail would be too difficult to maintain. Focus on the critical business functions and the processes that support them. Your long-run goal is that the business continuity planning process will become an integral part of how business will be conducted in the future.

Example criteria for success:

➤ Every department's continuity plan must provide for employee and visitor safety by detailing to them any dangers associated with this device or type of technology.

➤ Each department's continuity plan must be understandable to anyone familiar with that type of equipment or technology.

➤ A business continuity plan will be submitted for every critical piece of equipment or critical process in the facility.

➤ At the end of the project, the Contingency Planning Coordinator will submit a list of known weaknesses in our processes or equipment along with long-term recommendations to address them.

➤ All continuity plans will be tested by someone other than the plan's author and certified by the department manager as suitable for the purpose.

➤ This project shall commence on June 1 and be completed by December 31. By that time, all plans must be complete, tested and approved by the department managers.

In terms of a timeline, the length of your project will depend on how supportive the team members are of this effort, how complex your operations are, and how detailed your plan must be. Generally, these projects have an initiation phase and then the various departments break off and work in parallel to write their respective plans. During this phase, they also perform initial testing of the plan. At the end, all the plans are compared and modified so to avoid duplicate mitigation actions and to ensure one person's mitigation step doesn't cause problems for someone else. The capstone event is the system-wide disaster test.

As a general guideline, most plans can be completed in about 6 months, depending on the project's scope, the degree of management support, the number of locations to be included in the plan, and the amount of resources available. One month is spent on the start-up administration and training. About 3 months are needed to draft and test the departmental plans. Be sure to stay on top of these people so they don't forget about their plans! The final synchronization and testing should take an additional 2 months. However, as your team members are probably assigned to this project part time, their level of participation will vary according to their availability. The Contingency Planning Coordinator must be flexible but, in the end, is responsible for driving the project to its completion.

ADEQUATE FUNDING

One of the indicators of the seriousness of a project is the presence of a separate budget item to support its activities. It is the Contingency Planning Coordinator's responsibility to track the funds spent on the project and to demonstrate the benefit they provided. If a separate budget is not available, then clear guidelines on a spending ceiling for the project must be set.

Some of the items to include in the project budget are:

➤ The Contingency Planning Coordinator and key team members should attend formal business continuity planning training to obtain a thorough grounding in its principles. This speeds the project along and removes some of the guesswork of building a plan.

➤ You may need to pay a consultant to advise the project and mentor the Contingency Planning Coordinator as the plan is being developed.

➤ Sometimes the folks with the most knowledge about your processes are not available during normal working hours. For these people, you may need to schedule meetings on weekends or off-site to gain their full attention. This may incur overtime expense or the cost of a consultant to backfill the person while they work on the plan.

➤ Temporary help might be needed for administrative assistance, such as documenting the wiring of your data networks, transcribing notes for those without the time or inclination to type, conducting an asset inventory, etc.

➤ It is amazing what a few pastries brought into a meeting can do for attendance.

➤ It is a good practice to build a team spirit for the project to carry you over the rough times. This might be shirts, hats, special dinners, performance bonuses, and many other things to build team cohesion. Visible recognition helps to maintain the team's enthusiasm.

Visible Ongoing Support

If the goal of this project were to determine which employees deserved to have their pay doubled, you would be inundated with folks clamoring to join your team. Unfortunately, an assignment to a business continuity planning team may not be considered a high-profile assignment. This could discourage the enthusiastic support of the very people you need to make this project a success. To minimize this possibility, the visible, vocal, and ongoing support of the sponsor is very important.

Once the sponsor and the Contingency Planning Coordinator have agreed on the scope, the sponsor should issue a formal memo appointing the Contingency Planning Coordinator in a letter to the entire organization. This letter should inform all departments of the initiation of the project and who has been appointed to lead it. It should also describe the project's scope, its budget or budget guidelines, major milestones and timelines, and alert the other departments that they may be called upon to join the project and build their own recovery plans. This memo will detail who, what, where, when, why, and how the project will unfold. The closing paragraph should include a call for their assistance in ensuring the project will be a success.

SELECTING A TEAM

Once the sponsor and the coordinator have defined the scope of the project, the next step is to create a team. As you begin the project and start selecting your team, be ready for a chorus of resistance. Some departments will be indignant about being forced to join this project since they already have a plan (it's just no one can find it). Even if they have a plan, it does not mean that it is a good plan, or it may have interdependences with other areas and needs to be linked to other plans. Some will already have a plan being developed, but under scrutiny you see it has been under development for the last 10 years.

So with the naysayers in tow, prepare to select your team. In the case of existing, workable plans, ask that a liaison be appointed. For the plans under development, ask that you be able to enfranchise these hard-working people. As for any parsimonious financial people trying to kill your project's training request, ask the sponsor to override objections and allow the team to attend training on the latest business continuity best practices.

Identify the Stakeholders

As you form your team, take time to identify who the project's stakeholders are. A stakeholder is anyone who has a direct or indirect interest in the project. Most stakeholders just want to know what is going on with the project. Stakeholders need to be kept regularly informed on the project's progress or problems with which they need to assist.

For each stakeholder, identify what their goals and motivation are for this project. Based on this list, you will determine what to communicate to them, how often, and by which medium. Some stakeholders' interests are satisfied by a monthly recap report. Some will want to hear about every minor detail. Form 1-2 (see CD) is a Stakeholder Assessment Map. Use it to keep track of what the key stakeholders are after in this project so you do not lose sight of their goals. The strategy is an acknowledgment that you may need to apply some sort of specific attention to a particular person to keep them supporting this important project.

Form the Team

The size and makeup of your team depends on how you will roll out the project. In the very beginning, it is best to start with a small team. Always respect people's time. Don't bring anyone into the project before they are needed. The initial team lays the groundwork for the project by arranging for instructors, coordinating training on building disaster plans, helping to sharpen the focus of what each plan should contain, etc.

The core team should consist of the sponsor, the Contingency Planning Coordinator, an Assistant Contingency Planning Coordinator, and an administrative assistant. This group will prepare standards, training, and processes to make the project flow smoother.

Several other key people will eventually need to join the team. You may want to bring them in early or as they are needed. This may include people such as:

➤ **Building Maintenance or Facilities Manager.** They can answer what mitigation steps are already in place for the structure, fire suppression, electrical service, environmental controls, and other essential services.

➤ **Facility Safety and Security.** They should already have parts of a disaster plan in terms of fire, safety, limited building and room access, theft prevention, and a host of other issues. If they are adequate, this may save you from writing this part of the plan. Be sure to verify that these plans are up to date and of an acceptable quality.

➤ **Labor Union Representative.**

➤ **Human Resources.**

➤ **Line Management.**

➤ **Community Relations.**

➤ **Public Information Officer.**

➤ **Sales and Marketing.**

➤ **Finance and Purchasing.**

➤ **Legal.**

The next step is to make a few tool standardization decisions. The company's technical support staff usually makes these for you. Announce to the group what the standard word processing program, spreadsheet, and, most importantly, the project management software everyone will need on their workstations. Most people have the first two but few will have the project management software already loaded. Be sure that as people join the team, copies of the software are loaded onto their workstations and training is made available on how to use this tool.

You will get the best results by investing some time training the team on how to write their portion of the plan and providing administrative help if they have a lot of paperwork to write up (such as network wiring plans). Every person reacts differently to an unknown situation and being assigned to this team is no exception. If you will take the time to assemble a standard format for the plan and a process to follow to write it, then they will be a lot more comfortable being on the team.

A project of this type will generate a lot of paper. If possible, the accumulation of the various plans, wiring diagrams, manuals, etc. should be shifted from the Contingency Planning Coordinator to an administrative assistant. An administrative assistant will also free the Contingency Planning Coordinator from coordinating team meetings, tracking the project costs, etc. Although these tasks are clerical in nature, this person may also be the Assistant Contingency Planning Coordinator. Another value of appointing an Assistant Contingency Planning Coordinator is that it provides a contingency backup person in case something happens to the Contingency Planning Coordinator, as they will quickly learn about all aspects of the plan.

Once you are ready to roll out the project plan to the world, you will need to pull in representatives from the various departments involved. When tasking the department managers to assign someone, ensure they understand that they are still responsible for having a good plan so that they send the proper person to work on the team. This person need not know every aspect of their department, but they should understand its organization, its critical hardware and software tools, and its major workflows.

Depending on the project's scope, you might end up with someone from every department in the company. This would result in too many people to motivate and keep focused at one time. Break the project down into manageable units. Start with an area you are most familiar with or that needs the most work. Involving too many people in the beginning will result in chaos. Plan on inviting in departments as you begin to review their area. An example is fire safety. Although it touches all departments, it is primarily a Safety/Security department function.

Given all this, just what skills make someone a good team member? An essential skill is knowledge of their department's processes. This allows the team member to write from personal knowledge and experience instead of spending a lot of time researching every point in the plan. They should also know where to find the details about their department that they don't personally know. Another useful skill is experience with previous disasters. Even the normal problems that arise in business are useful in pointing out problem areas or documenting what has fixed a problem in the past. And of course, if they are to write a plan, they need good communications skills.

Department managers should appoint a representative to the business continuity planning project team by way of a formal announcement. However, the Contingency Planning Coordinator must approve all team members. If someone with unsuitable qualifications is sent to represent a department, they should be sent back to that manager with a request to appoint someone who is more knowledgeable about that department's processes. When rejecting someone from the team, be sure to inform your sponsor and the originating manager as to why that person is unsuitable.

The people on the initial project team are the logical ones to spread the good word of business continuity planning back to their departments. Time spent educating them on the continuity planning principles and benefits will pay off for the company in the long run. They can also learn more about the company by proofreading the plans submitted by the other departments. This has an additional benefit of broadening the company perspective of a number of employees. Use Forms 1-1 through 1-3 (see CD) to map out the responsibilities of each member of the team.

Rolling Out the Project to the Team

Team meetings are an opportunity to bring everyone together so they all hear the same thing at the same time. This is when you make announcements of general interest to everyone. It is also a good time to hear the problems that the team has been encountering and, if time permits, to solicit advice from the other team members on how to approach the issue. A properly managed meeting will keep the team members focused on the project and the project moving forward.

In the beginning, conduct a project rollout meeting with an overview of why this project is important and an explanation of what you are looking for. This is your most critical team-building meeting (you never get a second chance to make a good first impression). In most meetings, you will work to bring out from the people their thoughts and impressions on the project. But at the first meeting, be prepared to do most of the talking. Lay out the roles of each player and set their expectations about participation in the project. Information makes the situation less uncertain and the people can begin to relax. This is your first big chance to teach, cheerlead, and inspire your team! Sell your project to them!

Included on the CD is an overview of Business Recovery Planning written using Microsoft PowerPoint. It touches on the primary plan development activities of this book. Use it as a starting point for your own plan. Dates, contingencies, and departments covered all vary from place to place.

The team members should leave the meeting with a clear idea that this project is of manageable size—not a never-ending spiral of work. Use this meeting and every meeting to informally teach them a bit about business continuity planning.

As the project progresses, you will be surprised how hard it is to get business continuity information out of people. Some people are worried that others will use it to dabble with their systems. Some folks just don't know what they would do in a disaster and intend to ad lib when something happens, just like they always have. Have patience, ask leading questions, and get them to talk. When they have declared their plan complete (and you know it is only a partial plan), conduct a meeting with the team member, their manager, and the sponsor to review the plan. Step through it item by item. By the time that meeting is over, the team member will realize that they will be accountable for the quality of their plan.

PLANNING THE PROJECT

Refer to the sample plan included on the CD-ROM for ideas to include in your plan. Any plan that you use must be tailored to your site and management climate. Always keep your plan in a software tool like Microsoft Project. Such programs will recalculate the project's estimated completion date as you note which tasks are complete. It can also be used to identify overallocated resources.

OK, now it is time to build the project plan. This is best done with input from your team. There are four basic processes to building your plan: identifying the activities, estimating how long each task will take, deciding who should do what (or what skills this person should have), and then sequencing the tasks into a logical flow of work. The general term for this is a work breakdown schedule, which describes it quite nicely.

Identifying the Activities

What must be done? Your core project team can be a great help here by identifying the steps they see as necessary to complete this project. Although some tasks will logically seem to follow others, the focus here is to identify what needs to be done. How deeply you "slice and dice" each task is up to you. Unless it is a critical activity, you should rarely list any task that requires less than 8 hours of work (1 day). The times in the sample plan are calendar time, not how long the task will actually take. This is because your team members may only work on this project part time.

Write a brief paragraph about what each task involves. This will be very useful in estimating the time required to complete it. It also keeps the task's scope from spiraling out of control. You may understand what you mean for a task, but remember, someone else will probably execute the task, so an explanation will be very useful.

Always document your planning assumptions. When discussing the plan with others later, this explanation of what you were thinking at the time the plan was drafted will be very useful. By listing your assumptions, you can discuss them point by point with the team and your sponsor to avoid areas that the plan should not address and to identify why a specific course of action was followed.

Along with the assumptions, list all the known constraints for the project. This might be a specific due date to meet a business or legal obligation, it might be project funding issues, or even a limit on the number of people available to be on the team. A major benefit of listing your project constraints is that upon examination they may be less than you think or can be used to prevent the scope of the project from expanding.

Determining Activity Durations

Once the tasks are laid out, estimate how much time should be set aside for each task to be completed. Creating reasonable time estimates for someone else is tough. You may think you know what needs to be done, but you could underestimate the true work required. Also, not everyone has your strengths–or weaknesses. Therefore, the estimates you assign at this stage are a starting point.

When a task is assigned to a team member, take the time to discuss with them what each task involves and see how long they think it will require. Be sure that they understand what each task entails so they can estimate accordingly. Update the plan with their estimated task durations and start dates. It is unfair to the team members to drop a task on them and demand a date without any further explanation.

Once you negotiate the duration of a task with someone, encourage them to stick with it. Other people farther along in the project may be depending upon this task to be completed before they can start.

Who Should Do It?

Some tasks are easy to assign. If the task is to validate the key locker security, it will go to the security manager. If that person chooses to delegate it to someone else, then it is still their responsibility to ensure the task is properly completed on time. Some tasks will be more general in nature and need to be spread around the team fairly. If a task is not needed, don't hesitate to delete it. If it is necessary, don't hesitate to assign it!

This is a good time to identify any gaps in your available labor. If you see a large time commitment for the Data Network Manager and little likelihood that they will be available to do the assigned work, you might generate a task to bring in some temporary help to assist them. There may be other time issues on the horizon. For example, if you need to involve the Accounting Controller, and the project will run over the calendar time for closing the fiscal year accounts, then you would schedule their project participation so as to avoid this time period.

Sequencing the Activities

Now, put all the tasks in some sort of order. In this type of project, the beginning of the project is somewhat sequential and then there are many tasks running in parallel when the various groups break off to write their respective plans. Select an estimated start date and place some dates on your plan. With the plan held up against a calendar, check to see if any tasks need to be resequenced or noted that they conflict with some other critical company activity.

If your task contingencies are in place, the project management software will fill in the plan dates for you. If when you save the plan you select the option to save without a baseline, you can easily change the start date later.

Next, you should level your resources so one person isn't asked to complete 40 hours of work in 1 day. This occurs when people are assigned too many tasks that are to run at the same time.

Plan Risk Assessment

So now that you have a rough plan, with time estimates and in some sort of a logical flow, it is time to scrutinize the plan for problems. Are there any labor resources overobligated? Look at each task area. What is the risk that an item won't be completed on time? Yes, there is always a risk that a key person won't be available. List any other underlying issues.

Most projects share the same basic risks to their success. In addition, each project has its own risks unique to what you are trying to accomplish and to your environment. Common project plan risks include:

➤ The amount of experience the Contingency Planning Coordinator has in leading this type of project. Low experience adds risk to the project. Extensive experience would make for a lower risk.

➤ The level of management support for the project. If you have low management support, you will have high project risk, and vice versa.

➤ Adequate funding to complete the project with a top-quality result. Don't let needed training, support activities, or mitigation actions be cut from the budget.

➤ How many locations will this project involve at one time? The more locations that are involved, the greater the project's risk of failure. If possible, run a separate project for each site, and do not attempt to do them all at the same time.

➤ The number of departments involved with the project at one time. Like trying to work across too many sites, trying to handle too many departments will fragment the Contingency Planning Coordinator's time and increases the likelihood of failure. Consider tackling fewer departments at one time.

➤ The frequency and length of business interruptions to the project. This could be an upcoming ISO audit, it could be a quarterly wall-to-wall inventory, it might even be the end of the fiscal year, etc. The more interruptions to the project's flow you can foresee, the higher the risk of failure.

➤ The time required to complete your business continuity plans will depend on the knowledge and quality of the people assigned by the various departments. Typically, the data processing department has the most to write and will take the longest.

➤ A mandated completion date may not be realistic.

EXECUTING AND CONTROLLING

Now you have your sponsor, your budget, your plan, and a core team assigned. It is time to get your project underway! A Contingency Planning Coordinator must be the inspiring force behind the project. At those times when everyone is piling work on your team members' desks, you must be the driving force in keeping this job as a priority project until it is finished.

As the project progresses, you will make decisions as to what is included in your project charter and what is not. This is "scope verification" and it may mean that as you progress with your project, you see that it must involve specific actions that were not foreseen when the project was started. It may also involve the "nice-to-have" things that pop up as a project moves on. In either case, recognize these things as they occur and make a conscious decision to accept or reject them. Do not let anyone else add tasks to the plan without your approval or your tightly planned project will turn into an untamed monster!

Communications Plan

Every person within your organization has different information needs and preferred channels for receiving it. The sponsor shouldn't be burdened with minute details. The department managers want to track what their people are doing, etc. To provide the right level of information to the right person, at the appropriate time, you need to build a communications plan. The more people involved with your project, the greater your need for communication.

A communications plan details who needs to report about what, and when. For example, who should receive project status reports? Who needs copies of the team meeting minutes? Who needs to know about minor project delays, etc? To manage this, build a matrix that accounts for the information needs of all stakeholders. Your communications plan will address a wide range of audiences. Be sure to identify the person responsible for generating the communication and its major focus.

Evaluate every report and every meeting in your communications plan as to whether it will be worth the effort to prepare for it. Some reports may require more effort than they are worth. Some meetings are just a waste of time. Effective communications is important for focusing a team to a goal, but you must strike a balance between enough communication and the time wasted generating too much. Use Form 1-4 (see CD) to plan out who is responsible for what communications.

The communications plan will encompass more than memos floating around the office. It should include meetings with your team, meetings with your sponsor and presentations to the various departments. Another important communications task is to raise the awareness of the employees of your project and how it impacts them. Posters, newsletter articles, and open meetings all serve to answer their questions and are useful for instilling a business continuity culture in your company.

The information falls into three main categories:

1. Mandatory communications are things that must be done, such as status reports to the sponsor, meeting minutes to the team members, etc. Skipping a mandatory communication may affect your project's support or credibility.

2. Informational communications includes reports to the interested and curious. Many people will see the plan under development and believe that it directly or indirectly will involve them. Your informational communications will pass on project accomplishments, testing schedules, and things that may not directly affect them but they would want to know about. Informational communications can help to shape expectations so the interested people can better understand what is next instead of being surprised or disappointed.

3. Similar to informational communications is marketing communications. Here you are out to build a positive image of your project to the rest of the company. Your marketing communications will help to educate the company as a whole on the business continuity planning principles (risk analysis, mitigation, documentation, etc.) and how they can relate to their own work processes. One effective method is to give a presentation on business recovery planning to each of the various department staffs. The more they understand it, the greater your support is across the company.

Form 1-5 (see CD) is a sample stakeholder reporting matrix. Modify it to reflect your project team and business requirements. In this matrix, you will identify which persons might only want to see monthly status reports with summary comments, such as the sponsor. Who might need a weekly status report with specific accomplishments, like the department managers? Who might want short stories on accomplishments, like the facility's employee newsletter? The stakeholder reporting matrix also indicates the best way to deliver these reports. Do some of your executives ignore their e-mail? Do some require face-to-face reports? Indicate the method of delivery to which they would be most receptive.

Reporting Using the Communications Plan

As the project progresses, you should occasionally revisit the project's risk assessment. Things change; people come and go on a project and what was once a looming challenge may at closer glance appear to be nothing at all. In addition, business conditions are in constant flux and that must also be figured into the update of your risk analysis.

Controlling is the process used to identify variation from the plan in the areas of:

➤ Change control.

➤ Scope control.

➤ Cost control.

➤ Quality control.

➤ Performance reporting.

➤ Risk response.

Your best tool for focusing the team on its goals will be a weekly team meeting. There are many fine books dealing with the proper way to conduct a meeting, but a few basics follow:

➤ First, always publish an agenda before the meeting. It acts as an anchor to keep people from drifting too far off the subject.

➤ Second, keep the meeting pertinent. Focus on recent achievements over the past 2 weeks and upcoming events of the next 2 weeks.

➤ Third, keep it under an hour. People lose focus the longer a meeting drones on. Side conversations should be stopped and taken outside the meeting. If you are finished in a half hour, cut it off! People will respect the meeting time limit as much as you do, so set a good example.

➤ Have your meeting at the same place and time every week, even if not much is happening. Try to make it a habit for them.

➤ When planning your team meetings, involve a bit of showmanship to keep people involved. If they sit there passively, ask specific people questions, but never to embarrass them if they are late. If the discussions seem tedious, jump in once in a while to keep them focused and interesting.

➤ Use slack time in the agendas to fill in with short training topics and visits by the sponsor or department managers.

➤ Publish a meeting recap as soon after the meeting as possible. Detailed meeting minutes may become too burdensome but a recap of the high points gives you a document to talk from at the beginning of the next meeting.

➤ Always include a copy of the updated project plan.

Test "Completed" Plans

The quickest way to snap people out of lethargy is to publicly test the first plans submitted. You don't need to pull the plug on a computer to do this. An easy test is to verbally walk through it. If the plan authors know that it is really going to be read and see how you test it, they will be more thorough.

Do the first desktop walk-through with the plan's author. You will uncover glossed-over steps where they clearly knew what to do but where, based on the plan, you had no clue as to what was next. After updating that version, do the same walk-through with the author's manager (who may very well be called on to execute this plan) and look for gaps.

Reward those contributors who complete their plans on time. This is where your sponsor comes in. Everyone likes to be appreciated, and some liberal rewards for the first few completed plans will go a long way toward motivating the rest of the team. You'd be surprised how fast this kind of word spreads throughout a company.

Set Up and Enforce a Testing Schedule

As the departmental plans roll in, update the project plan's testing schedule. Testing will uncover gaps and inconsistencies in the current draft. Normally, this is a multiple step process:

➤ The team member and their manager initially check completed plans by using a desktop walk-through.

➤ The next level is to walk through the plan with someone familiar with the area, but not involved with the plan development.

➤ Run a departmental test.

➤ Once enough plans are ready, it is time to schedule a simulated major disaster. This might be over a holiday period or whenever the systems are lightly used. Testing will teach people some of what to expect in a disaster. It will also make them more familiar with the procedures of other functions.

Always follow testing or a disaster event with an "after action" meeting and report detailing the lessons learned and updates made to the plan. Be sure to praise its high points and to privately express what it is lacking. Depending on how well your group knows one another, you can use the team members for a peer evaluation. People must feel free to speak at these meetings without fear of retaliation or their full value will not be realized.

After-action reviews are a very powerful learning tool. They require a moderator to keep them focused and moving through the following five questions. An after-action discussion follows a simple format:

➤ What happened?

➤ What should have happened?

➤ What went well?

➤ What went poorly?

➤ What will we do differently in the future?

Appoint someone to take notes on these lessons learned. Send a copy to each participant, and the Contingency Planning Coordinator should maintain a file of these reports. Refer to this file when updating the plan.

CLOSING THE PROJECT

Once you have your plan written and the initial tests completed, it is time to close up the project. All good things come to an end as the plan is transformed from a project to an ongoing business process. The transition involves reporting the project results to management, closing out the project's budget, identifying known exposures for future action, and thanking your team for their efforts. Closing the project involves the following steps:

➤ **Turn All Files Over to the Plan Administrator.** What was once your project may become someone else's regular responsibility. If the Contingency Planning Coordinator is not to be the Plan Administrator, accumulate all files pertaining to this project and hand them over to the Plan Administrator. It is now their job to ensure the ongoing test plan is enforced, that plan updates are issued in a timely fashion, etc.

Make a final update to the project plan. It may be useful if sister companies want to use it for building their own business continuity plans. You can also refer to it when estimating task duration for future projects.

➤ **Reporting Results to Management.** To wrap up your project, draft a recap of the progression of the project to management. In this, point out any major successes that occurred during the project, such as low-cost solutions found to important problems, materials found stashed away in closets that could be put to good use, and so on. In the report, be sure to point out the benefit of the cross-functional training received by the project team as they worked with each other during plan development and testing.

You should provide a final account of the funds spent on the project, broken down as to what part of the project they supported. This will assist in estimating the funds required for similar projects in the future.

➤ **Identifying Known Exposures.** A business reality is that not every worthwhile activity can be funded. During your risk analysis and mitigation efforts, you very likely uncovered a number of areas where there were single points of failure that called for redundant solutions, unmasked obsolete equipment that must be replaced, or other mitigation actions that would make your business processes more stable.

Roll up these exposures into a report to management. List each item separately along with a narrative explanation of why it is important. Detail the advantages and disadvantages of this course of action along with estimated (or known) costs. These narratives may not be reviewed again for many months, so the clearer the business reasons behind funding this action, the better. When your capital budgeting cycle rolls around, use this list as input to the budget.

➤ **Thanking the Team.** Hopefully, careful notes were kept during the course of the project so that team members could be recognized for their contributions to the project. In particular, those team members who overcame major obstacles to complete their plan and thoroughly test them are due special recognition. Acknowledgement of a job well done should be made as soon as possible after the fact. At the end of the project, it is time to reacknowledge these well-done jobs to remind everyone and management of the individual accomplishments during the project.

CONCLUSION

After reading this chapter, you should now have a good idea as to the overall strategy for developing a useful business continuity plan. Your odds for a successful project increase dramatically when you have a well-thought-out plan. The major steps for getting your project off to a good start are these:

1. Make sure the scope of the project is clearly defined. You need adequate time, funding, and support to be successful.

2. Carefully select the right team members. They must have a good understanding of the important processes within their departments and be able to clearly communicate the importance of the project back to their co-workers.

3. Identify the activities required, their durations, and who should do the work.

4. Communicate not only within the team but with the entire organization, as what you are doing is important for everyone's survival.

5. Test, test, test. If a plan isn't tested, you won't know whether it will work until it's too late.

The remaining chapters in Part 1 drill down into the details of the process for meeting this objective. This chapter gave you the information you need to develop an effective infrastructure for developing your plan; now, it's time to get down to the business of developing the plan.

CHAPTER 2

RISK ASSESSMENT
Understanding What Can Go Wrong

Luck: 1a, a force that brings good fortune or adversity; 1b, the events or circumstances that operate for or against an individual; 2, favoring chance.

INTRODUCTION

The heart of building a business continuity plan is a thorough analysis of events from which you may need to recover. This is variously known as a *threat analysis* or *risk assessment.* The result is a list of events that could slow our company down or even shut it down. We will use this list to identify those risks your business continuity plan must address.

First, let's define the terminology we'll use when discussing risk:

➤ The potential of a disaster occurring is called its **risk.** Risk is measured by how likely this is to happen and how badly it will hurt.

➤ A **disaster** is any event that disrupts a critical business function. This can be about anything.

➤ A **business interruption** is something that disrupts the normal flow of business operations.

Whether an event is a business interruption or a disaster sometimes depends upon your point of view. An interruption could seem like a disaster to the people to which it happens, but the company keeps rolling along. An example might be a purchasing department that has lost all telephone communication with their suppliers. It is a disaster to them because they use telephones and fax machines to issue purchase orders. The facility keeps running because their mitigation plan is to generate POs on paper and use cell phones to issue verbal material orders to suppliers.

Risk is defined as the *potential* of something occurring. It could involve the possibility of personal injury or death. Insurance actuaries work to quantify the likelihood of an event occurring to set insurance rates. A risk could be someone you judge as reliable failing in his or her duties. It could be a machine failure or a spilled container of toxic material.

Not all risks become reality. There is much potential in our world that does not occur. Driving to work today, I saw clouds that indicate the potential of rain. Dark clouds don't indicate a certainty of precipitation, but they do indicate a greater potential than a clear sky. I perceive an increased risk that I will get wet on the long walk across the company parking lot, so I carry an umbrella with me. The odds are that it will not rain. The weatherman says the clouds will pass. I can even see patches of blue sky between the massive dark clouds. Still, to reduce my risk of being drenched, I carry an umbrella.

Some risks can be reduced almost to the point of elimination. A hospital can install a backup generator system with the goal of ensuring 100% electrical availability. This will protect them against the risk of electrical blackout and brownouts. It also introduces new risks, such as the generator failing to start automatically when the electricity fails. It also does not protect the hospital against a massive electrical failure internal to the building.

Some risks are unavoidable and steps can only be taken to reduce their impact. If your facility is located on the ocean with a lovely view of the sea, defenses can be built up against a tidal surge or hurricane, but you cannot prevent them. You can only minimize their damage.

Some risks are localized, such as a failure of a key office PC. It directly affects at most a few people. This is a more common risk and is not directly addressed in the facility-wide business continuity plan. Localized plans should be developed and maintained at the department level, with a copy in the company-wide master plan. These will be most used within the department as they address these challenges as they arise. But if the problem is more widespread, such as a fire that burns out just those offices, all the combined small reaction plans for that office can be used to more quickly return that department to normal.

Other risks can affect your entire company. An example is a blizzard that blocks the roads and keeps employees and material from your doors. We all appreciate how this can slow things down, but if you are a just-in-time supplier to a company in a sunnier climate, you still must meet your daily production schedule or close your customer down!

In building the list we try to be methodical. We will examine things in your business environment that you take for granted. Roads on which you drive. Hallways you walk through. Even the air you breathe. In building the plan, a touch of paranoia is useful. As we go along, we will assign a score to each threat and eventually build a plan that deals with the most likely or most damaging events (see Figure 2-1).

BUILDING A RISK ANALYSIS

At this point we can differentiate between several common terms. We will begin with a *risk analysis*. A risk analysis is a process that identifies the probable threats to your business. As we progress, this will be used as the basis for a *risk assessment*. A risk assessment (sometimes called a business impact

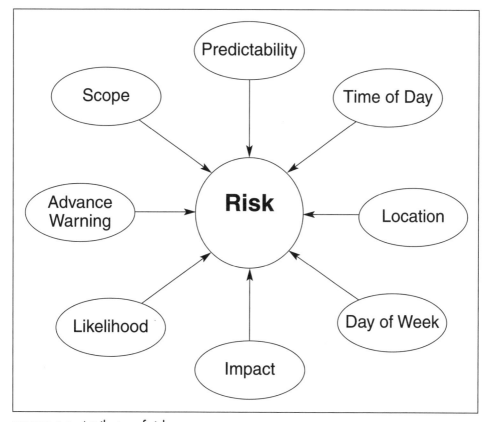

FIGURE 2-1: Attributes of risk.

analysis) compares the risk analysis to the controls you have in place today to identify areas of vulnerability.

The recommended approach is to assemble your business continuity planning team and perform the layers 1, 2, and 3 risk analyses (see The Five Layers of Risk) together. Your collective knowledge will make these reviews move quickly. Such things as the frequency of power or telephone outages in the past, how quickly these were resolved, and types of severe weather and its impact are all locked in the memories of the team members.

What Is Important to You?

A risk analysis begins with a statement of the essential functions of your business. This should be a written statement, as it will set priorities for addressing these risks. Essential functions could be business activities, such as the availability of telephone service. It could be the flow of information, such as up-to-the-second currency exchange rates. It is anything whose absence would significantly damage the operation of your business.

Most functions of a business are nonessential. You may think of your company as being tightly staffed and the work tuned to drive out waste. But think about the functions whose short-term loss would not stop your essential business from running. One example is payroll. Losing your payroll function for a few days would be inconvenient, but should not shut your business down. Most people can't delay paying their bills for long, so over a longer period of time, this rises to the level of critical. This illustrates how a short-term noncritical function can rise to be a critical function if it is not resolved in a timely manner.

Another example is a manufacturing site that states its essential functions as building, shipping, and invoicing its products. Anything that disturbs those functions is a critical problem that must be promptly addressed. All other functions that support this are noncritical to the company, although the people involved may consider them critical. On a more local scale, there may be critical functions for a department or a particular person's job. These are also important to resolve quickly. The difference is one of magnitude. Company-wide problems have company-wide impact and must be resolved immediately.

Another aspect to consider is the loss of irreplaceable assets. Imagine the loss or severe damage to vital records that must be retained for legal, regulatory, or operational reasons. Safeguarding these records must be added to your list of critical functions. Included in this category are all records whose loss would materially damage your company's ability to conduct business. All other records are those that can be reproduced (although possibly with great effort) or whose loss does not materially affect your business.

With all of this in mind, it is time to identify those few critical functions of your facility. These functions will be broad statements and are the primary purposes toward which this site works. The easiest way to start is for the top management team to identify them. Often the company's Operations Manager has some idea of what these should be. They would have been identified so that business continuity insurance could be purchased.

Another way to identify critical functions is for your team to select them. Based on your collective knowledge of the company, just what are they expecting you to provide? Another way to think of this is what is the essence of your site's function?

Some examples to get you thinking:

➤ **A Factory.** To build, ship, and invoice products. This implies that the continuous flow of products down the assembly line is critical, along with prompt shipment and invoicing (to maintain cash flow).

➤ **A National Motel Chain Call Center.** To promptly respond to customer calls, make accurate reservations, and address customer concerns in a timely manner. This implies that telephone system availability and speed of switching are critical, along with accurate databases to reserve rooms.

➤ **A Public Utility.** To provide electrical service to all the customers, all of the time. This implies that no matter what other crises within the company are underway, the delivery of this product is critical.

SCOPE OF RISK

The scope of risk is determined by the potential damage, cost of downtime, or cost of lost opportunity. In general, the wider the disaster, the more costly it is. A stoppage to a manufacturing assembly line can idle hundreds of workers, so of course this is a company-wide critical event. Even a 15-minute stoppage can cost many thousands of dollars in idled labor. Consequently, a problem of this nature takes priority on the company's resources in all departments to resolve the issue.

On a smaller scale, there may be a spreadsheet in the Accounting department that is used to generate reports for top management. If this PC stops working, work has ceased on this one function but the plant keeps building products for sale. The Accounting Manager can request immediate PC repair support. The problem and support are local issues peripheral to the company's main function of building, shipping, and invoicing material.

When evaluating the likelihood of risks, keep your planning horizon to 5 years. The longer the planning horizon is, the greater the chance that "something" will happen. Since the purpose of the analysis is to identify areas of concentration for your business continuity plan, 5 years is about as far out as you can plan for building mitigation steps. If the risk analysis is updated annually, then 5 years is a sufficient planning horizon.

Cost of Downtime

Calculating the cost of downtime is critical to determining the appropriate investments to be made for disaster recovery. But calculating the costs due to the loss of a critical function is not a simple process. The cost of downtime includes tangible costs such as lost productivity, lost revenue, legal costs, late fees and penalties, and many other tangible costs. Intangible costs include things such as a possible damaged reputation, lost opportunities, and possible employee turnover.

TANGIBLE COSTS The most obvious costs incurred due to a business interruption are lost revenue and lost productivity. If customers cannot purchase and receive your product, they may purchase from a competitor. Electronic commerce is especially vulnerable, because if your system is down, customers cannot make a purchase and can in many cases simply click on a competitor's website. The easiest method to calculate lost sales is to determine your average hourly sales, and multiple that value by the number of hours you are down. While this can be a significant value, it is simply the starting point for calculating the total cost of downtime.

Lost productivity is also a major portion of the total cost of downtime. It is usually not possible to stop paying wages to employees simply because a critical process is unavailable, so their salaries and benefits continue to be paid. Many employees may be idle while the process is unavailable, while others may continue to work at a much-diminished level of productivity. The most common method to calculate employee downtime cost is to multiply the number of employees by their hourly loaded cost by the number of hours of downtime. You may need to do this separately for each department, as their loaded cost and their level of productivity during the outage may vary. You will also need to include the employee cost for those who are assisting with any recovery or remediation processes once the process is back up. These employees may be doing double duty once the system is back up, doing their regular job and also entering data that were missed or lost during the downtime.

Other employee-related costs may include the cost of hiring temporary labor, overtime costs, and travel expenses. You may also incur expenses for equipment rental for cleanup or for temporary replacement of critical machinery, and extra costs to expedite late shipments to customers.

If the business interruption was due to damages such as fire or flood, the direct loss of equipment and inventory must of course be added in. Other tangible costs may include late fees and penalties if the downtime causes you to miss critical shipments to customers. You may also incur penalties if the downtime causes you to miss deadlines for government-mandated filings. Stockholders may sue the company if a business interruption causes a significant drop in share price and they believe that management was negligent in protecting their assets.

INTANGIBLE COSTS Intangible costs include lost opportunities as some customers purchase from your competition while you're down, and may not return as customers. You don't just lose the immediate sale, but possibly any future business from that customer. You need to calculate the net present value of that customer's business over the life of the business relationship. If you have repeated problems with systems or processes being unavailable, some employees may become frustrated and leave the company. The cost to replace them and to train the new employee should be considered. Employee exit interviews can help determine if this is at least a factor in employee turnover.

Other intangible costs can include a damaged reputation with customers, business partners, suppliers, banks, etc. who may be less inclined to do business with you. Your marketing costs may increase if customers defect to the competition during an outage and you need to work harder to win back their business. Calculating the true total cost of an outage is not easy, but it is important to know when determining the investment necessary to prevent and/or recover from a disaster.

THE FIVE LAYERS OF RISK

The impact of risks vary widely according to what happens to whom and when. Your reaction to a disaster that shuts down the entire company will be quite different from that which inconveniences a single office or person.

When considering risks, it is very helpful to separate them into broad categories (or layers) to properly prioritize their solutions. When evaluating risk we look at five distinct layers. The layers range from what affects everyone (including your customers) in Layer 1 down to the processes performed by each individual in Layer 5.

The first layer concerns external risks that can close your business both directly and indirectly. These are risks from nature, such as flooding, hurricanes, severe snowstorms, etc. It can also include risks from man-made objects such as railroads or airplanes. Risks of this type usually disrupt our customers and suppliers as well as our own employees.

The second layer examines risks to your local facility. This might involve one or more buildings—everything at this site. Some of these risks are due to the way your offices were constructed; some risks are a result of severe weather, etc. Second-layer risks include risks to basic services, such as electrical and telephone access to your building. We will also look into issues such as bomb threats, hazardous material spills, and medical emergencies.

The third layer is your data systems organization. Everywhere throughout your organization are computers, talking through a data network, sharing information, etc. In addition to operational issues, loss of data can lead to severe legal problems. Most data can be recreated, but the expense for doing so can be quite high. This layer deserves its own chapter as its disasters can reach across your company. In most companies, if the computers stop working, so do the people.

The fourth layer is the individual department. This will drive the main part of your plan. Fourth-level risks are the periodic crises we all confront on a weekly basis. Each department has critical functions to perform to meet their production goals and weekly assignments. These processes depend on specific tools to do this. Each department needs to identify the risk that might prevent them from performing their assigned work. These risks may not threaten the company's primary functions but over time can degrade the overall facilities' performance.

The fifth and final layer is your own desk. If you can't do your job in a timely manner, it may not stop the company from shipping its products, but it sure adds a lot of unnecessary stress to your life. Typically the risk assessment you perform on your own job will be more detailed (because you know more about it), make it easier for you to take time off (as you will be more organized), and making bouncing back from the crisis of the week look so very easy.

LAYER 1: EXTERNAL RISKS

Many natural disasters are wide-area risks. That means they not only affect your facilities, but also the surrounding area. As an example, we will consider a hurricane. The damaging winds from a hurricane can cover hundreds of square miles and then slowly move up the seacoast. These winds can bring on tidal surges and torrential downpour, spawn tornados, and result in downed power lines and many other calamities all at the same time.

Now consider your business in the midst of this. All companies are affected by this disaster including your customers, your suppliers, and your emergency services support. Damage can be widespread. Technicians and machinery you had counted on for prompt support are tied up elsewhere. Bridges may be out, your workers may be unable to leave the facilities, and fresh workers may be unable to come to work. Employees critical to your recovery may not be available due to damage to their homes or injuries to their families. The list of problems could go on and on.

Don't forget to consider how the disaster may affect your employees' ability to respond to the disaster. After the terrorist attacks on the World Trade Center, many disaster recovery plans called for surviving employees to be at the recovery site the next day. After watching their friends and co-workers dying around them, getting to the recovery site was not at the top of their priority list!

Don't live in a hurricane zone? How different is this than a major snow-storm? Power lines snap, which cuts off the electrical heat to your building, which causes sprinkler pipes to freeze and burst, etc. Impassable roads mean that help is slow to move around the area. Extreme temperatures reduce the productivity of power line technicians.

The risk to your site from natural disasters is determined by its topographic, hydrologic, and geologic conditions. This can be determined from maps provided by the United States Geologic Survey. The maps show elevations and drainage patterns.

The same goes for critical highways or railroads. Depending on where you live, a blocked highway may be easily bypassed. In some places, it may be the only practical route for tourists to reach your hotel. A damaged bridge on a key road could shut you down for days. A railroad derailment that spills toxic material may force an evacuation of your offices, even if it is quite a distance away.

With all of this "doom and gloom" in mind, let's break external risks into four categories: natural disasters, man-made risks, civil risks, and supplier risks.

WHAT SHOULD I DO?

Use Form 2-1, the "Risk Assessment Tool for Layer 1." It is on your CD-ROM included with this book.

Evaluate the risk to your site in each of the categories, over the next 5 years.

The columns of the tool are:

LIKELIHOOD is how likely is this risk to happen.

IMPACT is how bad you would believe the damage would be.

RESTORATION is the length of time to get your critical functions back into service, not the amount of time for a complete recovery. The shorter the restoration time, the higher the value in this column.

See section "Making the Assessment" at the end of this chapter for details on how to score each risk.

The risks listed in the tool are just a starting point. Add any other risks that you see for your site.

Natural Disasters

Natural disasters are the first thing that comes to mind when writing a disaster plan and are a risk that we all live with. They vary greatly according to the part of the country you live in. The damage from natural disasters usually covers a wide area. This not only affects your building, but also your employees, suppliers, customers, and the time required for a full recovery.

A major problem with wide-area disasters is that the help you are depending upon for recovery may not be available or able to reach you. If major electrical lines are down, then your power company may take a long time to rerun the wire from the downed power pole to your building.

How much warning will you typically receive of an impending disaster? For a hurricane, you should know days before it arrives. In the case of an earthquake, you may not know until it is upon you.

TORNADOES Tornados can occur at any time of the year. Where you live has a great deal to do with the likelihood of a tornado occurring, with the greatest risk per square mile in Florida and Oklahoma.

You can obtain information about the likelihood of tornados in your area from the Severe Thunderstorm Climatology web page of the National Severe Storms Laboratory of the National Oceanic and Atmospheric Administration at:

http://www.nssl.noaa.gov/hazard/hazardmap.html

This U.S. map displays the probability of tornados, wind, or hail for broad sections of the country. You can use this map, together with your team's collective memory, to determine the likelihood of these events happening to you.

EARTHQUAKES Earthquakes occur in all 50 states. Forty-one of these states are in the moderate- or high-risk category (see Figure 2-2). To see if your area has an earthquake risk, check out:

http://geohazards.cr.usgs.gov/eq/index.html

THUNDERSTORMS The typical annual threat of severe thunderstorms in the United States can be found at:

http://www.nssl.noaa.gov/hazard/totalthreat.html

Severe thunderstorms include winds in excess of 58 mph and hailstones greater than $3/4$ inches in diameter. These storms can include:

➤ High winds may rip off parts of your roof, exposing your equipment to damaging rain. High winds may also pick up objects and smash them into your windows, or even tip over semitrailers and close mountain passes.

➤ Hail can be smaller than a pea or larger than a softball. It can destroy field crops, put a massive number of dents in a car, damage unprotected material you have stored outside, and can be extremely annoying if you own a car lot.

➤ Deluge and flash flooding can cause roads to close, which slows the flow of customers, employees, and material in and out of your facility. Your

FIGURE 2-2: Seattle, WA, March 2001. Businesses in and around Seattle were damaged by the February earthquake in Washington State. (FEMA News Photo.)

building may change from a hilltop with a view to an island in a sea of muddy water.

➤ Lightning can damage electronic equipment without striking it. The charge can run up telephone wires to a PC modem and toast it easily. It can also damage electronics in your office without leaving a mark. Lightning is a danger to your employees, and steps should be taken to protect them from the danger of being struck and from lightning igniting flammable gases.

SNOW Heavy snow or blizzards can close access roads leading into and out of your building, keeping employees in and the next shift at home. Even if your local weather is manageable, you may still close if trucks full of materials cannot drive over snow-blocked roads. Snowstorms should be monitored for wind speed and the distribution of snow. Snow piled high against buildings or on roofs can lead to structural problems or failure (see Figure 2-3).

FIGURE 2-3: Little Rock, AR, December 29, 2000. Downed power cables are among the damage after a recent ice storm. (Photo by John Shea/FEMA News Photo.)

EXTREME TEMPERATURES Extreme temperatures, whether hot or cold, can wreak havoc on your facility, your materials, and your employees. These are also peak energy demand times, which will further throw off your operating budget. Like snow and other risks, your team can decide what an extreme temperature is and the risk it will occur within the next 5 years.

HURRICANES Hurricane occurrences can be predicted by the weather services, but they cannot provide an accurate warning of where they will strike landfall and at what strength. Hurricanes can spawn tornados, create tidal surges, cause flooding, etc. Evaluate the risk for hurricanes occurring by itself, and then evaluate the risk to each of the other categories separately.

FLOODS Floods or tidal surges are usually detected by the weather service, and thus you have some warning of what is coming. The Federal Emergency Management Agency (FEMA) reports that more than 90% of natural disasters involve flooding. The tidal surge may be the result of a hurricane or severe storm at sea. Floods can result from melting snow, severe downpours in the areas upriver from your location, and other natural causes. Usually, there will be some warning this is occurring but there may not be enough time to evacuate all your vital records and machinery.

Floods damage your property in many ways (see Figure 2-4):

➤ A flood will damage just about everything by soaking it in water. Office materials, computers, and manufacturing materials all can be seriously damaged by water. When the water finally moves out, mold can move in.

➤ The floodwaters themselves may contain raw sewage or chemicals that will end up inside your building.

➤ Debris of all sizes is carried in the floodwaters that can batter your walls, smash in windows, and be left strewn about when the waters subside.

➤ Floodwaters typically contain mud and sand that will coat the floors and walls as the waters recedes. This material will also be contaminated with whatever was in the floodwaters.

FIGURE 2-4: Mullens, WV, July 17, 2001. An office supply store is in shambles after floodwaters up to 9 feet hit earlier this month. (Photo by Leif Skoogfors/FEMA News Photo.)

OTHER NATURAL DISASTERS Forest fires or large brush fires may threaten your facility or the access roads to it. Landslides can close roads and damage facilities, depending on your topography. This is more common if your facility is located on or near a hill or your main roads pass along hillsides. Mudslides can result from heavy rainfall. Sinkholes (subsidence) are the result of surface collapse from a lack of support underneath, as might be caused by groundwater dissolving a soft material such as limestone, or from abandoned mine tunnels. Sandstorms resulting from high winds can damage vehicles, seep dust and grit into machine shops, and close access roads.

Man-Made Risks

All around you are potential man-made risks. If you are in the city, this is an even larger problem. These risks are the result of someone else's disaster or actions that affect your daily operations. Stand outside for a moment and look around. Drive around the nearby roads and make notes of what you see. Look for large outside storage tanks, semitrailers with gas, or hazardous warning signs.

How to identify man-made risks:

Get a map of your area from FEMA. It will show the routes taken by hazardous material carriers. It will have similar information on railroad usage and pipelines. Determine if a problem with these would block your only decent road access or if a toxic gas leak were blown your way, how close must it be to cause your facility to be evacuated.

Get a good local road map. Mark any obstacles that would hinder or prevent access to your facility if they were inaccessible, such as major bridges and primary highways. Now mark those things whose operation would stop or hinder access, such as drawbridges or surface-level railroad tracks. *This map will be further used when studying Layer 2 risks.*

Note any industrial sites with large outdoor storage tanks. What is in them? Do they contain distilled water or industrial chemicals? Other things to be on the lookout for are:

➤ **Access to Your Facility.**

◆ Major highways may be used to transport toxic materials through your area. If a truck flipped over and there was a major toxic spill, do you have another access road into your facility? (If this occurs close by, your building may need to be evacuated.)

◆ Bridges across large bodies of water or intercoastal waterways can be damaged by collisions with barges or boats. If you are on an island, do you have another suitable way in? If the bridge arches high into the air to allow seagoing vessels to pass underneath, is it often closed during high winds or ice storms?

➤ **Railroads also Transport Toxic Material.** Does your building have a railroad siding next to it where someone else's railcars with potentially hazardous cargo could be temporarily stored?

➤ **Pipelines.** Are there any underground pipelines in your area? These often carry fuels. A pipe rupture can force an evacuation lasting several days.

➤ **Airports.** Is your facility located on or near a flight path? This includes small dirt strips as well.

➤ **Harbors/Industrial Areas.** These areas are candidates for chemical spills and fires.

➤ **Chemical Users.** These are all around, often unknown to their neighbors. For example, many water treatment plants use chlorine to treat water. A chlorine gas leak can force an evacuation of a wide area.

➤ **Dams Require Regular Maintenance.** In extreme weather, they may overflow or become damaged; ask about soft spots.

➤ **Rivers.** Where are you on the 100-year flood plain? Is this measure long out of date due to massive building in your area? Use your local knowledge to determine the likelihood or frequency of flooding.

Civil Risks

The risk from civil problems is a tough area that covers a lot of ground. What is the risk of a riot occurring in your area? Is it higher in an urban area (where the people are) than in a rural area? In general, it would be less likely in an affluent area than in an area with a concentration of less affluent people. It might be less likely in the middle of an industrial park than on a busy street corner.

Another risk is from the potential of a labor dispute turning into a strike. The picket lines that usually accompany a strike might cause material and employee flow problems if truck drivers and employees refuse to or cannot cross the picket lines.

Similar to a labor stoppage is the risk of secondary picketing. If your labor relations are sound, but one of your suppliers is in the midst of a labor dispute, their employees may choose to publicize their dispute by picketing companies that continue to use products made by their company. Even though these picket lines tend to be much smaller, you may have union truck drivers who will not drive across them.

Suppliers

Another category of risk is how well your suppliers can maintain their flow of goods into your facility. Make a list of your key suppliers and ask yourself, in every case, what is the risk that they cannot manufacture and deliver your required material to your dock on time in the event of any of the aforementioned disasters. This is critical for manufacturers who depend on just-in-time deliveries.

You need to consider the condition of the access roads or rail service between your facility and your key suppliers. This could be interrupted by area-wide disasters such as blizzards or flooding.

SUPPLIERS RISK

What to Do:

1. Make up a list of key suppliers or service providers whose absence for more than 48 hours would shut you down. (You can change the 48 hours to whatever value you think is appropriate.)

2. Plot their location on a map (down to the road intersection if local, or to the town if distant). Pushpins work well for this.

3. Identify potential problems along their route, such as they are in St. Louis and they must cross the Mississippi River to reach your facility. So what is the risk they can't get across in the event of a major flood?

4. For local suppliers, check to see if they have multiple routes to reach you or have their own traffic flow bottlenecks.

Sources of Information for Layer 1 Risks:

Earthquakes: http://geohazards.cr.usgs.gov/eq/index.html

Tornadoes: http://www.nssl.noaa.gov/hazard/hazardmap.html

Severe storms: http://www.nssl.noaa.gov/hazard/totalthreat.html

Man-made hazards: Your local Federal Emergency Management Agency (FEMA) office can be found in the county or state sections of your local telephone book. They will be an invaluable source of the risks and mitigation actions for Layer 1 risks in your locale.

Access hazards: A road map and a topographical map.

LAYER 2: FACILITY-WIDE RISK

A facility-wide risk is something that only impacts your local facility. Some companies span many locations and will need to make a separate risk assessment for each location. Each assessment can be for one building or a cluster of buildings. In either event, a facility-wide risk involves multiple departments and would slow or stop the flow of business.

An example might be a facility that takes toll-free calls from around the country for hotel reservations. The loss of their internal telephone switch could idle hundreds of workers. Customers who could not complete their call would call a different hotel chain. This costs the company in direct revenue and is compounded by the loss of valuable customer goodwill through the uncompleted calls.

Another example is the loss of electrical power. Unless you sit next to a window on a sunny day, the loss of electrical power will mean all work stops when the lights go out. In addition, all your desktop PCs will "crash" and lose any data in their memory. Just the labor time alone to reboot this equipment can be substantial.

We will begin with the essential utilities we all take for granted, and then move into the important areas of people risks. There are five basic office utilities that we all take for granted, but without them, the doors might close quickly. They are:

➤ Electricity

➤ Telephones

➤ Water

➤ Climate Control

➤ Data Network

WHAT TO DO?
Use the local map that was marked up in Layer 1 and mark the location of the local fire department, ambulance service, hospital, and police station. Look for access problems.

Electricity

Electricity gives us lights. It powers our office and manufacturing machines. It is magically there every time we need it—just plug in! Stop and think of the complexity involved with generating electricity and then moving it hundreds of miles away to where it is needed. This is truly an engineering marvel. And it is very reliable. So reliable that when it is stopped, people become very annoyed as if something they have a right to expect has been taken from them.

To properly determine the risk of an electrical outage, begin with the team's own experiences with the frequency, timing, and length of outages in this area. Frequency is how many times might it occur within your 5-year planning window. Timing is what time of day or day of the week it usually happens. In some places, it seems most likely to occur during severe thunderstorms. In other locales, it might be most likely to stop during ice storms.

The second step is to consult your facilities maintenance department. Find out how many power feeds run into the building and if they enter from opposite ends of the building. It is not uncommon to only have one. If so, then you have just uncovered a potential single point of failure. It is better to have more than one power feed to your building.

One thing to understand is that even if electricity is unavailable across a wide area, the landline telephone system will still work. You can use this to notify the power company of the outage, to see how widespread it is, and to ask when they expect to have it operational again.

Telephones

Telephones are your window to the world. In the blink of an eye, you communicate with customers and suppliers in any corner of the world. Telephones also provide a crucial lifeline to emergency services during a disaster. Loss of telephone service hurts some companies more than others, but few companies can function without it for an extended period of time.

A critical aspect of telephone communications is that your external company data network often runs over the same cables. So if a backhoe operator cuts the cable to your building, you could lose both the telephones and the external data lines at the same time.

When evaluating your telephone risk, check out your local telephone service architecture. If the local central office were inoperable, would your telephones still work? If you can reach multiple central offices, then the answer is yes. If you are only connected to one central office, then its loss is your loss.

Most companies have their own Private Branch Exchange (PBX) system. Damage to this room could very effectively shut down your internal telephone system. How do you rate the risk or likelihood of this happening?

Water

One thing we can look forward to every winter is the breaking of water mains. As the ground is saturated with fall or winter moisture and then freezes, it expands and contracts, stressing older water main lines. Eventually, one will give way and a section of the town will be without fresh water until it is fixed.

If you are operating a restaurant, you use a lot of water for sanitation and for customers. So, of course, if a water main broke you could be closed for several hours. If this occurred during a particularly profitable time of day or day of the week, you could lose a lot of money. If it happened very often, you could lose customer goodwill.

Office buildings are also major water users. Many computer and PBX rooms are cooled by "chilled water" systems. If these units lose water pressure, they can no longer cool the air and the central computer equipment could overheat. If this occurred on a weekend, you might find out when everyone streams in on Monday. By then, the heat has damaged expensive electronic components and your systems are useless.

Office buildings also use water for sanitation. If your have 500 people in a building, you have a lot of flushes in one day. If your neighborhood water main were broken, how long would your building be habitable?

Climate Control

Loss of heating or air conditioning might be an inconvenience depending on the time of the year. In the depth of winter or the height of summer, this could make for very uncomfortable working conditions and be very damaging to your manufacturing materials and electronic systems.

Loss of heat in the depths of winter:

➤ Can cause your building to cool to the point of freezing. This could lead to frozen sprinkler pipes that could rupture and leak upon melting.

➤ Integrated circuits in electronic equipment are not designed for extreme cold and may malfunction.

➤ In a manufacturing environment, extreme cold may stop production as the viscosity of paint, lubricants, and fluids used in normal production is increased. Water-based products may be ruined if frozen.

Loss of air conditioning in the heat of summer:

➤ Heat can lead to office closures because the high heat could lead to heat stroke or heat exhaustion. Remember to consult the heat index for your area as humidity can make the air temperature feel much warmer and can impact people sooner.

➤ In a factory, high heat can lead to moving machinery overheating much faster and potentially beyond its rated operating temperature.

➤ Without air conditioning, the temperatures of your computer and PBX rooms must be monitored and shut down if in excess of the manufacturer's rated temperatures or risk losing warranty claims.

➤ Loss of humidity control may add moisture to your vital records storage room, leading to the potential for mildew growth.

Data Network

Most companies depend heavily on their data communication network to conduct daily business. It is the tool that allows desktop workstations to share data, send e-mail confirmations, receive faxed orders into their e-mail, and a wealth of other benefits. In many companies, losing their data network is as severe a problem as losing electricity. We'll discuss data communications issues more thoroughly below in Level 3, Data Systems risks.

Other facility-wide risks to review are those that endanger the people in the facility. These people risks include:

➤ Fire.

➤ Structural.

➤ Security.

➤ Medical.

Fire

What do you think the risk is of a fire occurring in your facility? This can be a fire of any size depending on what you see in place today to deal with it. There may be fire extinguishers in every corner but that does not mean there is a low risk of fire. This risk should take into account the local conditions (does it get very dry there in the summer time), the amount of combustibles stacked around the facility, and the construction of the building itself (wood, cement, etc.).

Another risk factor to add is the reaction time for fire crews to reach your site. If it is rural, it may take additional time to collect volunteer firefighters at the station house before they can respond (see Figure 2-5).

Structural

Structural problems may be caused by design flaws, poor materials, or even human mistakes. In any event, consider the risks of damage from the very building you are sitting in.

FIGURE 2-5: NOAA news photo. (From Frankel et al., U.S. Geological Survey, 1997.)

➤ Weather-related structural failure might arise from a heavy snowfall weighing on the roof or even from high winds.

➤ A fire on one floor of a building may be quickly contained, but the water used to extinguish it will seep through the floor and damage equipment and vital records stored below. Any large fire, no matter how quickly it is contained, has the capability to weaken an entire structure.

➤ Water pipe breakage can occur from a part of the building freezing from heating shut off over a holiday, or from a worker snapping off a sprinkler head with their ladder as they walk down a hall.

➤ Lightning does not have to hit your building to damage sensitive electronic components. However, if it does, you could lose valuable data and equipment in a very, very short time. Buildings must have proper grounding and lightning protection.

Security

The quality of security surrounding a workplace has gained widespread attention in recent years. Historically, the facility's security force was used to prevent theft of company property and to keep the curious away from company secrets. In more recent years, the threat of workplace violence, often from outsiders, has lead to a resurgence of interest in having someone screen anyone entering your facility. Issues that your security people must be trained to deal with include:

➤ **Workplace Violence.** What is the risk of someone in your facility losing their temper to the point of a violent confrontation with another person?

➤ **Bomb Threats.** Every occurrence of a bomb threat must be taken seriously. A bomb threat can disrupt critical processes while police investigators determine if there is a valid threat to public safety or if it is just a crank call. This risk can vary according to the public profile of your company, the type of products you produce, or even the level of labor tension in your offices.

➤ **Trespassing.** Employee and visitor entrance screening. What is the likelihood of someone bypassing or walking through your entrance-way security screening? You might wish to break this down further into the risk of a deranged nonemployee out to revenge some imagined wrong by an employee, to a thief looking to rummage through unattended purses. These things can tragically occur anywhere, but you can set this risk according to the team's experience at this facility.

➤ **Physical Security of Property.** This involves theft, either by employees or outsiders. The thief can steal from employees or from the company. It is expensive for a company to have a laptop PC stolen. It is even more expensive if that PC has company confidential data in it. Physical security involves employee identification badges, a key control program, and electronic security access to sensitive areas.

➤ **Sabotage.** Sabotage is the intentional destruction of company property. This can be done by an employee or by an outsider. There are some parts of your facility that are only open to authorized people. Examples are the PBX room, the computer room, and the vital records storage. What is the risk that someone will bypass the security measures and tamper with or destroy something in a sensitive area? Another thing to think about is to determine if all your sensitive areas are secured from sabotage.

➤ **Intellectual Property or Theft of Confidential Company Information.** What is the risk that valuable company information will miss a shredder and end up in a dumpster outside? This could be customer lists, orders with credit card numbers, or even old employee records.

WHAT TO DO?

Obtain copies of your company policies for security and safety. The security team often has emergency procedures for fire and police support. Add them to your plan.

Examine your security policy for a date that it was last reviewed or published.

Compare the written policy to how security is actually implemented at your facility.

Medical

The standard answer you hear to evaluating medical risks usually involves reacting by calling for an ambulance. This is a good answer. But when evaluating the likelihood of these risks, you might add to your disaster plans things that you could do in the interim until the ambulance arrives. Examples are such things as hanging emergency medical kits or defibrillators around the facility. Some companies register all employees who are certified Emergency Medical Technicians (EMTs) and pay them extra to carry a pager. In the event of a medical emergency, they are dispatched to the location to assist until proper medical support arrives. It may even make sense to staff an industrial nurse during production hours. Medical issues might include these:

➤ **Sickness.** What is the risk of someone coming down with a serious sickness while at work? Some serious illnesses can come on suddenly.

➤ **Sudden Death.** What is the risk of someone falling over dead? This risk should factor in the age of the workforce and the types of materials used in your facility.

➤ **Serious Accident.** Do you use heavy machinery or high voltages in your processes? Are serious accidents a real risk in your line of business?

➤ **Fatal Accident.** Along the lines of the serious accident, is there a risk of a fatal accident at your site?

What other Layer 2 Risks can you or your team identify? Add them to Form 2-2 on the CD-ROM.

WHAT TO DO?

Find out about local fire/ambulance service. What hours is it staffed? Is it full time or run by volunteers?

What is the distance from the station house to your door?

Are there obstacles that might delay an ambulance, such as a drawbridge or surface-level railroad tracks?

What is the distance to a hospital, and what hours are the hospital open?

LAYER 3: DATA SYSTEMS RISKS

Data systems risks are important because one problem can adversely affect multiple departments. Data systems typically share expensive hardware such as networks, central computer systems, file servers, and even Internet access. A complete study of data system risk would fill its own book, so this chapter examines these risks from an end-user perspective.

Your data systems architecture will to a great degree determine your overall risks. Its design will reflect the technology costs and benefits of centralized/decentralized software and data. A more common company-wide risk is a loss of the internal computer network. With a heavy dependence on shared applications and data files, many companies are at a standstill without this essential resource. Even a short interruption will lose valuable employee time as they reconnect to the central service.

A major goal in examining data systems risks is to locate your single points of failure. These are the bottlenecks where a problem would have wide-reaching impact. In later chapters, we will review our single points of failure for opportunities to install redundant devices.

Some of the hidden risks in data systems are processes that have always been there and have worked fine for a long period of time. It is possible that they are running on obsolete machines that could not be repaired if damaged in a disaster, and their software program likely could not be readily transferred quickly to another processor. Your only choice is to try to make your old program function on the new hardware. As anyone who has tried to use an old program while leaping generations of hardware technology can tell you, this can be a time-consuming process. Due to the sudden change to new equipment and operating software, your programs may require substantial fine-tuning to run. This "forced upgrade" will delay your full recovery.

Computer programs exist in two forms. The "English-like" source code is what the programmer writes. The computer executes a processed version of the program called "machine code." A typical data processing problem is finding the original source code. Without this, programs cannot be easily moved to a different computer. This leads to processes relying on obsolete languages or programs to work.

The risk analysis at this level is from the end-user perspective, as the data department should already have a current plan. If so, these items may be lifted from their plan.

WHAT TO DO?
Use the Critical Process Impact Matrix (Form 2-3) found on your CD. We will use this matrix for the final three layers.

The Critical Process Impact Matrix will become a very valuable part of your disaster recovery plan. Whenever the IS department wants to restart the

AS/400 over lunchtime to address an important error, you can sort the matrix by the platform column and see which systems will stop working during this time and thereby quickly see the impact of this action. You would also know which customer contacts to notify.

The matrix has the following columns:

➤ **System.** Enter the name commonly used to refer to this overall computer system, such as Accounts Payable, Materials Management System, Traffic Control System, etc. However, this does not have to be a computer-based system as it can apply to any important process.

➤ **Platform.** Enter the computer system this runs on, such as AS/400 #3, or a VAX named Alvin, etc.

➤ **Normal Operating Days/Times.** What times and days do you normally need this? Use the first one or two letters for the days of the week, and enter 24 hours if it must always be up.

➤ **Critical Operating Days/Times.** Use the same notation as for normal times and days. Some systems have critical times when it must be up for 24 hours, such as when Accounting closes the books at the end of the month, or end of quarter, etc. Use as many critical days/time entries as you need.

➤ **Support Primary/Backup.** Who in the IS department writes changes or answers questions about this system? These must be someone's name and not a faceless entity like "Help Desk."

➤ **Customer Contacts Primary/Backup.** Who should the IS department call to inform them of current or upcoming system problems? Often this is a department manager.

Fill in the matrix. This will take quite a while. Every system on this list must have at least a basic disaster recovery plan written for it—but more on that later.

Now that we have identified the critical processes, we need to break each process down further into its main components. Remember, this is only necessary for your critical processes. Use the Critical Process Breakdown (Form 2-4) found on your CD. This matrix helps to identify the critical components for each system. By focusing on the critical components, we can keep this sheet manageable. If your facility is ISO compliant, then much of this is already in your process work instructions.

➤ **System.** This name ties the Breakdown Matrix to the Critical Process matrix. Be sure to use the same system names on both matrixes.

➤ **Platform.** Enter the computer system this runs on, such as AS400 #3, or a VAX named Alvin, etc.

➤ **Key Components.** There may be more than one of each item per category for each critical process.

◆ **Hardware.** List specialized things here like barcode printers, check printers, RF scanners, etc.

◆ **Software.** What major software components does this use. This is usually multiple items.

◆ **Materials.** List unique materials needed, such as preprinted forms or special labels.

◆ **Users.** If this is widely used, list the departments that use it. If its use is confined to a few key people, then list them by name or title.

◆ **Suppliers.** Who supplies the key material? If the materials required are highly specialized, then list supplier information. Ensure this is included on the key supplier list. If the material is commonly available, then we can skip this.

Data Communications Network

The data communications network is the glue that ties all the PCs to the shared servers and to shared printers. Without the data network, the Accounting department cannot exchange spreadsheets, the call center cannot check their databases, and the Shipping department cannot issue bills of lading.

A data network is a complex collection of components, so the loss of network functionality may be localized within a department due to the failure of a single hub card.

Based on the collective knowledge of your team, what do you believe is the likelihood of a failure of your data network? Ask the same question of your network manager. Based on these two answers, plug a value into the risk assessment for this category.

Telecommunications System

Modern Private Branch Exchanges (PBXs) are special-purpose computers, optimized for switching telephone calls. They may also include voice mail and long-distance call tracking.

Your facility's telephone system is your connection to the outside world. If your company deals directly with its customers, special care must be taken because a dead telephone system can make them very uneasy. Telephones are used constantly internally to coordinate between departments and, in an emergency, to call outside for help.

Based on the collective knowledge of your team, what do you believe the likelihood is of a failure of your company's telephone system? Ask the same question of your Telecommunications manager. Based on these two answers, plug a value into the risk assessment for this category.

Shared Computers and LANs

There are many types of shared computers used by companies. They usually are grouped under the old name of "mainframe" but refer to shared computers of all sizes. It also includes the common term of LAN (Local Area Network). These computers typically support a wide range of programs and data. When evaluating the risks here, you have two questions:

➤ What is the risk of losing a specific shared application (like inventory control, payroll, etc.)? You should list each critical application separately.

➤ What is the risk of losing use of the machine itself? This could be due to damage to the machine or more likely through a hardware failure.

These risks should be based on the collective knowledge of your team. Ask the same question of your computer operations manager. Based on these two answers, plug a value into the risk assessment for this category. If desired, list each of the network servers individually.

Virus

What do you think the likelihood is of a computer in your facility contracting a software "virus"? How severely would this interrupt business? What would your customers think of your company if, before it was detected, you passed the virus on to them? What if it struck a key machine at a critical time? What if its mischievous function was to e-mail out, to anyone in your address book, anything that had the words "budget," "payroll," or "plan" in the file name?

Most companies have an Internet firewall and virus scanning software installed. When evaluating this risk, ask your data manager's opinion of the quality of his software. Ask how often the catalog of known viruses is updated.

Viruses can also enter your company through many other sources. Often they come in through steps people take to bypass the firewall or virus scanning, both of which take place only on files coming into your facility from the outside over your external data network:

➤ Does your company allow employees to take their laptop computers outside of the office, to their home? Are their children loading virus-laden programs? Are the employees downloading files from their home Internet connection that would be filtered out by their desk-side connection?

➤ Does your anti-virus software automatically update its catalog of known viruses, or must each person request this periodically?

➤ Do consultants, vendors, or customers bring laptop PCs into your facility and plug into your network to retrieve e-mail or to communicate orders?

➤ Is there virus-checking software to validate the attachments to your e-mail?

Data Systems

Theft of hardware (with critical data) can be a double financial whammy. You must pay to replace the hardware and then try to recreate valuable data. This risk spans your local site (do PCs disappear over the weekend?) all the way through laptop PCs taken on business trips.

Theft of software can be a major issue if someone steals a PC program and then distributes illegal copies of it. You may find yourself assumed guilty and facing a large civil suit. This can also happen by well-meaning employees loading illegal copies of software around the company.

Theft of data can occur and you will never realize it. This could be engineering data, customer lists, payroll information, security access codes, and any number of things. What do you believe your risk is of this?

Data backups are the key to rapid systems recovery. But what if you reach for the backup tapes and they are not readable? What is the risk that these tapes are not written, handled, transported, and stored correctly?

Hacker Security Break-In

One aspect of connecting your internal network to the World Wide Web is that it is a potential portal for uninvited guests to access your network. Even well-built defenses can be circumvented with careless setup or news of gaps in your security firewall software. In some cases, they invade your system only to mask their identity when they attack a different company. This way, all indications are that you originated the attack!

Hackers generally fall into several categories, none of them good for you:

➤ Curious hackers just want to see if they can do it. You never know when this person will advance to the malicious level, and they should not be in your system.

➤ Malicious or criminal hacking involving invading your site to steal or to damage something.

➤ In extreme cases, a hacker may conduct a denial of service attack and shut you down by bombarding you with network traffic, which overwhelms your network's ability to answer all the messages.

What other Layer 3 risks can you and your team identify? Add them to the list in Form 2-5 on the CD-ROM.

LAYER 4: DEPARTMENTAL RISKS

Departmental risks are the disasters you deal with in your own department on a daily basis. They range from the absence of a key employee to the loss of an important computer file. Most of these obstacles are overcome through the collective knowledge of the people in the department who either have experienced this problem before or know of ways to work around it.

So at this stage of the risk analysis we are looking at disastrous local problems. Consider for a moment what would happen if a worker changing light bulbs were to knock the head off a fire sprinkler. You know the ones I mean. A fire sprinkler nozzle typically protrudes from the ceiling into your office.

Losing a sprinkler head will put a lot of water all over that office very quickly. Papers will be destroyed, PCs possibly sizzled, and all work stopped for hours. The carpets will be soaked, water seeps through the floor to the offices on the floor below—what a mess!

A small fire is another localized disaster. It may spread smoke over a large area, making an office difficult to work in. Depending on how it was started and the extent of the damage, that area might be inaccessible for several days, especially if the Fire Marshall declares an arson investigation and no one is allowed near the "crime scene"!

Departmental risks also include the situation referred to in data systems where a unique device is used that is not easily or economically repairable. If this device is also a single point of failure, then you had better treat it like gold.

To build a departmental risk assessment, assemble a department-wide team to identify your critical functions, risks unique to your department, and risks to other departments that will cause problems in your group. Draft a fresh list of the critical functions that apply to your department. You can omit those functions already listed in the first three layers unless you are particularly vulnerable to something.

If a risk from an earlier layer will cause you to take particular action in your department, then include it here also. For example, if the loss of telephone service for your facility can be charged back against your telephone bill (based on your service agreement), then the Accounting department would need to time the outage and make the proper adjustment to their monthly bill. Another example is if you run the company cafeteria and an electrical outage threatens the food in your refrigerators.

Some examples of critical functions might include:

➤ **Payroll**

   ◆ To provide correct pay to all employees on time.

   ◆ To maintain accurate payroll records for every employee.

   ◆ To deduct and report to the appropriate government agency all payroll taxes that apply to every employee.

➤ **Materials**

   ◆ To maintain an accurate accounting of all material and its location in all storage locations.

   ◆ To maintain an accurate accounting of all materials issued.

   ◆ To ensure that material constantly flows to the manufacturing floor with minimal stock-outs, and with minimal inventory on hand.

➤ **Building Security**

   ◆ To provide immediate first aid to stricken employees until proper medical assistance arrives.

   ◆ To maintain the integrity of the building security cordon at all times, even in the face of disaster.

◆ To detect and notify appropriate authorities of any emergencies observed by security personnel.

◆ To monitor all personnel on the premises after normal business hours and during weekends and holidays.

WHAT TO DO?

Make a list of critical processes for your department.

Take a copy of the Critical Process list and pull off those processes unique to each department. Now expand it to include the critical processes in your department. Not all critical processes involve computers.

Break down the newly added critical processes into their components.

Key Operating Equipment

After identifying your department's critical functions, make a list of your processes and equipment. This list will drive your department's recovery plan. A process would be something like "Materials Management." That process requires (within the department) access to the materials database, materials receiving docks, order processing, etc.

Is there a critical piece of equipment in your department whose absence would hinder your ability to perform your critical tasks? Is there an important printer directly tied to a far-off office or company? Is your only fax machine busy all the time? Does your payroll department have a dedicated time clock data collection and reporting system whose absence might prevent accurate recording?

Make a list of all your critical equipment. Be sure to include unique items not readily borrowed from a nearby department.

Lack of Data Systems

Begin with a list of all the data systems you use in your department. Add a column of who uses each system and for what function (some people may perform updates, some people may only write reports from it). You will find this list very useful later.

Most data systems have a manual process to record data or work around when it is not available. But set that aside and examine the risk that each system on your list might not be available. Here is a good place where the team's collective experience can state how often a system seems to be unavailable.

Vital Records

What are the vital records originated, used, or stored by your department? List each category of records and where they are stored. Identify the risk (or damage) to the company if these records were lost or destroyed. Vital records are paper or electronic documents retained to meet business, regulatory, legal, or government requirements.

What other Layer 4 Risks can you and your team identify? Add them to Form 2-6 on the CD-ROM.

LAYER 5: YOUR DESK'S RISKS

This means more than avoiding paper cuts. You must examine every process (manual and automated), tool, piece of incoming information, and required output that makes up your job. Since you are so familiar with your daily work, this will be faster than you think. You are also familiar with your office priorities and can focus on the most critical functions.

Performing a Layer 5 risk analysis may seem to be a bit of overkill, but it closely resembles what was done at the department level. It is useful for ensuring that everything you need to do your job is accounted for in some manner, and may be in your department's disaster recovery plan as nice to have but not essential. Still, if you want to go on vacation sometime, this documentation will make slipping out of the office a bit easier.

Layer 5 risks are a bit different because it really includes all of the risks from Layers 1 through 4. You should be able to start figuring out your critical functions from your job description. Next, you add in what you actually do and then you will have your critical functions list.

Make a list of the tools and data systems that you use every day. All of these should be in the departmental risk assessment. What is the likelihood that one of these tools will be missing when you need them? This means that the tools are only missing from your desk. Everyone else in the department can do their job. Therefore, if your job is the same as the person's next to you, the risk at this layer is quite low that you could not complete your work since you could borrow the necessary equipment.

If you had confidential files on your PC and it crashed, that would be a risk. If you had a unique device that you used for your job, such as a specialized PC for credit card authorizations, then that is also a unique risk (but is probably in your departmental plan if it impacts one of their critical functions).

Another area to consider is vital records. Do you build or store vital records on or around your desk? Could there be a localized fire, water pipe breakage, etc. in your area that would soak these papers? This could be backed-up personal computer files, engineering specifications of old parts, employee evaluations, etc.

What other Layer 5 Risks can you or your team identify? Add them to Form 2-7 on the CD-ROM.

WHAT TO DO?

Make a list of critical processes for your department.

Take a copy of your Department's Critical Process list and pull off those processes unique to your job. Now expand it to include all the critical processes for your position. Not all critical processes involve computers.

Break down the newly added critical processes into their components.

SEVERITY OF A RISK

As you consider such things as fire, you quickly notice that except in the total loss of the structure, it all depends on where and when the fire occurs. In addition, it depends on the day of the week and the time of day.

Time of Day

Imagine a large factory. It's 7:00 A.M. and the assembly line has begun moving. Off to one side of the assembly line is a 300-gallon "tote" of paint, waiting for a forklift to carry it to another part of the facility. When the forklift approaches, the operator is distracted and hits the tote at a high rate of speed, puncturing it near the bottom with both of his forks. The punctured tote begins spewing hundreds of gallons of potentially toxic paint across the floor, into the assembly line area, etc. Of course, the assembly operation is shut down while a long and thorough cleanup process begins.

If this same forklift and the same operator were to hit the same tote after normal working hours, we would have the same mess and the same clean-up expense, but we could possibly have avoided shutting down the assembly line. With hard work, the assembly line could be ready for use by the next day. Therefore, the time of day that a disaster event occurs can have a major impact on its severity.

Day of Week

Along the same lines as the time of day, the day of the week (or for that matter, the day of the year) also determines the severity of a problem. If this same factory were working at its peak level with many temporary workers in an effort to deliver toys to stores in time for the Christmas season, this situation would be much worse than if it occurred during their low-demand season. If it happened on a Saturday instead of on a Monday, the severity would also be less as you have the remainder of the weekend to address it.

Location of the Risk

In terms of where this theoretical toxic material spill occurred, you can also quickly see that its location, near the assembly line, had an impact on how damaging it was. Some risks, like paint containers, float around a manufacturing facility. In an office, a similar situation exists. A small fire in an outside trash dumpster might singe the building and be promptly extinguished. The damage would be annoying, but your office productivity would not miss a beat.

The same small fire in your vital records storage room would be a disaster. Water damage to the cartons of paper would cause papers to stick together, cartons to weaken and collapse, and a general smoky smell that will linger for a long time. There is also a potential long-term problem with mold damaging the records.

WHO CAN YOU CALL FOR RISK ASSESSMENT INFORMATION?

The Federal Emergency Management Agency (formerly known as Civil Defense) can provide you with a wealth of local information about your Layer 1 risks. They have already mapped the approved hazardous materials routes. They know what the local natural disaster likelihood is. FEMA is listed in your telephone books and can also be found at http://www.fema.gov. Figure 2-6 shows a sample of the type of maps available from the government that show the likelihood of various hazards; this map shows the probability of an earthquake occurring.

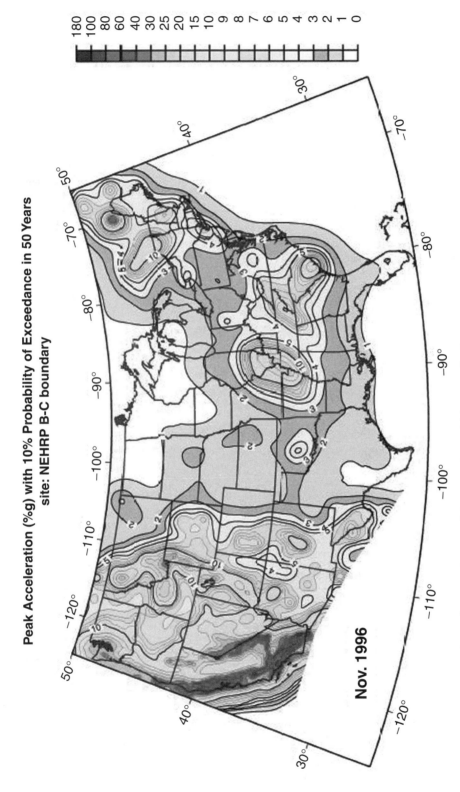

Peak Acceleration (%g) with 10% Probability of Exceedance in 50 Years site: NEHRP B-C boundary

Nov. 1996

FIGURE 2-6: U.S. Geological Survey National Seismic Hazard Mapping Project

Local fire and police departments are also likely sources for information on anticipated arrival times for help. If you have a volunteer fire department, you would like to know their average response time for your area and what you might expect for timely ambulance support. The longer the delay in responding, the more mitigation steps that your company should plan for. Some volunteer departments staff a few fulltime members to provide an immediate response and the rest of the volunteers join them at the accident site.

The local law enforcement authorities can also provide insight into crime activity patterns for determining your risk of theft or civil disorder.

MAKING THE ASSESSMENT

Wow! Now that we see that risks are all around us, that they vary in time, magnitude, and business impact, let's make some sense of all of this. This is a good time to bring your Disaster Planning Project team together. The more "institutional knowledge" you can tap for this list, the better tool it becomes.

Scoring

OK, now the risk analysis sheets have been filled and the scores calculated. Now it is time to identify the more likely risks and build plans for them.

Scoring the list involves your judgment of several factors. First, how likely is it that this will occur? If you think about, given an infinite amount of time, you could predict that about everything will occur at least once. So for this scoring exercise, let's use a 5-year horizon. Of course, you can use any timeframe you wish. Just be consistent.

We will use the electrical power outage as an example as we examine the column headings:

➤ **Grouping.** These are the overall categories provided to keep like issues together.

➤ **Risk.** This is where you list the various risks to your business.

➤ **Likelihood.** 0 through 10, with 0 being no likelihood at all and 10 as a sure thing. Remember your planning horizon. If it is 5 years, be sure to keep that in the forefront of everyone's mind. So over the next 5 years, what is the likelihood that the facility will lose electrical power at any time of the day, or any day of the week?

➤ **Impact.** 0 through 10, with 0 being no impact at all and 10 as a death sentence for the company. How badly would this disaster hurt us? To judge this, consider the problem occurring at the busiest time of the day, on the busiest day of the year.

➤ **Restoration Time.** 1 through 10, with 10 being a very short time and 1 as 10 days or longer. How long will this take to repair? Carrying forward the electrical service example, in the collective memory of your team, how long does it usually take to restore power? Use an average.

Sorting

The spreadsheet multiplies the Likelihood times the Impact times the Restoration Time to get a rough risk analysis score. As you can see, a zero value in the Likelihood or Impact columns makes the risk score a zero.

You should sort the spreadsheet on the "score" column in descending order. This will bring your biggest risks to the top. As you start your disaster recovery and mitigation plans, these risks deserve the most attention.

Setting Aside the Low Scores

It is true that there is a risk that the sun may quit shining within the next 5 years, but it is very low. So along with the risk of being run over by an iceberg, we will discard any of the extremely low likelihood risks. We will be fully occupied addressing the more likely ones.

Pick a point on each list and draw a line across it. All critical systems above the line will have plans written for them and plans for all below the line will come at some later time.

CONCLUSION

Your assessment of the risks faced by your operation is a critical piece of the business continuity puzzle. The steps in identifying the major risks to your operation as discussed in this chapter are:

1. First, determine the cost of downtime. This is critical when evaluating the potential avoidance and mitigation options.

2. Identify the potential risks at each of the five levels. Use a five-year time horizon to keep things manageable.

3. For each risk, determine the impact based on the time of day, the day of the week, and the location where the disaster occurred. Each of these factors has an impact on the severity of the risk.

4. Identify and use outside sources of risk information, such as emergency response operations at the local and state level.

5. Prioritize the risks based on the severity of the possible damage, the probability of the risk occurring, and the difficulty of available avoidance and mitigation options. You'll want to start with the risks that do the most damage, are the most likely, and are the easiest to avoid or mitigate.

Now that you've identified the risks that can affect your business, you are much better prepared to recover from any disaster. The steps required to identify risks are time consuming but are critical in building a foundation for your business continuity plans.

CHAPTER 3

BUILD AN INTERIM PLAN
Don't Just Sit There, Do Something

Build it and they will come.
—*Field of Dreams*

INTRODUCTION

Building an effective business continuity plan can take a great deal of time and resources. There is a considerable amount of information to identify and to gather, and a significant amount of time and effort required to organize people to interview. Until the primary disaster plan begins coming together, there are 11 steps you can take *right now* to provide some initial protection. The steps you follow in this chapter will be expanded in great detail in later chapters. Even if your disaster planning stops after this chapter, you will be noticeably better prepared.

Create an Interim Plan Notebook to organize your information. It should contain:

1. **Access to People.** Organization charts should be included to show who is assigned what areas of responsibilities and who their assistants are. Contact information for each key person: work phone, home phone, cellular phone number, pager number, and home address should be included.

2. **Access to the Facility.** A set of keys must be available to every door, cabinet, and closet that holds equipment you support, all maintained in a secure key locker. This includes copies of any special system passwords.

3. **Service Contracts.** Be sure you have the name, address, telephone number (day and night), contact name (day and night), serial numbers of equipment on the contract, contract number and expiration date. This section may also include a copy of the service agreement renewal calendar.

4. **Vendor List.** A list of companies where you have accounts set up for quickly buying emergency supplies. This includes contact information.

5. **Walkaround Asset Inventory.** This is necessary to properly build a plan. A thorough asset inventory will come later. What assets might you need to recover or to restore to service right away?

6. **Software Asset List.** What software are you protecting, insuring against loss, and supporting?

7. **Critical Business Functions.** What are the business functions we are trying to protect, to keep running with minimal disruption?

8. **Operations Restoration Priorities.** What do we fix first, and in what order do we restore functions to service?

9. **Toxic Material Storage.** Locations of toxic material anywhere on the company grounds.

10. **Emergency Equipment List.** Where are the equipment and materials you need to help clean up a mess?

11. **Trained First Responders.** Do you have any volunteer firefighters or Emergency Medical Technician (EMTs) on your staff? Does anyone have critical skills you can use in a crisis until emergency crews arrive?

In most emergencies you need the same several things: key people, keys to the doors, and key support account information. For your interim plan, you will pull together basic contact information on the people you would call on in a disaster, the service contracts you would invoke, and keys/passwords necessary to gain entry into where you need to be.

A quick way to gauge your current state of disaster readiness is to make unannounced visits asking for critical support information. Watch the people as you ask for this information and you will see how organized some are. See who can quickly provide a copy of their list and who has everything scattered about in a "sticky-note file." As you watch them fumbling through folders of documents, aren't you glad this isn't happening during a real crisis? How high would the quality of their hurriedly gathered information be? How quickly could they provide the correct answers? Rapid availability of this information is very useful even if the computer room is not on fire. Imagine the same people doing this during an emergency, and with the office only illuminated by emergency lighting.

As the information flows in, take time to carefully organize it. Label each item as to who sent it to you and the date you received it. If you later need an explanation about their information, you'll know who to call. The date indicates when you received it, not how old this information actually is. It never hurts to validate critical information like telephone numbers and contract agreements. Set up a tabbed three-ring binder to hold all the information. Later on, you will consolidate this information into your own lists and they will take a lot less space.

Remember that what you collect for an interim plan must be useful to anyone involved in disaster recovery. Readability, accuracy, and clarity are important. The various documents must be accumulated in a single binder and published to your various managers. Place a date on each document to show when it was created. This will also act as a built-in reminder to call for updated documents if you feel they are too old. Be sure to keep a copy of these documents at home; emergencies don't always happen during normal business hours.

Keep track of who has a copy of the binder. Then, as updates are created, you know who to pass them on to. Ensure all binders are tabbed for quick reference and clearly marked as Company Confidential in accordance with your company's document guidelines (remember, you have home telephone numbers in here).

At a minimum, each of the following people should have an up-to-date copy of this interim plan.

➤ Contingency Planning Coordinator (you—the person writing the plan).

➤ Disaster Recovery Manager (to be kept at home).

➤ Data Processing Department's Help Desk.

➤ Facility Security Manager (in a place the after-hours guard on duty can reach it).

ACCESS TO PEOPLE

Reaching key people is a two-step task. The first step is to know whom to notify. The second step is to know how to reach them. You should know not only how to reach your boss, but also the purchasing department, public relations manager, custodians' office; much more than just the people in your department.

Start with an organization chart that shows who works in what department from the top person down to the night-shift custodians. Current charts are often hard to come by. Organization charts reflect the formal lines of authority within an organization, not the actual day-to-day flow of authority.

The organization chart will help you to see who is responsible for what areas and who you might need to call if a given disaster occurs. Think of some of the ways this will be useful. If the accounts payable system crashes over a weekend, you might need to call in the accounting clerk who uses that system to test your fix before work starts on Monday. If there is a fire in the Quality Assurance office overnight, you need to know which manager to notify.

The second piece is a complete telephone list for all employees to include home telephone numbers, cell phone numbers, pager number, etc. In most cases, you will only notify the department managers, but by having a complete list, you should always be able to call in the "resident expert."

A funny thing about a telephone recall list is that some people lie to the company about their home telephone number. Imagine that! Others "forget" to pick up their pager every night before they go home. We can't change all the bad habits of the world, but for those key people who are critical to your disaster recovery efforts, ensure their numbers are correct even if you have to call them yourself.

An easy way to check this list is whenever it is used to call someone off-hours, make a small notation of the date next to their name. If the call went through, that is validation enough. Once every several months, take time to make a call to any of the unchecked phone numbers just to verify them.

Try to never call people after hours unless it is necessary (like checking the list). Check with your human resources manager to see what the impact is on hourly and salary workers compensation for calling people after hours.

If your company has multiple sites, you will need the telephone numbers for their key technical, support, and management people also. In an emergency, it is sometimes quicker to borrow material from a sister company than to buy it in a crisis. Also, instead of hiring unknown consultants to assist in your recovery, it is far better to borrow skilled people from sister companies. They are already familiar with your company's procedures, and they should have already had a security screening (something your emergency consultants may not have). All around, it is preferable to call on your fellow employees to supplement your recovery staff than it is to hire someone on the spur of the moment.

ACCESS TO THE FACILITY

Limiting access to the company's assets is not an optional activity. It is something your auditors will be checking. All sensitive areas must be secured, such as computer rooms, telephone switch room, vital records storage, and personnel files. There may be other areas unique to your company that must also be safeguarded. If in doubt, ask the auditors. They are a valuable source of information for disaster planning.

Don't be shy about asking detailed questions of your company's security force concerning the arrangements protecting your area of responsibility. Do not take for granted that they provide the proper protection for your equipment. Review their after-hours entry policy to ensure it meets your emergency needs.

Keys

Murphy's law says that problems will happen in the worst possible places. Wherever the problem occurs, you will need to get into the room it is in. Imagine a network problem. You may need to access a number of equipment closets checking data hubs until you find the defective equipment; another key to gain entry to the hub's cabinet, and still a third key to enter the secure area where spare hub cards are maintained.

In most facilities, the security force maintains copies of the physical keys to all doors and locks. If this is the case in your company, then you should review their key management policies and key locker procedure. Things to look for and for you to do if they are missing:

➤ There should be a formal request form for requesting a key. Each request should be properly authorized before a key is issued. People who feel accountable for a key will treat it more like a valued object. If someone keeps losing their keys, then they should not be given any more of them. Note how often their car keys turn up missing and you'll see that it is only your key that they don't care about.

➤ There should be a "Key Log" of who has what keys. Verify that people who work for you only have what is needed. Use this list to recover keys when people leave the company. If a theft of company property is detected, this list will be a valuable starting point for the investigation. If locks must be changed, this will tell you how many keys are needed for the new setting. Review this list at least quarterly to recover keys from people who no longer need them.

➤ A locked cabinet with copies of all keys must be maintained.

Sometimes paranoid people attach their own locks to cabinets to keep others away from their equipment. You may not even be aware there is an unauthorized lock on this door or know who to even ask for a combination. Personal locks on company doors and cabinets must be vigorously discouraged as it will hinder your recovery at a time when you can ill afford it.

Even if your facility security force has a key locker, you might want to have one just for your department in a place that you can get to quickly. For your own department, you might establish a "Key Locker" to hold a copy of every key to every door and cabinet in your facility. Then no matter who is on-site during a disaster, they can quickly enter the room or cabinet and begin containing the damage until the expert support team arrives.

For security reasons, only a few people should have access to this cabinet. Otherwise, you would be surprised how fast these keys will disappear. A sign-out sheet in the cabinet can be used to track what has been loaned out, to whom, when, and by whom authorized.

Note the phone numbers of local locksmiths who are available around the clock, every day of the week. If you are depending on the building security folks to provide this service, inspect their operation to ensure it includes all keys and that they are available 24/7. Whoever maintains the key locker should also have a large set of bolt cutters. This "master key" will open most locks by slicing through them. Use it liberally on all noncompany locks you encounter.

Master keys are keys that open more than one door. The way that door locks are keyed is such that security zones are created. This allows a master key to open all the doors in a given department and not in other departments. Master keys must be closely guarded and issued sparingly.

Electronic Keys

An excellent solution to the problem of propagating keys is electronic locks. Electronic locks are expensive to install but provide a wide range of benefits.

An electronic lock not only opens the door but it tells you who tried to open a door, when they opened the door, and how long it was open.

You see electronic door locks in most modern hotels. Hotels had a problem. Customers often lost their keys or continued their journey without turning them in. The hotel had to assume that someone was walking around with the key to a room that might use it to break in later. This forced them into an expensive rekeying of the doors. Rekeying cost their customers money and was a constant problem for the innkeeper. Now if someone checks out of a hotel with an electronic key, that key is disabled. Door locks no longer need changing and customers are no longer billed for re-keying.

Another problem with physical keys is that they get lost, get copied (with and without permission), and the people holding them may pass them on to less-trusted individuals. You can never be sure if a key is truly lost or has been intentionally stolen so that some miscreant can gain access to a particular area. This forces an expensive lock change. It also means that anyone else with one of these keys (those who are entitled to have one) must exchange their key for a current version.

There is not a law against copying keys. Even the keys stamped with an admonition of "Do Not Copy" have no legal standing. Key makers will copy them as they please. So anytime a key is provided to someone, they can easily make a copy. Once they surrender their key, you cannot be sure that door is still safe. For all anyone knows, they made a copy of that key for their friend in another department.

An electronic lock uses the digital number on a key or a key code to determine who has access to what area. All information is kept in a master database. When you try to open a door, the badge's number is read or the key code used is recorded and sent to a database. The database checks to see if you are authorized to open that door. If you are, then the door latch releases. If not, then usually nothing happens and the lock ignores the key. At the database, a record is saved of the key number trying to open a door, where, when, and if the door was opened or not.

In this way, people can be given access or denied access via the database without issuing or recovering keys to each door. If a key is lost, it can be disabled at the database and be worthless to a thief. Anyone that finds it has a useless piece of plastic. If an employee leaves the company, you can disable the key quickly. This of course depends on the individual to report the lost key and have it promptly disabled.

Whether you are allowed in or not, each attempt is recorded with a date and time for tracking who went where. Denied access can be used to see who is testing your security system. If something is missing from an area, you can see who entered each room. This log must be reviewed daily to see which unauthorized cards are attempting to get through which doors.

An electronic lock can also track doors that are propped open. Depending on how your system is configured, this may trigger a security alarm to see if this is a legitimate activity or if someone wanted a door left ajar. Since the log also told you who opened the door, it could be a good time to find out why they do this. If you wanted the door left open, you would save money and remove the lock!

Electronic locks also allow for master keys and security zones. This lets you set up the electronic key for the telephone systems technician to open all telephone room doors but none of the computer room doors, etc. Electronic keys are nice because it is easy to enable various levels of security at any time.

Like the physical keys, you should use the electronic lock software to generate a quarterly key access report to review which employees have access to what areas. This will catch those cases where someone's project once needed access to an area that is no longer required. It may also highlight more than one card issued to a person (they lost one, were issued a "temporary" replacement, and then kept it and the original). Usually this list is circulated among your managers to ensure people have the proper access. Keep in mind your after-hours support requirements or you'll be making some late-night trips to open doors!

Passwords

A system password is like a master key. Usually keyed to the user ID of administrator, they provide unlimited security access to every feature on a computer system. In our case, we may need them to perform an emergency shutdown of main computer systems. For this reason only, we need them kept in the key locker. These passwords have an unlimited potential for mischief so they must be closely guarded.

Establish a secure area to store system passwords. They can all fit on a sheet of paper and must include all administrator-level accounts. This is kept in a sealed envelope near your equipment in the event that a rapid system shutdown is required. Another place to store this is inside your key locker. Check the seal on the envelope from time to time to ensure it has not been tampered with.

You will need this information if you ever need to shut down or restart your computer system when the systems experts are not available. This might be due to a fire in an adjacent room where the loss of electrical power [and Uninterruptible Power Supply (UPS) power] is imminent.

SERVICE CONTRACTS

How could someone qualify the downtime on a piece of machinery as a disaster? You would if that was the only printer that could print pay checks and today is payday! These normally must be distributed at a given time and you may not be able to wait another 4 hours for a staff member to come in just to look at it. It might be critical if your primary data communications hub began emitting blue smoke. It might be critical if . . . but I think you get the picture.

A service contract isn't much good to you if you can't call for help when you need it. Round-the-clock service coverage is very useful for maximizing system uptime. This is especially true for critical hardware and software. Unfortunately, 24/7 service can easily double the cost of a service contract. So if you are paying out this large premium every month, take steps to ensure it is available when needed. People cannot call for it if they don't know how.

Obtain a list of all service providers you have service agreements with. Cross-check this list with a walk-around to ensure that all your major equipment is accounted for on the list. We will need to include all these service provider names later when we build our vendor contact list.

There are four basic types of contracts with endless variations:

1. **24/7.** Unlimited around-the-clock coverage for time and materials. Pay one price per month and leave your worries behind. This is necessary for mission-critical equipment and is the most expensive approach.

2. **8 to 5.** They will work on equipment problems during the business day and usually supply any parts that are needed.

3. **Time and Materials.** They will work on it and charge you by the hour for the repair technician's time. The costs of any parts required are also included on the bill. This is good for nonessential equipment that rarely breaks.

4. **Exchange.** Send them your broken equipment and they will either send you a refurbished replacement or repair it and send it back. This is good for devices where you have on-site spares, such as monitors, terminals, scanners, printers, etc.

Begin building your list of service agreements. This list will be very useful in many areas of your company—the help desk, the late-shift operators, the security guards, and many other places. Use Form 3-1 on the CD-ROM to develop your list. The essential information to gather from each of your service agreements include:

➤ **Contact Names.** Whom do I call? There may be multiple people involved with your account. There may be a sales representative, a dedicated technician, and even an after-hours contact name and number. When time is short, you need to know who to talk to for the fastest service.

➤ **Company Address.** Look at the city to see how far away they are. You can gauge an approximate response time for the technician. Any spare parts the technician may need will probably be that far away also. If the service company is too far away, make a note to look for someone closer to home. On the other hand, some companies use a work-from-home field workforce, so using the company's address is only a starting point for this inquiry.

➤ **Telephone Numbers.** This could be a rather long list. You may have a separate number for normal hours, their fax machine, the technicians' direct line, and an after-hours number. You need them all clearly identified. Like your recall list, when you use one, pencil in the date next to it so you know the last time that telephone number was validated.

➤ **E-mail Address.** Many companies use e-mail to pass noncritical information to their customers. This might also help if your sales representative was away from the office on a business trip and was checking for messages.

➤ **Customer Number.** The identification code number by which this contract is known to the vendor. You will need this when you call the problem in. Service centers normally will not budge until they verify that you are paid up and eligible for this service.

➤ **Hours of Support Under Contract.** This is VERY important. It will determine if you will be billed for the service call. If you are paying for 8:00 A.M. until 5:00 P.M. service and then demand a technician come out late at night, you will be billed for a hefty hourly fee. This may be acceptable, so long as you are aware of the potential costs. Paying for 8 to 5 service means that if the repair isn't finished at 5:00, the repair technician is going home and will be back tomorrow. Otherwise, you will again be paying a large overtime hourly fee.

➤ **When Does the Agreement Expire?** Some equipment inconveniently breaks on the wrong side of the deadline. All service contract expiration dates should be placed on a calendar so that you can see this coming and negotiate a new agreement before the old one expires. This information can also feed into your annual budget process.

➤ **Description of What You Buy from Them.** This could be a wide range of things. Some contacts provide everything for a fee to include materials and labor. Service companies you don't often need may be contracted under a time-and-materials scheme for all repairs. Whatever you buy from them, very briefly describe it here.

➤ **Your Internal Designated Contact Persons.** Many contracts require that several persons be designated as the company's representatives for contacting them to prevent their lines from being flooded by minor calls. Even though specific people are named in the contract, by declaring an emergency the service company should begin assistance until the named parties arrive.

Now that you have this list, assign someone to make up small cards for each machine covered by a service agreement. On this card, print all the essential information you have gathered. Firmly attach this information to the machine or inside of its cover. This is the ideal—information available at the point it is needed. Now if that device quakes, shakes, and begins to moan, the information on whom to call is immediately at hand.

When attaching these cards, check the machine over for advertising stickers. Some service companies attach them to whatever they repair. This is OK except when you change service companies and some well-meaning soul calls the number on the sticker to repair the machine. Without a service agreement, they may come out and send you an expensive bill. So when you see these stickers, remove them. People will get into the habit of depending on the cards you tape to the machines.

If you have a lot of equipment in the same room, make up an information station with a notebook attached to the wall that contains all the same information. Keep track of wherever you place this information for the times when you need to update your service providers or hours of coverage.

VENDOR LIST

Now that you know whom to call for a service call, make up a list of the other companies you routinely deal with using Form 3-2 (see CD). Since we have the major equipment covered, we can now focus in on the companies who provide your routine supplies. Why is that important?

Have you ever run out of something seemingly mundane like a special toner cartridge, and your usual purchasing agent is on vacation? The company kept moving along but there was someone out there that was very vocally upset. As you collect vendor contact information, you will quickly see how this can be very useful.

You want vendor contact information for the companies that supply your support materials such as custom cables, preprinted forms, backup tapes, any number of things you need to keep your operation flowing smoothly. Most suppliers don't list an after-hours number. They have one but it is not published. Try to get it from the salesperson. If they don't have it, get the salesperson's home number. Often when you really need something, a salesperson will go the extra mile to build customer loyalty.

Obtain a list of all support materials suppliers. This includes companies that provide off-site storage of your backup tapes, courier services, companies that provide preprinted forms, and companies that sell or lease you equipment as well as companies that repair it. Mandate that it be kept current. Essential data elements include:

➤ Contact names.

➤ Company address.

➤ Telephone numbers: normal hours, fax, and after-hours number.

➤ E-mail address.

➤ Your internal vendor number.

➤ Description of what you buy from them.

Public utilities are another set of vendors you need to know about. Loss of service from telephone, electric, gas, and water companies can shut down your operations is the blink of an eye. These companies all have 24-hour service support numbers. They may also have a special trouble reporting number for companies and major customers. For each utility, you will need:

➤ Contact names for sales, technical support, after-hours dispatch.

➤ Telephone numbers for each contact to include their normal hours number, fax number, and after-hours number.

➤ E-mail address for handling routine issues.

Public safety telephone numbers must also be prominent on your list. The ubiquitous 911 is always a good starting point, but you may find the normal telephone numbers for police, fire, ambulance, and the local hospital are all handy to have in a crisis. Use Form 3-3 (see CD) to start your list of whom to call in an emergency.

WALK-AROUND ASSET INVENTORY

Most companies have a lot of equipment to keep track of. We'll get to that later. Start by making a walk-though of your areas of responsibility (do not trust this to memory). Draft a list with key information on all your major equipment. A major piece of equipment is one that costs a lot of money, or that takes a long time to replace, or your operation depends on it and it is the only one like it you have. This will usually be your larger or shared pieces of equipment.

As you walk around, be sure to open all closet doors and look into boxes. You would be surprised what you will find stashed away by people for emergencies. Note the location of any spare equipment. Arrange to have it picked up later. It should all be collected into one central point to cut down on the number of duplicate spares. Computers and computer component parts are like fresh fish; they lose value quickly with age. If everyone is hiding something like a spare printer in case they have system problems, you could be paying for many more spares than you need. Consolidate and lock up all your spares in one location to minimize costs and so they will be available to whoever needs them. This may even free some equipment for use elsewhere.

When you examine each machine, look for indications of who sold or maintains the device. Sometimes repair services place large stickers with their telephone number on devices they service. Note these in case you cannot locate the service contract for this device.

Another sticker often found somewhere on the inside is a notice of the last time this device received preventative maintenance. Some equipment such as a network server may need as little as an occasional shake-out of the fan filter. Other devices, such as your UPS system, need their batteries checked every 6 months. The frequency that preventative maintenance is required can be found inside the manual that accompanies the equipment. Therefore, also begin locating the manuals you need. All preventative maintenance must be recorded in a log for that device. Note what was done and by whom. If the service was improperly done, and then the equipment fails, you may have a claim against the service company.

To continue with the thought on hardware manuals, the books should either be prominently displayed adjacent to the equipment or collected into a central place. This reduces the amount of time lost looking for answers. As you walk around, make a note next to each piece of equipment on your list as to whether the manual could be located.

In each room note the following information. Again, this is for critical systems, not a wall-to-wall inventory. Be sure to include all the equipment in your computer room, telephone switch room, and network closets (a chain is only as strong as its weakest link). The list should include:

➤ **Manufacturer's Name.**

➤ **Model Number.**

➤ **Serial Number.**

➤ **Warranty Expiration Date.** Tracking this will save on service costs and help you to know when to add that item to a service contract. Be sure to add it to your service contract renewal calendar.

➤ **Location.** You may need to work up your own notation for this if everything is not conveniently set up in an easily identifiable room.

➤ **Serviced by.** This may be a sticker right on the device.

➤ **Connected to.** This will take some asking around but will be very useful. Out of this, you may uncover the weak link in a chain.

➤ **Feeds into What.** Same benefits as connected to.

Think back to previous problems. Are there any other critical or unique devices around your facility that should be on the list? How about the UPS in your computer room? I bet there is another one on your telephone switch. Both rooms require climate control for the equipment to operate safely, so the HVAC repair number must be on there also.

Now that you have a list of your critical equipment, take time to cross-reference the equipment list to the vendor service agreement list. Are any of your critical devices lacking service coverage? Be sure to check the serial numbers because that is how service companies determine what is covered. Note the type of service agreement that each item has.

Consider each item on the asset list separately. Based on your experience, should any of the coverage be increased to include after-hours support? Should any of the items be reduced to 8:00 A.M. to 5:00 P.M. (or whatever they offer)?

With all this information at hand, draft a vendor list of whom to call and normal billing method (time and materials, flat rate, etc.). Consider making a matrix that allows you to quickly check to see who supplies services or materials per device, such as every vendor that supports your AS/400. Use Form 3-4 (see CD) as a starting point for creating your list.

SOFTWARE ASSET LIST

If you lose a server, a critical PC, or shop floor controller to a fire, you need to know what to replace it with. There is much more to a computer than what you see on its outside; there is all the very important software inside of it. Replacing the hardware without loading all the appropriate software (and data) will only result in a dark monitor staring back at you.

For each of the critical systems you have previously identified, you need to make a list of any software they require to drive them. This includes copies of custom software, any nonstandard driver programs, or operating system settings. (Cross-check this against your vendor list!)

This sometimes creates a problem if the machine that dies is old and only the latest hardware is available. You can reload the software from a data backup (you hope), but the hardware and existing operating system might create some conflicts.

In many cases, you can recover the software for that machine by reloading its full disk image backup. If you must reload the software from the original media, you need to be able to locate it. Once purchased software has been loaded onto a server, it should be stored along with your backup tapes at an offsite location.

CRITICAL BUSINESS FUNCTIONS

A key driver to your disaster planning is a clear identification of the critical business functions performed at your facility. You cannot protect everything equally, so you need to concentrate your recovery plans on the most important functions. Identifying this is a top management function.

Every company has a few essential things it does. Everything else can be delayed for a short time while the critical functions bring progress to a halt. Critical items must be recovered before all other areas. If you must draw up your own list, be sure to discuss them with your accounting manager or controller. Don't be surprised if they cannot rattle off a list to you. They probably never worked a list up either.

For each critical function you identify, explain why it is important. Does it involve cash flow? Does it fulfill a regulatory requirement? If you have a broad understanding of your business, your list may be quite long—too long.

Try to narrow it down to 10 or fewer items. The longer list is still very useful, but what we are after is a guideline.

In a later chapter, we will develop a cross reference between critical business functions and the data systems and critical equipment that support them. This will help to identify the impact of the loss of a specific server and the business systems it supports.

RESTORATION PRIORITIES

If three things break at once, which one do you fix first? That is a restoration priority. Based on the Critical Business Functions identified in the previous step, you now take your asset list and identify restoration priorities for every asset.

Some of these are easy. If there is a file server used by many departments across the company, it will have a high priority for service restoration. A telephone switch is the same high importance. But how important is your e-mail server? Is it more important than the Materials department's warehouse server? Probably not, unless it is the conduit for e-mailed and faxed orders from customers.

Consider this from another angle. If the electrical company called and said they were shutting off two thirds of the power to your building, which equipment would you shut down, which would you ensure stayed up, and which would you stand by to start as soon as the outage was over?

TOXIC MATERIAL STORAGE

For the safety of all concerned, you should know if there is any toxic material stored on the premises and where it is. If there is a fire, building collapse, or flood, you will want to help warn people away from that area.

Use a map of the facility to indicate where this material is stored and what it is. If it is flammable, be sure to note that also. This is an important part of your plan so ensure everyone is aware of it.

Everyone on the recovery team must know where these dangerous materials are located and how to identify if they are leaking. They should know what to do if they encounter them.

EMERGENCY EQUIPMENT LIST

When a disaster occurs, you're going to want to know where things are to help reduce the amount of damage to equipment and the facility. This includes things such as electrical shutoff, water valves, gas shutoff, sprinkler system controls, etc. You also want to know where any special equipment such as portable pumps, wet/dry vacuums, and special fire extinguishers are kept so that damage can be kept to minimum.

Everyone on the recovery team must know where these items are located and how to use them in the event of an emergency. See Form 3-5 (on CD) to start your list of emergency equipment. And yes! Don't forget the keys to the doors!

TRAINED FIRST RESPONDERS

Many rural communities depend on volunteer fire departments and ambulance crews to support their towns. If any of your employees are EMT qualified, this is important to note. If anyone is a trained volunteer firefighter, this is important; a ham radio operator, a homebuilder, any number of things might show up. An additional question is if they have any hobbies or outside interests that would be of use in a crisis.

If you have any military Reserve or National Guard personnel, the training for their military job classification may be useful. They may be military police, hospital workers, or a wide range of things. It is not unusual to work in an entirely different military field than is your civilian job. A possible downside to having these people on staff is that, in a wide-area emergency, these people may be called to government service and not be available to assist in your recovery.

Anyone that you identify with additional skills should be added to your recall roster. You need to indicate what skills each has, along with details on how to contact them during and after work hours. This list will have the same format (and be a continuation of) the emergency notification and recall list drawn up in the "Access to People" section of this chapter. You will need their work telephone number, home telephone numbers, cell phone numbers, pager number, home address, etc.

You should check this list with your Human Resources department to ensure you are not violating any company rules by calling on these people in an emergency.

CONCLUSION

Once you have finished the steps outlined in this chapter, you'll have created a basic interim plan that will drastically improve your ability to handle any disaster that occurs. This interim plan will provide the recovery team the critical information they need to:

1. Get access to key people that can get the recovery process started as soon as possible.

2. Get access to facilities and computer systems to get them back up and running.

3. Have the service contracts they'll need to get the vendors you've contracted with for outside support busy as quickly as possible.

4. Order emergency supplies quickly from critical vendors.

5. Document assets damaged using the walk-around asset list.

6. Order replacement copies of important software.

7. Identify the critical business functions that must continue during restoration.

8. Restore the operational functions in the best order.

9. Identify the location of toxic materials to cleanup crews for their protection.

10. Locate on-site emergency equipment and materials you need to help clean up the mess.

11. Ask for assistance from any volunteer firefighters or EMTs who are on staff.

If you have followed these steps and collected this information, you have the material for a basic business continuity plan. If your project stopped right now, your company is noticeably better prepared for a crisis than it was before. But don't stop now! There is much more important information to gather and mitigation actions to identify. What you have now is a good starting point. Continue reading to get the information you need to develop a complete plan.

CHAPTER 4

EMERGENCY OPERATIONS CENTER
Take Control of the Situation

Congress can make a general,
but it takes a radio operator to
make him a commanding general.
—USMC Radio Operator School slogan

This chapter is a bit different from the other chapters in this book. While the other chapters deal with problem recognition and mitigation, this chapter focuses on establishing a tool that must be ready before an emergency strikes.

INTRODUCTION

Emergency Operations Center—war room—command center:-these names invoke images of serious-faced people scurrying around feverishly trying to address one major problem or another. These terms imply action and direction of resources toward a goal. For the Emergency Operations Center, the goal is the return to service of whatever business emergency from which you want to recover. In this sense, you see that an Emergency Operations Center is a temporary tool to coordinate your containment and recovery efforts.

The radio school saying, trite as it is, provides a great deal of insight into a problem. Unless leaders can communicate with their workers, there is nothing but chaos. Imagine a horde of well-meaning technical people (and a few who amuse themselves with mischief) all scurrying around trying to fix a problem irrespective of what the person on their left or right is doing. Some people would be wiring equipment up and someone would come in behind them and disconnect every thing. No coordinated action, no focused activity, just confusion. Of course, you would have no clue as to the progress being made while your boss demands an accurate update every hour. Not a pretty sight.

Now consider the alternative. A disaster occurs, and everyone knows where to report. Someone at the recovery site is noting who is available and assigning them to teams based on the problem and the individuals' expertise. As a team fills, they are dispatched under the direction of one person. As the teams leave, their location and composition are noted on a status board. Relief teams are sent out so the teams assigned earlier can be rested. The status board and the disaster coordinator are up to date to answer executive questions about the recovery. Sound like a control freak's dream? No, it is just a focused effort.

A disaster recovery Emergency Operations Center is essential when addressing serious or wide-scale disasters. An Emergency Operations Center allows a company's management to reestablish organizational leadership, allocate resources, and focus on emergency containment and recovery. This command center minimizes the disruption of management and leadership caused by the chaos of the emergency. From a business perspective, it is a command and control center that is essentially a temporary project office to manage the special project of addressing the emergency. An Emergency Operation Center must be preestablished, presupplied, and its location well known to everyone before it is needed.

An Emergency Operations Center takes time and effort to start up and close down. Before a disaster strikes, you should have three Emergency Operations Centers identified. The first one is the normal emergency center. For short-term, contained disasters, you may already have a place where "everybody knows and everybody goes." This could be the security office with its radio network or the data processing help desk with its data network monitoring capability. Wherever your choice, it should be a telephone number that people would think to call during an emergency. Even smaller disasters have their own natural Emergency Operations Center of sorts. If your company lost its data network, then the Network Manager's office is turned into the hub of activity as a small team works to restore service. This works because the response team is a small group and the office is a natural place for them to work.

The second Emergency Operations Center is the one for addressing big problems and is the primary subject of this chapter. Imagine a winter storm that collapses the warehouse roof. The problem would require many people with a wide range of skills to restore warehouse services. Because the roof collapse was unforeseen, a plan to limit the damage and begin repairs would be made up quickly and modified as the recovery progressed. This type of Emergency Operations Center will be in use for many days and is therefore worth the effort to set up. The size and composition of the Emergency Operations Center team depends on how widespread the damage was and how many people are needed to address it.

The third type of Emergency Operations Center is a backup facility for the primary Emergency Operations Center. This facility would only be used if the primary Emergency Operations Center was unusable; for example, if a fire burned that part of the building and the rest of the building was in danger of collapse. You need a place to contact customers, suppliers, employees, etc. to keep them aware of the recovery progress.

A further variation on the command center is a mobile command center that uses a camping trailer or self-propelled recreation vehicle to bring the solution to the problem. This is a good solution for a large company with many sites, such as a large chain of department stores.

WHAT IS A DISASTER RECOVERY EMERGENCY OPERATIONS CENTER?

A Disaster Recovery Emergency Operations Center is a physical place where all the communications of the recovery effort are focused. Sometimes called a "War Room" to dramatize its importance, it provides a known place where all interested parties can report on the status of the recovery effort. The Emergency Operations Center also provides communications outward to all stakeholders external to the recovery process, such as company executives, the general public, suppliers, and customers. Another key function is to provide the administrative support to the recovery effort, such as purchasing, public relations, safety, and site security.

The phrase "a known place" is important. When disaster strikes, there is no time to announce to everyone where the Emergency Operations Center will be. It is too late then. In your company, the Emergency Operations Center should be some logical place where people would turn for information or assistance. Two logical places are the facility's security office and the data center's help desk.

An Emergency Operations Center has three essential functions:

1. **Command and Control.** This is where you will find the person in charge of the containment and recovery efforts. This person will set objectives and priorities and has overall responsibility at the incident or event.

2. Operational Control. Hour-by-hour control is exercised from here by the various functional areas, such as security, human resources, purchasing, communications, logistics coordination, etc.

3. Recovery Planning (which is separate from emergency containment) will begin here but quickly transfer to its own office.

If you would like to see what an Emergency Operations Center might look like, contact your local Federal Emergency Management Agency (FEMA) office. See how their office is set up to get some ideas for your own. Find out where in your state the next Emergency Operations Center exercise will be held and ask if you could observe the exercise. They may also provide some advice on the resources an Emergency Operations Center in your geographic area might require. If possible, ask for their help in selecting a site for the Emergency Operations Center within your facility. Your local FEMA office will be a wealth of knowledge as you work on your disaster plan, and it is a good idea to build a working relationship with them before disaster strikes your facility.

A Personal Experience

Imagine for a moment you are in a very large automotive factory with thousands of workers and lots of heavy machinery—a very busy place. Everyone is focused on keeping the production line moving, focused on doing their job right the first time. It's a weekday afternoon about 1:45 and— we lose electrical power. The assembly line stops, the overhead lights blink off, a roar of surprise arises from the assembly line workers, and then silence falls because all the noisy machinery has also stopped.

For the data center, the excitement has just begun. Computer programmers, whose workstations were now dead, began walking up offering to help. Some of the battery-operated emergency lights failed to come on. All the internal data processing offices were plunged into blackness only faintly lit by a small amount of light through the glass in the office door, which everyone migrated toward. The emergency lights had failed. Total chaos!

Meanwhile, in the main computer room, people are milling about wondering aloud how long the Uninterruptible Power Supply (UPS) battery backup units would hold and should we begin turning off servers and minicomputers. More volunteers were flooding in, all with their own advice, some forcefully offered.

The Data Processing Manager personally went to the UPS units to try and determine how their displays worked so to learn if they could estimate how long they would last. Still more volunteers were coming in, and others were leaving, loudly telling everyone that a bunch of idiots were in there since they did not act immediately on their advice.

Eventually everyone calmed down and we begin switching off noncritical system monitors used primarily to observe processes. We also shut down all printers, test servers, and servers to systems that could be restarted quickly. Without air conditioning, the equipment was beginning to heat the dimly lit (from emergency lights) computer room.

Eventually others joined the data processing manager to help figure out how much power was left. A few more flashlights appeared. Finally, a call back from building services that they have discovered the problem and we should be back online within an hour. An estimate, not a promise!

Outside the computer room, people were beginning to grab their coats and head outside into the daylight, loudly contemplating going home since there wouldn't be much of a workday left if the power came on in an hour. More confusion as people are reminded of their working hours—electricity or not. The group supervisors were unsure what to do and could not offer any other advice to their people but to wait and see how long it will take.

Finally, we have rounded up the various system administrators from the crowds and reminded them of how ugly these systems become if the UPS runs out of power before the servers are shut down gracefully (they kept hoping the power would reappear momentarily). We begin shutting down servers according to how long it would take to restart them. Our goals were to reduce the drain on the UPS batteries and extend the UPS battery support for the most critical equipment.

In the end, we worked through the issues and learned a few lessons that are included in the chapter on electrical service. The points relevant to this chapter are that:

➤ We did not have a predesignated Emergency Operations Center for a problem like this, so key people did not know where to report. In the end, the help desk proved to be the perfect place because it had plenty of telephone lines and everyone knew the number.

➤ The prime decision maker (the Data Processing Manager) was absent from the Emergency Operations Center, trying to learn about the UPS system because no one knew the details about it. This left decision making in limbo and fueled chaos. Managers need to focus on making decisions, setting priorities, and allocating resources. A technician should have been assigned to investigate the UPS units.

➤ Guesses were made about which systems to shut down instead of following a predetermined plan. Also, as some system passwords were not available, those machines, even if noncritical, were left drawing critical power from the UPS.

➤ Emergency lights failed because no one bothered to check them on a regular basis.

➤ The only people with flashlights were the ones who went through a similar facility blackout 5 years before. Basic tools were lacking when they were needed most.

➤ Many well-intentioned and skilled people were ready and interested in helping in any way possible, but when they saw the chaos around the manager, they left in disgust.

➤ Because the data processing people were focused on the computer room, we forgot that the telephone system was also on a UPS system but the telephone manager handled the problem on her own initiative. We just were not feeding repair progress information in that direction.

Where to Locate Your Emergency Operations Center

An Emergency Operations Center should be located as close to the problem site as is safe. This is rarely practical. If you knew for sure where a disaster would take place and what it would involve, you would take steps to prevent it. So unless you are the cause of the problem, you don't know where it will be. Therefore, when establishing an Emergency Operations Center, you evaluate the possible sites based on a few criteria, although the actual site is usually based on what is available.

Few companies can afford to leave a fully equipped room sitting idle just in case it is needed. What most companies do is convert an existing facility to an Emergency Operations Center as needed. For example, a Personal Computer training room is already wired for data and equipped with computers. If extra telephone lines were run to this room in advance, then with some rearranging of tables and plugging in of telephones, it can quickly be converted to an Emergency Operations Center. If a training room is not available, perhaps a large conference room was wired long ago to support a company activity. Ask your building services manager for some suggestions.

When picking a site, consider how close it is to a building exit and how likely it is to be flooded. A typical center is between 500 and 2000 square feet. It should have a large closet (with a strong door lock) to hold supplies for setting up your Emergency Operations Center. It must be easily accessible by road, have convenient materials loading and unloading available, and have ready access to delivery services, food service, and hotels.

Now you also need to set up a backup Emergency Operations Center. The backup center should be on a different power company electrical grid and be serviced by a different telephone central office. If you have another facility across town or in a nearby city, this makes a perfect choice. In this case, your primary Emergency Operations Center becomes their backup Emergency Operations Center, and their primary Emergency Operations Center backs up your operation. This saves money for the company and keeps your company's recovery actions "in house" rather than out in the public eye. Another advantage is that your backup site is already connected into your company's wide-area telephone and data communications network, allowing for faster Emergency Operations Center activation.

If this is not possible, consider partnering with another company for a backup facility. A close supplier or customer makes a good choice. Be sure to work through how telephone service can be rerouted to this location, and a clear legal agreement about company confidential information must be completed. Another alternative is a hotel that is wired for PC training and has sufficient outbound telecommunications capacity to support your telephone and data traffic. However, a backup Emergency Operations Center in a hotel might be in use by someone else in a wide-area emergency, so use this plan as a last resort.

A note on using a backup Emergency Operations Center to control your recovery operations: expect to relocate it closer to the disaster site within 48 hours, as it will quickly become unwieldy to control operations from a distance. However, for the first few hours, even a remote facility will be of immense value.

On the morning of September 11, 2001, the City of New York's Emergency Operations Center was preparing to execute a biohazard incident exercise. After the first aircraft struck the World Trade Center tower, the Emergency Operations Center sprang into action. Many of the key personnel were already on-site for the exercise. When disaster struck, additional teams were called in, and they began to coordinate containment and recovery actions.

This was made easier by its address: 7 World Trade Center. When the twin towers collapsed, the city lost its emergency "nerve center." Backup centers were quickly established, but rescuers struggled to make up for the equipment and trained staff tragically lost in the wreckage.

Mobile Emergency Operations Center for Large or Dispersed Companies

Depending on the number of sites you are supporting, you might consider a mobile Emergency Operations Center. Such a tool is normally a large "camping" trailer or self-propelled recreation vehicle. This vehicle is preloaded with everything necessary to establish a command center, including a generator and tent for expanding the work area outside of the vehicle. This reduces the number of Emergency Operations Centers required for dispersed companies. For example, if your company owned freight delivery hubs in major cities and one had a major fire, then you would immediately activate the mobile center and send it to the disaster site. The emergency staff could fly in or drive themselves over.

The mobile command center (lacking an immediate local telephone capability) will require multiple cellular phones for voice and data access. As you do not know in advance where you will be going, it should also include digitized floor plans and wiring drawings for every building, along with door keys to access critical places, or clear instructions on how to gain access. It should also include temporary security passes for the entire staff. To save space in the mobile unit, include electronic telephone books for all areas serviced to speed the location of local support services.

EMERGENCY OPERATIONS CENTER PRIMARY FUNCTIONS

When an emergency operations center is activated, there are two parallel teams working at the same time. The containment team works to stop the spread of damage. The recovery team works to restore a basic level of business service. One team has all the resources while the other may start with a single person. As the disaster progresses, the personnel gradually shift to the other team.

Containment Team

A containment team is formed as soon as the disaster is called. They begin work immediately to minimize damage from the disaster. This might involve draping large tarps over holes in the walls to keep the rain out; it might involve pumping water out of the building, or even salvaging soggy equipment from a computer room fire. The containment team quickly establishes a security cordon around the site and forms the initial damage assessments.

In the beginning, the containment team is the "Main Effort" as the early hours are occupied with minimizing the damage caused by the emergency. This will consume all your labor resources as you struggle to stop the damage from spreading. The Emergency Operations Center described in this chapter is primarily for damage containment.

As the spread of damage is stopped, the containment team will also take steps to safeguard assets (you don't need anyone taking any valuables home as "souvenirs of the great fire"). Sometimes helpful employees might sincerely try to safeguard their computers by taking them home so as to ensure the data on their hard drives do not get lost. Whatever their reasoning, nothing can be removed from the site until cleared by law enforcement authorities, your insurance adjuster, and then by your security force.

Even though the spread of damage has stopped, there is still much work to do. There are equipment and materials to sift through to determine what is salvageable. There may be artificial walls to erect (usually canvas or something to protect the contents), there are rooms to inventory, etc.

Recovery Team

The leader of the recovery team may begin work even while the damage is still spreading. This team is charged with restoring the facility to a minimal level of service as quickly as possible. Usually, this begins as a team of one and gradually gains labor resources as the events come under control.

The recovery team leader contacts the insurance company immediately and is their primary point of contact. Even as containment activities continue, this person is scurrying around taking pictures and documenting damage to aid in the damage assessment and the insurance claims. This person works closely with the insurance agent to ensure they gather the critical information for filing their claim. You will need the insurance money to rebuild and need it fast!

The recovery team begins to fill out as soon as the initial damage assessments are ready. Starting with a small group, they begin the planning of how to return the damaged area to full service. This might involve shifting the operation to another location or bringing in replacements for a few pieces of damaged equipment. As the containment effort winds down, executive management will shift their attention to the recovery effort and may replace the recovery manager with a more senior executive. This is normal to monitor the large flow of cash required to restore a severely damaged facility to service.

Emergency Operations Center Specific Functions

There are three essential functions for the Emergency Operations Center to perform. They are to command, to control, and to communicate. Keep these basics in mind, as you tailor a plan to support your facility. Some functions are listed here for you to think about, but what you actually need depends upon your own situation. The best way to find out what your command center requires is to run several exercises based on different types of disasters.

COMMAND A disaster, like any traumatic surprise, is full chaos. A lot of chaos! The person in charge of the Emergency Operations Center must make decisions about containment activities based on very limited amounts of information. Indecisive people should never be placed in this position. If your command center does not pull all-important decision making into it, then you will have small pockets of people making potentially hazardous and expensive decisions for you. There will be no vacuum of command, just whether the company's representative exercises it or individual employees do. This person will set objectives and priorities and has overall responsibility at the incident or event.

Disasters never seem to happen the way they are planned for, and this person must adapt plans as events unfold. When the problem occurs, the first action is to open the disaster recovery plan to see if that situation is specifically covered. If it is, then adapt the plan to the situation. If it is not, then develop a short-term reaction plan based on anything else in the plan that may be close to it. Emergencies vary according to their circumstances, priorities, and needs. Disasters are never as clear cut as the recovery plans seem to make them. As the problem unfolds, decisions must be made that may be different from the approved recovery plan. Keep in mind the plan is only a guideline and was never intended to be followed mindlessly.

Command activities include:

➤ Gathering damage assessments.

➤ Developing action plans based on current information.

➤ Assigning scarce resources where they will do the most good at that point in time.

CONTROL Control involves obtaining and dispatching resources based on the direction of the Emergency Operations Center Manager. Control handles all the administrative duties that are the tools for implementing the directions of the manager.

Control activities include a wide range of support activities:

➤ Ordering materials from food for the crews to pumps for pumping out floodwater to tarps for covering equipment.

➤ Tracking the recovery effort to ensure all personnel are accounted for at all times.

➤ Implementing the allocation and reallocation of resources as circumstances require.

➤ Gathering raw information and summarizing it for the manager's ongoing damage assessment.

➤ Controlling information about the facility to ensure it is available for all to use and not letting it be borrowed and lost.

COMMUNICATIONS Communications is the primary tool for the commander to control the resources. Beyond this, the command center will also communicate with the news media, with vendors, with customers, with the community, with a wide range of very interested stakeholders. Communications becomes the primary tool of the leader to mobilize teams toward a specific action. As was noted at the beginning of this chapter, it takes a radio operator (a communications medium) to make someone a *commanding* general.

ADMINISTRATIVE FUNCTIONS A primary Emergency Operations Center function is to receive information about the status of the problem. The first action is to identify what the problem is. We'll use the electrical outage example to illustrate our points. The first information we need to know is what the problem is. The problem is not that the lights went out. That is a symptom. The problem was a loss of electrical power. Proper identification of the problem allows you to focus on solving the problem rather than treating the symptoms.

Here is a list of some of the things that might be needed based on the type and severity of the problem. A key consideration of the administrative function is to ensure that records are maintained on what was done, when it was done, and how money was spent. Otherwise, at a later date, the "armchair quarterbacks," in their comfortable, no-pressure surroundings, will begin criticizing your actions. Administrative records also allow the company to later acknowledge their gratitude to those who did so much for them during the disaster.

➤ Keep a log of the steps taken toward problem resolution so you can later conduct an after action: lessons learned.

➤ Keep a list of who was working on the problem and when. A thank-you is in order later.

➤ Keep track of who is in each repair team and where they are. Use this to ensure teams are rotated and rested. Tired people make mistakes.

➤ Track expenses: sometimes we cannot wait for purchasing to issue POs. In the heat of the moment, money may flow for supplies, but all of that will be forgotten next month when the bills become due. Keep track of all expenses!

➤ Maintain communications logs for telephone traffic, radio traffic, electronic mail, and fax; any message traffic into or out of the Emergency Operations Center. This enables you to later refer back to who said what, and when.

➤ Ensure the essential human functions of food, water, and rest are addressed. Cater in food, order plenty of bottled water, and make arrangements with nearby hotels for the crews to rest. In the cases of being "locked in" your facility by flood, hurricane, blizzard, etc., this support must be provided from in-house services.

➤ Carefully track the location of the company's vital records that are governed by legal or regulatory agencies. If they must be relocated away from their usual storage area, a guard may be required.

➤ Maintain a list of injuries and any follow-up actions taken.

➤ Assist in documenting the damage for the insurance adjusters.

➤ Provide material safety data sheets to damage control teams and emergency service providers.

PREPARING AN EMERGENCY OPERATIONS CENTER

Basic Emergency Operations Center Materials

There are many things to consider when establishing your Emergency Operations Center facility. Here are some items to consider. The more time and resources you have, the more you can improve on this basic list.

➤ **Electricity.** The Emergency Operations Center will need a steady, reliable supply of electricity. This may mean a portable generator and a UPS battery system. The size of these units is based on the amount of electricity they will be called on to provide. Be sure to consult closely with your equipment suppliers about this.

Before you can size your electrical support units, you must know what they will need to support in the Emergency Operations Center. Hopefully you won't need them, but be prepared for the worst. If in doubt, go for larger units. Once you start adding copiers, personal computers, cellular telephone chargers, etc. to the load, you will appreciate the extra capacity.

If you are located in an area that is prone to wide-area disasters such as flooding, hurricanes, or earthquakes, then your own emergency power generation capability is essential and might be required to run for up to a week.

➤ **Emergency Lighting.** You will need to provide emergency lighting for the Emergency Operations Center in the event that power is lost and the generator is not ready yet. Emergency lights are battery operated and come on automatically when normal lighting is lost. These lights must be installed well in advance and checked regularly to ensure they will be ready when you need them.

Other forms of emergency lighting are flashlights (keep plenty of batteries on hand) and light sticks. Both batteries and light sticks lose their potency over time, and your emergency stock must be replaced at least every other year. Pack plenty of these away in your Emergency Operations Center supplies storage closet. Remember that recovery efforts are an "all-out" affair and will consume supplies around the clock. In a wide-area disaster, it may be some time before you can obtain additional supplies such as flashlight batteries.

➤ **Readily Available Sanitary Facilities.** If your Emergency Operations Center is open for any length of time, then sanitary facilities are essential. If water pressure is lost, then some sort of external facility must be obtained for the duration of the emergency.

➤ **Medical Kits.** It is always useful to keep several medical kits on hand for medical issues. These kits should be used by trained personnel to apply first aid until proper medical help arrives. Include in the kit blankets to keep patients warm. In addition to the kits, encourage employee first aid training and make a list of any trained Emergency Medical Technicians (EMTs) on your payroll. Many rural communities make extensive use of volunteer emergency services, and you should know if any of these trained people are on your staff.

➤ **Office Supplies.** Every office lives on a steady diet of paperwork and a disaster is no exception. Ensure there are sufficient materials packaged and stored in your materials closet so you don't lose time chasing them down in a crisis. As you detail what you might need to recover and who might need to help, it becomes obvious what sort of supplies might be needed. Some common materials required include:

➤ **PC Workstations and Printers, Connected to a Data Network.** If necessary, connect via cellular modems. Notebook PCs make it easy to take the PC to the worksite. Be sure all PCs are preloaded with your standard software. If your key disaster recovery staff are issued notebook PCs for use in their normal work assignment instead of desktop PCs, they can bring them to the Emergency Operations Center.

➤ **Chairs, Tables, Secure Filing Cabinets, Folding Tables, Bookcases, and Wastebaskets.**

➤ **Portable Radios and Battery Chargers.**

➤ **Telephones, Telephone Books, Fax Machines, Copiers, Paper Shredder.**

➤ **Video Cameras and Still Cameras.**

➤ **Copies of the Business Continuity Plan.**

➤ **Local Maps, Building Floor Plans.**

➤ **Basic Office Supplies, Such as Pens, Paper, Staplers, Paper Clips, Tape, Notebooks, and Special Company Forms, Checks, Postage, etc.**

Communications

Communications is critical to focus the maximum effort on where it is needed. In an Emergency Operations Center this will consume most of your effort. Ideally, your communications network will allow for rapid discussions with all members on your team. Emergency Operations Center communications also include company executives, news services, the public, suppliers, customers, and other groups.

When reporting the recovery project's status, be sure that your information is correct and complete. Make a note documenting who is reporting each information element that flows into your official management updates. If you pass on someone else's bad information, then the integrity of the entire containment and recovery project will be questioned.

Basic infrastructure needs include:

➤ **Telephone.** there must be multiple telephone lines into the Emergency Operations Center. At a minimum, you need one line for incoming calls, one for outgoing calls, and one for the disaster containment manager. The more telephone lines in service beyond this minimum, the better the information will flow. In case the loss of telephone service is the problem, make a list of who on your staff carries a cellular telephone so the traditional telephone equipment can be bypassed. If necessary, add external cellular antennas to the roof of the building to ensure a clear signal. Note that in a wide-area disaster, the cellular telephone network may quickly become overloaded.

➤ **Radio Communications Is Essential for Maintaining Contact with Work Crews in the Field.** If the problem is with a data hub in a closet on the 22nd floor, there is probably not a telephone connected in the closet. However, if the repair technicians carry a radio, then you have taken this problem out of the picture. Your security force normally already has a radio network in place for communications within the facility. If your location is remote and prone to wide-area disasters, such as flooding, you might also want a shortwave radio to maintain contact with emergency services in your area. Be aware that radio communications can be intercepted and interrupted by third parties. As such, it is not a good medium for passing sensitive information.

➤ **Data Communications Are Essential for Communicating with Other Sites.** Additionally, it provides an e-mail pipeline for publishing press releases on recovery progress.

➤ **A Web Site Can Be a Valuable Tool to Communicate with Employees and the Public.** Be sure to use lightweight pages that are quick to load and easy to update. Keep the information current, and the tone compassionate.

➤ **Messengers Are Sometimes a Vital Communications Link When the Amount of Information Is Large and It Is Already Written Down.** It is also a more private way to communicate information that should not be sent over the public radio waves.

➤ **Television and AM/FM Radios.** It sometimes helps to hear what the rest of the world is hearing about your problem. In addition, if this is a wide-area disaster like a blizzard or hurricane, then there may be important public announcements broadcast over the television and radio.

Information flow is critical every step of the way. Ensure you are using the appropriate communication channel when communicating with stakeholders.

➤ To management, to request people, equipment, tools, material and money, use regular voice communications such as direct or conference telephone calls. To provide management updates, use periodic updates via e-mail or voicemail box. This should be a different voicemail box than the one for all employees.

➤ To employees not present at the recovery site and their families, use a voicemail box with regularly updated announcements. Be sure the telephone number is widely published before an emergency occurs.

➤ To customers, to apprise them of the status of their orders, try to call each individually to assure them of shipment or to advise them of the estimated delay. If there isn't sufficient time or telephone lines available to call them individually, consider a "fax blast" to broadcast the same message to everyone.

➤ To the public and news media, let them know what is happening with the recovery effort. If things are going well, this is a chance to showcase the management expertise of your company. E-mail, fax, and on-site interviews can get your message out.

➤ To the people working on the recovery, use a large whiteboard with the status of the various efforts. Choose your words carefully.

➤ To suppliers, the materials managers must have telephone access to notify suppliers to hold shipments if appropriate and to assure other suppliers that you still need their goods on time.

➤ Insurance companies want to know immediately of disasters, as they may want to send in their own damage assessors before any cleanup effort begins. Use telephones to contact them.

Ignorance flourishes in the absence of truth. Time must be spent ensuring that factual information concerning the scope of any disaster is properly communicated. Your Corporate Communications staff must handle all communications external to the facility (especially to public news services). An ambiguously worded announcement can do more damage than no news at all.

To maintain a flow of information to employees who are not on the site, establish a voicemail box and prepare a recorded message of the progress of the recovery. It should include information such as the type of emergency, locations, time of occurrence, injuries, extent of damage, possible cause, and what action is being taken. These people are worried about their co-workers and their ongoing employment. Keep them on your side by updating this message often. The best way to make this work is to use this voicemail box for routine company announcements on a regular basis. Then when a disaster strikes, everyone knows where to turn for information.

If you set the standard of publishing regular updates, then the calls from executives will be fewer. If you force management to call for updates, then the staff will waste a lot of time responding to the same questions repeatedly. Try to stick to a containment and recovery progress announcement schedule even if there is nothing new to report.

An Emergency Operations Center needs some basic items to efficiently channel information in and out. Things to think about include:

➤ **Status Board.** Rather than field many of the same questions repeatedly, set up at least one large marker board. Marker boards make great temporary posters for sharing information of interest to a wide range of people. A marker board reduces calls to people doing the work asking "Are we there yet?" If your small children have ever repeatedly nagged you during a car trip with "Are we there yet?," then you can imagine what it is like for workers laboring through a problem being interrupted and inundated with progress report requests from a wide range of people. Post the progress on this board and refer all inquires to it.

A status board is invaluable for seeing the "big picture" of what is happening and how the recovery is unfolding. Some of the things you may want to post on your recovery progress board are:

◆ **An Updated Status of the Recovery**

◆ **The Name of the Current Recovery Manager on Watch**

◆ **Any Important Upcoming Activities**

◆ **Key Telephone Numbers**

Decisions are made and actions are taken based on information pro-vided by everyone on the recovery team. It is important that this infor-mation be complete and accurate. When using a status board, only the clerk assigned to update the board should write on it. Inaccurate infor-mation may lead to major delays or costly mistakes. The clerk controlling the status board should log the origin of every piece of information used to update the board.

If practical, use two status boards. The one in the Emergency Opera-tions Center is for keeping track of fast-moving details. The one posted outside of the Emergency Operations Center is to inform whoever walks up of the progress of the recovery effort and is a tool to reduce casual de-mands for information.

➤ **Inbound Communications.** The purpose of the Emergency Operations Center is to command, and the key to commanding is communications. Using telephones, radios, e-mail, facsimile machines, and any other com-munications tools at hand, information will pour into the center. It is im-portant that every inbound communication be logged and identified with a number (usually based on a date/time group). This will make it easier to later track back to see who said what, and when.

Inbound communications might include such things as:

◆ Work crews reporting the status of their recovery efforts

◆ Requests for tools, specific people, or skills from work crews

◆ Current locations of crews

◆ Status of inbound materials to aid in the recovery

◆ Inquiries from the local news services

◆ Offers of help

◆ Questions by the police and fire department

◆ Injury reports

➤ **Outbound Communications.** A large recovery effort will generate a steady stream of outbound messages to a wide range of stakeholders:

◆ **Status Updates to Executives.** Keep them informed or they will show up asking questions.

◆ **Public Relations Spokesperson.** They need the facts in case the disaster is considered a public event.

◆ **Suppliers.** They need to know if they should hold shipments, or even turn around loads on the road.

◆ **Customers.** They need to know if their goods will still arrive on time, especially if this facility provides just-in-time service to another company. If you are a just-in-time supplier, then it is crucial that you must maintain a steady flow of recovery progress reports to your customers.

Emergency Operations Center Security

It is nice to have a lot of help, but too many curious people will just get in the way. If someone is not assigned to the Emergency Operations Center staff, they should not be there except by invitation. This isn't intended to cover up anything or to keep the truth from anyone. It will cut down on the casual questions and well-intended actions that interfere with work.

Assign someone to oversee (and keep under control) visitors to your site. Visitors should have a comfortable place nearby to congregate and to be briefed on the progress. These people might be a valuable labor resource to draw from as the recovery progresses. As employees show up to volunteer their services, log them in and note their departments and the areas in which they normally work.

The primary source of identification during a disaster is your company ID card. If possible, hand the responsibility for the Emergency Operations Center and recovery work site security over to your facility security force. If you do not already have a company security force, then you should arrange an on-call support agreement with a local firm. With a standing agreement, this reduces their response time to your site and frees your staff to concentrate on the recovery.

Beware of people walking through your area looking for some loot to take home. It is prudent to limit the number of access points at a recovery site. Nothing should leave without a materials pass. Remember that a diskette or

CD full of customer information is easily picked up and fits neatly in a thief's pocket.

UNITY OF COMMAND

Emergency Operations Center Staffing

It is important to identify the Emergency Operations Center staff well in advance of a disaster. They need to know to automatically head for the Emergency Operations Center when a disaster occurs. There is no time to go looking for them. To facilitate this process, periodic recovery Emergency Operations Center staff exercises should be held. If you practice it, you'll better understand what to do at a time when your thoughts are distracted by the emergency and concern for others.

Who should be in the Emergency Operations Center? The number one person is the Disaster Containment Manager. This person is like an orchestra conductor who keeps everyone focused on the task at hand. There can only be one boss, and they should have a direct communications pipeline to the top executives. If some well-meaning vice president comes on-site, they deserve a briefing on containment and recovery efforts but they should not be allowed to begin issuing orders. The caveat to this is if they are advising on their own area of responsibility; then, their advice is valuable and should be seriously considered.

The company must decide in advance who the Disaster Containment Manager will be and what their authority will be. Since a disaster can happen to any part of the business, this should be a senior executive who has broad experience in the company. In a crisis it must be someone who can be spared from the regular job for up to several weeks to focus exclusively on disaster containment and recovery. This person must be authorized to spend money on the spur of the moment to bring in emergency assistance and materials without lengthy consultations with top management. Given this description, a company is wise to identify this person in advance and ensure they are intimately involved with the facility's disaster recovery and mitigation planning. The greater this manager's prestige in the company, the greater the support will be for your mitigation, training, and testing programs.

Declaring a disaster invokes a prewritten directive identifying the disaster containment manager and placing them under the direct control of the top company executive until they are relieved. Such a directive must be prepared in advance and published to all company officers. They are issued by the Disaster Containment Manager when activating the Emergency Operations Center. This action eliminates confusion among the employees. Typically, this prewritten declaration is intended to authorize prompt action for the first 24 hours or until the top executive decides to appoint someone else or to reaffirm it as ongoing through the recovery period.

An important staffing consideration is for every person to have a predesignated and trained backup. Every effort must be made to cross train the staff on the other functions of the recovery effort. Remember that your Emergency Operation Center will quite likely be tasked to run around the clock to speed the recovery. If you are only "one deep" in job skills, that person will quickly burn out. Everyone in the emergency operations center must be prepared to wear several hats at once.

A recovery staff "rest plan" should be in effect for around-the-clock efforts. A rest plan ensures that recovery teams are rotated regularly to allow for rest. Team members on their rest break should sleep or otherwise rest their minds and bodies. They should not assist in other recovery activity. Tired people make mistakes and get hurt.

STAFF RESPONSIBILITIES

Disaster Containment Manager Responsibilities

The Containment Manager is responsible for protecting and preserving the company's assets and resources. They have a dual role to ensure the impact of a disaster is minimized and to begin recovery operations. This position is most crucial during the first few hours of the recovery. As the containment phase passes into a recovery phase, this person may be replaced by one of the company executives to oversee rebuilding the damage areas.

The Containment Manager makes the tough decisions, sets the recovery effort objectives, directs staff toward priorities, and keeps the recovery team focused. They are also your primary contact with public emergency services on the disaster site. These organizations (fire, police, and government agencies) are legally mandated to control the site, safeguard lives, contain the incident. and preserve any criminal evidence. By working closely with these organizations, the Recovery Manager can determine which parts of the site can be entered and addressed at that point in time. They can also pull together a damage assessment and begin recovery planning.

Disaster Containment Manager responsibilities include:

> ➤ Declaring that a disaster exists and identifying which outside assistance is required. This includes the need to activate an off-site data center. Note

that this declaration to an off-site data center service provider incurs a major cost as soon as this call is made.

➤ If there are any emergency services on-site, the Disaster Containment Manager coordinates with them to gain access to the site as soon as they can be released.

➤ Making an initial damage assessment and beginning planning for emergency containment. As the event unfolds, updates the damage assessment and uses that as the basis for all future recovery actions.

➤ Selecting a site for the Emergency Operations Center by determining if the primary site is suitable, if the backup site must be activated, or if there is an opportunity to set up an Operations Center very close to the disaster.

➤ Activates the disaster recovery teams, assigning people to either business continuity or business recovery efforts.

➤ Personally ensures that adequate personnel safeguards are in place.

➤ Assigns staff to maintain a 24-hour schedule for containment and recovery. Drafts and enforces a rest plan.

➤ Maintains the official status of the recovery for executive management.

➤ Coordinates incoming material with the materials receiving staff.

➤ Coordinates use of skilled trades with the facility Engineering management such as for contract labor, electricians, welders, and millwrights.

➤ Assesses personnel strengths and weaknesses in terms of knowledge, skill, and performance to balance labor expertise and staffing.

➤ During a recovery operation, watches for signs of excessive stress and fatigue. Even exceptionally good performers grow tired and reach a point where they no longer can think clearly and are prone to serious error.

➤ Identifies "at-risk" employees, those who are deeply affected by traumatic stress. Moves them to a safe environment under the care of counselors or friends, and assesses the need for professional intervention.

➤ Designates a backup person to assume the Containment Manager's role while they are resting or not on the disaster site.

Facility Engineering Manager

The Facility Engineering Manager's responsibilities include:

➤ Ensures floor plans are current as to electrical, data network, fire, and environmental considerations, and that copies are maintained both in the Emergency Operations Center and in the off-site vital records storage facility.

➤ Prearranges for on-call contract skilled labor to supplement the facilities repair staff and to fill in any gaps in expertise.

➤ Ensures the facility's safety alarms and emergency lights are in good working order through periodic testing.

➤ Restores utilities: electrical, water, sewage, telecommunications, and HVAC as soon as possible.

Other Essential Emergency Operations Center Staff Members

Everyone in the company can play an important role in helping the firm recover from a disaster. This includes:

➤ **Purchasing.** The purchasing agent must have the authority to spend whatever funds are necessary to assist in the immediate containment and recovery effort. The purchasing buyer will need a checkbook for situations where a purchase order is not appropriate. Some companies also use a company credit card for this function. The purchasing agent is responsible for tracking the expenses incurred during the containment and recovery.

➤ **Public Relations Coordinator.** This person controls all official announcements concerning the disaster. This person is critical if injuries have been suffered by anyone during the disaster. Accidents can also occur during recovery, so this person must be fully aware of what is happening so that a minimal but truthful statement can be issued to the press.

➤ **Human Resources.** We need someone to make the decisions on personnel issues that are consistent with company policy. This person will probably be the one who calls in emergency staff from home and deals with employees who refuse to assist in the after-hours recovery. The Human Resources Manager is also the one who can send people home (with or without pay according to your company's disaster guidelines). They ensure that employee engineering and skilled trades skill assessments are up to date.

➤ **Security Manager.** This person will be fully occupied securing the disaster site to prevent material from being stolen. If you do not have one, then appoint someone to this important post and hire a security service to safeguard your equipment.

➤ **Safety Person.** This person is very concerned that anyone entering or exiting the damaged area is accounted for on the status board and provided with the proper safety devices. The safety person briefs the teams on safety issues before they enter the disaster area and debriefs them after they come out (to learn if there are any new hazards).

➤ **Materials Manager.** You will need someone to contact all inbound materials shipments and have them held at the terminal or redirected to a warehouse for temporary storage. Shipments that have not left the suppliers' dock may be canceled. This person should be skilled at traffic management for expediting shipments of emergency supplies.

➤ **Sales Manager.** Needs to get on the telephone to critical customers and keep them apprised as to the viability of their orders. Customers may see a splashy news report that sounds like your facility has been flattened when in reality all you lost were a few offices. Timely calls will prevent nervous people from canceling orders at a point when a continuous flow of business is very important.

➤ **Facilities Engineer.** If there was any structural damage, no one should enter the building without engineering approval. If heavy equipment is needed to move debris, this person will be very busy directing that operation.

➤ **Data Processing Support.** Needed for the operations center and the recovery effort.

➤ **Medical Director.** Needed if you have an in-house medical staff.

➤ **Vital Records Manager.** This person provides advice for recovering vital records or safeguarding undamaged records.

As time moves on, don't forget to reach out and request help from your vendors. Just as you will "go the extra mile" for your customers, so will they for your future business. As you make emergency material orders, bring their sales representatives on-site for advice. They may even send over technical experts to help you recover. After all, if you don't recover well, then you won't be a very good customer in the future. However, your vendors will not know you are having a problem *unless you tell them!*

EMERGENCY OPERATIONS CENTER: WHEN A DISASTER STRIKES

Now that your Emergency Operations Center plan is ready, what do you do when an emergency strikes? It takes time to bring together the proper people to begin addressing the problem. This time gap between when the disaster strikes and when the disaster recovery team is assembled is a critical time where events must not be allowed to take their own course. When a disaster strikes, the Disaster Recovery Manager must take immediate and decisive steps to protect people and property. This prompt action buys time to organize a proper reaction. Drilling the Disaster Recovery Manager and his team during Disaster Plan testing will make this an automatic process.

When the problem strikes, you have three major actions to accomplish at the same time. These may occur in rapid succession and overlap. In an emergency there will be massive chaos, so be prepared! Your three initial actions are to protect human life, to contain the damage, and to communicate with management and fellow employees.

Protect Life

Your first action is to provide for the safety of all employees, visitors, and by-standers—everyone! Work in the area of the disaster stops and the people are evacuated while an assessment is made. This can be expensive but is a very wise precaution. If, for example, this is a 10-story building and there is a fire on the second floor, everyone on the floors above needs to get out in case the fire climbs higher and to avoid smoke inhalation. Everyone on the floors below must leave due to water damage (from the fire hoses) and to avoid the potential of a building collapse (full or partial). By evacuating everyone, you can account for who is missing and may need rescue inside. You can also identify which managers and supervisors are on-site and ask them to keep their staffs together. You may need their help in the immediate recovery efforts.

Predesignate rendezvous areas by department. Someone (or several people) should be assigned as assembly area leaders whose job it is to account for everyone. They will need a roster of all active employees to check off names. Many companies identify the rendezvous points by attaching signs on the parking lot light posts. People need to know where to go!

To signal an evacuation, use an in-building page to alert everyone. In a noisy factory, you may need to set off the fire alarm—even if the problem is not a fire—just to get their attention. The important thing is to get everyone out safely with a minimum of panic. It is better to use a prearranged signal but in an emergency you must use whatever is at hand.

Besides a fire, you might need to evacuate due to a toxic material leak, a sudden structural problem, or even someone waving a gun around in an office. There are many reasons why this might be necessary. Everyone must know what an evacuation alarm sounds like and what to do when it goes off.

Contain the Damage

Once everyone is out, a quick assessment can be made to determine the extent of the damage. How this assessment is done depends on the nature of the problem. The first action is to call for help. If there is a fire, call for the fire department. If it is a toxic leak, activate your environmental hazard containment team (you should have one if you keep toxic material on-site). The on-scene manager must be sure the call gets through and must not delegate this important task without following up.

Next, notify top management of the situation. If this is a weekday, they may already be there. However, if this is a Saturday night and you just evacuated the building, then they need to be tracked down and told. This is not a time to be a go-it-alone hero. You need their support for the immediate recovery steps.

Determine if there is anything you can safely do to contain the damage. This is a judgment call. If everyone is out of the building, and accounted for, then you might want to await emergency support. If anyone is missing, try to determine where they may have been in the building so this information can be passed on to the rescue crews. They have the equipment to go in there and you do not. If the building has structural damage, do not reenter it without the clearance of a structural engineer.

As you work to contain the damage, you need to establish security around the building. Chaos is a momentary opportunity for a thief to snatch and run, so try to identify anything leaving the building and who has it. Use your idle employees to assist your security team. Ask for volunteers. Make a list of who is helping with this before they move out.

Communicate

For the first few moments, people will tend to follow whoever seems to be in charge and knows what to do. In times of crises, leaders tend to emerge. Unfortunately, some of these will be misguided and could tend to pull people in the wrong direction. So after the previously mentioned actions are taken, get an announcement to every assembly point that:

➤ Briefly describes the problem. Don't speculate. If you don't know, say so.

➤ Tell them what actions you need from them. If the problem appears severe and it is close to quitting time, asks the assembly point leaders to account for everyone. If you know whom you need to stay and help, or if you want to ask for volunteers, do so now. Send the rest of the people home. Keep all the department managers on-site so they can better understand if they should call their people to cancel work for the next day.

Keep the executives informed with hourly status reports.

1. Assess the extent of the damage.

2. List what is needed to recover the site in people, data, hardware, and software.

3. Choose to recover on-site or at the alternate site.

4. Keep everyone informed of the situation. Use the Public Relations department as a spokesman for all external contacts.

5. Activate the Emergency Operations Center and assemble the recovery team.

6. Request priority on purchasing support from the facility's accounting manager.

CONCLUSION

The goal of the Emergency Operations Center is to help return the business to normal as quickly as possible. While you can't eliminate the damage to your business from a disaster, a well-designed plan for managing the recovery will dramatically reduce your recovery time and speed the return to business as usual. As with most management functions, communications is the key to the commander controlling the situation and leading the recovery to a successful conclusion.

CHAPTER 5

WRITING THE PLAN
Getting It Down on Paper

No one plans to fail;
they just simply fail to plan.
—*Disaster Recovery* Journal

INTRODUCTION

Now that you've done your risk assessment, developed some interim plans, and identified your emergency operations center, it's time to start writing the official business continuity plans. Writing a plan is not difficult. It is as simple as telling a story to someone. It is the story of what to do. It addresses the basic concepts of *who, what, where, when, why*, and *how* of a process. Although you cannot predict exactly *what* will happen *where*, upon reflection, you can identify the basic steps that must be done in any emergency.

Throughout your plan writing process, keep in mind that emergencies affect people in different ways. Some will panic, others will sit and wait for the expert (but many are really waiting for someone else to take responsibility for any recovery errors), some will make excuses and leave. The goal of your plan is to minimize this chaos by providing some direction to the people on-site to get them started on the containment and recovery. Once the team is in motion, the chaos lessens and their professional training will kick in.

Writing your plan is simply documenting before the fact what should be done when a disaster strikes. The basic steps to follow are:

1. **Lay the Groundwork.** Here the basic decisions are made about who will execute the plan, what processes need a plan, the format of the plan, etc.

2. **Develop Departmental Plans.** Departments are the basic structure around which organizations are built; they are a good place to start developing your plans.

3. **Combine Your Departmental Plans into an Overall Corporate Plan.** Here you check to ensure that departmental recovery activities do not conflict with one another and that any interdependencies are considered.

LAY THE GROUNDWORK

Your first step in developing continuity plans is to establish a standard format. This will give at least the first few pages of each plan the same "look and feel." When drafting your plan, keep in mind the following:

➤ **Who Will Execute It?** If you are the local expert on that process, then why do you need a plan? The odds are, you don't. In a crisis, you would know what to do. But if you like to take days off, occasionally get sick, or even take a vacation, then whoever is on the spot when the emergency occurs must be able to stand in for you and address the problem. So your plan must consider who may be called on in an emergency if you are not available. Another consideration is that if you are the manager over an area, and you want to be able to recover a process in case the "expert" is promoted, transferred, quits, or is discharged, a written plan is essential. You should especially look for highly stable processes that never break and no one has experience working on. They must have a plan on file since whoever worked on them may have already left the company.

➤ **How Obvious Is the Problem?** Some problems, like magnetic damage to backup tapes, are invisible, until you try to read them. Other problems, such as the entire building shaking in a massive earthquake, are a bit easier to recognize. If a problem is hard to detect, then step-by-step troubleshooting instructions are necessary.

➤ **How Much Warning Will There Be?** Is a severe thunderstorm in your area often a prelude to a power outage? Will the weather forecast indicate a blizzard is imminent? On the other hand, if a local building contractor cuts your connection to the telephone company's central office, then there is no warning of an impending problem at all. Emergencies that provide warning, like a weather bulletin, often trigger automatic containment actions. This might be to purchase extra flashlight batteries, install sandbags, or to have essential technical personnel pitch camp within the building in case they are needed.

> ➤ **How Long Must They Continue Running with This Plan Before Help Arrives?** Should they have enough information to contain the problem for 10 minutes or 2 hours?

> ➤ **How Soon Must the Process Be Restored?** This is called the "recovery time objective" for this process.

> ➤ **Are There Any Manual Workaround Actions That Can Be Used Until the Process Is Restored?** For example, if your payroll computer system dies at the very worst moment, can you write 40-hour paychecks for everyone and then correct the payroll amount later when the system restarts? This makes a mess for the Accounting department to clean up later, but in an organized labor facility, the worker's contract may allow them to walk off the job if their paychecks are late.

What Needs Its Own Plan?

Is the answer anything that could break? Some processes are like links in a chain, where the failure of any single item brings the entire process to a stop, such as a data network. In this case, any number of items along a chain of equipment could be at fault. The plan would step you through the basic fault-location steps and tell you what to do to address the problem you find. Some problems are more isolated to one or a few devices, such as a web server failure. In this case, you would focus all efforts on the server and its connections to the network.

The answer is that you must have a plan for every *critical business function*. This includes manual processes and every piece of critical equipment that supports your facility. For each critical business function you must explain the steps necessary to restore *the minimal acceptable level of service*. This level of service may be achieved through manually doing the work of the machine. It may be achieved by shifting the work to another company site or even paying a competitor to machine parts for you. Your goal is to keep your company going. Optional plans may be written to support those functions essential to your own department (and peace of mind) but not essential to the facility's critical business functions.

Keep in mind how a plan will be used when you write it. Your goal is not a single large soups-to-nuts document. Usually a department has an overall plan for recovering their main processes or machinery and then specific action plans for specific problems. For example, Vital Records may have detailed plans for recovering documents based on the media they are stored on. This information should be readily available to the department. But some specific action should be kept on laminated cards and provided to the security guards (for after-hours emergency action) and posted on the walls of the rooms it affects. Examples of these laminated pages might be immediate actions to take for a water leak, for an electrical outage, for a fire, etc. See Form 5-1 (on CD) for an example.

Another example would be in the event of an electrical outage in the computer room. The overall plan will contain information on calling the power company and who to call for emergency generators, etc. But on the wall of the computer room will be specific power shedding instructions and immediate steps to take to monitor and potentially reduce the load on the UPS.

Word Processing Guidelines

PAGE LAYOUT Your company may have some specific guidelines in place for important documents like this. If not, consider these guidelines for the plans:

➤ Set your word processor to default to 12 point, Arial font (don't make me search for a pair of glasses in the midst of a crisis!).

➤ Set the page footers to include a page number in the center and the current date in lower-left corner. This date will help to indicate which files are the latest. The footers should also include the phrase "Company Confidential" on every page.

➤ Each document should read from major topic to minor topic—or broad view to narrow view. The beginning of the document deals with actions that would affect the entire process, and as you move further into the document, more specific issues would be addressed.

DOCUMENT FORMAT

➤ On the first page, include a brief narrative (one paragraph) of the business function of equipment that this particular plan supports.

➤ The name of the primary support person.

➤ The name of the secondary support person.

➤ Name of the primary customer for this process (Accounting, Manufacturing, Sales, etc.) It is better that you tell them what is wrong than they find out there is a problem the hard way.

➤ Immediate action steps to contain the problem.

➤ Known manual workaround steps to maintain minimal service.

➤ In the case of telecommunications, data networks, or data processing services, include the names of other technical employees in sister companies with expertise in this area.

DEPARTMENTAL PLANS

A departmental recovery plan has several components. The main component is the plan itself, a narrative that explains the assets involved, the threats being addressed, the mitigation steps taken, and what to do in the event of a disaster. This sounds simple enough but such a plan could easily fill notebooks. Our plans will be based on a primary scenario with specific threats addressed in attached appendices. Additional, more abbreviated instructions for security guards, computer operators, etc. will also be included as part of the departmental recovery plan.

The main part of the plan has three major components:

1. **Immediate Actions.** Steps that can be taken by anyone to contain the damage. This is to do simple things like shut off the water main to stop a leak, evacuate people if there is a toxic spill, or to open the computer room doors if the air conditioning fails. Once people are safe, an early action in "Immediate Action" is to alert the appropriate people for help. It takes time for them to drive to the disaster and the earlier you call, the sooner they will arrive.

2. **Detailed Containment Actions.** To reduce the spread or depth of damage. What else can be done until the "experts" get there? What actions should the "experts" take after they arrive to stop the damage from spreading?

3. **Recovery Actions.** To return the process to a minimal level of service is an important third component of every plan. This is the part that most people think about when considering disaster recovery planning.

There are four inputs into building your plan. First, begin with your Critical Process Impact Matrix that was developed in your risk assessment. This lists the critical processes and the time of day that they are essential. This list was further broken down in the Critical Process Breakdown Matrix. These two tools can provide the essential information for building your plans.

Add to these lists your risk assessment and your process restoration priority list. With these items, you have everything necessary to write your plans. Write your primary plan for the worst case scenario—complete replacement of the process.

In many cases, the damage is caused by multiple threats but their associated recovery steps are the same. Therefore, a plan that details the steps of what to do in one particular disaster situation is probably applicable in many cases. For example, the loss of a critical computer server due to a fire, physical sabotage, or a broken water pipe would have essentially the same recovery steps. Separate plans are not necessary, although the mitigation steps for each threat in the example would be quite different.

Begin by drafting your plan to address this central situation. Add to the central plan an appendix for any other specific threats or recovery actions you think are appropriate. All together, this is your department's (or critical processes') disaster recovery plan and should be available in your office, a printed copy at your home (and your assistant's home), and a copy available for general review in your department. In addition, the plan administrator must maintain both a printed copy and an electronic copy.

Looking at your department's main plan, you still have a document that is too unwieldy to use in the first few moments of the crisis. Remember, emergencies are characterized by chaos. Some people are prone to act and some are prone to run in circles. We need to have something quick and easy to follow in the hands of those that will act. These terse instructions must detail basic disaster steps to safeguard people and to contain the damage. They are usually laminated and posted on the wall. Include them as an appendix to your plan identified with their own tab.

As you write your plan, consider the following:

1. Who Will Execute This Plan?

At a minimum at least three people must be able to execute a plan: the primary support person, their backup support person, and their supervisor. Usually, the weak link here is the supervisor. If they cannot understand the plan then it is not sufficiently detailed or it lacks clarity.

Most facilities operate during extended first-shift hours, from Monday through Friday. However, if this plan is for a major grocery store, it might be open 24 hours per day, 7 days per week. Problems occur in their own good time. If they occur during normal working hours, and your key people may already be on-site, the emergency plan is to summon these key people to the problem. Referring to the written plan will also speed recovery since time is not wasted identifying initial actions.

However, if the problem arises at 3:00 A.M. on a Sunday morning, and is discovered by the security guard, he needs to know what containment actions to take until help arrives. Since this is the worse case scenario— someone unfamiliar with an area tasked to contain a problem—this is the level of detail you must write to. One of their first action steps is always to notify the appropriate person of the problem. This gets help in motion and then the person on the spot works on containment until help arrives.

That approach works well with things that are somewhat common knowledge or understanding within the general population, such as fire alarms, burst water pipes, or power outages. But for some of the technical areas, such as data processing, writing such a level of detail would make a volume of instructions so thick that the computer room would have long since burned down while the containment team struggled through the text. In those cases, the level of detail should be sufficient for someone familiar with the technology, but unfamiliar with this particular piece of equipment, to work through the steps. Also, specific containment actions should be posted on the wall so that the vital first few minutes are not wasted looking for a misfiled disaster plan book.

2. How Obvious Is the Problem?

Standing in an office with water lapping over your shoe tops is a sure sign of a problem. Smoke pouring out of a room is likewise a sign that immediate action is needed. When drafting your plan consider how obvious the problem might be to the typical person. Obvious problems are usually of the on/off type of problems, such as electrical service, air conditioning, machine-works-or-it-doesn't type of situations.

Problems that are difficult to pinpoint require step-by-step troubleshooting instructions. In these cases, something stops functioning but there isn't an obvious cause. In those instances, the call for help goes out first, but if there is anything that the person on the spot can do, then they should have detailed instructions on how to do it. For example, if a critical piece of shop floor machinery stops working, yet everything else in the factory is working fine, your immediate action troubleshooting steps would include tracing the data communications line back to the controller, and back to the computer room looking for a break in the line. The plan should identify all the system interdependencies so they can be checked.

3. How Much Warning Will They Have Before the Problem Erupts?

Most weather-related problems are forecast by the local news services. Flood warnings, severe thunderstorm warnings, and tornado watches are all fore-warnings of problems. If your facility is susceptible to problems from these causes, then you can prepare for the problem before it strikes. However, the first indication of many problems does not appear until the problem hits, such as a vital machine that stops working or the loss of electrical power.

4. How Long Must They Continue Running with This Plan Before Help Arrives?

Begin with immediate actions steps, sort of like first-aid. There are always some basic actions that can be taken to contain the damage and prepare for the recovery once the "experts" appear. Detail these in your plan.

Some plans have a short duration. For example, in the case of a computer room power outage, there is only so much electrical power available in the UPS before the batteries run dry. By turning off nonessential equipment, this battery time can be extended in the hopes that power will be restored at any moment. This assumes the person standing in the computer room knows which equipment is not essential or has a way to identify these devices. In this case, the time horizon for the containment plan is the maximum time that battery power remains available, or until the computer operations manager arrives to begin shutting down noncritical servers.

A different example is in the case of a broken water pipe. Shutting the water main to that portion of the building is the immediate action to stop the damage, at which time you switch over to containment efforts to prevent the water from spreading and the growth of mold. Your immediate actions steps would list the facility maintenance emergency telephone number or tell the person where the water shutoff valve is.

In any case, if people in the affected room or adjacent rooms are in danger, the first step is always to notify and evacuate them. Safeguarding human life is always the number one immediate action step!

5. Manual Workaround.

Most automated processes have a manual workaround plan. Unfortunately, this plan is rarely written down. If you know that one exists, put it on paper immediately. If you don't know about this, ask the process owner. Manual workaround processes may not have the same quality, they may require many more workers, and they may require substantial overtime work just to keep up, but they may quickly restore your process to a minimal level of operation (the least that a disaster plan should provide). Manual workarounds may allow you to go directly to the recovery phase with minimal containment actions.

Some manual workaround processes for computer systems will require a data resynchronization action when the computer system returns to service. In those cases, work logs must be maintained of the items processed manually so that the data files can return to accuracy.

I Still Don't Know What to Write!

Write your plan in the same way as if you were standing in front of someone explaining it. Overall, you start with the overview and then drill down to the details. For example, if you were writing a plan to recover the e-mail server, you would state what the system does, its major components, and any information about them. Then you would have a section for each major component explaining it in detail.

Imagine that you are standing in the room and the emergency occurred. Also imagine there are several other people in the room that work for you who will follow your directions. Now imagine that you can speak but cannot move or point. What would you tell them to do? Where are your emergency containment materials? Who should they call and what should they say? Write your plan conversationally in the same way you would tell someone to do these things.

It is sometimes useful to include pictures and drawings in your plan (for example, floor plans showing the location of critical devices in a building). Digital cameras can be used to create pictures that can be easily pulled into your word processing program.

It is also very important to include in your text references to the names of the service companies that have support contracts for your equipment. In the back of your notebook, include a copy of the vendor contact list so they know who to call with what information (such as the contract identification number).

So, the plan for your department will include:

1. Immediate Actions.

    a. Who to call right away

    b. Appendices: specific threats

        ◆ Loss of electricity

        ◆ Loss of telephone

◆ Loss of heating, air conditioning, and humidity control

◆ Severe weather and low employee attendance (perhaps due to a blizzard or flood; how can you maintain minimal production?)

2. Detailed Containment Actions.

a. What to do to reduce further damage

b. First things the recovery team does once on-site

3. Recovery Actions.

a. Basic actions

b. Critical functions

c. Restoration priorities

4. Foundation Documents.

a. Asset List

b. Risk Assessment

c. Critical Process Matrix

d. Critical Process Breakdown Matrix

5. Employee Recall List.

6. Vendor List.

7. Manual Workaround Processes.

8. Relocating Operations.

How Do I Know When to Stop Writing?

Your primary plan only needs to contain enough explanation for someone to restore service to minimal acceptable levels. Once you have established that, then your normal approach of handling projects can kick in. Some plans only cover the first 48 hours. As an alternative to setting a time guideline, link it to the function the plan is intended to protect and then it takes however long it takes.

Write as much detail as you need to explain to someone what they need to do. For the Immediate Action pages, assume they are unfamiliar with the details of the function and keep your instructions simple and to the point. For your primary plan, assume they are familiar with the function and understand basically how it works.

To be useful, your plan must be clear to others and include all pertinent details. The best way to know if your plan is sufficient is to ask someone to read it. Hand it to someone and then leave the room. See if they can understand and would be able to act on it. What is clear as day to you may be clear as mud to someone else. Then test it again without the involvement of your key staff members.

RECOVERY PLANNING CONSIDERATIONS

Prompt recovery is important to a company. It is also important to you since if the company has a hard time recovering, they may simply close your office and absorb the loss. For the sake of yourself and your fellow employees, include recovery considerations in your plan.

1. **Planning.** Each of these steps can provide valuable information for your plan development.

   ➤ Before an emergency arises, contact disaster recovery organizations that support your type of department. For example, if you are in charge of the company's Vital Records department, you might meet with and negotiate an on-demand contract for document preservation and recovery. Then you would know whom to contact and what to expect from them. They might offer some free advice for inclusion in your plan.

   ➤ Every department must have a plan for relocating its operations within the facility. A classic example of this is an office fire where the rest of the facility is intact. Your offices would be moved into another part of the facility until the damage is repaired, but the company's business can continue.

   ➤ Meet with local vendors and emergency services organizations before a crisis occurs to better understand what they can do for you and what their limitations are. Find out what sort of response times you can expect, and what their capabilities are to support you in an emergency and in the event of a wide-area emergency.

   ➤ Meet with your insurance carriers to discuss their requirements for damage documentation, their response time, and any limitations on your policies. This is a good time to review your business disruption insurance policy to see what it does and does not cover. Different parts of your facility may have different insurance specific to their type of work.

➤ Meet with vendors of your key equipment so you know how they can help in an emergency. Some equipment suppliers will, in the case of a serious emergency, provide you with the next device off of their assembly line. (Of course, you must pay full retail price and take it however it is configured.) If this is something you wish to take advantage of, then you must clearly understand any preconditions.

➤ Meet with the local fire, police, and ambulance services. Determine what sort of response time you should expect in an emergency from each. Identify any specific information they want to know from you in an emergency. Understanding how long it will take for the civil authorities to arrive may indicate how long the containment effort must allow for, such as for a fire or for first aid in a medical emergency.

➤ Consider shifting business functions to other sites in case of an emergency such as specific data processing systems, the sales call center, and customer billing. The effort is not trivial and may require considerable expense in travel and accommodations, but again, our goal is to promptly restore service.

2. **Continuity of Leadership.** When time is short, you don't have time for introductions and turf battles. Plan for the worst case and hope for the best. Assume that many key people will not be available in the early hours of an emergency.

➤ Ensure that your employees know who their managers are, and who their manager's managers are. A good way to approach this is to schedule luncheons with the staff and these managers and discuss portions of the plan.

➤ If you plan to use employees from a different company site in your recovery operations, bring them around to tour the site and meet with the people. Although an introduction is a good start, the longer the visit the better the visual recognition later during an emergency.

➤ When exercising your plan, include scenarios where key people are not available.

3. **Insurance.** Cash to get back on your feet again. Evaluating your current insurance and selecting additional coverage is a very serious step and

should involve insurance professionals to sift through the details. In light of that, consider this:

➤ What sort of documentation does the insurance company require to pay a claim? Do I need copies of receipts for major equipment? If I show them a burned-out lump of metal, will they believe me that it used to be an expensive server?

➤ If the structure is damaged will the insurer pay to repair the damage? What about any additional expense (beyond the damage repair) required for mandatory structural upgrades to meet new building codes?

➤ In the event of a loss, exactly what do my policies require me to do?

➤ What do my policies cover? How does this compare to my risk assessment?

➤ Am I covered if my facility is closed by order of civil authority?

➤ If attacked by terrorists, do we still have a claim or is that excluded under an "acts of war" clause?

➤ Can I begin salvage operations before an adjuster arrives? How long will it take them to get here? What about a wide-area emergency? How long must I wait for an adjuster then?

4. Recovery Operations.

➤ Establish and maintain security at the site at all times. Prevent looting and people from reentering the structure before it is declared to be safe.

➤ During recovery operations, keep detailed records of decisions, expenses, damage, areas of destruction, and where damaged materials were sent. Use video and still cameras and photograph major damage areas from multiple angles.

➤ Plan for a separate damage containment team and a disaster recovery team. The containment team focuses on limiting the damage and is very much "today" focused. The recovery team starts from the present and focuses on restarting operations. Their goal is to restore the minimal acceptable level of service.

➤ Keep employees informed about your recovery operations. They have a lot at stake in a recovery (their continuing employment) and are your staunchest allies.

➤ Protect undamaged materials from such things as water, smoke, or the weather by closing up building openings.

➤ Keep damaged materials on-site until the insurance adjuster releases them.

CONCLUSION

Writing a business continuity plan seems like a big project. But as with any big project, you can break it down into a series of smaller projects that are not quite so intimidating. Starting at the department level, you can work up the organization, combining department plans as you build toward an organization-wide business continuity plan.

Developing your plan is an iterative process, and you won't get everything right the first time. Testing your plan, discussed in the next chapter, will help you to verify what you've written and point out gaps in the plan. Your plan should become a living document, never finally done, but changing as your organization grows and changes.

CHAPTER 6

TESTING
Making Sure It Works

*What we have to do is to be forever curiously
testing new opinions and courting new impressions.*
—Walter Pater

INTRODUCTION

Testing proves that a plan will work. Every problem is different, but a plan that is tested has a much higher possibility of succeeding over a plan that has never been proven. The many benefits to testing include:

➤ Demonstrating that a plan is workable

➤ Identifying any unknown contingencies

➤ Verifying resource availability

➤ Determining the true length of recovery time

➤ Training people for their recovery roles

➤ Making more people aware of the actions required by them in the plan

Disaster recovery plan testing falls into three general categories: *tabletop* testing performed as a simulation, usually in a conference room with a made-up emergency; *small problem* testing, where parts of the plan are tested in the course of resolving small problems; and *full-scale* tests involving major system outages or facilities relocation. Tabletop testing allows you to review and test a plan under different scenarios. Small problems give us a chance to exercise plan components under more realistic conditions without the pain of a full-blown disaster. If we're unlucky, we may get to test our plan under severe conditions. Facility relocations also give you an opportunity to test portions of your plan. In many ways, relocation deals with the same issues as a disaster, as equipment and employees are disrupted in both cases.

TABLETOP TESTING

Tabletop testing of your disaster recovery plan gives you an opportunity to review the various elements of your plan without creating a disruption to your business. It is a useful exercise to demonstrate to management that the firm has the ability to continue functioning after a disaster. It also gives people in various parts of the organization an opportunity to come together and discuss corporate-wide issues that they might not otherwise have had.

The basic steps involved in creating a tabletop exercise are:

1. Select a facilitator to help plan and to lead the exercise.

2. Develop the objectives of the exercise with business process owners.

3. Create the scenario for the exercise.

4. Determine who should be involved with the exercise and schedule the exercise.

5. Perform the exercise.

6. Update the plan based on issues brought up during the exercise.

The tabletop exercise facilitator can be someone from within the organization or without, but should be someone with no vested interest in the outcome of the exercise or the business processes involved in the exercise. This person's responsibilities include:

➤ Ensuring that the appropriate people are present and understand their responsibilities.

➤ Keeping the exercise on track and on schedule.

➤ Ensuring that all issues uncovered are properly documented.

➤ Creating unexpected problems to add a real-life flavor to the exercise.

➤ Presenting a summary to management of the issues discovered and the plan for their resolution.

Other participants in the exercise should include members of the disaster recovery team, business process owners, an official note taker, and possibly other interested parties. Other interested parties might include senior management, business partners, audit teams, and regulatory agencies.

Disaster recovery team members are of course those persons who will be on the frontline if a disaster occurs. As part of their job, they should know in detail their role in a recovery effort and be familiar with other roles within the corporate recovery team. They should be prepared during the exercise to describe what actions they would take given the disaster scenario and what resources are required to perform their job. During the tabletop test they should be on the lookout for flaws in the plan and possible improvements that could be made.

Business process owners whose areas will be touched by the scenario can be helpful in making sure that the recovery solutions will in fact work within their area. They should also help in developing plausible scenarios for their area. They may also participate in the exercise, which will give them a greater understanding of how their area will be affected if a disaster occurs.

Someone should be designated as the official note taker for the test. This person must record all issues as they arise, record the resolution if one was developed during the test, record who is responsible for unresolved issues, and create a final report to management about the success of the exercise.

The tabletop exercise should be scheduled to last no more than half a day. A conference room large enough hold all the participants comfortably should be reserved for the exercise. Plenty of wall space or whiteboards should be available for making notes for everyone to see.

It is important that the disaster scenarios developed be plausible, yet exercise as much of the plan as possible. The facilitator may want to develop a long-range plan to exercise different parts of the plan using different scenarios over the course of several months. It is also important for some exercises to test multiple parts of the plan at the same time to make sure the different plans interact efficiently. Some sample scenarios might include:

➤ Power failure.

➤ Communication lines cut (Internet and/or telecommunications).

➤ Loss of heating in winter or cooling in summer.

➤ Important machine down in a factory.

➤ Server failure.

➤ Application software failure.

➤ Data corruption.

➤ Key vendor has a disaster.

➤ Transportation failure.

The cause of the failure can vary depending on the location of the facility, especially for a natural disaster. The destruction of an office by a hurricane or an earthquake may require the same recovery steps. Keep that in mind when designing future scenarios, as what is important is exercising the recovery effort, regardless of the cause of the disruption.

The facilitator is also responsible for developing an agenda for the exercise and making sure that it is followed. The agenda should be based on the objectives as determined by the business process owners. In general, the agenda should include the following items:

1. An overview of the objectives of the exercise and the business process involved.

2. An introduction of the participants and their roles in the exercise.

3. The staging of the scenario.

4. An outline of the procedures to be followed and task responsibilities of the participants.

5. Assessment of the disaster recovery plan(s).

6. A review of issues as they occur and possible modifications to the plan.

7. A wrap-up discussion of what was learned and next steps to be taken.

Steps 3 through 6 can be repeated if multiple scenarios are being tested. The facilitator must also establish the ground rules that everyone must follow to make the exercise as productive as possible. These rules should include:

➤ The facilitator can change the scenario as needed to best exercise the plan.

➤ Everyone must contribute.

➤ No interruptions from the outside are permitted. Cell phones and pagers must be turned off.

➤ The facilitator may table an issue for later resolution in the interest of keeping the exercise moving forward.

During the exercise, the facilitator will need to ask questions to keep the exercise moving in the right direction. Some possible questions include:

➤ Does everyone understand the process and their role in the exercise?

➤ Are there any additional assumptions we should make about the scenario before we get started?

➤ Who activates the disaster recovery plan?

➤ What is the first step taken when the plan is activated?

➤ How is everyone notified?

➤ Is the contact information up to date?

➤ How long does a particular step take?

➤ For each step, what could possibly prevent the successful completion of the step?

➤ Can the step be accelerated in some way?

➤ Are there alternatives to performing a step?

➤ What happens if a key person is unavailable?

➤ At what point are we "back in business"?

➤ Have all issues been recorded and a plan developed for resolving those issues?

SMALL PROBLEM TESTING

There are numerous problems that pop up from time to time that are not full-blown emergencies but provide an opportunity to test parts of your plan. This includes things such as lost end-user files, network glitches, power outages, and employee time off. Recording information about incidents that occur can help you see areas where improvements can be made to better protect important assets. Use Form 6-1, Incident Report (see CD), to record and track incidents as they occur.

Lost Files

Recovering lost or damaged files from backup media provides an opportunity to test the backup and restoration procedures, as well as the backup media. You may discover that your backup process makes it difficult to restore a single file. Many times only a small portion of a system is damaged, so being able to restore a single file can make restoration more efficient.

One of our clients had accidentally deleted an e-mail with a critical document attached. When they went to restore the user's mailbox, they discovered that they could not restore a single mailbox, but had to restore the entire corporate mail system. Their only option was to restore the mail store onto another machine, backup the needed mailbox, and then restore it to the live system.

Network Problem Debugging and Resolution

Communications outages and lost service are times when alternative communications can be tried. The lessons learned in the debugging of these problems can be used to strengthen the disaster recovery plan.

Short-Term Power Loss

Power losses exercise the UPS system and identify any unprotected systems. This is an opportunity to review your power supply needs, which may have changed over time. Review what is being protected from power loss and how long the devices can operate without outside power. You should also review your shutdown procedures to make sure that less critical systems are shutdown first to conserve backup battery power for your most critical systems.

Be sure to track the recovery activities performed so that trends or interdependencies can be discovered that can help you make improvements to your plan. Use Form 6-2 (see CD) to record your recovery activities.

TESTING THE PLAN

No matter what type of testing you're doing, you want to try and exercise as much of the plan as possible. The following activities and tasks should be reviewed and understood by the Disaster Response Team as part of their roles and responsibilities, or in use of the Disaster Recovery Plan:

1. Initial Disaster Alert.

a. Contact persons' phone numbers

b. Description of disaster

c. Preliminary damage and injury report

d. Other groups and persons to be notified

e. Location of the Primary Response Center and Alternate Response Center

f. Advisement of not making public statements

2. Disaster Damage Assessment.

a. Dispatch of Response Team

b. Initial tour of affected area

c. Determining facility damage

d. Determining equipment damage

e. Obtaining site access restrictions and personnel protective measures

f. Estimating recovery time

3. Activation of the Disaster Recovery Plans.

a. Reviewing damage assessment

b. Determining if the plan is to be activated in whole, in part, or aborted: notification of employees and management

c. Setup of an expedited procurement process

d. Notification of regulatory agencies

e. Obtaining guidance on contract and legal obligations

f. Ensuring that Public Relations is on-site

g. Monitoring response and recovery activities

4. Customer Reaction Plans.

a. Plans for relocating production to an alternate facility

b. Validation process for achievement of database sync-point and recovery of lost data

5. Alternate Processing Strategies.

    a. Go/no go decision

    b. Identification of alternate processing strategy

    c. Identification of downtime associated with alternate strategies

    d. Determining if damaged sites should be rebuilt

    e. Documenting costs for insurance purposes

6. Determining Which Equipment Is to Be Replaced, Salvaged, Leased, or Bought.

    a. Identifying salvageable items

    b. Identifying salvageable media

    c. Isolating salvageable items in defined spaces

    d. Ordering replacement items for nonsalvageable items

7. Site Preparations for Alternate and Primary Sites: Coordinating Deliveries.

    a. Coordinating installations

    b. Testing of systems

    c. Assuring supply availability

    d. Preparation of an emergency phone directory

8. Restoring the Operating Environment.

    a. Identifying media required for retrieval from backup site

    b. Personnel arrangements for transportation, travel, and lodging

    c. Notification of any operations staff to go to alternate processing site

9. Recovering Applications.

    a. Preparing for critical applications

    b. Creation of schedules

    c. Creation of information security at alternate processing site

    d. Review of salvageable magnetic media for possible use

    e. Reconstruction from backup media

f. Defining lost data, data to be held, and reprocessing needs

g. Verification of database sync-points

h. Review with users and management

i. Responding to requests for priority modification

10. Restoring Communications.

a. Restoring communications supporting critical functions

b. Restoring full communications

In addition to unexpected opportunities for testing your plan, you should also schedule regular tests of the various parts of your plan. Below is a possible testing schedule; your environment may cause you to create a different schedule for your plan.

Annually

Test recovery of main systems at your alternative site. This includes operating systems, applications, peripherals, etc. In addition, all managers should verify the accuracy of the plan and certify training of their people. The manager of the disaster recovery plan should:

➤ Conduct an emergency recovery drill.

➤ Review procedures from key vendors on after-hours support.

➤ Receive updated letters from vendors on emergency response time.

Semiannually

The information systems operations area should perform the following functions twice a year:

➤ Verify data backups.

➤ Test system backup system recovery.

➤ The plan coordinator should review all command center sites for availability.

Quarterly

All managers should:

➤ Exercise telephone recall list of home numbers.

➤ Update disaster recovery plan with any system changes.

➤ Review their portions of the plan with all their staff.

Operations should:

➤ Review plans with Help Desk and Operators to ensure understanding.

The plan coordinator should:

➤ Send updated copies of plan to each plan holder.

➤ Validate server recovery processes:

  a. Inspect backup logs to ensure currency and accuracy.

  b. Ensure all disks are accounted for on backups.

  c. How long is the tape rotation and how many old copies are kept (monthly, annual, etc.).

  d. Verify that the backup pool of tapes is sufficient for each system.

➤ Validate off-site processes:

  a. Visit storage vault to review handling and storage process.

  b. Verify that transportation of media is sound.

  c. Verify after-hours access.

On an ongoing basis, all managers should:

➤ Document events when plan was exercised to restore service.

➤ Review plan with all new personnel as a part of their in-processing training.

FULL-SCALE TESTING AND FACILITY RELOCATION

Full-scale testing involves pulling the plug on some part of the operation and letting the disaster recovery plan kick in. For obvious reasons, this is rarely done. However, relocation to a new facility is a great opportunity to completely test your disaster recovery plan. Many of the activities necessary during relocation are the same as those required in a disaster: new machines may need to be purchased, servers are down for some period of time, new communications infrastructure needs to be built, data need to be restored, etc. In fact, if a relocation project is not done properly, it may turn into a real disaster!

A relocation project is also similar to a disaster in that hopefully both are activities that do not occur very frequently within the organization. Because they occur infrequently, an organization usually does not have people on staff with a great amount of experience managing a relocation or disaster. By having your disaster recovery team involved with a relocation that does occur, they can gain valuable experience in managing the types of issues that come up during these types of projects.

CONCLUSION

No plan can be called complete until it has been tested. Beyond the initial testing, ongoing testing is critical to ensure that the plan is kept up to date. As the organization grows and evolves, the plan must be updated to incorporate the necessary changes. Periodic testing validates these changes and keeps everyone aware of their responsibilities when a disaster strikes.

PART TWO
THE ASSETS

CHAPTER 7

ELECTRICAL SERVICE
Keeping the Juice Flowing

Nothing shocks me. I'm a scientist.
—Harrison Ford, as Indiana Jones

INTRODUCTION

This chapter is provided so you will have some understanding of electrical power support for your critical equipment. Use this as a background when talking to your facility electrical engineer and your UPS supplier. While you'll not want to work on high-voltage circuits or equipment yourself (leave that to trained professionals), an overall knowledge of how your electrical systems work will help you to write a better plan.

ELECTRICAL SERVICE

Imagine a business where if you create too much product it is immediately lost forever. A business where people only pay for what they use, but demand that all they want be instantly available at any time. A product they use in varying amounts throughout the day. A product that requires an immense capital investment but is sold in pennies per unit. Welcome to the world of electricity. Electrical service is so reliable, so common, that people take it for granted that it will always be there whenever they want it. Electricity is an essential part of our everyday existence. Few businesses could run for a single minute without it.

Side-stepping the issue of the huge effort of the electric company to ensure uninterrupted service, let's consider the impact of electricity on our business. Without a reliable, clean source of electric power, all business stops. We have all experienced an electrical blackout at some point in our past. When we add together how important it is, and that we believe it is likely to occur again, we meet all the criteria for a requiring a disaster recovery plan. Because we cannot do without it and there are economically feasible disaster containment steps we can take, a mitigation plan must also be drafted.

In addition to recovering from an outage, our mitigation plan will reduce the likelihood of losing power to critical machinery. There are many other problems with electrical power beyond whether we have it or not. Therefore our mitigation plan must address ensuring a clean as well as a reliable electrical supply.

In the case of electricity, we need a process that:

➤ Monitors the line and filters out spikes.

➤ Provides additional power in case of a brownout or partial outage.

➤ Provides sufficient temporary power in case of a total outage.

➤ Makes the transition from normal power supply to emergency power supply without loss of service to critical devices.

Whatever power support plan you select, keep in mind that it must be tested periodically. With luck, you will be able to schedule the tests so that a power failure will have minimal impact. With a touch of bad luck, nature will schedule the power outages for you and, again, at that time you will know how well your power support plan works.

RISK ASSESSMENT

What sorts of problems are we protecting against? In an ideal situation, North American electricity is provided at 120 volts, 60 cycles per second, alternating current. If we viewed this on an oscilloscope, the 60 cycles would display a sine wave. There are many variations from "normal" that will play havoc with your reliable power connection.

A *voltage sag* is also known as a "brownout." Generally speaking, this is a reduced voltage on the power line and is caused by a number of things. You can see a brownout when the room lights dim. Brownouts are the most common electrical power problem. They can cause some computer systems to fail and occasional hardware damage by forcing equipment power supplies to work harder just to function.

Sags are caused by turning on power-hungry equipment. As they begin operation, these power hogs draw the amount of electricity they need to run from the power grid. This sudden electrical load causes a momentary dip in the line voltage until the electric company compensates for it. These power drains might be anything from heavy machinery to the heater under the desk next door. Most sags are of short duration.

Brownouts can also be caused by utility companies switching between power sources and, in some situations, be an intentional voltage drop by the electrical company to cope with peak load conditions. An example is the summer of 2001 power crisis in California with its rolling blackouts when the electrical utility company could not meet peak demand. The demand for electrical power is growing but the supply of electricity is not.

Once a voltage sag ends, there is typically a corresponding "spike" of "overvoltage" that can further damage equipment. Sharp or extended overvoltages can severely damage your electronic systems, which is not designed to receive and handle large voltage variations.

A *voltage surge* is a short-term substantial increase in voltage caused by a rapid drop in power requirements. A typical surge lasts for 3 nanoseconds or more (anything less is known as a spike). Surges are caused by major power users being switched off. For that brief moment, the power available for that item is still being supplied but is no longer needed and must be absorbed by other devices on that line. Examples of large users that may be switched off are factory equipment, air conditioners, and laser printers.

Surges frequently occur and usually go unnoticed. Some can be handled by the equipment's power supply, some must be absorbed by a surge protector, and the rare major surge will wipe out anything in its path. A common example of a major power surge is a lightning strike that surges down power and telephone lines into nearby equipment.

Noise is seen as jitters riding along on the 60-cycle sine wave. It is electrical impulses carried along with the standard current. Noise is created by turning on electrical devices such as a laser printer, electrical appliance in your home, or even fluorescent lights. Did you ever see "snow" on your television screen when using an electrical appliance? That is an example of line noise sent back into your electrical system. What you see on the screen is electrical noise riding on your local wiring that is too powerful for your television to filter out.

Noise is one source of irritating PC problems, such as keyboard lockups, program freezes, data corruption, and data transfer errors. It can damage your hard drives and increase audio distortion levels. The worse part of the problem is that you aren't even aware of what is happening when it occurs.

Voltage spikes are an instantaneous increase in line voltage that is also known as a "transient." A spike may be caused by a direct lightning strike or from the return of power after a blackout. Think of a spike as a short-duration surge that lasts for 2 nanoseconds or less.

Spikes can be very destructive by corrupting data and locking up computer systems. If the spike hitting the device is intense, there can be significant hardware damage.

An *electrical blackout* is a total failure of electrical power. It is any voltage drop to below 80 volts since, at that point, most electrical devices ceases to function. Blackouts are caused by a wide range of reasons from severe weather to auto accidents to electrical service equipment failures.

A blackout not only immediately shuts down your equipment, but most machinery is time consuming to restart from a "hard stop." Even though most blackouts are of a very short duration, from a business perspective a momentary blackout can be just as serious as a 2-hour outage. Additionally, some equipment may not have been turned off for years—and for good reason. There may be some doubt as to whether it will even start again!

Blackouts are very damaging to computer systems. Anything residing in memory, whether it is a spreadsheet or a server's cache, is immediately lost. Multiply this across the number of people working in a single building and you can see the lost time just for one occurrence. Compounding the data loss is the damage and weakening of your equipment. A further issue is that, from a recovery perspective, there may be network devices working out of sight in a closet deep within the building. If you don't know these exist or where to find them, just the process of restarting equipment can be very troublesome.

When recovering from blackouts, beware of the corresponding power surge that accompanies the restoration of system power. So when a blackout strikes, turn off your equipment and do not restart it until a few minutes after power is stabilized.

YOUR BUILDING'S POWER SYSTEM

Many years ago, your company's delicate data processing equipment was concentrated in the facility's data processing center. Often one whole wall was made of glass so everyone could see this technical marvel in action (hence the term "glass house" for computer rooms). This concentration allowed the equipment to be supported by a few Uninterruptible Power Supply (UPS) units and power line conditioning devices.

Now, the primary computing muscle for most companies is spread all over the facility in the form of PCs and departmental servers. Instead of a carefully conditioned and electrically isolated power feed, your equipment shares the same power circuits as soda pop machines, copiers, and factory machinery—all of which add noise and surges to the power line. None of this is good for your computer systems and network devices!

This variety of computing power creates a need to monitor electrical service to ensure maximum network and computer capabilities. I emphasize network because while personal computers are located comfortably on office desktops, network hubs, routers, and bridges can be found stuffed in any closet, rafter, crawl space, or under a raised floor. This makes the automatic monitoring of electrical service across your facility an important network management function.

Filtering the electricity as it enters your building is a good practice to minimize external influences. Sometimes, however, the problems are caused by equipment inside your building; this might be arc welders, heavy machinery, etc.

BUILDING A POWER PROTECTION STRATEGY

Power protection for business continuity is a five-step process.

1. The first step is to isolate all your electronic equipment from power surges by use of small surge protectors. Power surges sometimes occur internal to your building. Surge strips are inexpensive and simple to install.

2. The next layer is line conditioning. A line conditioner smoothes out voltage variation by blocking high voltages and boosting the line voltage during brownouts. This filtering should always be applied to the power line before electricity is passed to your UPS.

3. An Uninterruptible Power Supply (UPS) provides electrical power for a limited time during the event of a power outage. The UPS battery system can also help to protect against brownouts by boosting low voltages. A UPS is a critical device for ensuring that key components do not suddenly lose electrical power.

4. One of the best solutions for companies that cannot tolerate even small power outages is an on-site electric generator. These backup units instantly start and begin generating electricity to support your facility. Imagine a hospital's liability if all their life support equipment suddenly stopped from a lack of power. This added security is not cheap to install or maintain. Keep in mind that electrical generators of this sort are internal combustion engines and must conform to local air pollution and building regulations.

5. The last step, not directly related to electricity, is the physical security of the electrical support equipment. Few people require access to this equipment, and it must be safeguarded against sabotage. This equipment is unique in that if someone disabled it, the entire facility could stop with lost manpower quickly running into the thousands of dollars per minute. Additionally, the "hard stop" on machinery and computer servers will result in lost or corrupt data files.

However you secure this equipment, keep in mind the cooling and service clearance requirements for the UPS system. Also that the UPS control panel must be available to the disaster containment team in a crisis.

Surge Protection

One of the most common electrical protection devices is a "surge protector" power strip. Computer stores sell these by the bushel. For your dispersed equipment, a surge protector can provide some measure of inexpensive protection for your equipment. A typical surge protector contains circuitry that suppresses electrical surges and spikes. All electronic devices should be attached to electrical power through a surge strip to include all your PCs, network equipment, printers, and even the television used for demonstrations in the conference room. Even if your facility's power is filtered as it enters the building, a direct lightning strike can ride the wires inside the building and still fry your equipment.

There are many brands of surge suppressors on the market. There are places to save money and places to lose money. The old saying goes "for want of a nail, the battle was lost." When protecting your equipment from power problems, you may not want to skimp too much. Here are some things to look for when buying a surge strip:

➤ **Joule Ratings.** A joule rating is a measure of a surge protectors' ability to absorb power surges. A joule is a unit of energy equal to the work done by a force of 1 Newton through a distance of 1 meter. Generally, the higher the rating the better. A good surge suppressor will absorb between 200 and 400 joules. If greater protection is needed, look for a surge suppressor rated at least 600 joules.

➤ **Surge Amp Ratings.** The amount of above-normal amps the surge protector can absorb. As with joules, the higher the better.

➤ **UL 1449 Voltage Let-through Ratings.** Underwriter Laboratories(TM) tests to determine how much of a surge is passed by the surge protector on to the equipment it is protecting. The best rating is 330 volts. Any voltage rating less than 330 adds no real benefit. Other ratings of lesser protection are 400 and 500. Be aware that UL 1449 safety testing does not test for endurance.

➤ **The Surge Suppressor's Response Time Is Important.** If it blocks high voltages but is slow to react, then it is of marginal usefulness. Adequate response time is 10 nanoseconds or less. The lower the number, the better.

➤ **All-Wire Protection.** A high-quality surge protector guards against surges on the ground wire as well as the current-carrying wires.

➤ **Telephone Line Support.** To protect your modem from power surges riding on the telephone wire.

➤ **Clamping Voltage**. The voltage at which the surge suppressor begins to work. The lower the rating, the better. Look for a rating of 400 volts or less.

Some surge protectors provide basic line conditioning against noise on the line. This circuitry can smooth out minor noise from the lines.

An interesting thing about the ubiquitous surge protector strips is that in addition to protecting our equipment, they make handy extension cords. Over time, these surge strips may silently have absorbed any number of electrical "attacks" that have eroded or destroyed their ability to protect your equipment. Most people cannot see this because they still function quite nicely as extension cords.

Surge protectors often have lights to tell you when they are energized or not. High-quality surge protectors will have an additional light to let you know if their surge-fighting days are over. This light may say something like "protected," "surge protection present," etc. If your surge protector has such a light and it is no longer lit when running, then you may have a false sense of security that it is functioning as something other than an extension cord, because that is all it is anymore!

People traveling around the country using a notebook computer would be well advised to carry and use high-quality surge protectors when plugging their equipment into the local power grid. When you consider how big a typical surge suppressor is and how tiny notebook PCs have become, you can guess at how little room there is for surge suppression circuits in the notebook PC chassis. This is especially important for international travelers as the power in some countries is a bit rougher than it is in this country.

A few more things to consider when using surge protectors. As great a tool as they are, they cannot stop a nearby lightning strike from damaging your equipment. When a lightning storm approaches, unplug both the power strip and your modem line from the wall. (This is good advice for any sensitive electronic equipment that depends solely on a surge protector to defend against lightning.)

Also, never use a ground eliminator with a surge strip (a ground eliminator converts a three-prong plug into a two-prong plug for use in an older building). Doing so will make it difficult if not impossible for your surge protector to resist a major line surge.

Line Conditioning

Line conditioning ensures that your equipment always receives the same steady voltage. It also screens out noise on the power waveform. Line conditioning involves passing your normal electrical service through filtering circuitry before it is used. Many people don't realize that the "old reliable" electricity that magically comes out of the walls is susceptible to a wide range of influences. These influences take the "pure" 60-cycle alternating current and introduce fluctuations in the voltage or current as it passes down the line.

These fluctuations can have many sources but one that we especially want to avoid is lightning. Lightning can cause a localized one-shot power surge to roar down the electrical line into your equipment. When this happens, equipment power supplies and integrated circuits can be quickly melted.

Line conditioning is also advised for analog telephone lines connected to PC modems. The same lightening strike that induces an electrical charge in your electrical power lines can throw a jolt down your telephone line. Unfortunately, there is little in a PC modem to keep a power surge out and they are very easily destroyed. Many surge suppressors now include a telephone line surge suppression jack to filter these problems out.

A line conditioner should always be installed between a UPS and the electrical power source to reduce the load on the UPS batteries. Some UPS units include a line filtering capability. Check your model to see what it is capable of doing. A line conditioner reduces the number of times that the UPS jumps on and off of battery power (which shortens the life of your batteries).

A line conditioner is an essential component when generating your own emergency power. Use it to filter the electricity provided by the generator before it is passed on to delicate computer hardware. The power delivered by a generator is not as clean as that normally delivered by the power company.

Uninterruptible Power Supplies

An Uninterruptible Power Supply (UPS) provides several essential services and is best used in conjunction with surge protection and line conditioning equipment. A UPS can help to smooth out noisy power sources and provide continuous power during electrical sags. Its primary benefit is to provide temporary electrical power during a blackout. Depending on the model, it may also provide some measure of line conditioning protection.

Uninterruptible Power Supplies come in three basic types, based on their features.

1. The basic UPS is a "standby" UPS. A standby UPS provides battery backup against power outages (blackouts and brownouts) and a modest amount of battery-powered voltage correction.

2. The "line interactive" UPS is a step above the basic unit. It provides voltage regulation as well as battery backup by switching to battery power when line voltages move beyond preset limits. This type of UPS converts a small trickle of electricity to charge its batteries at all times. When power fails, the line interactive UPS detects the power loss and switches itself on. A line interactive UPS has a subsecond switching time from line power to battery power.

3. The third type of UPS is an "online" UPS that sits directly between line power and your equipment. The online UPS is always providing power to your electric circuits and has a zero transfer time between the loss of line power and the start of battery power.

UPS BATTERIES UPS systems provide power during a blackout by drawing on their battery electrical supply system. Most of these batteries are sealed lead acid batteries. Unlike the batteries found in many notebook PCs, these batteries do not have a "memory" and should be completely drained as few times as possible. Depending on how often your UPS draws on its batteries, they should last up to 5 years. Remember that brownouts and short-duration blackouts all wear on the batteries, so if your local power fluctuates very much, the life of your batteries will be reduced. The speed at which your UPS batteries age is also determined by their environment. Extreme heat or cold are not good for your batteries. Refer to your manufacturer's guide for the recommended operating temperature range.

As batteries age, their power-generating capability will decrease. Therefore, regular preventative maintenance is important. Preventative maintenance should include changing the air filters to help keep the UPS unit cool. At that time, all the batteries should be checked for damage, leaks, or weak cells. You should also consider a service agreement that includes the replacement of damaged batteries.

UPS systems use "inverters" to convert the DC battery power to AC power. An inverter is electrical circuitry to change the direct current to alternating current. High-quality UPS systems use a dual inverter system for smoother power conversion.

UPS "SIZE"   The first question people ask about UPS units is, "How big does it need to be?" This all depends on several things:

➤ What must be supported? This translates directly into how much electricity must be supplied at a given point in time.

➤ How many minutes must the battery pack provide this level of support?

➤ Is your area prone to power problems?

➤ Will this UPS be managed remotely through manufacturer provided software?

UPS units are rated according to the number of volt-amps they can deliver. Volt-amps are different from watts and you cannot equate the volt-amps provides by a UPS with the watts used by an electronic device. Typical power factors (which is watts per volt-amp) for a workstation is 0.6 or 0.7. So if your PC records a drain of 250 watts, you need a UPS with a 417 volt-amp rating (for a 0.6 power factor). Always be careful to never overload a UPS beyond its rated capacity. Doing so will severely damage it.

Most UPS manufacturers have a software tool for estimating UPS sizes. Where possible, use their programs to size your UPS. In the absence of that tool:

1. Begin with a list of all equipment for which you will need to provide electricity. This may include personal computers, monitors, servers, critical printers, network hubs, telecommunications equipment, whatever will be supported by the UPS.

2. Determine the wattage ratings on all these devices by checking their nameplates. The numbers may be expressed as watts. We need the numbers in volt-amps (VA) since that is a more accurate number for UPS sizing. Multiply the watts by 1.4 to get the volt-amps load.

3. If the power usage is provided in amps, then multiply that number by the line voltage (120 volts in North America and 230 volts for Europe) to get a volt-amp rating.

4. Total the volt-amp requirements for all the supported equipment.

This is the amount of load you need to support. From here you check with the manufacturer for the size of unit to support this load for the amount of time you select.

SWITCHING TO BATTERIES A UPS uses power line filters to address minor power disturbances, but its main weapon against a power loss or severe brownout is a near-instantaneous switch to battery power. This is good for keeping your systems alive but hard on the batteries. If your UPS must switch to batteries often due to poor power regulation in your area, then your battery life will suffer significantly. As the batteries rapidly age in this environment, they would not provide the length of time you may be counting on from your UPS.

Recharging the batteries is another issue. Some UPS systems allow you to choose between a fast recharge or a slow recharge. The frequency and duration of outages in your area should determine if you must recharge your batteries as fast as possible or use a more gentle slow recharge process. Fast recharging puts a large drain on your restored power supply.

If you switch to generator power, you do not want the batteries to recharge from the generator as it might take away too much of the power needed elsewhere. If you plan to recharge the batteries from the generator, be sure that is included in the power load plan when sizing the generator, and that the batteries are on a slow recharge cycle.

UPS LOCATIONS If you have concentrated your data processing main computers and servers into one room, then selecting a location for your UPS will be easy. Electricians will run a separate electrical circuit from the UPS to the equipment to be protected. Electrical codes require these outlets to be a different color so you will know which circuit you are plugging into.

Some critical machinery and computers will be located away from the central computer room. For these devices, consider smaller UPS units located adjacent to the equipment. These units will not have a long battery life and will be used to keep the machine operational long enough to shut it down gracefully. Be sure not to lose sight of these satellite units as they will need to be tested and their batteries maintained over time. Remote monitoring software is ideal for this situation.

ADVANCED UPS FEATURES Modern UPS units offer much more than battery backup. They possess microprocessor logic to support a wide range of services. They can provide alarms of error conditions both on the unit and through your data network. This is a very useful feature since they are often stuck in some dark back room where an audible alarm only serves to annoy the mice.

The network signaling of power conditions is a very useful feature. Depending on the capabilities of your UPS and data systems, a UPS can instruct the orderly shutdown of equipment to protect it before the UPS batteries are exhausted. This feature is very useful over weekends and holidays when no one is around. In some cases, it can order a restart when power is restored. A more sophisticated UPS system stores a log of the power supply status for later analysis. Do you know how noisy your power lines are? Do you know the frequency and magnitudes of sags and spikes that occur on your electrical power lines?

A UPS is a critical component of a data network. Remote monitoring software allows a network control analyst to monitor the status of each remote UPS and display the current line voltage and the voltage/current draw on the equipment. This helps to track which lines seem to have the most variation and potentially drive it back to a root cause in your facility. If some electrically driven machine in your facility is causing problems in your internal power grid, it needs to be identified and provided with better electrical isolation.

UPS TESTING It is great to have a UPS system set up and running, but it needs to be tested if there is to be a credible plan. So on a weekend in your slow time of the business cycle, you should plan for a UPS load test. This will demonstrate your power support system capabilities before a blackout strikes.

To set up the test, shut down the operating systems on all your computers but leave them running. The idea is to not lose any data but to still pull each system's normal electrical load. Bring in your UPS service technician to address issues during and after the test. Warn management you are going to do this. When all is in place, have an electrician cut the power to the UPS in that part of your facility and see what happens.

This test has several goals:

1. The first is to see what is not on the UPS that should be. Once the power is cut and the batteries are humming, you will see which server, computer, network device, etc. has been overlooked. Now look to see which low-value items are connected and wasting valuable emergency power.

2. Second, you need to know how well your UPS will support the load you have attached to it. If it is overloaded, you must plug some equipment into other power sources or get a bigger UPS unit.

3. When you shut down the servers' operating system, bring along a stopwatch and write down how long it takes. This will tell you the minimum amount of time the UPS must hold for you to perform orderly system shutdowns. If your servers are far apart in different rooms, and the same person is expected to shut them all down, that may add travel time to the time you must allow on the UPS. Plan your time for the worst case.

4. Observe exactly what information the UPS displays about the remaining minutes of power given the current consumption rate. Compare this to the operator instructions you have provided to the after-hours support team. Be sure to also train the facility electricians on how to read the UPS display panel.

5. Exercise your power shedding plan while someone observes the impact on the UPS. How much additional time do you get for each level shut off?

POWER GENERATORS

If your facility absolutely must maintain its power supply in the face of any sort of electrical problem, then you will need your own electrical generation system. This is a large leap in complexity above UPS systems and takes extensive planning. There are some industries that quickly come to mind as requiring this level of support. Hospitals need it to support electronic medical equipment, food storage sites need it to prevent spoilage, and even Internet hosting providers need it to ensure maximum application availability to their customers.

On the other hand, it is kind of nice to switch from having a problem to being in control of it. A properly sized and installed electrical generation system can return some benefits in the form of keeping your company running while other companies cope with a rolling blackout, by the potential of selling electrical power back to the utility company, and by running your generator during peak electrical usage times thereby avoiding the highest cost electrical power.

Sizing Your Generator

Once you decide the need for maximum power availability, you begin with determining what it is you need to support. If it is everything within a building or an isolated part of a building, you could contract for an electrician to monitor the amount of electricity used in that building or part of the building and use that as a starting point for sizing your equipment. If the generator is only supporting one portion of the facility, you must have a way to isolate it from the rest of the structure.

Next you need to know how long your generators must provide electricity. If you live in an area that experiences widespread natural disasters, such as floods, hurricanes, earthquakes, or blizzards, then you might want to allow for running this system for several days at a time. A good place to start here is to use your personal experience for the frequency and length of outages in your area to plan on system size. This will help to determine the size of your fuel storage system for running the generator.

Switching Time

Some industries, like hospitals, have a standard amount of time they can be without electrical service. Their generator must switch on automatically. However, mechanical engines take some time to start and run up to operating speed (ever start your car on a cold day?). Some of the fastest generators can automatically sense the loss of electrical power and start providing standby power in less than 10 seconds.

The question here is how long of a gap your company can tolerate. During this brief outage, UPS systems can maintain power to critical devices.

Some equipment, like refrigerators, can tolerate a brief gap since they are already chilled down. Some equipment, like lights, can ever so briefly be out if supported by a backup emergency lighting system. So when deciding how long your company can function without electrical power, be very specific of what is needed and why.

The alternative is to always run generators together with pulling power from the power grid. As you can quickly discern, this is yet another step in complexity that distracts you from your core business. Rather than take this step, most companies settle for quick-switching generators supplemented with UPS support at critical points.

Generator Testing

More than any other power support system, the engines on your generators will take regular care. Begin by running them monthly to ensure they function on demand. Next, they need to be tested under load. This can be arranged for a weekend where everything they are to support is turned on and the electricity disconnected for a few hours from the power grid. Periodic testing under load is a critical component of your power backup system credibility.

During your testing, monitor the actual fuel consumption to generate a given unit of power. Fuel consumption is also a matter of air temperature (height of summer or the depths of winter). Aside from the manufacturer's claim, use this to determine how long your on-site fuel supply will last for delivering electricity.

Testing also exercises the people supporting your generators. By drilling them on their duties, they will be able to respond more quickly in a crisis. Be sure to rotate personnel to provide sufficient trained backup staff.

Working with Your Public Utility

Unlike a UPS or line conditioner, a generator has the potential to help pay for itself. During peak electrical usage periods, such as the depths of winter or the oppressive heat of summer, running your generators will reduce your draw on the community's power grid. Some utilities base their year-long electrical rates on the peak usage at any point over the year. By using your generators on these days, you contribute to the overall containment of electrical rates. And even then the units don't need to run all day, just during the peak usage hours of the day. If your generation capability is sufficient to run your entire company site, then the utility may call you and ask that you run your generators at those times to reduce peak usage.

Another aspect of running your own generators is the selling of power back to the power utility. This must be investigated with your local board of public utilities as to how much you would be paid and what conditions must be met. But if you are in an area of unreliable power, you might be able to address your own problems and cover some of your costs at the same time.

Environmental and Regulatory Issues

Like all good things, there are some downsides. Running an internal combustion engine to make electricity puts pollution into the air. Some jurisdictions limit the number of hours per month that a generator can be run (except in a crisis). Before purchasing your generator, check for any requisite permits for such things as fuel storage, air pollution, taxes, etc.

ACTIONS STEPS FOR YOUR PLAN

If you have a UPS, be sure that it is properly maintained. Most UPSs require regular preventative maintenance, such as changing the air filters and checking the condition of the batteries. If you skip this step, then you are destined to discover how important it is the next time your UPS is needed.

Most large UPS units come with a small display panel that indicates the condition of the UPS's ability to supply power. Master this panel and all controls before an emergency arises. Never open the front of the UPS as the unit is an electrical shock hazard. It should only be opened by trained electricians.

In the event of a power outage, the front panel display can tell you how long the UPS batteries will be able to supply power to all the devices attached. This is a very important piece of information. Most computer servers take a long time to recover if they suddenly lose power. They require time to shut down "gracefully." You need to know the typical amount of time required to shut down each critical server.

Most UPS units include an audible alarm for when they are on battery power. It is important to know what these alarms are and what to do when you hear them. If the UPS units are in a place where a security guard can hear them after hours, be sure the guard knows what to do.

EMERGENCY LIGHTING

In a large building, it can get very dark very quickly in a blackout. Even if flash-lights are readily available, you need to be able to find them. Also, a sudden blackout can be very disorienting to some people. This only adds an element of panic to the moment. To address this, most legal jurisdictions require the installation of emergency lights that come on whenever power to the build-ing is lost. This provides some light for the safe evacuation of offices and work-places.

These lights depend on a battery to power the lights in a blackout. To be sure that the lights and the battery are ready when they are needed, they must be checked monthly according to the manufacturer's testing steps.

SOMETHING FOR YOUR SUPPORT PLAN

Following are three pages for you to consider as additions to your Power Sup-port Plan.

The first page is an insert for your immediate steps Contingency Plan to be kept at the help desk. When power drops, they are to execute the steps on this card to contain the problem while the technical staff is called in.

The second page is a wall notice on which equipment to turn off in what order so that your UPS and generator system can be freed to support the most critical systems.

The third page is a set of instructions for making up the power shedding tags described on the second page.

Power Outage Action Plan

1. Immediate Action.

   a. Notify your facility's Maintenance supervisor immediately.

   b. Notify your Supervisor.

          Primary: **(name and number here)**

          Alternate: **(name and number here)**

   c. Determine the scope of the problem.

     ➤ Look outside the office. Is there power everywhere else in the building?

     ➤ Send someone outside to see if the electricity is on outside of the building. (Do not go yourself. You must sit by the phone to coordinate action until your supervisor arrives). Are there lights on in any other buildings? Are traffic signals working? Are street lights on?

   d. Notify the facility's Disaster Recovery Manager.

   e. Begin a log sheet of all events to include when the lights went out, who was notified and when, any communications with the power company, etc.

2. Physical Layout.

   a. UPS Room

     ➤ Send someone to look at the UPS. Note how long the display indicates the batteries are projected to last.

     ➤ Execute the power shedding plan.

     ➤ Keep monitoring the UPS and continue shedding power using devices. When the UPS time falls below 20 minutes, begin shutting down all the servers.

     ➤ Call all system administrators and the network manager.

(Post this on the computer room walls.)

Power Shedding Priorities

When electrical power fails, or when the power company notifies us that a failure is imminent, the drain on the UPS batteries is minimized by turning off equipment according to its power shedding priority. After reliable power is restored, turn equipment back on according to its priority. Start the most critical systems first.

When a power outage occurs or is anticipated, notify the Help Desk, Facility Security, your supervisor, and the Data Processing Manager. Monitor the UPS systems to see how much time is remaining on the batteries (instructions are posted on the UPS devices).

This approach uses Power Shedding Priorities A through D, with A being least critical and D being most critical equipment to keep running. Priority is set according to:

➤ Which systems directly support facility production.

➤ Which systems will cause widespread problems if they stop working.

➤ Which systems are difficult to restart if they stop suddenly.

1. As soon as we lose electrical power, shut off nonessential systems and equipment identified with a green "A" power shedding label, , such as CRTs, terminals, printers, card processing equipment.

> ➤ Notify other company sites on your network.

> ➤ Update the Help Desk, Security, and the Data Processing Manager.

2. When the UPS units show 15 minutes of power remaining, shut off low-priority CPUs and devices identified with a Yellow "B" power shedding label. When you progress to this step, notify:

> ➤ The Help Desk and the Data Processing Manager

3. When the UPS units show 5 minutes of power remaining, shut off all remaining equipment and servers identified with a red "C" power shedding label. When you progress to this step, notify:

> ➤ The Help Desk and the Data Processing Manager

4. Let equipment identified with a tan "D" power shedding label "die" on their own as power drops off. This is equipment that can tolerate a sudden power drop.

Communications is important!

Ensure that management and the appropriate support people know when you start the next step of shutting down or restarting systems. Data Processing Management will call in the required system support people for a proper restart.

Power Shedding Tag Instructions

Labeling your equipment: make up labels on colored paper and then laminate them.

A = Green   B = Yellow   C = Red   D = Tan

> **Power
> Shedding
> Priority
> A**

Resources:

Liebert	www.liebert.com
American Power Conversion	www.apc.com
Tripplite	www.tripplite.com
Underwriter Laboratories	www.ul.com

CONCLUSION

Electricity is a powerful resource necessary to operate the modern business. Like any resource, we need to be familiar with its role within our operation and how its absence will affect us. In the absence of clean power from the electric utility, our main sources of electrical power are the battery-operated UPS and the generator. A thorough understanding of the electrical requirements of your organization will help you to design the most cost-effective plan to protect against its absence.

CHAPTER 8

TELECOMMUNICATIONS
Your Connection to the World

Everything is connected . . . no one thing can change by itself.
—Paul Hawken

INTRODUCTION

How important can a telephone line be? What's the cost of a telephone call? What is the value of a missed call? How much would you pay for 100 percent telecommunications reliability? Is such a thing even possible?

Consider this scenario. You are the Plant Materials Manager, sitting in your living room. Now as you watch the evening news, you see a video of flames rising out of the roof of a key supplier's main factory. You don't need trouble like this. What should you do? You try calling your salesperson and their company offices but no one answers. First thing the next morning and all the next morning you try calling them. They are over an hour drive away and you can't get away from the office that long and your calls still go unanswered.

Looking through your contact list, you select another supplier and place an order for a 2-month supply of goods to replace the other supplier. The setup costs are a killer but it is worth the money if we can keep your factory running. At least this problem is contained. Trouble is, the fire you saw on TV was isolated to their front offices, and their factory is fine. Their warehouse is bulging. At a time like this they need the cash, but they can't call out until their telephone switching room is replaced! They took care of the fire but forgot all about their customers.

All companies strike a fine balance between the cost of reliable telephone service and the cost of downtime. In a time of tight budgets (which is always), you balance the cost of premium services against the potential loss of telephone service. The more reliable that you want your telephone network to be, the more you must spend to get it that way. Telephone service is very central to the conduct of business in most companies. A failure here isolates customers and suppliers from your company—and that can quickly become a very lonely feeling.

Some companies are even more dependent on their telephone service than others are. If you work at a factory, you use the telephone to conduct business but your main concern is moving products down the line. The loss of telephone service does not slow down the assembly line one bit. However, if your facility is a call center for sales or service, then 100 percent reliable telephone service is crucial to your ongoing business. In the factory example, if the conveyor on the main assembly line breaks, the workers have nothing to do. In the call center, if the telephone service is interrupted, then they are likewise idled. How your facility utilizes its telephone service has a great deal to do with how crucial it is for your operations.

This chapter begins with a recap of telephone systems basics. If you are already a telephone system expert, skip the next section. If you are charged with writing a plan in an area in which you are not a full-fledged expert, then you should read on. A basic understanding of the main components will make it easier for you to develop an appropriate plan.

TELECOMMUNICATION SERVICE

The North American telephone network is designed to carry traffic from about 10 percent of all telephones in a given area. This approximates its load on its busiest times. In a wide-area disaster, this capacity is quickly swamped as people everywhere call to check on their loved ones. The cellular network doesn't fare any better because portions of it also use landlines and it has its own capacity limits. In today's fast-paced business environment, how long can your business afford to be without telephone service?

The disasters that can befall your delicate communications line are legion. Anywhere along its path the wire can be broken, switching equipment can lose power, or problems can even occur within your building. The high level of telephone communications reliability of our modern networks is the envy of the world. We must ensure that your company has reviewed the risks to its telecommunications pipeline and taken steps to reduce the likelihood of failure. Our job here today is to identify those risks and build a wish list of mitigation actions to make our company's telephone communications even more rock solid than ever before.

Where Does That Wire in the Wall Go?

The world of telephonic communications all begins with the telephone instrument on your desk. This modern marvel connects you to the world at large. The telephone is connected by wire to the wall jack, which is in turn connected to a wire closet. A wire closet may be one of those locked doors on your office building floor that you never get to look into. The same function can be served by running wires to a specific place on the wall of a factory (which is generally a wide-open space). In either place, you would see brightly colored wires running in spaghetti-like fashion to a telephone wire "punch-down block."

If you look at a punch block, it seems to be a "rat's nest" of colored wire routed in an orderly fashion, yet going in all directions. Each office telephone has at least one pair of wires running from its wall jack all the way back to the wiring punch block. The punch block also has wires running to the telephone switch for your building. This is where the two are connected to each other. If an office no longer needs a telephone line, this is a place where it can be disconnected.

Private Branch Exchange

From the wire closet, large bundles of wires run to the company's telephone switching equipment. In a larger company this would be a Private Branch Exchange (PBX). A PBX replaces the long-gone company telephone operator who would connect internal calls with a plug patch panel. The patch panel physically connects the wires from one telephone instrument into the wires of another. This is really a basic operation, but until electronics matured, it was the only way to do it. This is now all done electronically. In today's offices, a PBX takes these incoming wires and, using the signal on them, provides electronic switching of calls within the building. A simple way to think about a PBX is to consider it a special-purpose computer with all the support needs of a minicomputer.

The PBX determines which calls are intended for external telephone numbers and connects to the local telephone company Central Office using "trunk" lines. Trunk lines are used for inbound or outbound calls. The number of trunk lines the PBX has connected to the Central Office determines the maximum number of external (inbound or outbound) calls you are capable of supporting at a given moment.

The Telephone Company's Central Office

In the earliest days of telephones, it became obvious that every person could not be wired to every other person they might possibly want to call. This would result in an impossible maze of wires. To call someone new, you would first need to run a wire from your telephone to their telephone. Imagine the problems in asking a girl for her telephone number in those days!

To simplify this problem, all the telephone lines were run into a centralized building and then the switchboard operators would physically patch your telephone line into the switchboard, making the connection. These buildings would be located at various places around the city and were the central place where connections were made. Eventually, automated switching made it easier, but buildings were still needed to switch the calls. In more recent years with the advent of solid-state circuits, the floor space required for these buildings has shrunk dramatically. You still see them around. Small buildings without any windows, usually neatly trimmed grass, and a small telephone company sign by the front door.

The Central Office provides a service similar to your PBX by switching your call to another local telephone, to a different Central Office far away, or to a long-distance carrier's Point of Presence (POP). The long-distance company then routes the call through its switching center and back to a distant Central Office and down to the far-away telephone.

OK, well, this all sounds pretty straightforward. After all, telephone service has been around for well over 100 years and its technology is pretty well known. *What could possibly go wrong?*

RISK ASSESSMENT

Now that you know the basics of how the telephone system works, what are the risks to these components? We reviewed natural hazards in detail in an earlier chapter so here we will only address those natural hazards that have a major impact on your telecommunications system.

Natural Hazards

➤ **Ice Storms and Blizzards.** Ice can coat cables strung from telephone poles and, if the weight is great enough, potentially bring them down.

➤ **Thunderstorms and Lightning.** Severe rain can weaken the ground around a pole and cause it to sag when there are high winds at the same time pushing against it. Lightning can strike telephone poles and send a major charge flying down the line, burning up wire and equipment along the way.

➤ **Tornadoes.** A powerful destructive force that can snap lines and rip up telephone poles. High-risk areas are prime candidates for buried lines.

➤ **Hurricanes and Floods.** Can cover a wide swath of land and not only bring down a telephone network but also prevent crews from promptly addressing the problems.

Man-Made Hazards

➤ **Breaks in Buried Lines.** Sometimes emergency excavation is necessary (such as repairing a broken gas main). Sometimes the state is cleaning trash out of the ditches alongside the road. Sometimes a well-meaning person just digs without asking (including on your own property). In any of these cases, there is the chance that your tiny little cable will be dug up and severed.

➤ **Accidents.** Sometimes people miss the tight turn and break off a telephone pole. If this is your only line to the Central Office, your service is gone until the pole is replaced.

➤ **Central Office Failure.** A problem in a Central Office can quickly shut down your telecommunications, unless you are wired to a second Central Office.

Telephone Equipment Room

➤ **Temperatures** that are too hot, too cold, and that swing widely are all hard on your telephone switching equipment. Extreme temperatures stress the printed circuits. Large swings in temperature (hot to cold) cause expansion and shrinkage of circuit cards and again can weaken components over time.

➤ **Humidity** has an effect on temperature and the growth of mold on your equipment.

➤ **Loss of Electrical Power** will definitely stop a PBX. Pay phones and direct lines out should still be operational since the telephone circuits supply their own power.

➤ **Water Pipes Overhead** in your PBX room could release water onto your equipment. The same goes for your cable panels. Overhead pipes along external walls could potentially freeze and leak when thawing. Leaks from rooftop air conditioning compressors are also a problem.

➤ **Security.** This room is not set up to accommodate tourists and they should not be allowed in. Keep the door locked at all times.

➤ **Fire.** This equipment generates heat and is in danger from fire or the sprinklers used to extinguish a fire. Typically this room is unattended and a slow-starting fire may go undetected. Gas fire suppression is expensive but may save your equipment.

CABLING

Let's start off with cabling. The discussion earlier about the telephone wire closet had a purpose. Imagine the mess if an isolated fire in the wire closet melted all these wires. In terms of structural damage, you got off pretty easy. But in terms of damage to the telephone system, that entire area of the facility will be without service for some time. New wire would have to be run from the PBX to the closet and from the wall to the closet. The alternative is to splice an extension onto each wire and run it into a punch block. Either way is time consuming and expensive. So you can see how the wiring closet can be a single point of failure for your telephones. This makes it a good idea to keep everyone out of it and to not store anything in the closet that might cause a problem.

Internal Cabling

For disaster avoidance, our concerns begin with the wiring closet and patch panels. Take a walk with your telecommunications specialist and identify the location of all telephone patch panels in your facility. Things you are looking for:

1. In a closet

➤ The door and any windows are kept locked.

➤ There is fire suppression equipment (usually fused link sprinklers).

➤ There is nothing else in the closet except telephone equipment and data communications equipment. Combustible materials stored in the closet threaten your equipment. This is not the place to store holiday decorations, old files, office supplies, janitor supplies, etc.

➤ Very few people have keys—telephone support staff, security, and no one else.

➤ There should be sufficient light to work in the closet. Remember those little wires are color-coded and you need enough light to identify them.

➤ There will often be data network wiring and switching equipment in these closets. They are a natural fit here. The issue is that where the patch panel is simply a physical connection for wires, the network equipment is energized electronics, which will generate heat and introduce a potential fire source where there was none before.

2. Outside a closet

➤ Be sure it is covered and the cover is locked. Same rules for the keys as for the wire closets. Enough keys for the right people and none for anyone else.

➤ All wires leading into the external panel are encased in heavy conduit to inhibit tampering.

➤ If this is located in a warehouse or factory, be sure it is strongly protected from environmental influences (leaky ceilings, etc.) and from being crushed by a forklift or toppling stacked material.

External Cabling

The first rule of outside cabling is "cabling and backhoes don't mix!" A chain is only as strong as its weakest link. Your PBX is snugly locked up in its room, and the telephone company's Central Office is also secure. But the wire in between is exposed to the ravages of weather, men, and machines.

Experienced telecommunication professionals have their own name for backhoes—cable locators!

External cabling, which is cable run from your telephone exchange room to the telephone company's Central Office, is your biggest concern. The wire runs from your building to a telephone company access point along the road, usually on a pole. Then the wire runs through the countryside (usually along a road or railroad) to a Central Office. In the city, it might run through underground pipes to the Central Office. You have no control over where the wire is run and no capability to protect it! In some areas, you will even have separate cable runs to be concerned about—one for the local telephone company and a different run for the Inter Exchange carrier (long-distance service).

A term used by some telephone people is "the last mile." The last mile is about the wire from the telephone company's Central Office to the structure (and is usually more than a mile). This is also known as the "local access" or the "local loop." This part of the cabling is the biggest problem. It is often carried on telephone poles (susceptible to ice storms and errant vehicles) or underground.

Route Separation

The goal in telecommunications reliability is redundancy. This can be redundant equipment, redundant technicians, and redundant cabling. The more alternate paths that a signal can be routed, the more likely it is to get through. The principle of cable route separation should be an integral part of your telephone network design. Essentially this means that you have more than one cable between your building and the telephone company's Central Office, and between your building and your long-distance carrier's point of presence. This prevents a total communications outage from a single cable cut.

Few companies can afford to take this to the extreme, but there are some steps you can look into. Begin by asking the telephone company to show you the route that your telephone cable takes from the wall of your building to the Central Office. This will also show you how exposed the cable is to auto accidents (are the poles close to the road), to backhoes (is the cable buried along the road in some places) or any other number of threats.

With this experience in mind, negotiate with the telephone company a fresh cable run from your building (exit from the opposite end from the other cable) to a different Central Office. This will keep you operational in case your usual Central Office is damaged or experiences an equipment failure, or if the cable to the Central Office was broken. How likely is that to happen?

In May 1988, there was a fire in the Illinois Bell Central Office located in Hinsdale, IL. The two-story building was completely gutted. This building was an important hub for Illinois Bell as well as major long-distance carriers like MCI and Sprint. In addition to cellular service and data networks, approximately 40,000 subscriber lines and 6 fiber optic lines lost service.

To reduce the chance of a total system failure similar to the Hinsdale disaster, the telephone companies have gradually migrated their Central Office structure from a spoke-and-hub approach (with its obvious single point of failure) to a ring or mesh approach where multiple Central Offices are connected to each other. In this scenario, calls are routed around the damaged Central Office in a manner that is transparent to the caller. This is an ongoing process and may not yet have been completed in rural areas or small towns. If possible, you want routing separation with the wire running from your facility running to two different Central Offices on separate routes.

Route separation is more important than having multiple vendors. Most telephone routes follow railroad rights-of-way and the major carriers lines commonly converge at bridges. Imagine the number of places there are to cross a major river, etc. There aren't many to choose from. The lines from various companies often come together here and cross under the same portion of the bridge. What could go wrong? Vehicles crossing bridges might catch on fire, river barges can break free and strike bridge pilings, and major bridges are tempting terrorist targets.

Many telephone carriers define cable separation as a distance of 25 feet or more between cables. Others ensure cables are at least 100 feet apart and have at least a 2-foot separation at cable crossovers. Ask your local and long-distance carriers how they define cable route separation and how faithful they are to that standard. When using multiple vendors, even if their cables are separated, they share a common weakness if they join at the same Central Office or cross a river under the same bridge. Upon close investigation, you may even see that where you are using two companies, that one is leasing part of the same wire from your other provider!

What to do? Find out how many access points there are for your telephone service. Does it enter the building at more than one place (again, trying to separate the cables)? Ask the telephone company to identify the route that the cable takes from the Central Office to your facility. Drive along this route and look for potential problems.

In terms of your long-distance provider, where is their Point of Presence (POP) located? Where is the POP of their competitors? You can consider running a separate connection to a second POP to provide for multiple circuits. Depending on the distance, this separate line may be quite expensive to run and maintain.

Map It Out

Now that you know the cable route to the Central Office, map it out—from where it enters your wall to the Central Office. You might think, "Isn't that the telephone company's responsibility?" The answer is yes, but type up that excuse and paste it to your wall in case the line is cut. Try it on your boss! If you drive to work using the same route as your cable, you might see construction crews digging near where the cable is to repair a water main, snapped poles, or sagging wire due to accidents or severe weather, any number of threats too close to the wire for comfort.

So draw out a map of your wire runs from the telephone pole outside to the Central Office. Then make a detailed map of the run from the pole to the wall and on to the telephone room. Indicate which lines terminate in equipment provided by the telephone company and which lines provide essential services.

YOUR TELEPHONE SWITCHING ROOM

PBX: Your "Other" Computer Room

A Private Branch Exchange (PBX) is a telephone switching device used in most large companies. It automatically routes calls internally to other extensions without operator assistance. Inbound calls are routed to the correct desktop and outbound calls are passed to the telephone company. Modern PBX systems offer a wide range of additional services such as:

➤ Voicemail

➤ Telephone conferencing

➤ Call transferring

➤ Music on hold

Based on this, from a business continuity perspective, you have a large single point of failure device. You must plan to recover from a catastrophic failure of the PBX (e.g., burned to a cinder in a fire). A close examination of the PBX room and its ancillary equipment will show that it is essentially another computer room, requiring the same electrical and climate stabilization actions. Backup copies of the configuration data must be made for each device and handled with the same care as the backup data from your computer system. These data should be securely stored off-site and available when needed. Up-to-date backed-up data are the key to a prompt recovery.

Internal to a company, the telephone signals can be analog or digital. Digital PBX systems provide a wide range of services beyond simply routing calls. Most PBX systems use digital signals to communicate with the telephones. This allows for additional services such as one-touch dialing, preprogrammed telephone numbers, voicemail, etc. This is significant in the case where you want to use a modem to dial out of the office. A fax machine or a direct modem connection requires an analog line. If you have a digital PBX, then you will need separate analog lines.

Rather than run a multitude of analog telephone lines, most companies access the Internet via their external data network. This works fine for most office dwellers. However, some devices still need these analog lines and you should keep track of where they are. Examples of analog dial-out lines might be for an alarm service, which dials out to notify the repair service of an out-of-tolerance condition, validating a credit card in stores, etc.

Other Vital Equipment Located in the PBX Room

There is other important equipment typically located in the same room as your PBX. After the critical devices are identified, make sure they are protected and draft a plan to fully recover them. These devices may include:

➤ **Interactive Voice Response (IVR).** Gives callers information based on what the caller enters using the telephone keypad. You have heard the messages—please select 1 to talk to sales, select 2 to talk to . . . These audio tracks should be backed up and the queuing logic documented.

➤ **Automatic Number Identification.** This is the business version of what is sold to consumers as "caller ID."

➤ **Intelligent Port Selector.** Connects the incoming call to the first available line. This is used when you have multiple people answering inbound calls, as in a hotel chain's reservation center.

➤ **Call Management System.** To monitor the volume of telephone calls during peak periods, to identify the number of telephone operators needed, and to track operator efficiency.

➤ **Call Accounting.** Tracks calls made and assigns them to a billing account. This is also known as a "Station Message Detail Recording" (SMDR). This is used in various ways. Lawyers might use it to bill their time to a specific client. Some companies use this to track employees' long distance usage, etc.

➤ **Call Monitoring.** Tracks the level of call activity by showing the status of the trunk lines, the number of calls in progress, the number of calls waiting in queues, the wait time, the number of abandoned calls, and the status of the operators.

Inter Exchange Carrier Point of Presence

With the breakup of the AT&T long-distance monopoly in 1982 came the creation of independent long-distance telecommunications providers. These non-AT&T long-distance providers are known as Inter Exchange Carriers (IXC). Along with this choice came the opportunity to split your long-distance service across different carriers in hopes that all of them would not be knocked out in a disaster and therefore your communications traffic could flow out on the alternative pipeline. For that to be true, a lot of careful planning is necessary.

First, you must ensure cable separation so that you have a different wire path from your facility to the IXC's point of presence. Most companies are a mix of owning the network in high-traffic areas and renting from another carrier in a low-traffic area. This means your traffic separation may only be on paper. If you are in a high-traffic area, the carrier may run a separate cable to your facility. If you are not, then you will probably connect to the IXC in the nearest Central Office. Do not take for granted that because you use two companies that you are on two different wires. Ask them if they share lines and ask to see the route of the cable.

Some telecommunications experts believe that route separation is much more important than using multiple telecommunications companies. They feel it is easier to manage one supplier so long as the cable issue is addressed.

When evaluating networks, consider whether they rent their network or own it. Most are a mixture. The more of the network equipment that they own, the more control they can exercise over it. When choosing an IXC there are many things to consider:

➤ You need to know what their system availability time is and what they will guarantee.

➤ What are the consequences to the IXC of downtime? You can ill afford it. A few extra free minutes of service every month is poor recompense for missed customer calls.

➤ What is the restoration priority for the sections of the network that you will be using?

➤ What are their alternate routes for the places you normally communicate with? Don't automatically assume a new carrier will be a better alternative to your existing carrier. Is your service route a spur (single-threaded) service? Is it a ring architecture, which at least gives you two paths in case one has a problem?

➤ How often does the carrier practice their disaster recovery procedures?

➤ How easily can the IXC shift your inbound calls to another site?

ACTION STEPS FOR YOUR PLAN

What Are We Protecting?

As you know, the first step in building a plan is to make an inventory of your telecommunications assets. You will assemble at least three lists. The first list tells us all about every major item and who to call if it breaks. The second list shows us where in the building the main cable runs are. The third list is of all the telephone numbers used by the facility. In a crisis, we may need to reroute some of these to another location.

1. Begin with a list of all major devices in your telephone switching room, such as the PBX, IVR, etc. Include on this list:

➤ A description of each machine.

➤ The serial numbers of the main equipment and any major components.

➤ The name, 24-hour telephone number, contract number, and contract restrictions for whomever you have arranged to service that item.

➤ The location of every item, including a simple floor map of the telephone room.

> Be sure to back up your entire configuration data, either on magnetic media or, if the file is small, print it off and store it safely away.

2. Now make a wiring inventory of all the cable runs within your facility. We do not need to show individual runs to the offices. In a crisis, you can always shift someone to another office. This is best accomplished with computer-aided drafting software on a digitized version of the floor plan.

> Indicate on maps of each building or floor of a multistory building. Knowing the location of these cable runs is important to quickly assess damage.

> Indicate where the telephone service enters the building and its route to the telephone exchange room. Note any hazards along the cable path.

> If you have pay phones, indicate them on the map.

> If you have any independent direct lines that bypass your telephone switch, mark them on the map.

3. Make up a telephone number inventory with all the telephone numbers assigned to your building/facility.

> DID lines.

> Dedicated telephone lines that bypass your PBX, such as FAX machines.

> Pay telephones.

> Foreign exchange lines.

Identify Critical Circuits

Telephones are used to communicate, and every part of the company uses them differently. In an emergency, salespeople will need to contact customers, the warehouse will need to call suppliers, and the people at the disaster site will want to call home. In a disaster, you won't be able to please everyone right away, so we need a restoration priority guideline to know which circuits to recover (or protect) and in what order.

Start this analysis by reviewing the critical functions identified by your executives at the beginning of the Business Continuity Planning project. Next, meet with representatives from each department and ask them to identify their critical telecommunications needs and at what point in the disaster containment/recovery they would be needed. For example, early in the emergency, the Human Resources team might need to notify employees to not report to work or to come in at certain times, etc. Each department must prioritize their communications needs.

With your critical communications functions identified, we can determine which circuits support these key functions. If you trace out the top three or four circuits, you may see some of the same hardware, some of the same cables, and circuit paths common to them all. Working down your list, you can see which of your hardware devices (or cable bundles) has the greatest benefit to being restored first.

You must also include in your plan how you will relocate operations to another site. This is a twofold issue. In the first case, if a department must be moved off-site due to damage to their offices, you need to be able to shift their inbound calls to their new location quickly. In the second case, if your telephone equipment room is destroyed, you must quickly restore a minimal level of service. Some people might plan to build a new telephone room on-site. Others will contract with a service company who will bring a telephone equipment room to your site already set up in a large trailer. They just need to plug into your wiring (no trivial task). This could buy you time until your equipment room is rebuilt. If you elect to bring in the configured trailer, this agreement must be made in advance, and be aware that these might not be available in a wide area disaster.

Telecommunications Mitigation Plan

With these risks in mind, along with due consideration of the identified priority circuits, we can assemble a mitigation plan to reduce the likelihood of a threat or its impact if it occurs. The key to telecommunications mitigation is redundancy. Redundancy in equipment in case one machine must be repaired. Redundancy in communications routes in case a cable is severed or interrupted. Redundancy in communication methods, such as radios, cellular telephones, or satellite communications will provide at least basic communications support.

CABLE MITIGATION PLAN

➤ Multiple paths for the "last mile". Investigate the path from your telephone equipment room all the way to the Central Office. Ask the telephone company to make another connection from your PBX, out through the wall of your building at a point distant from the other exit point and on a different route to a different Central Office. Be sure that your in-house wiring staff understands what you are asking for before they start.

➤ Multiple paths for Inter exchange carriers. Investigate the path from your telephone equipment room to your service provider's point of presence. Avoid the same route as used for your local telephone service.

➤ From the pole to your wall, if the cable is underground, ensure it is clearly marked with "do not dig" indicators or other obstacles to keep digging equipment away (or at least delay them until the cable can be marked).

TELEPHONE EQUIPMENT ROOM MITIGATION PLAN Think of your telephone communications room like a computer room. Their environmental and security needs are almost identical.

➤ **Uninterruptible Power Supply (UPS).** When you lose electrical power, this is what will keep your PBX active until external power is restored or until your facility's electrical generators kick in. Conduct a power loss test to see which equipment is not connected to the UPS. If the device isn't essential or time consuming to restart, take it off the UPS. The fewer machines on the UPS the better. When conducting the power test, see how long the batteries can support the load. Be sure the UPS is properly maintained by your service company.

When Hurricane Hugo struck the southeast United States in 1989, it surged hundreds of miles inland with huge mounts of rain and wind. There were so many trees downed by the storm that in some areas it was days before electrical power was restored. Even the emergency batteries at the Central Offices were eventually drained. So, do not depend solely on your UPS for emergency power. Consider other power sources as well.

➤ **Fire.** This room requires the same fire protection as a computer room. An early-warning fire alarm system and gas fire suppression systems are highly recommended.

➤ **Security Access.** This room is normally unattended. It should be locked as no one has any business strolling around in this room. The telephone system administrator can normally perform their switching administration duties via terminal over the network.

➤ **Structural Investigation.** Although you can rarely select the room, a close inspection can identify problems. Water pipes running along the walls or along the ceiling are a potential source of problems. They may freeze or leak. They should be watched carefully. Consider installing a plastic shield attached to a drain placed under them to catch condensation or leaks. A roof-mounted air conditioner may cause a roof leak. External walls may stress the air-handling equipment as outside temperatures heat or cool the walls.

➤ **Temperature Variability.** Your equipment must stay within a specific operating temperature and humidity range for maximum life and to maintain your service agreement coverage. Proper air conditioning, heating, and humidity control equipment must be in service and well cared for.

➤ **Alarms Such as Humidity, Temperature, Fire, and Electric.** A bank of alarms will help you to monitor the condition of the room. These alarms must sound within the room as well as at the security guard station since the room is normally unattended. Early detection will reduce the likelihood of significant damage. Include automatic paging equipment for notifying the after-hours support team of problems. Consider installing automatic shutdown software for your equipment. This signals your hardware to shut itself down gracefully in the event of a problem.

➤ **Data Backups.** Like a computer, your switch and configurable devices need to back up their configuration data whenever these change. Store copies of these files in a secure off-site location.

➤ **Housekeeping.** Keeping the door locked will help to prevent others from using the switch room as a storage facility. Nothing should be stored in this room that does not pertain to the equipment. This will reduce the amount of combustibles available to a fire. Do not let this room become another storage or janitor's closet.

ALTERNATE COMMUNICATIONS METHODS You must have written procedures for quickly routing inter exchange carrier traffic to the local telephone service in the event that your IXCs have major problems. How hard is this to do, and then to switch it back again? Is it easier (or cheaper) to do this by splitting the load across two carriers and then shift the entire load to the functional carrier? Other items to consider include:

➤ Do you have company-owned cellular telephones and cellular modems for communicating when the telephone system is inoperable?

➤ Develop written procedures for how to work with the telephone company to shift specific telephone numbers or all incoming calls to a different company site.

➤ Do you have any employees who are "ham" radio operators? It is nice to have alternative channels when the primary ones are not available. In a wide-area emergency, radio communications will also get congested. Radio conversations are not secure and anyone with the proper equipment can listen to them. Radio communications is also slow and not suitable for large data volumes.

➤ Other communications alternatives include satellite and microwave, both susceptible to problems if the antenna has been shifted by a storm or earthquake.

SOMETHING FOR YOUR SUPPORT PLAN

Most companies contract emergency recovery of their telephone equipment through the same company that services their equipment. A problem arises if there is more than one service company involved. An alternative is to arrange with a company to come on-site if your telephone equipment room is destroyed and to set up a trailer adjacent to your building with a ready-to-go telephone switch. To support this, companies often run cables to the front of the building for a quick connection.

Another consideration is that pay phones do not route through your PBX. They are direct lines to the outside service; so if your PBX is inoperative, use pay phones. Keep a list of where they are and their telephone numbers.

Cellular telephones are also common. Cellular traffic can be somewhat limited in a wide-area emergency as the local cell towers become saturated with calls. Use this as an alternative communications channel, not as the primary backup.

A branch office is an ideal place to shift operations to until the disaster-struck site is recovered. The key is how far away the backup facility is located from the affected site. It should be far enough away to be unaffected by the same disaster. There is no set mileage distance but it should at least be on a different power grid and telephone Central Office. If it is too far, then you must also provide lodging for the relocated people.

One problem is how to relocate to these sites in a crisis. If this is during an area-wide disaster, mass transit such as air travel may be disrupted, and driving there yourself may be difficult. One side aspect of the attack on the World

Trade Center in September 2001 was that it shut down all air travel. Companies scrambling to activate their out-of-state recovery sites had a difficult time shifting key personnel and material to the site. No one had planned for a complete shutdown of the air transportation system.

Things to consider after a disaster:

➤ Do not make any unnecessary calls—only for emergencies.

➤ When calling, you may need to wait several minutes to get a dial tone. Do not hit the switch hook, because every time you do, you are placed at the end of the line for the next available dial tone.

➤ When you receive a dial tone, quickly dial your number. In a time of low telephone service availability, the dial tone is offered for a much shorter time.

TESTING

Plans are written by people with the best of intentions but, unless they are tested, you will never know what you don't know. Testing a plan exposed gaps and omissions in the process steps. It points out incorrect emergency telephone numbers and emergency equipment that no longer exists.

Test exercises are a great way to train the people on what to do. The more that they practice their emergency steps, the faster they will be able to perform them as they become familiar actions instead of something new. Where possible, include your emergency service providers. They will be a great source of recovery information.

When testing your plan, include some of your contract service providers. They may be able to point out some gaps in your planning or things that can be done in advance to make their assistance to you flow much easier.

Also, over time, your communications flows will shift. As this occurs, update your testing accordingly.

CONCLUSION

The modern business relies on telecommunications to perform its role in the marketplace. Like any resource, we need to be familiar with its role within our operation and how its absence will affect us. Redundancy is your best defense against a disaster removing your ability to communicate with customers and suppliers. A thorough understanding of the telecommunication requirements of your organization will help you to design the most cost-effective plan to protect against its absence.

CHAPTER 9

VITAL RECORDS RECOVERY
Covering Your Assets

Every vital organization owes its birth and life
to an exciting and daring idea.
—James B. Conant

INTRODUCTION

What are your personal vital records? Are they your car title, your home's deed, a marriage license, or even a divorce decree? Whatever they are, you spend a lot of time and effort to be sure they are safe because you know they may be difficult and time consuming to recreate later. The same holds true for your company's business records. They need a well-thought-out emergency management program if they are to be there when you need them.

Throughout this chapter references will be made to documents and records. In all cases, these terms apply to information stored on any media, possibly paper, magnetic, or microfilm. There may be a bit of difference in how they are stored, but the issues for their handling and management are essentially the same.

This chapter is focused more toward mitigation actions than recovery as that will address most of the emergency situations that you will encounter. Also included are recovery actions for small, contained records damage. There is always a chance that an emergency will overpower the best defenses and a recovery action will be needed. Few facilities are staffed or equipped for a large-scale recovery. Your best plan is to prearrange for a professional recovery service to come on-site to assist in the recovery effort. They are also a resource for designing your records mitigation processes. Remember that in a wide-area disaster, an outside service may already be engaged, so be prepared to take the initial preservation actions on your own.

A professional storage facility can be a safe and secure place for storage of documents not needed to run the business day to day and can also be a good source of information. Companies that provide this service include:

Fireproof Records Center—www.fireproof.com
Iron Mountain—www.ironmountain.com
American Archives—www.americanarchives.com
Archive America—www.archiveamerica.com

The whole point of storing your vital records is that they will be available when you need them. If they are not accessible, then why are you spending all this time and money to store them? Every company has a set of records that it must safeguard for future reference. These records might be contracts, customer lists, or personnel files. Vital records can encompass just about anything.

But typically, vital records refer to documents that your company must retain to comply with legal requirements. This could be accounting records to support tax reporting. This could be hazardous waste disposal forms. It could even be quality verification records to defend against future product liability lawsuits. Other types of vital records might be engineering plans and drawings, product specifications, trade secrets, and computer database backup tapes.

Vital records can be stored on many different forms of media. Some are piles of paper. Some vital records are stored on microfiche. Many vital records are electronically recorded onto CDs, data backup tapes, or removable disks. What is your company's vital information stored on? The answer is probably all of these. Where are they stored? All over your facility! They are squirreled away in closets, under desks, on CDs, and even at employees' homes. Even the vital records that are properly situated in routine storage—how well are they climate controlled for preservation? If they are stored off-site, who ensures they are well cared for? Will they be accessible and readable when you need them?

Whatever the media your vital records are stored on, and wherever they are stored, you must have a plan for safeguarding them and recovering them in the event of a disaster. Each type of media requires its own recovery strategy. Each type of document has its own level of recovery urgency.

Our goal in this plan is to safeguard these documents, whatever media they are stored on. In an emergency, your best plan is to call in a records recovery company that you previously contracted with to come in on an as-needed basis. In an emergency, you will not have the leisure time to shop around for the best service and the best price. Every hour counts.

In our plan, we will review the different types of primary vital records storage media, action steps you can take to safeguard them, and steps you can take to recover them yourself. Even if you have a company lined up for an emergency, they may be busy with another customer when you call if this is a wide-area emergency (like a flood or earthquake).

A company's records retention plan should address destroying out-of-date documents, and detail how to store records and how to identify each container. If we uncover out-of-date or unmarked documents, we can use the records retention plan as authority to get the records custodians to clean up the storage areas. It is also a chance to educate people as to what the records retention and storage standards are. This information will be very valuable as we work to build our plan.

If your company does not have a written Records Management and Retention program, you may need to write one. It will make your recovery planning a bit easier.

VITAL RECORDS INVENTORY

By now you know that our first step is to make an assessment of what we are going to protect. This will tell us how big the issue is. In the case of vital records, we need to know, at a minimum, four essential things. Refer to Form 9-1 on the CD-ROM. The inventory, also known as a shelf list, can be combined with the risk assessment spreadsheets. Other information elements may also be useful, such as the document's expiration date, but we wanted to keep this plan basic:

➤ **Records.** What are these documents about? Are they customer records with credit card numbers, personnel files with legally protected information, or legal documents referring to lawsuits and court actions? The information content of a record will help determine its recovery priority.

➤ **Media.** Is this information stored on paper, magnetic tape, microfilm? This will tell you what its storage conditions should be to protect its readability.

➤ **Originating Department.** This helps you to track down someone who may know something about this document to properly prioritize it in the event of a recovery.

➤ **Location.** Vital records turn up in the strangest places, so you need to know where they are all stored. Otherwise, you may lose those vital first few hours after an emergency and the records will be damaged or unrecoverable.

Locate Your Records

The location for storing your records is extremely important. If most of your vital records are stored far away at some distant corporate headquarters, then that saves us from a lot of mitigation and recovery actions. Mitigation and recovery will be their responsibility. We can then focus our efforts on ensuring a safe delivery to them for storage.

The best place to begin your vital records inventory is with your company's records retention plan. This will detail what types of records you are expected to keep and how long each type of record must be maintained. If we are lucky, then most of these records are stored in the same place, or in only a few places. The key thing is that we know where they are. Ask your records custodian for a copy of their records inventory or a listing of what types of documents are stored at which locations. Your next step is to visit these file rooms and see how much volume is involved. Vital records tend to be bulky collections, so expect to see a lot of boxes.

We all admire those companies who keep their records in top shape. The rest of us probably have outdated records lingering everywhere. Our concern here is not the housekeeping aspect, but rather that these excess records distract us from dealing with the truly vital records. Once the records custodian sees us looking at their records, we hope they will wake up and purge the storage areas of outdated documents. Just like cleaning out their garage or seeing the dentist, some people won't do what they should until they must.

It is time well spent to speak to the originators of these records. They can explain to you what is vital and why. Add to your documents inventory the retention period for each document type. Try to uncover any other vital records storage sites not listed, such as interim storage sites, various offices where vital records are stored for office use, and any other records storage. Most departments keep their own cache of records irrespective of the need to safeguard or environmentally protect them. Now is not the time to fight that battle. Some of these are in boxes under a desk. Some are in the bottom of the coat closets. Some are even stored in people's homes as if that would be any safer. As you work with each department, find where these records are stored and add them to your records inventory.

Make a list of the locations and the types of media stored in each. Knowing which type of media is stored there helps you to quickly form a containment and recovery plan based on whether the room suffered water damage, smoke damage from a fire in an adjacent room, deep-freezing due to loss of power in the winter, etc. Each type of media has its own preferred storage conditions to protect their readability. Paper can tolerate freezing so long as it is not wet. Airborne particles and pollution can damage microfiche. Extreme heat or cold can damage magnetic media such as tapes, diskettes, and fixed disk cartridges.

So now with the records inventory list in hand of the types of media you need to protect, the quantities of material and the locations, we can begin to figure out how to protect these records in an emergency.

Prioritize Your Records

The biggest time saver you can do for your vital records disaster recovery plan is to classify your records according to how valuable they are to your business. This single action will help everyone involved to know which records are to be kept safest or to be recovered first. Skip this step, and valuable time may be wasted on low-value records.

Record priority can be determined by legal requirements. It may be based on the cost to reproduce the same information from other sources. It can be determined by who the originating department is. Select a system that suits your business. Be sure you understand the legal retention period for all document types. If in doubt, consult a lawyer. Do not guess!

Once priority has been established, tag every record or records container. Priority tags should be a simple color code to speed the containment effort. Consider using 1-inch-square stickers with different colors to indicate their priority, such as red for top priority, black for do-not-recover records that have copies at a backup site, etc. Post the color code explanation on the walls and be sure it is documented in your plan. Color-coding is especially helpful when there is a fire and someone other than the company employees (fire/police) is performing the salvage operation.

Next, ensure that all your top-priority records are stored in the safest locations. This might be in a fireproof cabinet. This might be in special moisture-proof containers. Typically, the safest place for your documents is on the middle shelf—midway between the floor (moisture, vermin, etc.) and the ceiling (sprinkler heads).

With all the records marked with their recovery priority, make up a floor plan for each storage site indicating the location of your top-priority records. Keep this plan posted in all copies of your recovery plan books. The facility security office should have this also for immediate action during a late-night disaster.

Another classification is who the originating department is. A visual identification tag is needed so you know which records belong to Human Resources, Finance, Legal, etc. Refer to your company's records retention plan for your standard marking information block. As these documents are recovered, be sure the originating departments are involved in the effort. They may be reluctant to have others perusing their stored documents for reasons of legal or privacy issues.

You might mark or stamp the originating department's name in the recovery priority colored tab.

RECORDS TRANSPORTATION

Just as important as your storage process is how your records are handled during transportation. Do you have an off-site storage facility? Most companies have off-site storage for their backup computer media. Imagine how valuable this information would be to an outsider. They can't hack through your network defenses but could they easily snatch your tapes while en route to or from the storage room?

Just because records are traveling to somewhere, don't let your guard down about their security or environmental controls. Once outside the cozy confines of your storage room, they are susceptible to the ravages of all sorts of environmental dangers. Their security must be safeguarded just as well as when they are locked in your storage room. Their environmental "comfort" must also be protected. Improper handling can negate all the careful handling we have used so far. Prudent actions when shipping these records will ensure that they return to you as fresh as they were when they were sent out.

Security

Security during transit is not a lot different from security in your storage room. Keep the curious and the criminal away from your documents. Safeguard the documents from environmental threats so they will be readable upon arrival. Limit access to your records by starting with locked shipping containers. If the records are of very high value, employ a courier to personally carry these records to their destination.

Shipping of vital records should be by way of overnight express delivery. This minimizes the amount of time the records are exposed to security and environmental threats. Shipments should be adequately insured to cover the expense of recreating the material and should be in as inconspicuous a container as possible. Always require a signature from the receiving party. The shipper should provide a tracking number so the progress of the shipment can be monitored. This provides valuable clues when looking for materials missing in transit.

Magnetic Recordings

If a magnetic recording is being sent to someone to review, make a copy of it and send them the copy. Never ship the original.

➤ Open-reel magnetic tape should be wrapped in bubble wrap or shock-absorbing material and packed snugly into containers. This will reduce their movement within the container and reduce the likelihood of damage during transit. It also acts as an insulator against temperature swings.

➤ Cassettes with a locking hub should have their hubs locked and be placed in a rigid container for shipping.

➤ Temperatures in transit should not exceed 110 degrees F. The best time of the year to ship these materials is the spring and the fall.

➤ Tapes and cassettes should be shipped in the same way that they are stored, on their edge. The weight of the media should be supported by the hub.

RECORDS RETENTION

Every company has its own records retention requirements. If your company does not have any, then either you are accumulating massive amounts of paper (creating a fire hazard, housekeeping issues, and storage charges), or you are throwing out documents that you should be retaining to meet legal requirements. Either situation is a problem.

The details of the many things that go into a records retention plan are beyond the scope of this book. An important issue is the elimination of obsolete documents. This means we will have fewer documents to protect and to recover. Some organizations like historical societies try to keep everything. That is the nature of the service they provide. But a business cannot afford to hang on to stored documents that have no value. It takes floor space to store them. It takes energy to maintain them within an acceptable environment. It takes people to move them around. Check with your lawyers, check with your accountants, and properly dispose of the excess. Some laws and regulations may require that the original documents be retained even if they are also recorded on other media.

As we implement our plan, we will be working to identify those critical records that must be restored after a disaster. This is a very time-consuming and expensive process. But it begins with being able to quickly find these critical documents. The less clutter there is to wade through, the easier the plan will be to exercise.

The records retention plan will detail a standard way to identify documents. Know what each of the markings mean and where they are supposed to be placed. Be sure that all the high-priority records encountered are properly marked according to this standard.

When documents reach the end of their useful life, they are destroyed. When this happens, a record is made of the event so we know what happened to that document. A portion of a records retention plan will deal with how your company will record document destruction. In an emergency, documents not at the end of their useful life may be destroyed. A part of your recovery effort will be to make a list of what was destroyed. Be sure that your emergency procedure for reporting accidentally destroyed records agrees with your overall records destruction documentation policy.

MEDIA STORAGE

Most business records have a fixed useful life, usually less than 10 years. If your records collection includes documents of historical or artistic value that you must retain indefinitely, then the storage and recovery of those types of documents are beyond the scope of this book. Always consult a restoration professional for questions about storing or recovering these types of artifacts.

In general, your vital records can be reasonably stored at room temperature. This is true for records whose useful life is 10 years or less. The ideal situation is for your records storage facility to be a separate room or set of rooms, with its own air filtration, heating, air conditioning, and humidity controls. The storage environment of your records will be the major determinant of their useful life. The more controlled the environment, the longer they will be readable.

In general, your storage room should be between 62 and 68 degrees F with a relative humidity of 30 to 40 percent humidity all year long. Temperature and humidity should not vary more than 10 percent of your established settings. If your room is cooler than this, allow magnetic media time to slowly warm to room temperature before use. Temperature and humidity will vary in different parts of the storage room so keep the air circulating with a strong air-handling unit.

As the seasons change, so will the weather outside. Be sure your environmental control equipment can compensate for the temperature and humidity variations of the change of seasons and those that occur between day and night.

To monitor the climate in your storage area, install a thermograph and hygrometer. They will chart the conditions inside of the room over the course of a week. Pay particular attention to how well the humidity and temperatures stay within tolerance between daylight and nighttime hours—and between winter and summer. If something occurs when no one is around, these charts will indicate when the problem began. You might discover someone is turning off the heat to your storage room over the holidays and weekends, not realizing the impact on stored magnetic media.

Many smaller companies will assign a trusted employee to take the backup tapes home as a remote storage solution. This is not a good idea, as there are security and accessibility issues and risks involved. While we would like to trust all our employees, corporate espionage and damage caused by disgruntled employees is not unheard of. You wouldn't want to be in a position where you have to deal with performance issues with the employee who is storing your corporate data at his home. A private home is also not going to be as secure as a professionally managed storage facility. Accessibility could be a problem if a disaster occurs and the employee is not at home due to vacation or other reasons. Listed below are some of the different media types you may have in storage and their particular requirements:

➤ **Paper Document Storage.** Paper is sensitive to humidity and to temperature. It slowly deteriorates. Rapid swings in either or both accelerate this process. If the documents are exposed to low humidity and high temperatures, they gradually dry out and become crumbly. If they are exposed to high humidity and warm temperature, they become susceptible to mold.

To protect your most important records, store them on the middle to lower-middle shelves. This keeps them well off the floor in case of a flood or pipe leak and away from the sprinkler in case of a fire. It also keeps the records in the middle of the room's temperature range (cooler near the floor, warmer near the ceiling).

➤ **Microfilm Storage.** The first key to safeguarding your microfilm is to store it in an airtight container. This will protect it from dust, humidity, and impurities in the air. The container should be made from a noncorroding material such as anodized aluminum or stainless steel. If your microfilm is on a roll, the reel should be made of the same material as the container. Always use lint-free gloves when touching the film.

Store your microfilm on shelving and storage racks made from non-corroding material. Special cabinets designed for protecting microfilm can be obtained from industrial equipment suppliers. If possible, do not store your microfilm in rooms containing pressboard or particleboard as these may give off fumes that will damage the film.

The storage room should have its own temperature and humidity controls. Humidity should be between 30 and 40 percent, and it should never change more than 5 percent within a given day. Large swings in temperature and humidity are damaging to microfilm. The temperature should stay around 65 degrees F and vary no more than 5 percent in a given day.

Fire is always a threat to a storage facility. If possible, install a gas fire suppression system. Water from sprinklers is very damaging to microfilm. If you choose to use fireproof cabinets, be sure they are rated for microfilm storage. A cabinet designed to keep paper from burning will not be able to keep damaging heat away from your microfilm. The cabinet must be able to hold the internal temperature below 150 degrees F.

➤ **Magnetic Media Storage.** Magnetic storage media requires every bit as much care as printed documents. The useful life of a tape can be sharply reduced by improper storage or handling. Unlike paper, you cannot readily look at a tape and determine if it is still readable or not. Improper handling can result in a tape becoming unreadable.

Steps must be taken to ensure that no contaminant of any kind comes into contact with the recording media. You should never touch the magnetic surface at any time. Therefore, magnetic media, such as reel tapes, cassettes, floppy disks, etc., should only be stored and used in a very clean environment. In these rooms, smoking, eating, and drinking must be prohibited. Ideally, an air filtration system will be employed to screen out airborne contaminants.

Magnetic media are susceptible to variations in temperature and humidity. If storage and operating temperatures vary more than 15 degrees F, you must allow time for the media to adjust to the different conditions. Allow 4 hours for every 15 degrees F of temperature difference. Strong sunlight will also damage magnetic tape.

The components that make up magnetic tape will react with moisture and slowly begin a process of breaking down the chemical bonds. Carefully avoid water and moisture when tapes are exposed.

Before using a tape, inspect it for surface damage. Look for any debris on the tape (but never touch the media itself without lint-free gloves). If in doubt, clean the tape surface before use. Always return tapes promptly to their protective containers. Minimize how much tapes are handled. Ensure that any tapes being returned to service are first thoroughly bulk erased.

Magnetic tapes should never be dropped or treated roughly. When in storage, they should always be stored on end and never stored "flat" (with the reels parallel to the table). Magnetic tapes are susceptible to damage from magnetic fields. Never store tapes on or near machinery, on windowsills, or on top of electronic devices.

Magnetic media is worthless without the proper equipment required to read the media. As your storage media ages, periodically check to make sure you still have the proper equipment for reading the media. Work with your data processing hardware support team to make sure you are involved when new backup hardware is being considered. Software can also be an issue, as formats may change slightly as backup software and operating systems are upgraded. You may need to copy the old media to a new format as the technology changes.

RISK ASSESSMENT

This is a good place to conduct a risk assessment of the threats facing your vital records. Refer to Form 9-1 (see CD). We will use our inventory list of documents to fill in the left side. Once all the documents are listed, we will identify the storage risks faced by these documents, based on the type of media and where they are stored.

If life was fair, you would be able to select your own storage facility. It would be a secure place without water pipes in the ceiling, with a reliable, steady environmental control system and no external walls. The facility would be located in a place not susceptible to natural disasters with a separate clean room for magnetic media storage. Unfortunately, vital records storage is usually on the low end of the floor space priorities and you must compete for adequate floor space with everyone else. Vital records storage is an overhead cost and does not bring in any revenue. Therefore, it is treated like the coat closet, important to have but must fit in wherever it can.

A key part of the risk assessment is to identify the types of documents to retain and their priorities for restoration. With computers, many of these records can be duplicated from stored media—unless it was in the midst of the fire zone.

Storage risks include:

➤ **Water.** This could be caused by a leaking roof, a burst water pipe, a sheared-off sprinkler head, a water leak on the floor above—any number of things. If this storage area is below ground, is it susceptible to flooding? Are the temperature and humidity automatically controlled? Never establish a records storage area in a room under a rooftop air conditioner, as they tend to collect water. Also, keep away from rooms with overhead water pipes, steam pipes, and exterior walls. Spot coolers used in storage rooms collect water and are a haven for mold and bacteria. Subfloor cooling in computer rooms also collects water.

➤ **Smoke.** If there is a fire in this room, what is the potential for smoke particles to penetrate the packing crates?

➤ **Structural.** Does the roof leak? Is it strong enough to withstand a very heavy snowfall or an unusual downpour? Look at the ceiling. Is it discolored at any place as if moisture were collecting there or had previously leaked?

➤ **Fire.** Is there adequate fire suppression? Does this include fire-suppressing gas or are you relying solely on sprinklers? Is the room clear of clutter? Is anything stored against an electrical appliance or receptacle? Are extension cords in constant use? Are the walls fireproof? Is a fire hazard on the other side of any of the walls?

➤ **Humidity.** How much humidity is floating about in this room? Does it vary appreciably during the year? Is a functioning humidifier/dehumidifier in operation?

➤ **High Heat and Deep Cold.** Excess heat or cold can be very damaging to stored documents—especially for magnetic media and microfiche. Is this room well insulated and climate controlled?

➤ **Wide Temperature Swings.** Wide temperature swings can age your material and cause humidity variations. The best long-term storage environment for your materials is a stable one that varies in temperature no more than 5 degrees F.

➤ **Theft.** If there is something of value in these documents, you must take steps to reduce the likelihood of theft. This can be personnel information, credit card numbers in your customer files, or any number of things. Securing the room with a lock and key is a good start.

➤ **Sabotage.** Similar to theft, except in this case, they just want to destroy what you are safeguarding. Like theft, sabotage may be difficult to detect.

➤ **Insects and Rodents.** No food or drinks should ever be allowed in the storage area. Look around for signs of animal or insect infestation.

➤ **Magnetic Fields.** If you are storing magnetic tape or diskettes, your materials may be susceptible to damage from magnetic fields. Be sure there are none present in your storage areas and also be aware of what is going on in adjacent rooms. Over-the-weekend construction work may not be reported to you yet could damage your media. This hazard includes small magnets and magnetized tools in the storage room.

MITIGATION

Now we will identify the mitigation actions to be taken to minimize the threats we have identified. Risks to your records depend on the types of media that they are stored on, how carefully they are stored, and how accessible they need to be.

Using the table in Form 9-1 (see CD) where you have previously identified the threat to each document, now identify the mitigation actions you will use to reduce the impact or likelihood of that threat.

Fire Control System

➤ **Smoke Alarms and Fire Detection System.** An early warning of a fire is your best deterrent against losing records to a fire—and most likely is mandated by local fire code. These alarms must not only alert anyone in the storage area of the danger but also your facility's security team so that the local fire department is dispatched immediately. These alarms are often used to trigger the gas fire suppression system. Special fire alarms are available that detect fires in their earliest stages. This permits quick intervention with a fire extinguisher before the sprinklers can kick in.

➤ **Sprinklers.** These are necessary to contain fires and save the building. They also provide valuable time for people to escape an inferno. Most of the material stored in the records room will readily burn, so sprinklers are essential. A problem is that the tool you are using to save the room is damaging to what is stored in there. Sprinklers are an inexpensive fire suppression tool and regulated by local fire code. Do not defeat the sprinklers' action by lining your shelves with plastic. It will only allow the fire to grow larger before the plastic melts (and is likely a violation of local fire codes).

➤ **Gas Fire Suppression.** Gas fire suppression is the best first line of defense against a fire. It can snuff out a fire before the sprinklers' fusible link melts. Although the gas discharge may spew some particles in the air, the damage is far less than from sprinklers. A gas fire suppression system is expensive and requires a sealed room for best effect, so be sure the doors close automatically and snugly.

➤ **Fire Extinguishers.** These come in several types based on the type of fire they can be used for. In general, they should be of the "A" type, which is for combustible materials. Fire extinguishers must be inspected monthly. Employees should know where they are and how to use them.

➤ **Fireproof Containers.** Use these for cash, checks, and vital records that cannot be replaced. After a fire, never open these containers until they are completely cooled, inside and out. If the inside is still hot, sudden exposure to fresh air may cause a flash fire. Documents protected from a fire by a fireproof container may be charred but readable.

➤ **Fire Drills.** Drills should be conducted at least every 3 months, or more often if required by your local fire code.

➤ **Good Housekeeping.** This minimizes the amount of rubbish in your storage areas. Rubbish accumulation is nothing more than fuel for a fire or food for vermin. Be sure it is removed daily. If possible, do not allow trashcans in the storage areas at all.

➤ **Minimize Electrical Equipment in the Storage Areas.** This is a potential source of fire and magnetic pollution.

◆ Move all possible electrical equipment out of and away from your storage area. This reduces the possibility of a fire starting in this equipment. Also, some equipment, such as copiers, stir up paper dust.

◆ Electrical outlets should not be overloaded as this could start a fire. Always use equipment with properly grounded plugs.

◆ Extension cords are another potential fire source. Be sure to only use heavily insulated extension cords and never on a permanent basis.

Environmental

➤ **Moisture Sensors and Alarms.** These alarms alert you to the presence of moisture in your storage room. These are very useful if you have a raised floor or an area that is difficult to see such as a drain in the room. These alarms may alert you to water buildup or excess moisture due to temperature changes.

➤ **Humidifier/Dehumidifier.** This device will help to keep your records storage area within the proper humidity range.

➤ **Temperature Control.** Some records may be stored on media that is susceptible to temperature damage. Actually, all media is susceptible, but some, like magnetic media, has little tolerance for high or freezing temperatures. These extremes even work to degrade your paper records but not as severely. Steady temperatures will reduce the load on your humidifier/dehumidifier.

➤ **Magnetic Check.** Wherever magnetic media is stored, be sure to run a periodic check of magnetic influences on the storage area. Magnetic influences are difficult to see but will degrade or damage the data stored on magnetic tapes, diskettes, cartridges, etc.

Other Issues

➤ **Secured Access.** Eliminate the people problems by limiting who has access to the storage areas.

➤ **Off-Site Duplication of Key Records.** If you have very critical records, one of your best solutions is to store copies of these records off-site. Then if a crisis occurs, you will not need to labor through an expensive records recovery process. This would require, however, that you maintain the off-site storage facility to the same high standards as used in your primary records storage facility.

➤ **Pest Extermination.** These creatures are not welcome in your storage area. Insects, rodents, and anything else that might want to dine on your documents must be vigorously kept away from your records.

➤ **Proper Storage**

◆ Identification tags must be attached to every container. In a crisis, these tags will be used to prioritize the records to be recovered. Records recovery is an expensive and time-consuming process. Proper identification allows everyone to focus on the most critical records first.

◆ Any documents containing water-soluble ink should be stored on microfilm. If these documents get wet, they will probably not be recoverable.

◆ Store your most critical records on the middle shelf. This keeps them off the floor in case of a water problem, and the records above will slow down the flow of water from a sprinkler or broken water pipe.

◆ Store all vital records at least 4 inches above the floor. If shelving is not available, use clean pallets.

◆ Do not store anything within 6 inches of the ceiling or lights.

◆ Do not store anything within 18 inches of a sprinkler head. That would interfere with the sprinkler's ability to put out a fire.

◆ Do not store anything in contact with an electrical device or obstructing any of the air-handling ducts.

A quick note on alarms. We talked about moisture sensor alarms, excess temperature alarms, and fire alarms. Alarms are useless unless people know what they mean and know what to do when they hear one. During your training exercises, let your staff hear each kind of alarm and explain what to do when it sounds. Repeat this step with every exercise! Ensure that alarms in the closed storage room can be detected and acted on during the weekends and evenings.

Security Mitigation Actions

Unfettered access can lead to theft problems, increased insect issues (people bringing in food), potential for sabotage, and, in some cases, just nosy people rifling through documents. Always secure your vital records storage areas. If they are climate controlled, then the less often the door is opened, the better.

Begin with controlled access to your vital records. This may be as simple as locking the door to the storage closet. Controlling access is important to prevent someone from these actions:

➤ **Reading Your Records.** If these are trade secrets, such as customer lists, you may not want anyone to casually peruse them. Someone reading your records and copying the information can be difficult to detect. If documents are worth keeping, they are worth keeping in secured storage.

➤ **Stealing Records Is a Form of Employee Sabotage.** If these records are required for regulatory compliance, a disgruntled employee could attempt to damage a company's reputation or an executive's job performance by removing records. This can go undetected for a long time. Sometimes companies victimized in this way find out as the documents are published in newspapers. An angry employee could also steal the records in an effort to damage your ability to prove company compliance with legal requirement or even to hide their own crimes.

➤ **Damaging Your Records Is a Variation of Employee Sabotage.** Similar to stealing, someone trying to hide their own actions or trying to damage a company's reputation could damage records. Often this is done on a wide scale rather than stealing a few select documents; the miscreant may opt for damage through arson or heavy water damage.

Rodents and Insects Mitigation

Your vital records may be very appetizing to insects and rodents. Basic housekeeping steps can minimize your exposure to these pests. Clutter, dirt, and dust should never be allowed to accumulate. Eating and drinking should never be allowed in your records storage area. Break rooms and cafeterias should be as far from the storage room as possible to reduce exposure to these pests.

These pests also like to be comfortable. They prefer high temperatures and high humidity. Keep your storage room at the optimal temperatures for storing your media; this provides a built-in defense against pests. Ensure that there are no "dead spots" in your air circulation that might create a safe haven for these creatures to base their operations in.

A key way to prevent these creatures from setting up housekeeping is to not invite them into the room in the first place. Doors, windows, and vents should be opened as little as possible. Seal cracks in the walls and ceiling promptly. Inspect incoming materials for signs of insects before admitting them to your storeroom. Remove packing material before entering the storeroom as that is a conduit for the spread of insects.

If an infestation is discovered, the quickest method is to bring in a professional exterminator. Rodents are easier to treat as they can be trapped. Poisons should be avoided as a contaminant to the room's atmosphere.

Insect eradication is a tougher job. If possible, take an example to the exterminator so they can apply the proper solution. Isolate all documents around the infestation. The best solution is to carefully freeze infested paper documents and all the containers around them to kill the insects.

ACTION STEPS FOR YOUR PLAN

In an emergency, you will have an immediate need for damage containment supplies. These supplies should be purchased in advance and storage in a locked room far across the facility from the records storage area. The goal is that an emergency in the storage room will not also destroy your containment supplies. If possible, store the emergency materials on a cart for rapid deployment.

A list of the recommended supplies is found in Form 9-2 (see CD). What you need for your site depends on your risk assessment (things likely to go wrong) and your inventory (what types of media you are protecting).

The materials needed for an emergency fall into several general categories:

➤ General items are basic items needed to clean up a mess. Some of these materials age over time (like flashlight batteries) and should be rotated at least annually (out of the closet and into general use, fresh batteries into the closet). Some of these items may be in regular use in departments across the facility from the storage area and a separate storage stockpile may not be necessary. Not listed here but useful will be a wide range of hand tools.

➤ Portable equipment is the heavy tools you may need to address more severe problems. Smaller items like water vacuums and portable dehumidifiers may be kept in your storage closet. Larger items like water pumps may need to be obtained from the facility's maintenance department. In addition, you must list the telephone numbers of ALL local companies that will rent trucks with freezer compartments in case you must freeze and/or ship documents for off-site recovery.

➤ Individual equipment is the safety equipment for the recovery team. Be sure to inspect this annually and rotate out the older materials to the facility's cleaning staff.

➤ Drying and cleaning materials will be quickly consumed in a large emergency, so be sure you know who the local suppliers are.

➤ Containment material; if the floodwaters are rising, if the roof or wall is missing, if the fire is now out, these materials can slow the spread of damage or prevent additional damage from occurring.

Maintenance Activities

Now that you have your storage facility safeguards in place, we need to ensure that we don't let our guard down. Plan to make these activities a part of your normal routine:

DAILY ACTIONS

➤ Trash emptied.

➤ During off hours and weekends, ask your security guard to step into the room and see if it feels too hot or humid.

➤ Check locks on windows and doors.

➤ Look for ceiling leaks, especially after a major storm.

EVERY WEEK

➤ Housekeeping inspection: ensure all trash is promptly removed.

➤ Change the paper on the hygrothermograph's plotter.

➤ Check the corners of the room for warm, moist air circulation "dead spots."

QUARTERLY ACTIONS

➤ Pest control quarterly. Check sticky traps, doors, foundations, walls.

➤ Test fire and humidity alarms.

➤ Test water detection sensors.

➤ Fire extinguishers inspection.

➤ Magnetic check or, whenever neighboring rooms change, including the floor above and below.

➤ Meet with local emergency officials.

➤ Rotate supplies out of your emergency stock. Be sure that emergency recovery supplies are stored away from the vital records storage so they aren't lost at the same time.

➤ Be sure air filters on all equipment (such as air conditioning) are changed at least quarterly.

You may also want to consider hiring a records storage professional to perform an audit on your off-site storage location, the security procedures in place, and the retrieval process. Whether you perform the work yourself or use a dedicated storage company, this can help you to identify gaps in the company's storage and retrieval process.

IMMEDIATE ACTIONS IN AN EMERGENCY

In an emergency, the first concern is the safety of your people. You must wait until the vital records areas are structurally safe to enter. Buildings are substantially weakened by fire, flood, and any major shock to their structure. In the event of a fire, you must check with the on-scene fire marshal in case they want to seal the site for a criminal investigation. This is where your predisaster liaison with local emergency services will pay off. An investigation may not start for days. Work with local officials to gain access to remove your undamaged records—but only do so with the permission of the proper authorities. Before entering, put on the hard hats stored with your emergency supplies. Ceilings are easily weakened in a structural emergency.

In the meantime, scramble around to line up emergency supplies to be ready to act once the go-ahead to enter is given. Contact your company security team and inform them where your records recovery operation will take place so they can assign a detail to keep the curious away from your documents. Immediately call sister companies requesting help from their records custodians. Begin setting up your damage mitigation area so recovery operations can begin as soon as the teams are ready.

When entering a damaged area begin your initial damage assessment. This is a quick walk-through to see which records are obviously damaged. Determine which vital records are damaged. Color-code your containers to indicate the recovery priority of all damaged containers and their type of damage (heat, water, exposed to air, etc.).

Before opening any file cabinets, use your hand to feel their outside temperature. If they are still hot, allow them to cool thoroughly before opening. A fireproof cabinet prevents a fire by sealing the contents from an oxygen supply. If the contents are sufficiently hot, and you open the cabinet too soon, you will see your documents turn into a flash fire and quite possibly injure someone.

Based on your initial damage assessment, divide your helpers into teams. There is no set size on a team since each emergency is unique:

> ➤ **Damage Containment Team.** These people focus on containing the damage. If there are now holes in the walls or ceiling, they should hang heavy ply plastic to keep out further weather damage. If documents are strewn about on the floor that are too numerous or for whatever reason cannot be picked up, the damage containment team will locate and lay plywood to protect the documents from foot traffic.

> ➤ **Assessment Team.** These folks will identify the records to be retrieved from the storage area based on their preestablished priority color code. They should take many photographs during all phases of the operations. Assessment pictures can be reviewed for understanding the amount of damage and may be useful to the insurance company. Pictures taken during the recovery can be used as source material for the after-action report.

> ➤ **Shuttle Team.** These are the people who are carrying documents from the storage room to the recovery area or for transportation to the off-site storage location.

> ➤ **Triage Team.** This team will log all documents as they are received from the damaged storeroom to begin tracking them through the recovery process. They will examine incoming documents and assign them to three categories: not damaged, damaged, or beyond recovery. Damaged documents will be categorized by the recovery technique to be used. They also ensure that the priority documents are addressed first. The triage team

will monitor the flow of documents to the recovery team and may identify documents to send on for immediate freezing and later recovery.

The triage team will also identify those documents that are unlikely to be
salvageable. They may be charred beyond recovery, or deteriorated due to
water or physical damage. Note these on your recovery log, tag them and, if
made of paper, freeze them for later evaluation.

Some teams may use a color code for documents to indicate their dispo-
sition. Take care not to confuse these with the color codes assigned to the documents in normal storage. Use whatever color system suits your situation, but
a suggested one is this:

➤ Green for undamaged documents: send these on to storage.

➤ Red for priority documents: to be recovered first.

➤ Yellow for lower-priority documents: to be frozen and reviewed for potential recovery later.

➤ Black for documents beyond hope of recovery.

What If the Emergency Missed Me?

In many instances, your building may be damaged but your records are intact. In those cases, you must decide if they are safe where they are or if they
must be evacuated to a safer place. Safety involves both physical security and
environmental security. If the air conditioning system still works, plan to stay
where you are. Work to return the storage area to its proper environment to
inhibit the growth of mold.

Before the emergency, you had a secure building. There were secure
walls, locks on the doors, guards at the front door, and other security measures. Once a major structural emergency is contained, there may be holes
in the roof or walls, strangers wandering about, and less than adequate
physical security for your records. In addition, power may not be functioning in the building until major repairs are completed. You must decide to
stay or go.

If you stay, and if your temperature and humidity control equipment is
not working, then it is just a matter of time until problems begin. Insects may
begin to creep in, mold begins to grow, and your records begin to deteriorate.
Still, it is a major effort to pack everything up and move out. Packing, trans-

portation, reestablishing a controlled atmosphere at the new site, and then moving everything back later is a frighteningly difficult challenge. What to do?

The key to this question is how soon electrical service, air conditioning, heating, and humidity control can be restored to your storage areas. If your rooms are unharmed, turn off the air circulation immediately until the air has settled. This should prevent circulating smoke fumes throughout your storage areas. After the emergency has been contained, try to maintain the flow of clean, filtered air at the proper temperature and humidity levels to avoid a forced move of your records.

If you stay, ensure there are adequate air filtration, ventilation, and climate controls in your storage room. This may require the use of a large portable electrical generator and portable air-handling units. With wire runs all the way from the generator in the parking lot up to your storage area, and then with the expense and effort involved with portable air-handling units, you can quickly see what a major job this will be.

If service restoration is likely to be soon, then seal the storage area as tightly as possible and press for prompt temporary repairs to the storage area.

What If the Emergency Hit Me?

There are detailed recovery steps later in this chapter, but the issue here is that if your storage facility is unusable, you must relocate it to an off-site facility. This off-site facility must have security for your documents. It should have as much of the climate control capabilities as your old site. On short notice this could be a problem, so if possible, contract with a storage company to be used on an as-needed basis. If practical, ship the documents to another company site. This will greatly simplify the security arrangements.

Once the disaster has passed and the document recovery process is underway, the new records storage room must be carefully prepared. Be sure that it is completely dry. All the old carpeting, shelving, furniture, and anything else that may harbor mold or fungus must be replaced. Walls, floors, and ceiling must be treated for mold and fungus before returning documents to this room. Be on the lookout for hidden water under tile or raised floors.

Allow fresh paint to dry for at least 2 weeks. This allows the solvents to dissipate and the airborne paint particles to settle.

When all the excitement is passed, sit down and write an after-action assessment. This is where you can recognize the people that helped through the crisis and critique how realistic your plan was. Include the photographs taken during the emergency. You should also review actual expenses incurred for future budgeting.

RECOVERY TECHNIQUES

There are many recovery processes that can be used. Most companies turn this over to a professional recovery service as they lack the expertise and equipment to do this in the face of a major emergency. Document recovery is a very delicate business that, if not properly done, will complete the destruction of your vital records. If you expect to recover your own documents, here are some of the steps to take. You should also study the finer details of document recovery from books dedicated solely to that subject. Time spent practicing before an emergency is an excellent idea.

Water Damage to Paper Records

Water is a threat to all your vital records. Just about any paper documents can be recovered from water damage (except those containing soluble ink, which should be microfilmed before storage) if promptly treated. Paper records begin deteriorating in as little as 3 hours. Within the first day, mold, fungus, and bacteria begin growing on paper. Recovery is basically to remove the documents from the water, and then remove the water from the documents. If the document is not to be immediately recovered, then it should be quick-frozen until it can be processed. Freezing can protect a paper document for up to 5 years.

Begin your paper recovery process by stabilizing the atmosphere in the work area to between 50 and 60 degrees F, with a humidity level between 25 and 35 percent. Temperatures and humidity in a room tend to vary based on how close you are to the heater or dehumidifier, so use fans to circulate the air and equalize the conditions. Remove from the room any wet things that are not the documents being treated, like wet clothes, unneeded packing material, etc.

Review paper documents for damage. Water-soluble inks will not likely survive a good soaking. The wettest records are usually the ones that were on the lower shelves or directly under the fire sprinkler (so be sure not to store your most valuable records in either location!). Among your priority records, process the wettest ones first.

Remove all metal fasteners from the documents. This will prevent rust from forming on the fastener and then spilling over onto the document. Use plastic milk crates to transport documents because they allow for some of the water to drain off. Never pack them more than three quarters full as the weight of the wet papers will further damage your documents. For the same reason, you should not stack books atop each other in these crates.

Wrap the documents in freezer paper before placing them in the crate, about 200 sheets at a time. Wrap books and set them in the crate with their spine toward the bottom. Always make a list of any document you have found, their condition, and where you sent them. Mark the identity of the documents on the outside of the freezer paper.

AIR-DRYING PAPER RECORDS Air-drying is the easiest but most labor-intensive process for recovering paper documents. It is most suitable for small amounts of documents or lightly damp books. Drying documents in the open air requires a lot of space and time. After drying, the documents will never look the same and may be permanently stained by soot and water. Note these considerations:

➤ Wet paper is easily torn. Handle every document very carefully.

➤ Individual sheets of coated paper are very difficult to air-dry. Send them to a freeze-dry facility. If they are to be air-dried, carefully separate them immediately. Books printed on coated paper should never be air-dried. They should be frozen immediately and sent for professional recovery.

➤ Books suffer the most from air-drying. Most will be distorted from the moisture and will require rebinding. Very wet books should always be freeze-dried. If you decide to air-dry books, interleave absorbent paper every few pages. Do not stress the spine. Place absorbent paper inside the front and back covers. Change the absorbent paper every several hours. Dampness will persist in the spine and the covers for quite some time, so you must check often for mold. Never return books to shelves until fully dry to reduce introduction of mold into your facility.

➤ Air-dried documents, especially books, are susceptible to mold.

➤ Mold can be brushed from dry documents. Trying to remove mud while the paper is still wet simply pushes the mud into the document fibers.

As you begin your recovery efforts, use the nylon fishing wire in your emergency supplies to string some drying lines. Take care where you place the wire as it is hard to see, especially in low light, because people may run into it. Separate the sheets of paper and hang them on this drying line.

In your drying room, keep temperatures lower than 70 degrees F and humidity below 50 percent to inhibit the growth of mold. Use fans to circulate the air to the dehumidifiers to accelerate drying. If your drying efforts are conducted outside, keep in mind that prolonged exposure to sunlight will accelerate the aging of paper.

An alternative to a drying line is to spread the documents out on tables covered with absorbent paper. Interleave sheets of paper with absorbent paper if they are very wet or in a book. Change this paper as needed, depending on how wet the documents are. Use your fans to keep the air circulating around the room to the dehumidifier.

Other recovery methods include photocopying damaged documents and discarding the original. This solution may depend on any legal requirements for maintaining the original document. Another is to use a low-heat clothing iron to gently heat the moisture from the paper.

Dried records always require more storage space when finished. Photocopy water-damaged documents if possible and keep the copy (assuming there is not a legal requirement to keep the original).

FREEZE-DRYING PAPER RECORDS Freezing is a way to stop the progress of damage to your damp paper-based documents. Those documents that cannot be recovered quickly or those which will be transported off-site for recovery should be frozen. If the quantity of documents is small, use dry ice to freeze them during transport. If the quantity is large, call in freezer trucks. Freeze documents to between 20 degrees and –40 degrees F. Freeze as quickly as possible to prevent damage from the formation of ice crystals.

If a commercial recovery service is used, they will freeze your documents and possibly vacuum dry ("freeze-dry") them. This process reduces stains and odors caused by smoke and also eliminates mold. Freeze-drying is a passive process and may take several weeks or more to complete. Freeze-drying is the best solution for recovering wet books. In the case of slightly damp books, this will kill any mold. In the case of very wet books, this will reduce the damage to the book in addition to killing any mold.

Wrap bundles of documents in freezer paper and place in interlocking milk cartons. Document bundles should be about 2 inches thick. The milk cartons allow for air circulation and moisture drainage. Be sure to label the bundles so you know what they are without unwrapping them. Books should be wrapped separately. Never fill the cartons more than three quarters full, as damp paper is weak and easily damaged.

When preparing books for shipment to a freeze-drying facility, support the bindings to reduce the likelihood of swelling. This will reduce the amount of rebinding required for your recovered material.

Even though your records are in a recovery facility, you must still ensure their security. Depending on the sensitivity of your data, you might want a security guard present in the drying room at all times. Now is not the time to drop your guard.

UNRECOVERABLE DOCUMENTS The destruction of any document must be carefully recorded. Be sure to clearly identify what the document was, any identifying titles or routing codes, and why (or how) it was destroyed.

Fire Damage of Paper Records

Fire damage to your records can be just as severe as water damage. Fire will char documents, cover them with soot, and make them more brittle. They may also be wet and smell of smoke. Even portions that are not burned may be darkened by heat and smoke. If you can do without the original document, make a photocopy and discard the original. Handle these documents as little as possible as they may be quite brittle and crumble in your hands.

Place every fire-damaged document on paper towels or absorbent paper. Move these documents by picking up the absorbent paper, not by touching the document itself. The absorbent paper will also pull some of the moisture out of the document.

Microfilm

Wet microfilm must be delivered to a film duplicator as soon as possible. Line containers with clean trash bags and fill them with clean cool water. Submerge the film in the water and deliver them to a professional recovery service within 48 hours. The recovery service will professionally wash the media and dry it.

Optical and Magnetic Media

Wet magnetic media should be placed in bags of cold water for transportation. The media should never be frozen. Use distilled water when rinsing magnetic materials. Tap water may contain chemicals or other materials that would dry on the media. Air-dry the magnetic media in a clean room within 48 hours. Conduct a quick check of the recovery area and ensure no magnetic sources are present, including magnetized tools.

Once magnetic storage media is dry, promptly copy it onto fresh media. Clean the read heads frequently.

> ➤ **Tapes.** Immediately rinse dirty water and mud off magnetic tapes. Be sure to never touch the magnetic media with your bare hands. When touching the media, use lint-free gloves and handle as little as possible. Whenever possible, handle the tapes by the hubs or the reel. Air-dry in a clean room to prevent the settlement of dust and other particles on the media.

> ➤ **Compact Disks.** Handle the CD carefully to avoid scratching. Air-dry to remove moisture.

> ➤ **Floppy Disks.** Pack wet disks vertically in bags of cold water. Rinse thoroughly before air-drying.

CONCLUSION

Vital records protection is not difficult, but requires some thought and action before a disaster strikes to keep the damage to a minimum. The key is a good records retention policy, so that you are storing as little as possible and destroying records you no longer need.

CHAPTER 10

DATA
Your Most Irreplaceable Asset

640K ought to be enough for anybody.
—Bill Gates, 1981, co-founder of the Microsoft Corporation

INTRODUCTION

Most of what you lose in a disaster can be relatively easy to replace. Buildings can be rebuilt or new offices leased, furniture is easily replaced, and even new computers can be purchased at the click of a button. What is not easy to replace is your competitive advantage that is stored in the files and databases within your computer systems. This critical information is stored in accounting files, customer lists, part lists, manufacturing drawings, etc. This information is unique to your company, and contains information that makes your company special to your vendors and customers. It is the very essence of your company. Unlike physical assets, this information is difficult if not impossible to recreate once it is gone.

There are two types of risks to your infrastructure that supports your data assets: physical loss due to a device failure or a disaster at your location, and logical loss caused by an application or user error. Physical loss is the less likely of the two, but is potentially the most damaging. It includes incidents such as a hard disk failure, server failure, or environmental disasters such as fire or floods. It can affect just a single device or your entire location. Physical loss accounts for about 20 percent of all incidents affecting information technology resources. Logical loss includes incidents such as application errors, user errors, or a security breach. Logical failures account for approximately 80 percent of all incidents. A logical failure can be easier to repair, but may also not be noticed for some time.

COMPONENTS OF AN INFORMATION TECHNOLOGY INFRASTRUCTURE

A modern corporate computing environment consists of several components that build on each other to support the functions of the business. You must understand each of these components and how they relate to your business process to create an effective recovery strategy. At the foundation of this infrastructure are data. Figure 10-1 shows the typical components of an information technology (IT) infrastructure.

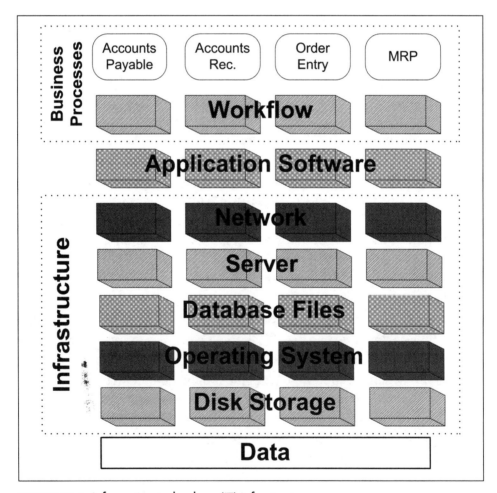

FIGURE 10-1: Information technology (IT) infrastructure.

Each layer builds on the layer below, building up to the application that the user sees. The applications interact in varying degrees depending upon the requirements of the organization. But no matter what the specific architecture, the foundation is the data that are stored on various media somewhere within the organization.

RISK ASSESSMENT

Your data are susceptible to loss or damage or both from several sources. Some key causes of data loss include:

➤ **Viruses.** These malicious programs can get into your system at any time, and strike when you least expect it. Once you're infected, the virus can spread from system to system, destroying data along the way.

➤ **Natural Disasters.** Fire, flood, and high winds can all cause disruptions to systems and make your data unavailable or unreadable.

➤ **Man-Made Outages.** Systems can be damaged by a sudden loss of power, or worse yet, a small part of a data stream can be lost, causing damage that may not be readily apparent.

➤ **Hard Drive Crash.** It's not *if* a hard drive will fail, but *when.*

➤ **Laptop Loss or Theft.** The value of the data stored on a laptop usually far exceeds the cost of replacing the hardware.

Market research firm IDC estimates that approximately 60% of all corporate data reside on laptop and desktop PCs.

➤ **Software Failures.** Operating systems and storage area network software can fail, corrupting existing data.

➤ **Application Failures.** Applications are not guaranteed to be bug free; a bug in an application can cause incomplete or incorrectly formatted or calculated data to be written into your files.

➤ **Vendor Failure.** If you are hosting e-commerce or other applications with an application service provider, your data could be at risk if the vendor suddenly goes out of business.

Less than 5% of application downtime is attributed to a "disaster"
40% is caused by application code failures
40% is caused by operator error
20% is caused by system/environmental failure

Source: Legato Systems

There are both tactical and strategic issues surrounding the loss of critical corporate information. Tactical issues include:

➤ **Compromised Information.** Your valuable information could fall into the hands of competitors if stolen by hackers or by losing a laptop. Your competitors having this information could be more damaging than if it were simply destroyed.

➤ **Lost Productivity.** Recreating lost data can be very expensive, especially if it must be recreated from paper records.

➤ **Employee Downtime.** Employees need their information to do their jobs; this includes sales, customer service, accounting, etc.

➤ **Loss of Customer Information.** Loss of important customer records can seriously hinder your ability to serve your customers.

➤ **Increased Help Desk Costs.** Not only might your help desk people be needed to help restore your data, but they will be bombarded by users requesting assistance and information.

A recent Gallup poll calculated the average cost of a data loss incident at $10,000.

Strategic issues surrounding data loss are those that have an impact on some critical operation within your business processes. This might include:

➤ **Loss of Opportunity.** Without up-to-date and accurate information about your customers and your company, data loss can cause you to lose sales. If you don't have accurate inventory information, customers may order from someone else who can guarantee delivery from stock. Follow-up calls to customers might be missed if your CRM data are lost, also resulting in lost sales. Future sales could also be in jeopardy.

➤ **Increased Operational Costs.** The lack of access to data will result in a greater reliance on manual processes, which will drastically increase your operations costs.

➤ **Inability to Support Customers.** Without access to customer data, you will have a difficult time supporting your customers, or incur unnecessary costs providing support to which they are not entitled.

➤ **Increased Systems Costs.** Your total cost of ownership (TCO) will increase, making it more difficult to make money if margins are thin.

➤ **Noncompliance Issues.** Without accurate data, you might not be able to prove compliance with government mandates, resulting in fines and legal fees.

CREATING YOUR DATA RECOVERY PLAN

Just like any other project, there are several distinct steps required to develop your plan to successfully recover your data after a disaster. The steps we recommend are these (see Figure 10-2):

1. Planning

2. Identify critical data

3. Create appropriate policies and procedures

4. Determine type of backups

5. Develop recovery processes

6. Plan testing and maintenance

PLANNING

As with any project, a successful data recovery plan begins with proper planning. Your first step should be to review with key stakeholders what their data recovery expectations are. Find out what their business needs are, and if there are regulatory requirements that they are concerned about. Few organizations have not done any data recovery planning, so your next step can be to review the existing backup and restoration strategies. Find out what is currently being backed up and how often. Are there procedures in place to periodically test the backups? How are the backups transported and stored? What

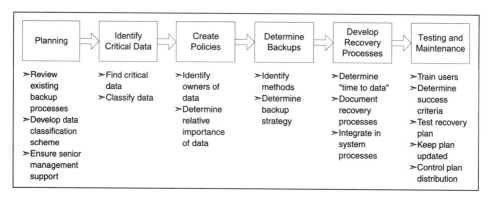

Planning	Identify Critical Data	Create Policies	Determine Backups	Develop Recovery Processes	Testing and Maintenance
➤Review existing backup processes ➤Develop data classification scheme ➤Ensure senior management support	➤Find critical data ➤Classify data	➤Identify owners of data ➤Determine relative importance of data	➤Identify methods ➤Determine backup strategy	➤Determine "time to data" ➤Document recovery processes ➤Integrate in system processes	➤Train users ➤Determine success criteria ➤Test recovery plan ➤Keep plan updated ➤Control plan distribution

FIGURE 10-2: Data recovery steps.

new systems have come online since the backup documentation was last updated? Are old files being backed up that could be archived and removed from the live systems?

Begin researching the most efficient and effective ways to store your backed-up data. Do you have multiple facilities that can store each other's data? Make sure that the data being stored cannot be destroyed in the same disaster; they should be at least 20 miles apart.

You must also plan for an analysis and classification of data: what is the importance to the firm of each file being backed up? The cost of protecting the data should be proportional to the value of the data. You don't want to spend a lot of time and resources protecting data that are easily restored by other means.

There are numerous strategies for backing up and restoring of data. They include traditional offline storage methods such as hardcopy printouts, magnetic tape, CD-ROM, and microfiche. Online methods include synchronous and asynchronous backups, which allow for faster restoration of your data. The evaluation and selection of the appropriate strategies are critical to the success of your recovery plan. Other things to consider are whether your backup hardware and software tools are the latest versions from the manufacturer. Many firms have had a disaster only to discover that the software needed to read their backup media was outdated and difficult and expensive to obtain, or simply no longer available.

Where your data will be stored is also an important consideration. It's most convenient if your firm has multiple locations that can store each other's data. You might also have a reciprocal agreement with another noncompeting firm to store data for each other. Of course, you need to be reasonably sure that both locations won't be affected by the same disaster. You'll also need to make sure that both locations can handle the extra workload if one site is down. This option is difficult to manage and does not always work well in practice.

Another option is to use a commercial storage vendor, who will have an environmentally controlled facility to protect the integrity of your media. They will also have tested procedures for storing and retrieving data in an emergency and can offer advice on your disaster recovery plans.

You might also set up or contract with a vendor to have an off-site facility ready if your location experiences an incident. There are several basic types of remote sites:

➤ **Cold Site.** A cold site is simply a place to store your data and has adequate space and infrastructure (power, communications, and environmental controls) to support your systems. This is the least expensive option, but also requires the most time to get up and running in the event of a disaster.

➤ **Warm Site.** A warm site has systems and communications ready to go, but requires the data to be restored onto them before they are ready to use.

➤ **Hot Site.** A hot site is an active duplicate of your live systems, with both systems and data ready to go at a moment's notice. Hot sites are usually staffed 24 hours a day, 7 days a week, and are prepared for immediate action if an incident occurs.

➤ **Mobile Site.** A mobile site is a self-contained transportable office custom-fitted with IT and communications equipment. They are usually transported by truck and can be set up at the desired location. The mobile site needs to be set up and configured before it is needed to be a viable recovery solution. If using an outside vendor, a service-level agreement is necessary to make sure the vendor is committed to meeting your needs in an emergency.

➤ **Mirrored Site.** A mirrored site is an exact duplicate of your production site, with data stored there in real-time. This is the quickest way to get your business back up and running, but is also the most expensive.

The different recovery site options offer different cost and recovery time tradeoffs. A mirrored site gives you the best protection against a disaster, but is obviously the most expensive. At the other extreme, a cold site is the least expensive to implement, but it requires the greatest amount of time to restore your operations. The other options fall in the middle of these two extremes; your organization's restore time requirements and the results of your business

Type of Site	Cost	Equipment	Communications	Setup Time	Location
Cold	Low	None	None	Long	Fixed
Warm	Medium	Partial	Partial – Full	Medium	Fixed
Hot	Medium-High	Complete	Full	Short	Fixed
Mobile	Medium-High	Servers only	Varies	Varies	Mobile
Mirrored	High	Complete	Complete	None	Fixed

FIGURE 10-3: Recovery site selection criteria.

impact analysis will determine which option you choose. Figure 10-3 compares the resource requirements for the different recovery site options.

Restoring data in the fastest time possible will minimize the revenue loss caused by damaged or lost data. "Time to data" is a critical metric to evaluate when creating your recovery plan, and is defined as how much time it takes for your users to have access to their data after a disaster occurs.

Rapid "Time to Data" is fundamental in achieving reduced downtime, maximizing productivity and system I/O rates.

Source: Strategic Research Corporation.

Asset management is an important key to recovering your systems. You'll need an accurate and complete hardware and software inventory list. You'll need to know when and where it was purchased and the warranty status. You'll need to know where the hardware was located and how it was configured. Your original software licenses will be necessary to facilitate getting new media from your software vendors. You'll also want to research what the vendor's policy is in a disaster situation. You'll want to know what to do if you need to quickly obtain replacement software.

Identify Critical Data

The first problem you'll face in creating your data recovery plan is **finding** the data. The amount of data being produced by business today is growing rapidly. These are not just data stored in traditional databases, but also include graphics, word processing files, spreadsheets, sound clips, and other enhanced forms of data. In many organizations, terabyte (approximately 1 trillion bytes) databases are becoming common; petabyte (1024 terabytes) size databases are right around the corner. And of course, paper is still an important repository of data; these paper files are stored in file cabinets, desk drawers, etc. Microfilm and microfiche are also still used in many organizations. For data that are stored electronically, there are products available for automatically discovering files and databases throughout your network.

The next issue after you have found the data is **categorizing** the data. Like paper files, much of the electronic data that are created are never referenced again. You'll need to identify the critical data required to restore critical business operations. Don't forget to review ancillary data and documentation and data that must be preserved due to legal requirements.

Nonessential Data

Much of what is stored on your file servers by users is data that are not essential to the operation of the business. This includes space-wasting data such as e-mail attachments, Internet cache files, and personal files such as digital pictures. This nonessential data can add to the cost of backup and recovery in many ways. If you have a hot-site facility, it will require more disk storage space. If you are performing backups using tapes or CDs, additional media will be required for backups. If you are using replication to a remote location, additional bandwidth may be required to support the transfer of all these files.

A place to start in reducing the volume of unneeded files is to have policies in place that prohibit the storage of personal files on company servers. Strict enforcement of these policies can dramatically reduce the amount of data that are backed up. You should also consider limiting the amount of storage place available to each user, which will force them to consider carefully what to store in their personal folders.

Create Appropriate Policies and Procedures

Most companies do not have policies and procedures for storing and classifying data. And many that do have policies do a poor job of enforcement. Having policies that aren't enforced can create a false sense of security, which can be worse than having no policies at all.

The first step in creating policies for storing and classifying data is to identify the owners of information. All data in the company should have an identified owner who is responsible for understanding the importance and use of the data.

Once the owners of the data have been identified, develop a policy for determining the relative importance of data. You can then develop an information classification scheme. Some categories you might use include business critical, sensitive, legally required, and noncritical.

➤ **Business Critical.** These are data that you must have to run your business. This can include customer lists, production drawings, accounting files, etc.

➤ **Sensitive.** These are data that you would not want your competitors to see. This might include customer lists, employee lists, production process documentation, etc.

➤ **Legally Required.** This is information that you need for compliance with government regulations, such as Occupational Safety and Health Administration (OSHA) compliance data, Environmental Protection Agency (EPA) information, hiring data, etc.

➤ **Noncritical.** This is information that you can live without. Up to 90% of all information stored in file cabinets and databases is never retrieved, so this category can include a lot of data.

Determine Type (or Types) of Backups

Different types of data and different time to data requirements will require different backup processes and media. Types of backups include:

➤ Regular backup to tape or other removable media.

➤ "Electronic vault" storage via a wide-area network.

➤ Remote mirroring.

You will probably use a combination of techniques, balancing time to data versus cost tradeoffs. Traditional tape backups are still widely used and can be effective, but they can create transportation issues, storage issues, and restoration issues. If not handled and stored properly, tapes can fail without warning. They require that the application also be reloaded, and software to read the tapes must be available. Electronic vault storage allows you to save your data over a wide-area network such as the Internet, and can be easier to restore than tape. Remote mirror ensures that there is little or no data loss, but is the most expensive option.

Develop Recovery Processes

The last step is to develop and document the process for both backup and recovery of data. It does no good to have a plan in your head, or one that sits on the shelf. Schedules will need to be developed to ensure that backups are made in a timely fashion. Some criteria to be considered when evaluating which recovery techniques to use include:

- ➤ **RTO (Recovery Time Objective).** How quickly must the data be restored before business is adversely affected?

- ➤ **RPO (Recovery Point Objective).** How much data can we afford to lose before the business is adversely affected?

- ➤ **Availability.** Can the system be down while we do the backups?

- ➤ **How Sure Do We Have to Be That We Can Restore the Data?**

- ➤ **How Much Is It Worth to Protect the Data?**

- ➤ **What Are the Performance Requirements of the Application?**

You must also consider how effective each recovery technique is in protecting from the different types of loss. Each business process may have a different recovery process.

SOMETHING FOR YOUR SUPPORT PLAN

Your plan will need to be tested and updated periodically to keep it effective. Testing allows you to identify any deficiencies in your plan so that they can be corrected. This includes not only equipment and backup issues but personnel issues as well. Each component of your plan must be tested to verify the accuracy and completeness of your recovery procedures and to determine the overall effectiveness of the plan. Some areas to review when testing your plan include:

- ➤ Ability to restore critical applications from backups

- ➤ Performance of recovery personnel

- ➤ Performance of backup equipment

- ➤ Communications

To remain effective, your plan must be kept up to date with changes in your production systems. Changes in your IT infrastructure can be caused by business process changes, technology upgrades, regulatory requirements, employee turnover, or new policies. Any of these events should trigger a review of your recovery plan. It is therefore essential that your plan be reviewed and updated frequently to ensure that new processes are documented and that the recovery process is updated to reflect these changes. Items to be monitored for changes include:

➤ Hardware, software, and peripheral equipment.

➤ Business operation requirements.

➤ Security requirements.

➤ Technology changes.

➤ Recovery team contact information.

➤ Vendor information.

➤ Regulatory requirements.

Because your recovery plan contains potentially sensitive personnel information, its distribution must be controlled. Copies should be stored at the home of key recovery personnel, at your production location, and at your off-site recovery location with your backup media. The individual in charge of recovery planning must maintain a list of who has copies of the plan, and a record of when changes were made (use Form 10-1 on the CD as an example).

CONCLUSION

Data are the lifeblood of modern businesses; by having an effective data recovery plan you can help ensure that your business will survive an unexpected emergency. The steps are simple, but must be diligently performed to be effective:

➤ Identify what's important.

➤ How soon do you need it?

➤ What is it going to cost not to have it?

➤ Test your recovery procedures.

CHAPTER 11

NETWORKS
The Ties That Bind

*Every improvement in communication
makes the bore more terrible.*
—Frank Moore Colby

INTRODUCTION

All but the smallest firms today have one or more networks within their organization. We use networks to share applications, files, schedules, e-mail, and to access the Internet. The network connects us with our coworkers, and allows us to collaborate in doing the business of the firm. This chapter reviews the attributes unique to networks that require special processes to restore them after a disaster.

A network consists of one or more servers that are connected to one or more workstations and allows users to share information and resources. This connection can be by copper wire, by fiber optic cable, or even by radio frequency (RF). Rarely are workstations connected directly into a server. Typically they plug into the wall jack, which is connected to a wire closet. In the closet will be one or more "hubs" that will connect the local devices to a hub in the computer room. This room is often the same closet as contains the telephone wiring.

In the computer room (either a central location or possibly sprinkled about the facility) sit the servers. A server is a computer that runs software to provide access to resources attached to the network, such as printers, disk storage, and network applications. A server can be any type of computer that supports the sharing of resources: it may be a standard desktop PC, or a dedicated device containing large amounts of memory and multiple storage devices that can support hundreds of PCs at the same time.

NETWORK BASICS

The term local area network (LAN) is typically used to describe workstations and servers that are all physically in the same location. A LAN can be implemented using two main architectures:

➤ **Peer-to-Peer.** Each computer on the network communicates directly with every other computer. Each computer is treated equally on the network. Communication between computers is coordinated using a network hub.

➤ **Client/Server.** Each end-user PC is connected to a central server, which coordinates communication and supplies resources to the end users. Typically the server contains file storage, printer, backup, and other resources that are shared by the end-user client computers.

Figure 11-1 shows a typical client/server LAN, with five PCs connected to a server. The server has attached a network printer and a backup tape drive that can be accessed from any end-user client computer on the network.

A wide-area network (WAN) is a data communications network that consists of two or more local area networks connected together to allow communication between geographically dispersed locations. Most companies have some sort of WAN connection, either connecting to other locations within the organization or to the public Internet. There are several different types of WAN communication links available. The most common ones are:

➤ **Dialup.** This is the most basic type of connection, using a modem and a plain old telephone system (POTS) line. This is also the slowest and most unreliable type of connection available, supporting up to 56 kilobits per second (kbps).

➤ **ISDN.** An ISDN (integrated services digital network) connection uses a POTS line using an enhanced communication standard to speed up the connection to 64 or 128 kbps.

➤ **T-1.** A dedicated connection that supports data rates up to 1.5 megabits per second (mbps). A T-1 line consists of 24 individual channels, each supporting 64 kbps of data.

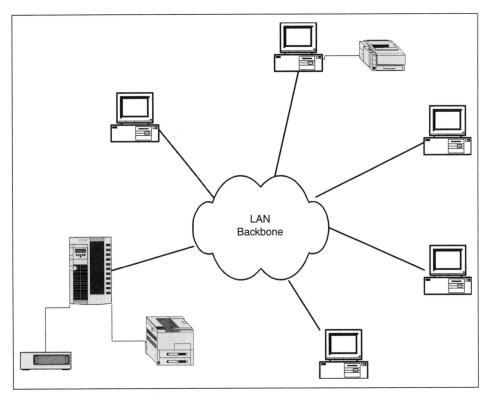

FIGURE 11-1: Typical LAN configuration.

➤ **T-3.** A dedicated connection that supports data rates up to 43 megabits per second (mbps). A T-3 line consists of 672 individual channels, each supporting 64 kbps of data.

➤ **Frame Relay.** This is a packet switched protocol for connecting devices on the WAN. It supports data transfer rates up to T-3 speed.

➤ **ATM.** ATM (Asynchronous Transfer Mode) is a means of digital communications that is capable of very high speeds; suitable for transmission of images or voice or video as well as data.

➤ **Wireless.** A wireless LAN bridge can connect multiple LANs for distances up to 30 miles with a direct line of sight.

➤ **VPN.** A VPN (virtual private network) uses encryption in the lower protocol layers to provide a secure connection through the public Internet.

Figure 11-2 shows a corporate wide-area network, with two remote locations linked to the headquarters, which is in turn connected to the public Internet.

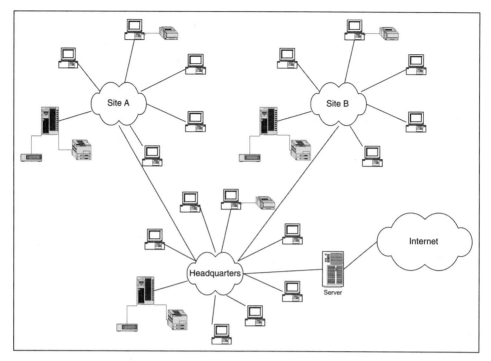

FIGURE 11-2: Typical WAN configuration.

RISK ASSESSMENT

When developing your disaster recovery plan for your network, look for single points of failure that will adversely impact your critical business processes. These critical processes should have been identified in the business impact analysis. Threats to your network include cables being cut, interference from electromagnetic sources, and damage from other hazards such as fire or water. Your best defense is to have duplicate service running to each desktop. As it is usually not cost effective to run duplicate cables, an alternative is to install an extra jack every few cable drops. If a problem occurs in an end-user's cable, the extra jack would be available as a backup until the problem cable is repaired.

Don't forget to review your vulnerability to problems with the devices that connect your network together, such as routers, switches, and hubs. Your business impact analysis should determine the level of threat that these devices pose if they fail. Look at having redundant devices installed that can take over if the primary device fails.

Wireless network connections can provide an effective backup strategy if the wired network fails. Wireless networks have no wires to fail, and can be quickly installed if needed after a failure in the wired system. The major drawback to using a wireless network is that the transmissions can be intercepted; make sure encryption and other security measures are implemented to avoid others intercepting your network traffic.

You should also consider using network monitoring software that can detect problems on the network. Network monitoring software can alert you immediately if a node on the network is having problems or has failed, which will allow you to restore service more quickly and help prevent problems from cascading. Most network monitoring software can be configured to look for system parameters that fall out of the desired range and then generate a page to a support person to take action.

Your recovery plan for your WAN will address many of the same issues as the plan for your individual LANs. Your WAN is also susceptible to single points of failure issues. Threats to your WAN include cables being cut, interference from electromagnetic sources, and damage from other hazards such as fire or water. Your best defense is to have duplicate service running to each location. If you go this route, ensure than the two providers are not sharing the same physical cable. Their lines should come in on opposite ends of the building to reduce the likelihood of damage by the same incident. Trace the physical route of each provider's cable to see if they converge into a single point of failure along the way.

Don't forget to review your vulnerability to problems with the devices that connect your networks together, such as routers, switches, and hubs. Your business impact analysis should determine the level of threat that these devices pose if they fail. Look at having redundant devices installed that can take over if the primary device fails.

Wireless network connections can provide an effective backup strategy for a WAN if the facilities are close enough to be connected using a point-to-point wireless connection.

If an Internet connection is critical to your business, consider having two independent connections to the Internet from two separate locations. If one connection fails, the other can handle the traffic until the original connection is restored. One issue with multiple Internet connections is that there are now two points of potential entry for hackers; be sure to work closely with your security team to adequately protect your WAN.

DATA STORAGE OPTIONS

Although off-site storage will allow recovery of data after an incident, data that were added or modified after the last backup will be lost. A good complement to this strategy is to use some method of data storage redundancy, such as disk mirroring, RAID, and load balancing. Using network attached storage or a storage area network as part of your data storage strategy also provides a degree of data protection.

Disk Mirroring

With disk mirroring, data are written to two different disks to create two identical copies to increase the odds that at least one copy of the data is available at all times. The main disk used to store the data is called the protected disk, and the disk to which the data are replicated is called the backup disk. The two disks can be in the same location or in different locations. A WAN is used if the backup disk is at a different location from the protected disk. Installing the backup at a different location provides protection against a disaster that occurs at the location of the protected disk. While this is an effective approach, beware of its impact on your network traffic load.

Two different types of disk mirroring are available, synchronous and asynchronous. Each provides a different time to data recovery, and each has different performance considerations.

Synchronous mirroring works by writing to the backup disk first, then writes to the protected disk once it has confirmed that the write to the backup disk was successful (see Figure 11-3). This type of mirroring ensures that the backup data are always up to date, but is slower and more expensive than asynchronous mirroring. Special disk controllers are required to enable the two-way communication between the disks, and there is inherent latency between the writing of the data to the backup disk and waiting for the confirmation.

Asynchronous mirroring (or shadowing) works by sending the data to both the protected and backup disk at the same time (see Figure 11-4). It is cheaper than synchronous backup, and more than one system can write to the backup disk. It is also quicker, since the application does not have to wait for a confirmation on the write to the backup disk. The downside to asynchronous mirroring is that you cannot be guaranteed that the last transaction before a disaster was successfully written to the backup machine.

RAID

RAID is an acronym for redundant array of inexpensive (or independent) disks, and is used to provide fault tolerance to disk storage systems. RAID

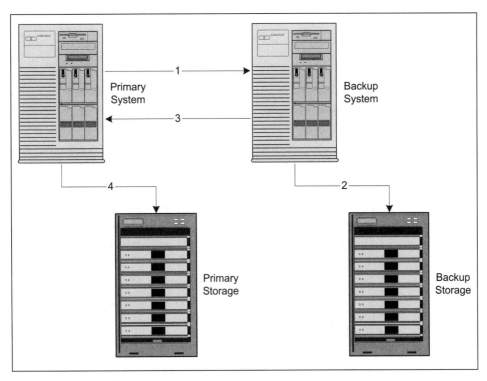

FIGURE 11-3: Synchronous mirroring.

works by combining a collection of disks into a logical array of disks using a special disk controller that does not require all disks to be functioning to maintain data integrity. It can be implemented using either hardware or software. The RAID drives are seen as a single device by the operating system. RAID also increases disk performance and reliability by spreading the data storage across multiple drives, rather than a single disk. The terms used when describing a RAID implementation are defined below:

➤ **Duplexing.** Disk duplexing involves the use of two RAID controllers writing the same data to two separate disks simultaneously. A system using duplexing can survive the failure of either a disk controller or a hard disk.

➤ **Mirroring.** Disk mirroring involves the use of a single RAID controller writing the same data to two separate disks simultaneously. A system using mirroring can survive the failure of either hard disk. Both duplexing and mirroring can slow down system performance because the data is being written twice.

➤ **Striping.** Striping involves breaking up the data into smaller pieces and writing the different pieces to multiple disks. The data may be broken up

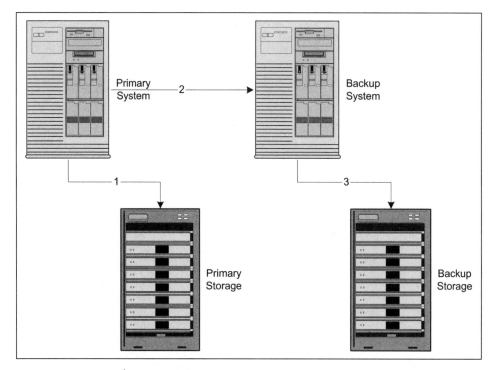

FIGURE 11-4: Asynchronous mirroring.

into bits, bytes, or blocks depending upon the RAID implementation used. Striping is faster than either duplexing or mirroring.

➤ **Parity.** Parity is a way to achieve data redundancy without the disk space overhead of mirroring by storing logical information about the data being written to facilitate recovery. Parity is used with striping and requires at least three disks. The parity information is either stored across multiple disks or on a separate disk.

There are several levels of RAID operation, each with its own balance of redundancy, fault tolerance, cost, and complexity.

➤ **RAID 0.** Disk striping. This implementation of RAID uses disk striping. The data are divided among several disks, which allows for good performance but with no redundancy. This level offers no protection against data loss if a disk were to fail and is not recommended for data recovery purposes.

➤ **RAID 1.** Mirroring and duplexing. This level of RAID involves mirroring or disk duplexing of the data across two or more disks. This provides for redundancy in case of a disk failure. Performance is slower than with

RAID 0, especially during data writes. This level is simple and inexpensive to implement, but 50 percent of the storage space is lost because of the data duplication.

➤ **RAID 2.** Bit-by-bit striping. This level stripes data bit by bit across multiple drives, and is used with disks without built-in error detection. Since most modern disks have built-in error detection, this level of RAID is rarely used today.

➤ **RAID 3.** Byte-by-byte striping. This level stripes data byte by byte across multiple drives, with the parity information stored on a separate disk. The parity disk can be used to restore data if a failure occurs. The parity information is at risk because it is stored on a single drive.

➤ **RAID 4.** Block-by block striping. This level of RAID stripes data at the block level. Just like RAID 3, the parity information is stored on a separate disk. Performance is greater than with RAID 2 or 3 because the data are handled in block sizes.

➤ **RAID 5.** Striping with distributed parity. This level is similar to RAID 4, except that the parity information is stored among the available disks. RAID 5 is a common implementation of RAID.

➤ **RAID 10.** Mirrored striping. This level of RAID (sometimes called RAID 0+1) is a combination of RAID levels 0 and 1. Data are striped across multiple disks and also mirrored. It provides the best fault tolerance of all the RAID levels but is obviously the most expensive.

Load Balancing

Load balancing is used to distribute network traffic dynamically across a group of servers running a common application to prevent any one server from becoming overwhelmed. Using load balancing, a group of servers appears as a single server to an application on the network. The load balancing process is part of the network operating system; the process monitors each server to determine the best path to route traffic on the network to increase performance and availability. Load balancing also allows the application to continue running even if one of the servers goes down. So long as at least one server is available, the application will continue running. Load balancing can be implemented on different servers at a single location or at different sites. If load balancing is implemented on servers at different sites, it can act as a method to allow access to applications in the event of an incident at one of the locations.

Network Attached Storage

A network attached storage (NAS) environment is a common storage area for multiple servers. NAS environments are useful for storage or file server applications, such as mail and web services. A NAS server runs a minimal operating system, and is optimized to facilitate the movement and storage of data. Using a NAS environment creates a centrally managed storage pool, which allows new storage devices to be added without requiring network downtime. Storage volumes from a down server can be easily reassigned, or new storage can be easily added if needed. The flexibility provided by a NAS environment increases the availability and reliability of network storage, adding value to your disaster contingency plans.

Storage Area Networks

A storage area network (SAN) is a high-speed, high-performance network that allows computers running multiple operating systems to store data on a single virtual storage device. A SAN is designed to handle backup traffic more efficiently than a NAS environment. The SAN can be local or remote, and usually communicates with the server using a fiber channel. By moving the storage off the LAN, backups can be performed without affecting the performance of the applications on the LAN.

Figure 11-5 is a comparison of the relative availability value of the different options described here.

ACTION STEPS FOR YOUR PLAN

The key issues for creating your plan to protect your network are:

➤ Document both the physical and logical layout of your network.

➤ Develop appropriate backup strategies.

➤ Identify single points of failure.

➤ Install redundant devices as needed.

➤ Monitor the health of your network.

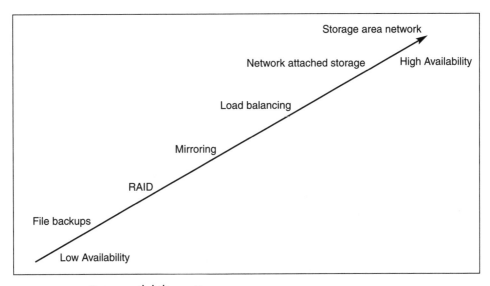

FIGURE 11-5: Data availability options.

The goal of your plan will be to identify what is where and connected by how! A network outage is caused by the failure of some device along the chain. The failure can be electronic, in its programming, or because it was roasted to a crisp in a fire. The plan should be clear and readily available in an emergency.

A continuity/disaster plan is useful for the network manager in a crisis but is very valuable for the data processing manager to understand the network layout and any threats to it at your facility. It is the primary tool for the backup network manager to use when the normal support staff is unavailable.

Begin your plan with a set of blueprints for your facility. These can be on paper or on a CAD system—whatever is easiest for you. Note on the drawings the location of every network closet and the main cable runs between them. This isn't always straight lines; it is where the cables actually run. You may need to crawl through some tight spaces to see where they run. Note if the runs are copper wire or fiber optic. These cable runs should be added to the drawing all the way back to your computer room.

It is not necessary to add the cabling from the closet to the workstations, unless it is unique in some way or the device supports one of your business critical functions. However, you should include the wiring runs to every RF node. This also identifies where these nodes placed.

With these plans in hand, when someone calls to report a network outage in one part of the facility you know where the closet is that supports that part of the facility and the cable that connects it to the computer room (either could be out). More importantly, if you must send out several people to check several different things, you can use the floor plans to point out where they are going. Network devices can be stuffed into the most out-of-the-way places and a wiring plan is a good way to keep track of everything.

Wiring plans will be useful for the facility manager when planning construction projects. Cables may need to be moved or avoided, but at least this way they shouldn't be cut. In the event that a fire damages a cable, you would know where it went from/to and about how much cable is required to replace it.

The second step is to inventory all your hardware in each closet. Like all solid-state electronics, network equipment becomes obsolete before it stops working. Sometimes, older specialized equipment must be maintained to support critical business functions. Adding it to your hardware list should also include adding it to your service contracts after comparing the two.

Another valuable use of the list is to ensure everything that you want in a service contract is covered—and that you are not paying for support for devices that are long gone. Take the time to compare the network inventory against the support contracts item by item. Add the service contract information to the service contacts list for your facility along with any information relevant to that vendor. If you have multiple service vendors, attach a sticker to each item indicating who to call for what service, the contract number, and the hours of service coverage. When the network is ailing, there is not time to look things up to determine who to call.

Network hardware changes at a rapid pace but, in general, you should try to standardize network devices to minimize the number of on-site spare parts. These spares are expensive! However, spare equipment is required if you are to promptly restore the network to service.

Over time, try to drive out the nonstandard network technologies and equipment. It will greatly simplify your job. Some spares are easy. Often one or more jacks on a hub are left unused. If an active jack fails, then the line can be quickly moved. The number of spares and what to store in your closet is determined by:

➤ Your experience as to how often something breaks.

➤ How long it takes to get a replacement.

➤ How long it takes for the contracted service technician to appear.

➤ How critical the circuit is.

➤ The technical experience of the staff.

Adequate spares will quickly restore your equipment to service. Additionally, adequate spares coupled with a trained staff will allow you to reduce your service contract expense. Instead of 24 by 7, you can change it to time and materials. Broken devices can be sent in for repair since spare devices are swapped into the network to replace them.

Spares should always be located as near to the bulk of your equipment as possible and securely locked away. The key should be held by several different people (so a key is always around). One approach to managing the spares is that when new equipment is ordered, it becomes a spare and the oldest spare device is placed into service instead.

The third item in the plan is physical security. No one but the network support staff should be allowed in the network closets. The network administrator must work with the facility's security manager to ensure that these doors are always locked. Depending on the airflow in the closet, some vents may be added to the doors. These rooms are not for storing holiday decorations, old documents, unwanted furniture, etc.

Sometimes network equipment is in freestanding cabinets instead of closets. These cabinets must be locked just like the closets and the keys held by only a few people. In a large facility, this can add up to a lot of keys. Your goal is to minimize the number of keys by using a sub-master key for all closets, and if possible, a sub-master key to all cabinets. These keys must be tracked and, if lost, a determination made whether to rekey the locks.

The fourth plan item is logical security. The network software on the servers and in the network devices will be, in some cases, password protected. These passwords should be protected like any other and known only to the key network support staff. However, they should also be written down and locked in the data processing manager's office in case the network staff is unavailable. (In a wide-area emergency, the network manager or key staff members may not be available or able to come in.)

The fifth plan element is a policy that no one is permitted to plug anything into the network. That is the exclusive job of the network support team. This is to stop people from plugging in their home notebook PCs and bringing down your network. In addition, contract employees should never be permitted to connect into your network. The same policy should cover your RF nodes.

Because servers can support a large number of users and are used to host critical applications, loss of a server can have a severe impact on the business. Some processes to ease the restoration of servers include:

➤ **Store Backup Tapes and Software Off-Site.** Follow the procedures discussed in Chapter 17 for handling and storing backups. Backups of data and application installation media should be stored off-site in a secure, environmentally controlled facility.

➤ **Standardize Hardware, Software, and Peripherals.** Standard configurations of these items will make restoration much easier. The standard configurations for hardware, software, and peripherals should be documented in your plan.

➤ **Document the Network.** The physical and logical network diagram must be kept up to date. The physical documentation should include a diagram of the physical facility, where the primary cables are routed. The logical diagram shows the network nodes and how they interconnect. Both diagrams are critical in restoring the network after a disaster.

➤ **Document Vendor Information.** Maintaining up-to-date information on the vendors you use for hardware, software, and peripherals will make it easier to restore your operations.

➤ **Work with Your Security Team.** The more secure your systems are, the less likely you are to have a data loss due to a security breach. You'll also want to be sure you can restore the latest level of security if you must configure new servers after an emergency.

CONCLUSION

We all need to stay connected to do our jobs. A well-developed network recovery plan will help ensure that your people can get reconnected and back to work as quickly as possible after a disaster.

CHAPTER 12

END-USER PCs
The Weakest Link

Why is it drug addicts and computer aficionados
are both called users?
—Clifford Stoll

INTRODUCTION

At the user end of our networks are typically personal computers. Over the years, personal computers have evolved first to supplement mainframe computer terminals (dumb terminals) and then to replace them. Few companies still employ dumb terminals. PCs have become so inexpensive that they can be found all across companies performing a wide range of functions. And from a business continuity point of view, this is exactly the problem.

Mainframe computers centralized computing power and also centralized data storage. To view data stored by the mainframe required a password, and data files had various levels of security to protect them. Important data were stored in a central location, making backing up the data relatively easy. But a problem with mainframes was that programmers could never keep up with demands for their services. Personal computers, along with their easy-to-use programs, gradually migrated this capability to the individual's desk (hence the "personal" in Personal Computing). As this occurred, all the environmental, electrical, and physical security protections that are provided for the backroom mainframes were no longer available to the PCs and the data residing in them. You've got a problem!

As we discuss critical PCs, keep in mind that servers (shared PCs optimized for storage speed and other services) located outside the protection of the computer room are always considered critical units and must be protected as such.

RISK ASSESSMENT

As always, begin with your risk assessment. Normally personal computers are listed in the departmental risk plans. Are there any critical PCs in your department? Before answering, think about what a PC can be today. It can be a desktop unit. It can be a notebook PC that a manager uses at work and then carries home at night to catch up on urgent projects. It can be the PDA (personal digital assistant) unit carried around by the inventory manager to track shipments. It can even be a web-enabled cell phone. In a factory, it could be a machine tool controller. In a hospital, it could a testing or monitoring device. Computing power is now everywhere!

So what to do? The first thing to do is an asset inventory. Check to see how many of each type unit you have. Categorize them by what they are (notebook, PDA, desktop) or what they are used for. Every computer has several things in common:

1. At some point, the hardware must be repaired or replaced.

2. It runs a stored program, often from a hard disk. In some cases, the program is stored in a ROM chip and rarely changes.

3. In almost every case, it stores data.

4. They are delicate flowers adrift in a cruel world.

So let's take these one at a time. We said at some point the hardware must be repaired or replaced. Funny thing about PCs is that their usefulness fades away long before they stop working. If your processes depend upon a specific machine to always be available, then imagine what would happen if some day it stopped working. Often you can replace it, but if the machine was quite old and uses an older operating system, you might have difficulty getting the old software to run on the new machine. In general, if a PC is used in your business, it should be replaced no less often than every 4 years. If the PC is critical, the hardware should be upgraded no less than every 2 years. Your concern is maximum availability. If a change in hardware forces a change in the software, then at least it will be a planned event with time to address the issues that arise instead of something patched together in a crisis.

The second item common with every computer is that it is running software of some sort. This is true, even if it only runs the same software application over and over again. Like hardware, software has a useful life. If it gets too old, you should rework the PC to use more contemporary hardware and operating systems. This assumes you have the source code. If you cannot find it, then recreate the same software functionality immediately. Do not wait for the other shoe to drop! If the software was purchased as a "package" from a company, periodically check with the company to ensure the software is still supported. The supplier will provide updated versions of the software that will run on current operating systems. If not, then this must also go on your controlled upgrade list. Without support, the software may not work on replacement hardware in an emergency.

By keeping your software up to date, you reduce the number of spare PCs necessary to keep on-site. If a PC running a critical application stops working, you can quickly exchange the hardware, reload the data from backup and proceed with your business with a minimum of downtime.

Also, software sometimes has upgrades to apply. These both update the software's function and repair problems in the code. Unfortunately they may introduce new problems into the machine. Have you ever installed an operating system upgrade that killed the PC it was supposed to save? Controlling versions and testing software is a subject for a data processing book. The key here is that you need to be aware of any changes to a critical PC's software. Always keep backup copies of critical software. The ability to restore a PC's software from a backup copy is critical to a prompt recovery.

Be sure to include on your asset list all software used in critical units to support critical business functions. When in doubt, list them.

The third item that all computers have in common is that they store data. Most data are not worth retaining or can be lost without damage to the company. Those files are not our concern. Do your PCs hold any critical data? We will delve deeper into this subject deeper a bit later, but as you make your asset inventory, note any critical files or general categories of files these units hold. Your list of data files should indicate:

➤ **Size.** Determines optimal backup/recovery method.

➤ **Format.** Is it in Access? Excel? WordPerfect?.

➤ **Data Origin.** Does this PC create or modify it?.

➤ **Volatility.** How often does it change?.

The fourth item that computers have in common is that they all can be subjected to environmental stresses that may weaken the hardware. Always use a properly rated, functioning surge protector to protect your PC. This includes notebook PCs carried by travelers. Notebook PCs have an advantage in that if they lose power from the wall plug, they fail over to the unit's battery. This acts as a built-in Uninterruptible Power Supply (UPS). Critical desktop PCs also need the protection of a UPS to ensure they do not suffer a "hard stop" when losing electrical power. This reduces the likelihood of a power outage resulting in a corrupted data file. After installation, ensure your users do not burden the UPS by plugging nonessential devices into it.

In addition to clean power, PCs are designed to exist within a range of temperature and humidity as established by the manufacturer. Stray outside of this and your hardware will weaken and eventually fail. A typical office environment is usually fine. But a hot, dirty factory stresses the equipment. Notebook PCs left overnight in a car during the depths of winter can be damaged by freezing—or baked in the hot sun on a scorching summer day. Problems may not immediately appear but any marginal components may begin to fail.

So far, we have the risk assessment for each department that identified their critical assets, plus our own asset inventory we made walking around and looking at what we have to support. How can we mitigate the risks (or threats) to our equipment, programs, and data? The most basic step involves the physical security of these assets. As we work through these steps, keep in mind our focus is on supporting our critical business functions, but from time to time you will want to extend this to other machines as well.

Physical Security

Physical security involves preventing unauthorized access to the unit or its theft. It also seeks to prevent someone from sabotaging the unit. Sabotage can be temporary, such as unplugging a cable, or permanent by destroying the unit. Physical security is also important for your software and your backup files. Stolen software can end up copied across the company by well-meaning individuals but creates significant legal problems later.

Unauthorized access is prevented by locking the computer in a room where only authorized people can reach it. This might be in a computer room or an executive's office. The computer room is always locked and the executive's office is watched by the secretary or locked whenever they are not present. Locking the room or watching over the unit provides a barrier to prevent theft and sabotage.

There are other PCs in your company like this. One would be the PC that controls the electronic door locks, such as in a hotel, or to your employee entrances. Someone sneaking in to steal something would gladly steal or destroy the records of their entry in this unit. Therefore it is also normally locked away.

How about the PC that records the time attendance for your employees? Some companies use a barcode on their employee badges to indicate when they arrive at or depart from work (punch in/punch out). This information is recorded in a database for payroll purposes. Such a PC must be secured in a place where it cannot be stolen (there would be a lot of employee private information in there) or sabotaged.

Most PCs are not kept in locked rooms. They are out where the workers are with coworkers, visitors, and who knows who else walking by. For some companies, a lot of people pass by the desks or float through the offices. It is not always possible to be sure who belongs there and who does not. Over lunchtime when everyone has abandoned the office, it takes but a moment to snap shut a notebook PC, slip it into a briefcase, and out the door you go! Desktop units are still fair game but are a bit bulky and more likely to disappear overnight or on a weekend. Handheld PCs barely make a bulge in the pocket of (stylishly) baggy trousers.

One way to hang on to your equipment is to strap it down to your desk. This is typically a steel cable through a loop in the back of your PC. You can also buy a similar device for your notebook PC. To remove it, you must have the key to the lock. True, this can be defeated with brute force but it drastically reduces the number of units stolen. However, it will not stop the deliberate attempt to damage the unit, so do not keep anything critical out in the open when it can be hit, burned, shocked, crushed, etc.

PCs used in warehouses and on the factory floor should be housed in locked cabinets. Factories are a harsh environment for electronic components. A monitor and keyboard are all that a user requires access to. Ensure that the cabinets are well ventilated to avoid overheating the components. Locking the cabinet protects the unit against theft and sabotage. It also prevents someone from loading unauthorized software onto it.

Another important physical security issue for personal computers involves safeguarding the PCs' vital records. It is important that all PC software licenses are gathered after purchase and filed for future reference. Some companies create a software "image" of the operating system and all standard programs. This image is then copied into each PC they own. The serial numbers on the software then all read the same. By holding these licenses in a secure location (often the same off-site storage used for your backup media), you can readily prove how many copies of a program that you own.

The other vital PC records are the backup media. These devices (CD-ROMs, tapes, removable fixed disk, etc.) all contain confidential company data. They must be correctly labeled and safeguarded as such.

Backing Up Your PC Programs and Data

The key to a rapid recovery from a theft, damaged PC disk, or sabotage is to restore from your last good backup copy. Mainframe computers typically make a full copy of everything they have stored on disk once per week. Every day, they make an incremental copy of whatever has changed that day. In this way they capture all the data and software necessary for them to function. The storage media (usually magnetic tape) is carefully transported and stored. Over time, some tapes are kept for historical copies and others are rotated back into use.

PCs are another matter. Their data are often scattered about their hard disk mixed in among programs, obsolete data, and pictures of Aunt Meg, and following a naming convention that defies most logic. Although a complete (image) backup of each PC is desired, it is expensive and most users will not faithfully do it. In addition, there is the cost of the backup hardware, handling the backups and all the media necessary to copy these disks.

Selecting a Personal Computer Data Backup Strategy

Hard disk capacities in PCs have grown rapidly over the years, and the smallest available disk sizes are more than most users can fill. Still, your backup tool must be capable of copying everything on the disk onto the media selected.

Before beginning your data backup strategy, *require* users to store all mission-critical files on a computer room file server. Make this a firm rule, and whenever you find such a file stay after it until it is migrated properly. These files should not be left to chance, and the computer room staff will ensure they are included on the normal backup tapes. This category should include databases, spreadsheets, legal documents, and anything that is truly mission critical. Mission critical includes all documents that must be retained for legal or regulatory reasons. For a few individuals, this may mean that all their files will reside on the server. So be it! The end-user's PC can still access these data as if they were present on their PC's disk.

That said, your first consideration is, "What do I want to back up?" PCs hold a lot of programs that may not even be used but could require a considerable amount of space to back up over and over again. A PC's operating system may require several gigabytes just to back up the software. Applications software can easily triple this number. Most of these programs rarely change. If a PC were stolen or otherwise rendered unusable, you should be able to install your standard software image on a new PC and load any additional authorized programs from your support staff copies. Then the data can be loaded and you are finished. Therefore, for most PCs, it is not necessary to make backup copies of the programs—just the data.

Special-purpose PCs may have special configuration settings in the software or operating system that are necessary for it work properly. For these PCs, you may want to make image backup copies (the entire disk).

This is important because the larger the amount of data to back up, the longer it will take. It may also drive your backup strategy into a more expensive choice if most of what you are copying is unnecessary.

Now that we have trimmed down the job to only copying data, consider which data you want to save. If you are keeping copies of old files and correspondence on your PC for historical purposes, consider moving that off to a CD and deleting it. Again, why copy something over and over when once will do. The archive CD should have the proper level of security on it. Either store it off-site with your other vital records or in a locked vital records storage on-site. Mark every CD legibly as to the originator, date created, and contents. Do not stuff it in your desk if it contains any sensitive information.

Another valuable space saver is to delete those files you no longer need. Some people never clean out their attic and others never delete any files from their PC. If it isn't needed—delete it! If in doubt, copy to a CD and then delete it.

So with only active data files left, containing data that are useful, the last and very important step is to store all your data under one master directory. A common choice is to use C:\Data. Under this are folders by topic and by product such as Excel. To back up all the data, copy them to a CD-ROM for storage with a drag and drop. Click on the Data directory, drag it over to the CD-RW drive, and drop it. The operating system copies it for you and then waits for you to tell it to burn the CD. You can type away while the copy is made.

CDs are so inexpensive, roughly less than 20 cents each, that they are practical for data backup so long as the older, unneeded copies are properly destroyed. For most end-user PCs, this will be the easiest way for them to make their own copies. Be sure they understand and comply with your standards for marking backups (for easy identification when it is needed for a restore). Also, simplify the collection and filing of backups. From time to time, check off who is handing in backups to identify the ones who are forgetting their good data processing practices.

With that said, here are the factors to consider when selecting a backup strategy for your users.

➤ **Storage Volume Requirements.** The backup media used should be capable of handling the anticipated volume.

➤ **The Length of Time to Make the Backup Copy.** Huge amounts of data take huge amounts of time to copy. However, a typical end-user PC should not require more than a single CD to backup their data, if storage intensive files such as audio, movies, and pictures are stored separately from the data.

➤ **Interoperability.** The backup media should ideally be compatible with the operating systems and applications in use today and in the future. In 2003, most major PC assemblers announced their intention to drop the 3.5-inch floppy disk from their new PCs.

➤ **Backup Software.** Ensure that users know the process for making backup data copies and that their tools are easy to use. This will improve the chances that backups are regularly made.

Backup Technologies

There are many different backup technologies available for end-user backups. Whatever is used, be sure to mark the backup with the date and the users' name. The most popular include these:

➤ **Tape Drives.** These are readily available for desktop computers. Most tape backup software can be set up to have the backup run automatically. Tapes provide the greatest amount of storage space; depending on the technology, a single cartridge can hold several hundred gigabytes. However to fill such a large tape may require a considerable amount of time. Also, the higher the capacity, the greater the cost per cartridge. Multiply this by the number of PCs needing to be backed up and this can be an expensive proposition. Tape is best suited for server backups.

➤ **Removable Media.** this includes products such as Zip cartridges from Iomega, and are used similar to floppy disks. They are faster and easier to use than tape drives. The cartridges are comparable in cost to tape media, but have a lower capacity.

➤ **Compact Disk Read Only Memory (CD-ROMs or CD).** CD drives are standard on new PCs and have replaced the old floppy disks as a way to load software and data. Many PCs include a CD-RW (Read Write), which can also write to a CD. CDs are low in cost and have a capacity of about 700 MB of data per disk. One drawback is that most CDs (known as CD-R) can only be written to once. However, given the low cost per disk, this is the most cost-effective way to back up end-user PCs. If all your data are consolidated under one master directory, you may be able to fit them all onto one disk. If individual CD-RW units are not practical, consider purchasing portable CD-RW drives with USB connectors.

➤ **DVD-Rs (DVD Writers).** These are a step up from CDs in that a DVD holds approximately 4.2 GB per disk. The disk is the same compact size as a CD. These devices are gradually dropping in price and over time may be combined into a single unit with the CD-RW.

➤ **Internet Backup.** This is normally a commercial service that uses the public Internet to backup data from the end-user PC to a remote server connected to the Internet. Software is loaded onto the end-user PC that is used to schedule the backups, select the files to be backed up, and to communicate to the backup server. Data are normally encrypted to ensure security during transmission. A major advantage of this method is that the user does not have to deal with backup media, and the backups can be run unattended. One disadvantage to this approach is time. It may be slow if attempted using a dial-up connection.

However, this is a very useful tool for "road warriors" as it allows them to back up their data while traveling. Remember, only back up the critical files that have changed. Hotels are now installing broadband services for travelers, so this option is becoming more attractive.

➤ **Network Storage.** If the PC is connected to a network, that unit can back its data up via the network to a server. The network file servers are then backed up daily so your files eventually end up on tape. There are two basic ways to use the network:

1. **Backup Initiated by the Server.** The server can be configured to read the data from the end-user PCs and store the data either to the server hard disk or to a backup medium.

2. **Store Data to the Server.** A networked disk can be configured for use by the end users. The end users configure their application software to write to the virtual drive rather than to a local drive. The networked drive is then backed up as part of the normal server backup process.

There are several problems with backing up to a server. The first is space. Most servers lack unlimited disk space so they limit how much space an end user can use. Once this limited space overflows, the backup dies. Estimate the size of your typical PC data directory. Multiply it times the number of users and this approach, while elegant, may not be practical.

The second obstacle is bandwidth for all these PCs to clog the network with massive data transfers. Also, the server disks can only run so fast.

END-USER BACKUP ISSUES

It is important that the data recovery plan emphasize the availability of the data, protect the data's confidentiality, and ensure the data's integrity. Some processes to follow to make restoration of desktop PCs easier include:

➤ Train end users on the importance of backing up data on a regular basis. If the process is simple and easy to follow, they will usually cooperate.

➤ Document vendor and configuration information for all specialty PCs.

➤ Establish a mail slot-type dropoff for backup media in the data center where they can be dropped off securely. Provide labels that may prompt them to fill in essential information. When tapes are recycled (old backups no longer needed), provide them to users at a pickup point. From time to time, test these backups to ensure they can be read. Sometimes data backups look like they worked but they did not.

Hard Disk Recovery

Sometimes you are just sure whatever was on your hard disk is lost forever. This could be a PC that was melted in a fire, or it could have been submerged for days in a flood. It could have suffered a head crash. Don't be too depressed. There are companies who specialize in recovering data from severely damaged disks. They can also recover data from deleted files (the ones that the usual file recovery software cannot rebuild).

These companies use specially trained engineers to disassemble the hard disk unit in their clean rooms and extract the data. The services can be expensive but the savings to your company can be considerable.

MOBILE DEVICES

Mobile PCs are the wave of the future. The ideal is a unit that can accompany you throughout your workday. A unit that is unobtrusive, light, and always ready for use. Today we have notebook PCs, PDAs, and web-enabled cell phones. Once these devices depart the cozy confines of the office, they introduce a new range of issues to be addressed.

Mobile Security

Unlike desktop PCs, notebook PCs advertise how light and easy they are to carry. This portability also makes them easy to steal. Once a mobile PC is taken out of the office, it loses whatever protection your facility's security force provides. Several steps should be taken to protect this equipment:

1. Keep it out of sight if possible.

2. Do not carry it in a carrying case that is obviously for notebook PCs. Use a standard briefcase or pack it in your luggage.

3. When it is not in use in your hotel room, store it out of sight.

4. When attending seminars or business meetings outside the office, never leave it unattended.

5. While it is in your car, keep it out of sight. Then if you go to a restaurant for lunch, it isn't visible sitting in your car.

6. When passing through airport security, ensure no one is ahead of you before laying it on the scanner's conveyor. This way it should arrive at the other side the same time that you do.

Essentially the same holds true for PDAs. While it is carried on your trip so it could be used, if a thief cannot see it, they cannot target it. Airports are a favorite place to steal notebook PCs, and there are many ways to waylay the unsuspecting. Targeting a company's executives in an airport and stealing their notebook PC is a very effective tool for industrial espionage. You think it was just a thief but your competition may now know many hidden details of your operation.

Some managers take their notebook PC or PDA home to catch up on work. The problem is that if they have an accident on the way, someone must know to promptly remove the notebook from the vehicle as soon as possible (with the permission of the police). A notebook is an easy theft item that could be removed from a wreck and not be missed for several days. More than the PC itself, it is the data you are safeguarding.

Mobile Data Backup

Mobile devices present their own particular backup issues. This is even more of a problem for other mobile devices such as PDAs, smart phones, and pagers, which are less likely to be connected to the corporate network. Users are also a problem, as most think that a disaster such as a lost or damaged device will not happen to them. These devices are much more fragile and more easily stolen than desktop PCs.

Always make a full backup of your notebook PC before a business trip. This will lessen the impact on your job since the replacement unit can be restored from the backup. If necessary, a new unit can be loaded and sent out to you.

If your PC has critical data files (such as legal briefs of contracts), they can be burned to a CD and stored in a different piece of luggage. Again, if the PC is lost, the CD can be loaded onto a new unit. Guard the CD carefully—your coat pocket will do!

The average IT-enabled person uses at least three portable devices and spends more than 1 hour per day trying to keep these devices synchronized.

PROTECTING END-USER VITAL RECORDS

Ensure that your department's vital records program includes the handling of your data backups. PCs tend to be somewhat secured but if a competitor can lay their hands on your data backups, in most cases, you would never know. Further, to break into your PC they must hack past the password but the backup tape would be clearly readable. Therefore, always treat backup media as critical data and store it properly.

Another vital record is the paper copy of your PC software licenses. These are essential to prove the number of licenses you have purchased in the event of a software audit. If your equipment was lost in a fire, the licenses can be used to demonstrate ownership and the software copied onto your new equipment (always consult your company's attorneys if such a situation arises).

Along with the licenses, the original software media must be secured as a vital record. This reduces the likelihood of someone installing unlicensed software in multiple PCs. On the one hand, they may believe they are helping fellow employees by providing programs for their use. On the other hand, they may be ready to resign and are setting you up to be turned in for using pirated software! Don't take chances. After installing programs promptly gather the media and store it with the vital records. Then if you are accused, you can show you have taken prudent steps to control and stop it.

Vital records can turn up in several unwanted places. Before recycling tapes from storage, be sure to erase them because they may not end up with the same user every time. Backups on CDs cannot be recycled and should be rendered unreadable, usually by crushing them.

Another set of vital records to protect is found in your surplus PCs. When a PC is ready for donation to charity, remove the fixed disk and destroy it. Some people crush it; some use a heavy drill and make holes completely through it. There is a lot of sophisticated technology in the world that can recover data from your disk no matter how thoroughly you format it. The charity receiving the PC will need to find someone to loan it old hard disks. *Never* send one out in your surplus PC.

Additional Resources

www.globalcomputer.com—Devices for securing PCs to a desk, backup hardware, and media.

www.bsa.org—Business Software Alliance. BSA educates consumers on software management and copyright protection, cyber security, trade, e-commerce, and other Internet-related issues.
(from http://www.bsa.org/usa/about/).

CONCLUSION

When supporting personal computers, it's not a matter of if it will break, but when. Periodic upgrading of both hardware and software is necessary to ensure that support will be possible if a critical PC fails.

Although the proliferation of personal computers has produced many benefits, it has made life more difficult for those charged with protecting vital corporate assets. Physical security is now more of a problem, as these systems are scattered throughout the organization. Data security is also more difficult, as data are no longer concentrated in a central location. But proper policies and procedures for managing these devices can help you keep these assets safe and sound.

CHAPTER 13

CUSTOMERS
Other People to Worry About

If we don't take care of the customer . . . somebody else will.
—Author Unknown

INTRODUCTION

Successful businesses are built on the basics: supplying your customers with the products and services that they want, when they want them, and at a price they are willing to pay. What would they do if you could not supply them with what they needed to run their business? How many times could this happen before their confidence in you as a supplier is eroded or fails altogether? Good customers are hard to find. It is always cheaper to keep the ones you have than to find new ones. Don't wait until it is too late! Action steps must be identified to support your customer in the face of a disaster in your facility. A disaster plan that considers the customer is important!

The most basic step is to develop a customer notification plan. Properly implemented, a customer notification plan builds a valuable image in your customer's mind about your company and its usefulness to them. We have all experienced troublesome suppliers to our own businesses and value the ones that do not create problems for our operations. When a disaster strikes, it is imperative that your company's hard-won reputation not fall victim to the calamity. You must consider the disaster's impact on your customers and act decisively.

Our plan development steps by now should sound familiar. We list what it is we want to protect, what the threats are, and then take mitigation actions to reduce the likelihood of occurrence or severity of a disaster. Of course, we then need to test it. A successful customer notification plan will strengthen the relationship between you and your customer. Just as your parents told you, "When life gives you a lemon, make lemonade," this plan will demonstrate your commitment to top-quality customer service.

Throughout this chapter we will use the term "product" to mean all manner of goods and services provided to your customer.

Once a catastrophe occurs, crews will be assigned to contain the damage and restore a minimal level of service. How will your customer find out that their orders will be delayed or not coming at all? Will they see it on the evening news? Will it be in the trade press? Don't let competitors tell your story in a manner that is out of your control. It is unlikely that your sales force will be among the crews repairing your factory walls. Don't leave them idle. They can assist in the long-term recovery by using their experience in dealing with your customers.

From a business continuity perspective, the best we can do at this point is to control the indirect damage this causes to our customers. As the saying goes, "perception equals reality." To control the perception, the sales force will inform the most important customers personally. They will also assist the customer to minimize the shock a possible materials shortage will cause to their operations. We do this by notifying them of the situation, explaining to them what is already en route or available from intact warehouses, providing a realistic timeframe for restoring the flow of goods, and, if necessary, assisting them in locating equivalent products elsewhere.

These are the actions of a partner, not an adversary. Your customer still has a crisis, but now there are two of you working on it! Long after your facility is operational again, the customer will only remember the time you forced them into scrambling for components. Use the tragedy to strengthen your supplier-customer bond by helping keep their business running. The long-term goodwill will be invaluable.

KEY CUSTOMER ASSESSMENT

Our first step is an inventory of who our key customers are (use Form 13-1 on the CD-ROM). Then we will examine their buying habits to see which times of the year they are most sensitive to a problem. Third, we will add to the list any one-time customers that we currently are contracted to support.

Who are our customers? If you are like most businesses, the 80/20 rule applies to your revenue stream: 80% of your revenue stream comes from 20% of your customers. We would like to be all things to all customers, but our efforts will focus on protecting our core customers. This information might be extracted from historical shipping and billing data. Set a time frame to reach back, perhaps 2 years, perhaps more, and total the amount of business each customer gives us. Place the big customers at the top of the list by sorting the list in descending order, based on the amount billed. Drop the bottom 80% of customers from the list. Now add back to the list any specific customers whose business you are cultivating or who have other significance to you.

Using this list of names, add contact information, such as contact names, addresses, phone numbers, and e-mail addresses. There may be multiple locations that buy from you or that you deliver to. Next, add in the name of the salesperson that covers this account. In tough times, relationships are important. Now the list says who to call, where to call to, and who should do the calling. The salesperson's name is important because they may be sitting idle during disaster recovery.

For the customers on your list, for the time period you specified, produce a month-by-month report of total orders or of total billings (either one should do). Your goal is to dig out the buying patterns for the customer. You want to understand when their busy season is, which is when they depend on you the most. The salesperson for this account can adjust the report based on experience with that customer. Before submitting that request, add to it a second report to break down the same time period by the specific products they buy. If you offer more than one product, in a disaster you may find your warehouse "fat" on some items and lean on others. It is likely that a disaster will affect some customers more than others.

In the case of specific contracts, either for one-time or ongoing purchases, you must check for a clause dealing with *force majeure*. This describes actions beyond your control, also known as "*acts of God*" that prevent you from fulfilling the terms of your contract. This is especially important for contracts with penalty clauses. Note on the customer inventory sheet, next to the customer's name, any agreements that contain penalty clauses and the products they cover. Invoking a *force majeure* clause means that the event could not have been avoided. A tornado isn't avoidable, but an argument could be made that a warehouse fire could have been avoided. If the other party demonstrates that you were careless in your fire prevention, they may invoke any penalty clauses in the agreement. To do so, it must be established that your nonperformance was avoidable.

Some questions to consider:

1. If we cannot fulfill a contract will we incur any penalties?

2. What is the financial and operational impact on your key customers?

3. In the event of a prolonged outage, how long can your customer withstand a loss of services or products?

4. Does your customer have alternative suppliers and supply channels?

5. How many days of inventory do your customers normally carry, or are normally in the supply chain to them?

A Just in Time (JIT) supplier must have a documented and tested Business Continuity Plan. Disasters happen to us all. One supplier's failure can close down a customer's production if they fail to deliver on time.

Exceptions may exist, but most customers just want their goods delivered on time. Delivery credibility can be a positive (or negative) selling point for your company. Many materials managers maintain supplier scorecards to weed out unreliable providers.

With your plan in place (and tested), invite your customers to comment on how to keep them supplied in a crisis. It is in their interests as well as yours that you have a good plan. Invite them to observe a test and even allow them to select one of the disaster scenarios from a list you have prepared. They will see chaos, they will see people scrambling around, but more importantly, they will see how quickly order is restored to the situation and action begins.

This is a good time to further cement your relationship with them and ask them about their own recovery plans. This street runs both ways. Just as they want to ensure you are always ready as a supplier, you want to ensure they are always in business as a customer. This dialogue will be useful in developing or modifying your Supplier Notification Plan.

RISK ASSESSMENT

Looking at the other side of the issue, what are you to do if your major customer suffers a disaster? You need their future business.

A quick risk assessment of the customer's facility location may uncover those who might be closed by the same problem:

➤ Hurricane (you are both on the coast)

➤ Blizzard (scenically located in the Rocky Mountains)

➤ Earthquake

➤ Other wide-area disaster

To prevent Mother Nature's destruction from closing your business, make a conscious effort to obtain customers spread over a wide geographic area. Customers are where they are and you handle as many as you can, but your risk will be reduced if they are spread out. Don't let poorly prepared customers drag down your business as well.

DEVELOP A COMMUNICATIONS PLAN

OK! Now that you have an inventory of your customers, we need to determine how we will communicate with them in an emergency. As always, the best way is by telephone, person to person. Face-to-face contact is fine but much too time consuming. While traveling to the customer's site, you are out of touch with the latest containment and recovery results.

It is much better for the customer's purchasing agents to hear the first news of the calamity from you rather than from a newscast or your competitors. A newscast by nature consists of an attention-grabbing headline and few details. Your call will provide real information.

Before calling anyone, try to obtain a list of open and pending orders. Call those customers first. Lacking a list of orders, it is an executive decision as to which key accounts to call.

Contact your customers three times:

1. As soon as possible after the disaster.

2. Within 24 hours after the disaster with a clear picture of how this problem affects them.

3. When services have been essentially restored. Recoveries take a long time and your customers will be looking elsewhere. Do not wait until the last new nail is driven but when you can provide predictable delivery dates for their goods.

To facilitate the first call, a standard, written statement needs to be developed that can be used to inform customers of the problem. The statement would acknowledge the calamity, provide a few brief details, and promise to call them back within 24 hours with an update. If the disaster struck the factory but left the warehouse intact, don't be afraid to say so. However, for the first message, all callers must use the same approved, guarded text.

An example text might be:

"This is to notify you that ABC Company has experienced a serious incident. A ___*(fire, earthquake, hazardous spill)*___ occurred that has temporarily halted ___*(shipping, production, baking your cakes)*___. This may impact your order by ___*(late shipments? Can't be built?)*___. A detailed recovery assessment is now underway. We will contact you again within 24 hours with a full update to the situation and any impact it may have on your open orders. Thank you for standing by us in this moment of adversity. If you have any questions, please contact xxxx at xxx."

For the first call, it helps to know what they usually buy and when. Keep your conversations positive, but honest. You would want nothing less from them. If this is their busy season, they should be the first called. After reading the text, ask them how this will impact their operations. If it will be significant, then consider assisting them to quickly locate alternative suppliers.

The second call, 24 hours later, should provide specific and useful information to your customer. Tell them when you can deliver their products to them.

➤ If the recovery will be long, help them to locate another supplier. You may protect your relationship by acting as an intermediary between the customer and another supplier. It is doubtful you can charge a markup for your services but you are protecting a very valuable relationship.

➤ If the recovery will be short, provide a best estimate for the resumption of shipments. If the goods now in shipping are sufficient for several days, this may keep your customer supplied for the short term. Once production resumes, send the next several shipments by express freight until the normal shipping channels are filled again.

This may sound somewhat strange but your competitors may become your supplier or your customer during a crisis. It all depends on whether you have the disaster or they did.

Do you have reciprocal processing/servicing agreements with your competitors? In the event of a disaster, reciprocal-processing agreements should be available for immediate execution. For instance, a competing bank may clear funds for the customers of their competitor bank if the competitor bank cannot clear funds because a disaster has taken down their network; or a competing airline would honor air travel tickets from other airlines in the event of a disaster that grounds the competing airline. It is good business and in the best interest of all competitors in the marketplace to make these kinds of reciprocal arrangements with each other, if possible, to minimize the impact of a disaster and be able to fulfill your obligations to your customers.

ACTION STEPS FOR YOUR PLAN

A customer notification plan is not necessary for small or well-contained disasters. It is only executed when your ability to deliver goods and services has been greatly diminished or temporarily halted. It is also used if a disaster is well publicized. The key items to cover in the notification are:

1. Conservatively estimate how long the facility will be out of service and what products are affected.

2. Establish what finished goods are available for shipment and allocate according to those customers who need them the most or as required by contract.

3. Gather the sales force and explain the situation. Provide general details of what may be damaged and what is intact.

4. Provide a copy of the preprinted text and explain any limitations on what should be said.

5. If the sales offices are not available, cover all expenses for them to call from home or from their cell phones.

6. For products affected by the disaster, identify alternative sources of materials.

7. Prepare the follow up message for customers to set an expectation as to when the facility will be back to normal.

CONCLUSION

Don't allow a disaster to become worse by failing to communicate with your customers. Most customers will work with you to get through the disaster if they are kept informed about the progress of your recovery efforts and status of their orders. Instead of a disaster becoming an opportunity for your competitors, make it into an opportunity for you to show your customers what a reliable business partner you are.

CHAPTER 14

SUPPLIERS
Collateral Damage

Advice is the only commodity on the market
where the supply always exceeds the demand.
—Author Unknown

INTRODUCTION

Every business has suppliers. If you have not been far sighted in dealing with the impact that a disaster may have on your ability to work with them, it may result in financial and operational hardships for your company. Some disasters have the ability to not only shut your business down for a time but could also affect your suppliers' ability to provide your business with the necessary goods for your business. If this happens, your business is shut down. For example, if a tornado hits a section of the community where your supplier for raw materials is located, that supplier might not be able to produce the goods you need for your operation. Their building may be damaged and their employees cannot get to work. Even if they still could operate, their distribution channel may have been affected. They may not be able to get trucks to their building so they can ship their products to you. Either way your business will be in trouble; your supplier cannot deliver the goods required for your business, which results in you not being able to satisfy and ship your customer orders, your customers in turn won't pay for unshipped orders, and you suffer serious financial problems.

KEY SUPPLIER ASSESSMENT

All companies, large and small, need to address this issue concerning suppliers and how they will be affected by a disaster. Businesses are linked together in the supply chain, each needing one another to complete the business cycle. The adage "you're only as strong as the weakest link" is so true when it comes to the strength of the supply chain. Every business must work out with their trading partners how to deal with disasters that may result in the link breaking between the businesses. As you conduct a review of your business practices and operations, identify the suppliers that are critical to your business. These suppliers can be local, national, or even international. Also, don't overlook third-party influences. For example, if you buy products or services from abroad, then don't just look at your supplier's ability to supply the products or services you need, but also consider the risk of the shipper not being able to operate or a delay or failure in supporting import/export documentation. Your supplier may be healthy but the transportation method may be affected by the disaster. This was all so apparent when the disaster struck on September 11, 2001. For days after the attack, airline travel and even air cargo transportation was either completely at a halt or severely curtailed. Even though the disaster took place in New York City, Pennsylvania, and Maryland, the whole nation was affected. How prepared were you? Did you have an agreement with your suppliers on an alternative transportation plan or how they would supply their services to you?

Identify all areas in your business that pose a major risk in your business operations if your suppliers are unable to continue to supply you with the raw materials, supplies, or services that you require. It is all too easy to concentrate on the major suppliers of products and services in your business, such as telephone, electricity, raw materials, etc., but do not forget to examine the role of all the firms you deal with, both large and small. Your small suppliers could be equally or even more important than your larger suppliers. For instance, your supplier for raw materials may not be affected by the disaster, but what about your advertising agency or printer? Your ad agency or printer, more times than not, is a small local firm but may be very critical in your recovery efforts. Without additional advertising or collateral you may not be able to advertise or market your products effectively, even though you can manufacture them. If your ad agency or printer were affected by a disaster, would you have an alternative supplier?

There are times that there is no other supplier you could use; one option to an alternative supplier is to store enough of the types of supplies that could be used in the event of a disaster until you could get re-supplied. For instance, if your business relies on printed material such as direct mail pieces to generate revenue, print up additional pieces and store them in an off-site storage facility. In the event that your printer cannot supply you with these materials, you can simply go to your offsite storage area and use your stored supplies. Storing these supplies may have an additional cost, but not doing so could result in reduced sales and loss of revenues if a disaster occurs and you haven't identified an alternative supplier in a timely manner. What if you can manufacture your products but you can't use a local transportation company to deliver your products to a larger shipper? Could these local suppliers be affected by the same disaster that has affected you? What alternatives do you have if you don't have access to your local distribution channel? Can you rent your own vehicles to transport your products to your national shipper? Is there an alternative shipping method that you can use?

Several years ago a regional shipper had a work stoppage because of a union strike. There was no natural disaster but an outage just the same. Those customers who didn't have an alternative shipping method for their products lost millions of dollars in revenue because they couldn't get their product to market.

Do not take for granted that your smaller and other third-party suppliers are not important in the supply chain; they just may be your "weakest link."

Managing your vendors or suppliers in the aftermath of a disaster is critical. As with your customers, prioritization for your vendors is the key. Focus your business continuity planning on those suppliers that have the largest impact on your recovery efforts and are the most critical to the support of your business. Again, these may not be your largest suppliers! Set priorities for the management process on this priority basis.

Do you know who your supply chain partners are?

➤ Large and small suppliers?

➤ Service providers?

➤ Security alternatives?

➤ Public infrastructure service providers?

➤ Other agencies and business partners?

➤ Regulatory bodies?

➤ The public?

➤ The news media?

RISK ASSESSMENT

Failure of an important vendor can have a devastating impact on your business. Whether due to a natural disaster or bankruptcy, your plan must include the steps you plan to take to manage the failure of an important vendor. This vendor could be supplying a critical component on a just-in-time basis, or it could be your ISP (Internet Service Provider) that is hosting your online ordering system. Quick action on your part could mean the difference between keeping your customers happy and losing business to your competitor.

The basic steps involved in handling the loss of an important vendor are to quickly assess the situation, mitigate the risks to your business, and develop a plan to keep the business moving while the vendor recovers or is replaced. Put together a small team of three to five people to handle the crisis; a larger team can cause you to waste valuable time arguing things in committee, and this is a time for quick decision making.

The selection of the right team members is important to the success of this effort. The team should have at least one member who understands the technical issues involved. Depending on the vendor, this might require someone familiar with the company databases, Web servers, or network infrastructure. Someone on the team should also have enough authority to cut through any red tape that might be in the team's way. The team should have experience with legal contracts, and should also be able to evaluate new vendors if necessary. The team may also need to be able to negotiate service-level agreements with possible replacement vendors.

If the likelihood of the vendor not surviving is high due to a bankruptcy or major disaster, you may want to consider suspending all payments to the vendor. This is especially important if you have prepaid for some services. This will help to prevent any financial reclamation issues down the road.

The next step is to review carefully all legal contracts between you and the vendor. Make sure you understand your rights and obligations during this time. If a lawyer is not on your team, make sure you get advice from the corporate legal counsel. In many cases you will have a service-level agreement (SLA) that guarantees you a minimum level of performance and should provide for penalties if the vendor cannot meet the minimum service levels. An SLA should cover the following issues:

➤ What is the minimum acceptable level of service?

➤ What is the standard for measuring the service level?

➤ How and when are service statistics calculated?

➤ What is the process for notifying customers if service is affected?

➤ Are there alternative sources of the service?

Once you have a complete understanding of the situation, your next step is to contact the vendor to discuss the problem. Work with the vendor if possible to help them through the problem. If the vendor is providing technology, make sure you work out what you will need to continue operating. This may include software licenses, source code for custom software applications, architecture documentation for infrastructure providers, etc. Whether you ultimately switch vendors or see this one through the crisis, you first responsibility is to keep your own business functioning.

ACTION STEPS FOR YOUR PLAN

There are five steps to developing your plan to protect against supplier problems affecting your organization. These steps are:

1. Data collection.

2. Investigation.

3. Assessment.

4. Agreement.

5. Mitigation.

Data Collection

The first step in managing your suppliers is to collect your supplier's vital information and data. Each internal department should appoint a supplier coordinator responsible for ensuring that the critical suppliers for that department or business unit are identified and documented. The department coordinator should document the process and specific approach of identifying the key suppliers. One good source for the initial identification process is to run an accounts payable list of current and past vendors. It's pretty obvious that you need to identify and document the vital information of your current suppliers, but what about past suppliers? Past vendors are important because they may become your alternative vendors in the event that your current vendors cannot fulfill their obligations. Maintaining a dialogue with your past suppliers is extremely important for this reason. Some past suppliers may not want to work with you since you don't buy from them any longer. Make sure you identify and document these as well so that if you need to select an alternative supplier, you don't waste time finding out after a disaster occurs that a certain supplier doesn't want to work with your business any longer.

Other means of identifying your suppliers should also be used because not all suppliers may appear on the account payable list. The supplier may not be paid through normal channels or there is no payment involved for the service or product. Research "other" suppliers by conducting interviews with key personnel and research product documentation to determine if there are other suppliers of material or services that are being used that are not on the account payable listing. For instance, the supplier that packages your product may be a subsidiary of your company and no money changes hands for payment of their services. Their "payment" for their services is only a journal entry in accounting. Missing this supplier as a key vendor may mean that if a disaster occurs to you or your subsidiary, your products cannot be packaged and therefore they cannot be shipped to your customers. After each department has researched and compiled their supplier list, each coordinator should note the product or service that is supplied by the vendor or organization and how critical the product or service is to the organization. Each supplier coordinator should then assign an impact score for each supplier based on the criticality of the supplier's product or service.

Apply the "KISS" (Keep It Simple Stupid) principle for developing your scoring system. Don't overly complicate your decision process by dreaming up a complicated scoring process that requires a Ph.D. in mathematics to figure out and to maintain. A simple 1 to 10 scoring system is adequate, where 1 is very little impact and 10 is very high impact. The supplier impact score should relate to the impact on the organization based on the Risk Assessment for your entire organization, ranked by type of disaster and how critical the product or service is to the organization. Don't give suppliers high impact scores simply on the basis that they are your largest suppliers. As we saw earlier, your smallest supplier may just be the supplier that has the largest impact on your organization if they cannot supply you with their product or service in the event of a disaster. Use Form 14-1 on the CD-ROM to organize the data on your suppliers.

Investigation

The next step in this supplier process is to communicate with suppliers to determine how you will operate with them in the event of a disaster. After you have collected and analyzed the data and completed your master supplier list, get in touch with them to investigate their capabilities and to get agreement on how to operate in the event of a disaster; yours or theirs. Don't forget it's to their advantage to work with you during this process. If you find a certain supplier is not cooperating and find this process unimportant, then it may be time to find an alternative supplier. This supplier may be your weakest link in your supply chain; you must take measures to strengthen it!

The first step in forming a dialogue with your suppliers is to compose a letter that lays out the process that you are using for all suppliers and how each supplier fits into your supply chain. Let them know how important they are to your success in the event of a disaster. In the letter, ask a series of questions concerning their own ability to recover from a disaster. Some questions that you might ask them are:

➤ Do you currently have a disaster plan?

➤ Does your plan provide for supplying products to my business?

➤ How important is my business to your supply chain?

➤ Do you maintain safety stock for my products?

Form a dialogue with your suppliers to make them aware that you are formulating a business continuity plan and that their input into the plan is important and necessary in the event of a disaster. The next step is to mail out the letter to each supplier. Make sure you indicate when you want the questionnaire returned to you. Once you have received all the questionnaires back, make arrangements with them to discuss in person any concerns you may have in regards to their ability to keep you supplied with products or services. With each supplier, perform the appropriate level of investigation according to the priority and criticality of the product or service. Determine if the supplier has completed a business continuity plan and to what extent they have considered your operation in their planning process. Determine if their plan adequately protects you, their customer, in the event that your supplier has a disaster and has to implement their plan. If the supplier does not have a plan, offer to help them develop one. You may even be able to charge them for this help.

Discuss with them the role that they would play in the event that you would have a disaster. Discuss alternative processes in the event that your supplier could not deliver on their contracts to you. You might also want to explore changing your purchasing policy for certain products and services. Historically your business might have purchased single orders from the lowest cost supplier. This may not be the best approach to help you through a disaster, as you might not be confident that the cheapest supplier on any one day will be able to supply you after a disaster occurs. An alternative policy could be to form a longer-term relationship with a smaller number of trusted suppliers so that you can work with them to ensure continued supply in the event that you have to declare a disaster. This might cost slightly more money than a completely open approach to purchasing but it might pay off in the long run.

Assessment

Some questions that can be asked about a supplier to assess the impact criticality should include:

➤ What happens if the supplier is struck by a disaster?

➤ Will the supplier's failure have an immediate affect on your business, financial and operational?

➤ Will the failure result in total or partial loss of support levels from your supplier?

➤ Can you insulate your operations from this supplier?

➤ Is there a workaround for this supplier?

➤ Is this supplier a sole, primary, or secondary supplier?

➤ What is your exposure based on alternative suppliers?

➤ How long can your company function without the services or products from this supplier?

➤ How does the supplier affect your operational processes?

➤ Does your supplier have a business continuity plan in place?

Once each department has completed their individual supplier list and has scored the suppliers, combine the departmental list into one company supplier list. This list now will become the Master Supplier List that has documented every supplier, large and small, that the business uses in conducting its affairs and has given each supplier an impact score to determine the criticality of each supplier. Once the master supplier list is completed, categorize each supplier by type of service or product they supply. For instance, combine suppliers by raw material for production of your product; combine suppliers who supply communication services; combine distribution suppliers that are used for delivery of products. The category type of suppliers will depend on your particular business and also on the number of your suppliers. If you have a large number of suppliers, you may want to break them down into very narrow categories; on the other hand if you have a small number of suppliers you may only have three or four categories; it all depends on your business.

Categorizing your suppliers is extremely important because it will allow you to see relationships of which you may not have been aware. It may point out that you have a number of suppliers that you may be able to consolidate to a smaller number that will enable you to decrease your costs for certain supplies and streamline your supply channel, thus strengthening your supply chain. It may also point out alternative suppliers for the same products or services that you can use in the event that one of your suppliers has been affected by an outage. You may also find that any one supplier may be the only supplier in a particular category. This would indicate a potential weakness, or a single point of failure in your supply chain. Make sure that you address this issue immediately and determine if there is a quick fix for this potential risk. If there is not a quick fix then develop a separate plan to rectify this situation in the near future as soon as you are able. Once rectified, make the solution a permanent part of your business continuity plan.

Agreement

Agree with your critical suppliers on how you will deal with problems that surface as a result of a disaster. For instance, how will the supplier communicate with you if your communications lines are down? Do you operate with your supplier via EDI or other electronic means of communications? In today's environment, look for ways to utilize the Internet to facilitate communications with your suppliers. Look for web-enabled software that allows you to communicate orders, invoices, and other documents and information. Get your suppliers to agree to utilize these same communications methods in dealing with you. Document these agreements, develop operating policies, and document how these policies will be enforced if necessary. Investigate workarounds, such as producing paper copies for use rather than relying on computer-generated documents; this solution may not be elegant but it might just save your business. After a disaster occurs, communications lines or electronic means to communicate with your suppliers may be offline. The main point to remember is that during a disaster a reliable process is one that is repeatable and standardized, and where terminology and techniques are clearly defined. The process doesn't have to be elegant to work; it just has to work until you are able to bring up your standard operating procedures.

One very important point is to agree with your suppliers on the framework for resolving any disputes that may arise during a disaster, theirs or yours. For instance, it may be pointless sticking to the letter of your supply contract in the event of a disaster. While you and expensive attorneys are arguing over the point in court, you still might not be getting the products, parts, or services you need for your business. Your business would not only suffer severe financial problems from not getting the products you need; but you will also spend valuable resources, time, money, and personnel on legal issues that could have been worked out in advance. You must avoid litigation during a disaster. You have leverage with your suppliers during this planning process to work out the details of how you will operate, utilize workarounds, and how to deal with problems if a disaster occurs. If you wait until the disaster strikes your bargaining power is diminished greatly. It is always to your suppliers' best interest to work with you during the planning stages of putting together your plan to settle on how you will work outside the contract if the need arises. This planning process will also help you in future negotiations with other suppliers by putting these agreements directly into the contract before you and they commit and sign a contract for supplies and services.

Depending on how important any particular supplier is to your business, you might want to investigate alternative sources of supply. If you adopt this means, do not forget that merely identifying another vendor is not sufficient. You must ensure that the alternate supplier is in a position to supply you with your product or service as soon as possible after a disaster. The same assessment should be taken with any alternative suppliers as you did with your current suppliers.

Mitigation

As with any associated risk, events and factors that cause or even contribute to supply chain disruptions cannot always be stopped or even predicted. Any associated risk to your supply chain should be viewed as a possibility, and plans should be put into place to mitigate those threats.

Mitigation of these disruptions can be accomplished in several ways. One of the best methods of mitigating these risks is to establish a technology-based framework that will allow the prompt exchange of data and information about your supply chain activities. This framework allows the integration of data and information between your supply chain partners; it monitors your supply chain partners' activities to detect irregularities and disruptions in the "chain." It also provides for rapid resolution of disruptions as they are detected and provides a framework to manage the entire process to ensure continuity of resolutions as they occur. Some other mitigation factors to consider are these:

➤ **Current Inventory Information.** Know what products you have in stock, where your products are being stored, who is shipping your products, and if any are in transit. Knowing when your products are arriving or the scheduled arrival of products can be crucial to determine how you will respond to a disaster and how you might deploy products to your customers in the event of a disaster.

➤ **Knowing How to Communicate to Your Suppliers.** As stated before, good communications to your suppliers in the event of a disaster is crucial! If your suppliers don't know what is going on, how will they be able to respond to your request? Knowing how to and who to communicate that you have had a disaster may mean the difference in getting products or not.

➤ **Test/Test/Test.** Having your plans of what you will do in the event of a disaster documented is essential but not nearly enough. Exercising or testing your plan is crucial to the success of your recovery and the health of your company. Don't just let the plan sit on your bookshelf and draw dust. Make sure it becomes a living breathing document within your organization. The way you will interact with your suppliers in the event of a disaster will depend on how accurate and up to date your plan is and if you have actually tested your plan. Like any procedure you have in your organization, if you have never tested it how will you know if it will work?

CONCLUSION

In summary, the five elements in supply chain management continuity are these.

1. Data Collection.

Identify every supplier you have within your organization, the products they supply you, how they supply you, the product supply schedules, and how you will operate with them in the event of a disaster. Collect data on your products or services, how they are manufactured or delivered to your customers. Who are your alternative suppliers? Be certain that you collect all the data concerned with your supply chain.

2. Investigation.

Investigate alternative strategies with your supply chain. Can they ensure product delivery if you or they have a disaster? Do they have a disaster recovery plan in place and are you an important element in their plan? Can the product be drop shipped directly to customers? Can existing inventory meet the demands of high-priority customers? Who are your weakest supply chain links? Can you strengthen these weak links through better communications or alternative processes or suppliers?

Recoveries have a much greater likelihood of success when a company has already investigated their supply chain and have means in place to quickly react to a disaster with an appropriate and tested procedure and policies.

3. Assessment.

Once all your data have been collected and a thorough investigation of possible weaknesses and appropriate responses has been conducted, assess the risk associated with each supplier if a disaster or an event occurs. Identify by supplier the associated risk and the impact that may occur if the supplier is not able to fulfill its obligation to supply you with products or services. This assessment will determine the correct course of action to be taken if a disaster would occur and any additional cost that may be associated with the recovery.

4. Agreement.

Form agreements with your suppliers on how they and you will react to a disaster if it should occur. Don't wait until a disaster occurs to determine if there are any associated additional costs if your supplier has to use alternative shipping methods to supply you. Get agreement from your suppliers how to deal with contract points. Don't try to negotiate new contract terms while you are in a recovery process; and for sure don't try to litigate a solution while you are trying to recover from a disaster!

5. Mitigation.

As a company you want a supplier who is a strong and viable partner, one who has planned for business interruption and has your interest as well as their own in mind. To ensure this you should put into place a vendor management program while creating your disaster recovery plans. A vendor management program is a partnership between your company and your suppliers. Ensure that you have communicated to your suppliers the development of your disaster recovery plan and how they are important to its success. Work out any concerns they or you might have if they are not able to fulfill their commitment due to a disaster. If they do not have a disaster recovery plan in place, help them to develop one. The effort you take in helping them will be well worth the time if it clarifies everyone's role in the event of a disaster.

Remember, business continuity planning in your supply chain is your responsibility; it is not your vendors' or suppliers' responsibility for managing the impact to your business.

PART THREE
PREVENTING DISASTER

CHAPTER 15

FIRE
Burning Down the House

Books have the same enemies as people:
fire, humidity, animals, weather, and their own content.
—Paul Valery

INTRODUCTION

A fire can severely damage a business. The amount of damage is determined by the fire's location, its timing, and its size. Fires damage a business' property through heat, through smoke damage, and through damage caused by trying to put it out. (Did you ever see the gusto with which a volunteer fireman swings his fire ax?) Stolen objects can be recovered and returned. Water-damaged objects can be cleaned and restored. But burnt objects and documents are destroyed forever.

A fire can have far-reaching impact on a company's profitability. Depending on the size and location of the fire, the damage may include:

➤ **Structural Damage.** A fire can destroy or weaken walls, floors, ceiling/roof assemblies, and structural support. Smoldering fires often make a home within walls, which must be opened so the fire can be suppressed.

➤ **Loss of Valuable Documents and Information.** Financial records, personnel files, and a wide range of vital company records can disappear in a fire. Some of these documents can be reconstructed from other information sources; some of this knowledge can never be recovered.

➤ **Injury or Death.** Fire threatens the lives of your valuable employees. Some of the physical injuries will take a long time to heal, and the mental injuries can take even longer.

➤ **Customer Relations.** Your customers are expecting that the goods they have ordered will be delivered on time. A delay due to a fire will lessen their confidence in your reliability and may cost them lost profits.

➤ **Vendor Relations.** Vendors deliver their goods on credit (terms often delay payment for 60 days or more). A fire that temporarily disables your business may delay your payments to them, thereby damaging your credit— or they may demand immediate return of goods already delivered!

➤ **Building Security.** A fire is a major security threat to your business. Massive volumes of smoke pouring through your facility will sow panic among the employees. This makes an ideal opportunity for theft. Intentional fires are also set to cover up crimes.

THE ANATOMY OF A FIRE

A fire is a chemical reaction in which a fuel mixes with oxygen and is heated to a point where flammable vapors are created. A typical workplace contains numerous items that can become fuel for a fire, including furnishings, business records, interior finishes, display cabinets, office equipment, laboratory chemicals, and machining lubricants. Look around your office or workplace. Anything that contains wood, plastic, paper, fabric, or combustible liquids can fuel a fire.

The key ingredients of a fire are:

1. **Fuel.** Any combustible material.

2. **Oxygen.** The air we breathe is about 20% oxygen, more than enough to nurture a fire.

3. **Heat.** Something to raise the fuel's temperature until it combusts.

Remove any of these elements and a fire will cease to burn.

A typical fire begins as a slow-growth, smoldering process. The smoldering stage may last from a few minutes to several hours, depending on the fuel type, arrangement, and available oxygen. During this stage, heat will increase and the fuel will begin producing smoke. A smell of smoke is usually the first indication that a fire is underway. Early detection (either human or automatic) at this early stage can trigger fire suppression efforts before there is significant loss.

As the fire reaches the end of the smoldering phase, flames will become visible. Once flames have appeared, the fire will begin to spread. The temperature of the burning object will quickly exceed 1800 degrees F. At this point, a room's contents will ignite, structural fatigue becomes possible, and occupant lives become seriously threatened. Within 5 minutes, the room temperature will be high enough to ignite all combustibles within the room. At this point, most contents will be destroyed and human survivability becomes impossible.

As a fire progresses from the smoldering phase into open flames, there are some chemical interactions underway. Let's use a piece of wood as an example. Wood contains all sorts of stuff like water, minerals, and volatile organic compounds. As the heat source applied to the wood exceeds 300 degrees F, the volatile organic compounds begin evaporating. This is typical of a smoky fire. Eventually, the fire gets hot enough and these vapors begin to burn, which is typical of a fire with a lot of flame and not a lot of smoke.

Fires are classified according to their fuel. As we shall see later, the method used to attack a fire is generally based on the type of fuel that is burning. Each class of fire has some basic concepts that can be used to reduce the likelihood of occurring. The classes of fire are:

➤ **Class A Fires** are made of up ordinary combustibles, such as paper. Class A fires can be prevented through good housekeeping practices such as keeping all areas free of trash and the proper disposal of greasy rags.

➤ **Class B Fires** are based on gases or flammable liquids. These fires can be prevented by never refueling a running or hot engine, storing flammables away from spark-producing sources, and by always handling flammable liquids in well-ventilated areas.

➤ **Class C Fires** are fires that were ignited by electricity, such as may be caused by an overloaded wall outlet. Sometimes, the electricity is still present when you move in on the fire. Class C fires can be prevented by inspecting for worn or frayed electrical wires and promptly replacing them. Never install a fuse with a higher rating than called for by the manufacturer. Keep electrical motors clean and monitor them for overheating. Always have a wire guard over hot utility lights to prevent accidental contact with combustibles.

➤ **Class D Fires** feed on flammable metals, such as magnesium. These fires are very difficult to extinguish and must be suppressed by use of a special fire fighting agent.

RISK ASSESSMENT

Given the seriousness of a fire, what can we do? The easiest and cheapest thing you can do is to identify potential fire hazards and eliminate them. Every company should implement an employee awareness program to identify and eliminate potential fire hazards.

Begin by identifying what it is you are trying to protect. Offices move around, interiors get redecorated, and vital records repositories spring up in new executive offices. Rarely are a company's fire protection plans updated to protect this ebb and flow of equipment and documents around an office. Begin by making a list of your facility's critical areas and ensure they are adequately protected.

Next examine your building's layout. Minimal fire safety is governed by local building codes and fire safety regulations. Violating these codes can shut your business down more thoroughly than any fire! Hire a fire safety engineer consultant to evaluate the adequacy of your existing fire alarm and suppression systems. If money is an issue, invite in the local fire inspector. They will provide a free evaluation of areas that should be changed and those that must be changed.

An added benefit to using the local fire inspector is that they can explain something about the fire potential of other occupants in your building or surrounding buildings. They would be aware of nearby facilities that store or use combustible liquids, etc. They can provide a wide-area picture of your fire threat and the ability of local services to contain it. Is there something in your facility that will require special fire suppression equipment to control a fire? For example, how quickly should you expect the first fire truck to arrive on scene (this indicates the volume of fire suppression you should provide yourself). Is your facility in the country or in the city? If your facility is in a rural location, do you have a pond nearby to refill the fire trucks?

Evaluate your facility's fire program. If it isn't written and available to employees, then it isn't worth much. Ensure that the fire safety plan is incorporated with your other emergency plans as well. Things to look for include:

➤ Automatic fire suppression systems to contain a fire. The most common approaches are gas fire suppression systems or sprinkler systems.

➤ Internal barriers to a fire in the form of fire doors and firewalls to hinder the spread of a fire. Place special fire barrier emphasis on expensive computer and telecommunications rooms.

➤ Well-marked emergency exits that are kept free from clutter.

➤ Automatic fire detection to alert occupants and the local fire department. Automatic fire detection systems are especially important in areas that are not normally occupied, such as closets, attics, and empty rooms.

➤ Manual fire alarms as a means to quickly alert all occupants to evacuate.

➤ A system of fire extinguishers and fire hoses that can be used to contain small fires. Both types of equipment required trained operators.

Many fire hazards in the workplace are employee-related items such as space heaters and coffee pots. Review any existing policies concerning the use of these items. Consider including these issues the next time that your company safety policies are reviewed:

➤ **Personal Space Heaters.** These are popular in colder climates in the winter time. As companies economize by lowering workplace temperatures, some people compensate by purchasing personal heaters to sit under their desk. The danger here is the heaters can start a fire. Heaters provide the elevated temperature necessary to start a fire, and fuel is all around it. Heaters may be overturned, left on after hours, or have something pressed against them that could catch fire. If possible, heaters should be banned. If that is not practical, then an acceptably safe heater must be identified by the company for all who need one.

➤ **Coffee Pots.** Banning coffee pots is a fast way to make enemies all across the company! However, like all electrical appliances, the issue is not that they are in the building but that they may be of low quality or left on with no one to attend them. The best strategy is to select a high-quality coffee maker that is as safe as you need it to be in your environment (office, factory, warehouse, etc.). Require that someone occasionally checks to ensure that the appliance is turned off when not in use. A timed electrical outlet set to normal business hours can be used to ensure the pot is turned off at night.

➤ **Overloaded Outlets.** Sometimes the tendency is to add more and more extension cords and surge protectors to a single outlet to feed the ever-growing flood of office electronics. This should not be allowed. A periodic safety inspection should be made of all work areas, and overloaded outlets should be immediately addressed with either the addition of more outlets or the removal of the extension cords.

➤ **General Housekeeping.** Simple housekeeping can be a major source of fire prevention. Some people seem to want to keep their offices and workspaces as simple and uncluttered as possible. Others seem to be following them around and stuff their papers into the recently cleaned-out areas. Excess papers and other materials are potential fuels to a fire. If you have valuable documents that you must retain, then treat them as such and store them properly. Utility closets and rarely used facility areas must be inspected regularly to ensure no one has started an unauthorized storage depot.

Another easy housekeeping issue is to ensure that nothing is blocking your emergency exits or the paths to them. Sometimes boxes and factory components find their way into aisle ways and around exit routes. These must be moved immediately. If they are truly needed, then an adequate storage place will be found. Otherwise, they need to go! Use Form 15-1, Sample Fire Poster, on the CD-ROM to help get the message out about fire safety.

BUILDING A FIRE SUPPRESSION STRATEGY

Once you have controlled the possible sources of fire, the next step is to look at how you will suppress a fire if it occurs despite all your efforts. Handheld fire extinguishers and automatic detection and sprinkler systems are the most common means of fire suppression.

A thorough understanding of fire safety systems can help you to evaluate your company's existing safeguards to ensure they are current, adequate, and focused on employee safety. Before tackling a section in your plan for fire safety, be sure to inspect your existing company plans. This area may already be adequately covered.

Fire Extinguishers

Fire extinguishers can be used to contain very small fires. They lack the capacity to attack large fires. The contents of a fire extinguisher's bottle determine the type of fire for which it is best suited. For example, using a water-filled fire extinguisher to fight an electrical fire would be a bad thing to do. Electricity from the source that started the fire may still be active and travel up the stream of water and injure the extinguisher's operator. The "class" of the extinguishers corresponds to the previously described class of fires. The types of extinguishers include:

➤ Class A uses pressurized water to cool the material below its ignition temperature. This deprives the fire of its fuel. Never use a class A extinguisher on an electrical fire!

➤ Class B uses foam, carbon dioxide, or a dry chemical to smother grease or flammable liquid fires. This deprives the fire of its oxygen.

➤ Class C uses carbon dioxide, dry chemical, or halon to smother the fire.

➤ Class D uses a dry powder specifically for the metal fire being extinguished. In most cases, the powder dissipates the heat from the burning materials so it will cool below its combustion level.

➤ An ABC-rated extinguisher is a multipurpose dry chemical extinguisher that is good for class A, B, or C fires. However, the extinguishing agent may leave a residue that is mildly corrosive and potentially damaging to electronic equipment.

➤ A BC-rated extinguisher is a dry chemical extinguisher that is good for flammable fluids and electrical fires, but not suited to containing class A fires.

Fire extinguishers have conspicuous labels that identify the class of fire for which they are suitable:

➤ ABC-rated extinguishers are almost always red and have either a spray nozzle or a short hose. Halon extinguishers look identical to ABC-rated units. These units are lightweight.

➤ Water-based extinguishers are generally chrome colored and are quite large.

➤ Carbon dioxide (CO_2) extinguishers are usually red with a large tapered nozzle and are quite heavy. Care must be taken when handling these units because the contents are under very high pressure. CO_2 extinguishers must be weighed to evaluate the volume of their contents.

After any use, fire extinguishers must be inspected and recharged. You cannot "test" a unit and then return it to its rack. It may not be ready for you when it is needed most!

Most organizations have an ongoing maintenance program to inspect fire extinguishers monthly and to promptly recharge and repair leaky or discharged units.

Fire extinguishers are useless if no one knows how to use them. Include basic fire safety and the proper use of fire extinguishers in your company's annual safety briefing. Rules for using fire extinguishers are:

1. Always fight a fire with your back to your escape route. If the escape route is threatened, leave immediately.

2. Remember the acronym **P.A.S.S.**:

P ull the pin.

A im at the base of the flames.

S queeze the trigger.

S weep from side to side.

In summary, know the location and type of fire extinguishers in your work areas—and in your home. Ensure they match the types of fires that are most likely to occur in these areas.

Detection Systems

Fire detection systems are required in most states to protect human life. They also alert you to the presence of a fire so it can be contained with minimal damage. The earlier that an alarm is equipped to detect a fire, the more expensive it will be, and the greater maintenance it will require. However, in some areas of your facility the extra expense will be well worth the money.

Detection systems provide early warning to allow for evacuation and fire containment. Fires do not always occur when people are standing nearby. They can occur at night, in vacant rooms, in back closets, or even behind cabinets. Be sure that you have the proper detection system in all these places—and a way for someone to react to it. A fire alarm system that sounds at night when no one is there does you little good. It must be connected to a remote alarm monitoring facility (usually the same company that monitors your burglar alarms).

There are two signs of a fire that can be detected: heat and smoke. Both these can damage your facility without flames ever touching an object. In a previous section we briefly discussed the characteristics of a smoky fire and a fire that was more flame than smoke. As we cannot be sure if a fire will be a slow starter (smoky) or fast and furious (little smoke), you should install both types of alarms in sensitive areas.

There are three basic types of fire detection alarms.

1. Photoelectric detectors detect smoke from smoldering fires. These are fires that generate a lot more smoke than heat, due to the fuel that is burning and the temperature of the fire. This is the most common type of detector.

2. Ionization detectors are better at detecting fires that have more flame than smoke. Flash fires can be ignited based on the fuel and heat source combination, such as in some industrial applications.

3. Temperature detectors detect excessive temperatures from fires or other heat sources.

A fire alarm system must do more than just ring a bell. It should

➤ Trigger the closing of fire doors.

➤ Activate the early fire suppression system (usually CO_2 or halon) if the fire is in that room.

➤ Release electronic locks so that people can get out and rescue crews can get in.

➤ Notify the people within the facility to evacuate. This should at least include both audible and visible (strobe lights) alarms.

➤ Notify the fire department of the emergency.

➤ In some cases, shut down automatic factory equipment.

Sprinkler Systems

Fire protection experts believe that automatic sprinklers are the most important feature of a fire management program. Properly designed, installed, and maintained systems are your first line of defense again a fire.

Fire sprinklers are the cheapest method of containing a fire while people evacuate a facility. They are most effective during the fire's initial flame growth stage. Sprinklers will contain a fire's growth within a few minutes of their activation. More than half of all fires are contained by two or fewer sprinklers. A typical sprinkler system will deliver 25 gallons of water per minute. Sprinkler systems offer several benefits to building owners, operators, and occupants.

Television dramas give sprinkler systems a bad name. It is highly dramatic to see a matrix of sprinklers begin spewing water across a large open office. Life, however, is a bit more mundane. Sprinkler systems only spit water from activated sprinkler heads. They do not waste water on a place where there isn't enough of a fire to activate a sprinkler head.

These benefits include:

➤ Sounding the alarm. Most sprinkler systems are connected to an alarm system that sounds when the sprinkler head is activated. Sometimes this is by detecting the flow of water in the pipe.

➤ Sprinklers are always on duty. Even if no one is present when a fire starts, the sprinkler will activate.

➤ Early detection reduces the amount of heat and smoke damage and allows for a more orderly evacuation of the facility.

➤ Sprinkler control of fires minimizes intrusion opportunities because the fire is contained and detected early.

➤ Insurance companies normally offer reduced premiums for buildings with sprinkler systems as compared with buildings without them.

When selecting a sprinkler, consider:

➤ Desired response time. How fast do you want the sprinkler to kick on?

➤ Criticality of what you are protecting. The value or importance of what the sprinkler protects can move you to a more expensive quick-reacting sprinkler system.

➤ The volatility of what you are protecting.

➤ Aesthetics.

➤ Normal room temperature.

For most fires, water is the ideal extinguishing agent. Fire sprinklers apply water directly onto flames and heat. Water cools the combustion process and inhibits ignition of adjacent combustibles. Basic sprinkler systems are a relatively simple concept that consist of three primary elements:

1. The first element is a dependable water supply. Water must be available even if electrical service is lost.

2. The second key element is to connect the sprinkler heads to the water supply through a network of water pipes. Rusted, weak, clogged, or too-narrow pipes will reduce the effectiveness of a sprinkler system.

3. The third element is the sprinkler head. At intervals along these pipes are independent, heat-activated valves known as sprinkler heads. The sprinkler head distributes water onto the fire.

The sprinkler head is a valve attached to the pipe that is "plugged" by a fusible link. This link might be plastic, solder, or anything that will melt at the desired temperature. While a fire is in the smoldering stage, the heat output is too low to activate a sprinkler. As the heat increases, the sprinkler's thermal linkage begins to deform. If the temperature remains high as it would in a growing fire, the sprinkler's thermal linkage will fail within 30 seconds to 4 minutes. This releases the sprinklers' seals and allows water to flow.

A sprinkler head has five major components: a frame, a thermally operated linkage, a cap, an orifice, and a deflector. Sprinkler heads vary among manufacturers but all use the same basic components.

➤ **Frame.** The frame provides a structure that holds the sprinkler components together. Frame styles can be low profile, flush, standard, or concealed mounts. Selection of a frame type depends on the area to be covered, the type of hazard to protect, and visual effect desired.

➤ **Thermal Linkage.** The thermal linkage controls the water release. In normal use, the linkage holds the cap in place and keeps water from flowing out of the pipe. When the link is heated and gives way, the cap is released allowing water to flow. Common linkage types include soldered metal levers, frangible glass bulbs, and solder pellets.

➤ **Cap.** The cap provides the watertight seal over the sprinkler orifice, held in place by the thermal link. When the thermal link fails, the cap is released and water flows out of the orifice. Caps are always made of metal.

➤ **Orifice.** The opening in the water pipe at the base of the sprinkler valve is called the orifice. As its name implies, this is the opening in the water pipe where the water comes from. Orifices are about 1/2 inch in diameter. The orifice size may vary from larger for hazardous areas to smaller in home sprinkler systems.

➤ **Deflector.** The deflector splatters the water stream shooting out of the orifice into a pattern that is more efficient for fire suppression. The deflector styles vary: mounted above the pipe, mounted below the pipe, and sideways in a wall mount. Deflectors mounted above the pipe are found in ceiling plenums. Below-the-pipe deflectors are commonly found in office ceilings—just look up!

➤ **Water Source.** A key element in your sprinkler system is a reliable water source. This can be from public water systems, rural lakes, or water cisterns. Wherever your water comes from, it must be ready when the sprinkler cap pops off or it has all been a waste of time.

If your water source is not reliable, then water must be provided from more than one source. The supply of water must be sustained until the fire is extinguished. Along with the sprinklers, the water supply may be called upon to support the fire department's fire attack hoses. If so, then both requirements must be met. Things to consider when evaluating your water supply:

➤ It must be resistant to drought. Dry conditions outside increase your fire chances. If drought dries up your water supply, sprinklers may not work to full capability.

➤ Pipe failure can keep water from where it is needed. If your pipes cannot support the water flow, then again the sprinklers will not work to full potential.

➤ In conjunction with the need for water flow is a need for water pressure. The water supply must be able to maintain a steady water pressure or a pressure tank system must be added.

Sprinkler water pipes are the way to ensure a steady water flow to the sprinkler head. Steel is the traditional material used. There are many other features available for sprinkler systems:

➤ **Alarms.** The most basic fire alarms that are built into a sprinkler system are based on gongs that sound as water begins flowing in the sprinkler pipes. There may also be pressure switches and detectors at the sprinkler head to identify where the water is flowing to.

➤ **Control Valves.** A control valve allows you to shut off the flow of water to sprinkler heads. If the fire is out, the sprinkler cannot stop by itself. Remember, that open sprinkler head is spewing about 25 gallons of water per minute over your carpets, desk, and down the hall. Once the fire is extinguished, the sprinkler's water source must be shut off promptly. Shutting off the water to the sprinkler system is also useful for allowing periodic maintenance on the pipes and sprinkler heads. There is also a drain valve to allow the water in the pipes to drain out for easier maintenance. The control valve is kept locked to prevent an arsonist from disabling your sprinklers, so ensure a key is available when needed.

There are four basic types of sprinkler systems:

1. **Wet Pipe.** By far, this is the simplest and most common type of sprinkler system. In a wet pipe configuration, water pressure is constantly maintained in the sprinkler pipe. The advantage is that the only delay in action is however long it takes for the link to fatigue. The disadvantage is that the pipe may leak or the sprinkler head may become damaged and accidentally discharge.

Wet pipe systems have the fewest components and are the easiest to install. They are the easiest to maintain or modify. After a fire, they are the easiest configuration to restore to service.

The major disadvantage to a wet pipe system is that the pipes must not be allowed to freeze. Frozen pipes may burst or weaken joints. Therefore the temperature of the building spaces with these pipes must be maintained above freezing at all times. This can be particularly troublesome if the pipes are run along exterior walls or in high ceilings in buildings located in very cold climates.

2. **Dry Pipe.** A dry pipe system uses a valve to hold the water out of the pipe. Instead of water, the pipe holds pressurized gas or air. When the thermal link is melted by the fire, the cap is released and the air in the pipe escapes. The water pressure pushing against the valve overcomes the declining air pressure and water flows to the sprinkler head.

Dry pipes are useful in unheated areas in cold climates. This prevents freezing of pipes, especially for exterior applications. Some people believe that a dry pipe is superior to a wet pipe because, if the sprinkler head is damaged, the surrounding areas will not be hurt by unneeded water. This is not the case. A dry pipe system would also leak and just deliver the water a bit later.

There are several disadvantages to using dry pipe systems. First, they are more complex to install and maintain. Second, the maximum size is limited, which makes it difficult to add on to an existing system later. Finally, there may be a delay of up to 60 seconds in the water flowing to a fire.

> **3. Pre-Action.** The most sophisticated approach is through the use of a "pre-action" configuration. A pre-action system uses a dry pipe approach, but the valve controlling the water is activated by a fire detection system.

The pre-action system uses a two step process to fire suppression. The first step is when a fire detection system detects a fire. This releases the valve and allows water to enter the pipe. The second action is when the sprinkler head's thermal link fatigues and allows water to flow onto the fire.

Disadvantages of the pre-action system include higher initial costs and higher maintenance costs. There is also a short delay while the air in the pipe is displaced by water.

A variation of the pre-action configuration is the deluge system. A deluge system is triggered by a fire detector and releases water through all the sprinkler heads over a given area. Deluge systems are used wherever high-velocity suppression is required, such as a paint booth and in chemical storage areas.

> **4. Water Mist Systems.** An emerging technology is a sprinkler system that uses a water mist to suppress fire. Micro mists discharge fine water droplets at a very high pressure, which has been shown to control fires with very little water. This technology minimizes secondary water damage to your property.

An automatic sprinkler system is your best first line of defense against fires. A properly designed and installed system is very reliable. If your sprinkler water pipes will be subject to freezing temperatures, use a dry pipe or pre-action system. Remember, most system failures are due to poor maintenance. Always consult a sprinkler system professional before selecting or modifying a sprinkler system.

ACTION STEPS FOR YOUR PLAN

Two areas that should be included in your plan are storage that can resist the fire for your important documents and the evacuation of personnel safely from the building.

Fire-Resistant Storage

One defense against the damage caused by fire is the use of fire-resistant storage, which can be anything from a small cabinet to a large room. Fire-resistant storage is based on preventing combustion by removing oxygen from a fire (remember the three key ingredients to a fire?).

"Fireproof" containers consist of thick walls and a tight-sealing door. These containers are called fireproof because their thick insulated walls will protect documents and other valuables against a small, short-duration fire. The containers themselves are fireproof and will not burn, but the contents are what you really want to protect.

In a large or long-duration fire, the benefit of these containers is less complete. As the heat outside the container rises, the thick insulation walls slow the flow of heat into the container. If the container remains in the midst of a hot fire, eventually the interior temperature can rise high enough to begin a smoldering fire. This incipient fire will quickly die as soon as the oxygen within the container is consumed.

Depending on the amount of heat applied to the container, the contents can still be seriously damaged. At high interior temperatures, flammable materials will still char (until the oxygen runs out). Magnetic media will deform at temperatures above 125 degrees F and 80 percent humidity, much less than the heat required to burn paper.

Underwriter's Laboratories has a standard for evaluating the protection value of a storage container. A "one hour fire rating" interior will not exceed 350 degrees F when exposed to an external temperature of 1700 degrees F. A "two-hour-rated" container would withstand this temperature for 2 hours and withstand a drop of 30 feet (since a fire of this magnitude would probably also cause structural failure).

After the fire has passed, you must allow adequate time for the interior to cool below the fuel's flash point. Remember, the container starved the fire for oxygen. The interior still has fuel (your valuable documents). If high heat is still present and you open it, then you get to see your documents flash into smoke before your eyes! Always allow plenty of time (at least a day) before opening a fireproof container after a fire.

What does a typical business need to store in a fireproof container? Begin with:

➤ Cash, checks, and securities

➤ Software licenses

➤ Magnetic backup media (use a container specifically rated for this)

➤ Engineering documents, including work in progress

➤ Any legal papers difficult or impossible to replace, such as tax documents

➤ Works of art

➤ Precious materials

Other steps to take include these:

➤ Make copies of critical documents and magnetic media and store them in a different building.

➤ Place fireproof storage containers in your facility where they won't fall through a floor weakened by a fire (such as in the basement or on a ground floor) and where there is minimal material overhead to fall on it and crush the container. Ruptured containers will let the fire in to burn your documents!

Evacuation Planning

An essential part of any emergency plan is to provide a way to safely evacuate the building. A well-thought-out evacuation plan will ensure that everyone has left the building and that no one was left behind. This helps the fire and rescue squads to focus their efforts on locating people known to still be in the building. Without an accounting of who may be still inside the structure, the fire department may needlessly risk their lives searching the entire structure, wasting time they could be using to contain the fire damage.

Evacuation plans come in many forms.

1. **Evacuate the Building.** Everybody out, due to perhaps a fire or earthquake.

2. **Evacuate the Area.** Everyone must leave to avoid a natural disaster such as a hurricane or a forest fire.

3. **Evacuate into a Shelter.** Leave your offices for the storm shelter for safety against a tornado, etc.

Normally, evacuation involves getting everyone out of the facility as quickly as is safely possible. Evacuation planning is an 11-step process.

1. Determine the conditions that would trigger an evacuation.

2. Establish "evacuation supervisors" to ensure areas are clear, to assist others, and to account for everyone at the rendezvous site.

3. Pull together a system for accounting that everyone is out of the building or in the storm shelter.

4. Assign someone to assist anyone with disabilities and those who may not speak English. This is important in your customer areas, reception room, delivery driver lounge, or any other area where outsiders may be in your facility. They need someone to show them what to do and where to go.

5. Post evacuation procedures around the facility. Also, post maps showing the nearest building exits. Identify primary and alternate evacuation routes. Ensure they are clearly marked.

6. Designate key people to shut down critical or dangerous operations during the evacuation. This might be transferring toxic chemicals, halting automated paint spraying operations, or disconnecting power to high-voltage equipment.

7. Designate someone to quickly secure the petty cash box, close the safe, and lock all cash registers before evacuating the area.

8. Ensure evacuation routes are always kept clear and unobstructed by material. They should be wide enough to handle the volume of people that may need to use them. The route should not take anyone near other hazardous areas in case the disaster spreads rapidly.

9. Install emergency lighting in case electricity fails during the evacuation. Some companies also install "knee-high" exit signs near the floor so that anyone crawling under the smoke can still find a building exit.

10. Designate outside assembly areas for each section of the building. Assembly areas should be well clear of the structure and clearly marked so they are easy to find. Some companies use signs on their parking lot light poles. Assembly areas should be located away from the roads required by the emergency crews so they do not interfere with incoming fire trucks.

11. Actions in the assembly areas should be clearly understood by the evacuation supervisors. To facilitate the headcount, department rosters should be kept adjacent to the evacuation exits so they can be picked up on the way out. These rosters list the name of every employee and long-term contract worker by department.

a. Keeping rosters up to the minute is an impossible task. Instead, use the roster to see if the normal staff is accounted for. Ask if the missing are out sick that day or known to be working elsewhere in the facility.

b. Ask if any other contract employees were working in the area that day.

c. Ask if any visitors were in the area that day.

d. Forward the completed roll call results to the Evacuation Command Center as soon as possible. Note the names and last known locations of any missing people. **DO NOT** reenter the building as these people may be at a different rendezvous point.

In some emergencies, you will evacuate your workspaces and head to the storm shelter. This might be as protection from a tornado. Evacuation supervisors will ensure the orderly entry and exit from the shelter and ensure that space is fairly allocated.

Employee training is essential if plans are to be executed as written. Training should be a part of initial employee (and long-term contract worker) orientation. An annual refresher class along with an evacuation drill will improve employee understanding and reduce some of the panic and chaos of an actual emergency.

FACTS ON FIRE

Fire in the United States:

➤ The U.S. has one of the highest fire death rates in the industrialized world. For 1998, the U.S. fire death rate was 14.9 deaths per million population.

➤ Between 1994 and 1998, an average of 4,400 Americans lost their lives and another 25,100 were injured annually as the result of fire.

➤ About 100 firefighters are killed each year in duty-related incidents.

➤ Each year, fire kills more Americans than all natural disasters combined.

➤ Fire is the third leading cause of accidental death in the home; at least 80 percent of all fire deaths occur in residences.

➤ About 2 million fires are reported each year. Many others go unreported, causing additional injuries and property loss.

➤ Direct property loss due to fires is estimated at $8.6 billion annually.

Where Fires Occur:
➤ There were 1,755,000 fires in the U.S. in 1998. Of these:

◆ 41% were outside fires

◆ 29% were structure fires

◆ 22% were vehicle fires

◆ 8% were fires of other types

➤ Residential fires represent 22 percent of all fires and 74 percent of structure fires.

➤ Eighty percent of all fatalities occur in the home. Of those, approximately 85 percent occur in single-family homes and duplexes.

➤ Causes of fires and fire deaths:

◆ Careless smoking is the leading cause of fire deaths. Smoke alarms and smolder-resistant bedding and upholstered furniture are significant fire deterrents.

◆ Heating is the second leading cause of residential fires and the second leading cause of fire deaths. However, heating fires are a larger problem in single-family homes than in apartments. Unlike apartments, the heating systems in single-family homes are often not professionally maintained.

◆ Arson is the third leading cause of both residential fires and residential fire deaths. In commercial properties, arson is the major cause of deaths, injuries, and dollar loss.

Source: National Fire Protection Association (1998) Fire Loss in the U.S. and Fire in the United States 1987–1996, 11th edition.

Additional information can be found at:

The National Fire Protection Association at www.nfpa.com.
The U.S. Fire Administration at www.usfa.fema.gov.

CONCLUSION

Fire is one "natural" disaster that knows no geographic boundaries. Where there is fuel, oxygen and heat, you can have a fire. The key elements to avoiding a disaster caused by fire are:

1. Assess the risk to your business.

2. Have policies in place to reduce the risk from fire.

3. Have appropriate detection mechanisms in place.

4. Know how to extinguish a fire as quickly as possible.

CHAPTER 16

HUMAN RESOURCES
Your Most Valuable Asset

You win with people.
—Woody Hayes

INTRODUCTION

Your Human Resources department has an important role to play in Business Continuity Planning. Major business emergencies are very stressful events. From a business perspective, stress reduces the productivity of the workforce. The Human Resources department ensures that the "people side" of an emergency is addressed for the best long-term benefit of the company. They can also take steps to ensure that the essential human needs of the workforce are addressed so that they are ready to resume work as soon as the problems at hand are addressed. In manufacturing jargon, the Human Resources specialists are the "human machinists" who maintain the "people" machines.

Employees spend a great deal of their life at work. Their workplace becomes a separate community for them, somewhat paralleling the one around their home. They make friends, celebrate life's milestones such as marriage, childbirth, or death, and develop an identity with those around them. When this is properly cultivated by the company, the employees become more productive. If this aspect is ignored by the company, then this can turn negative and become a drag on employee efforts. Business Continuity Planning for Human Resources works to address the employee concerns during a crisis to minimize the negative impacts and position the work force for a successful recovery.

Most Human Resources departments already have in place approved procedures to handle some of the things addressed here. These processes should be incorporated into the plan insofar as they touch on Business Continuity Planning.

HUMAN RESOURCES ISSUES

Stress

Probably the biggest issue with employees in the aftermath of a major disaster is stress. The mental injuries caused by serious incidents have long been recognized. Like a physical injury, if it is properly treated, it will heal—if ignored, it may fester and grow worse over time. Different people react in different ways to the traumatic incidents around them. Everyone has their own way of coping with the sights and sounds of a disaster, which is shaped by their personal environment, faith, family, and many other factors.

Any major emergency can bring on a great deal of stress to your employees. It could be a co-worker who was injured or killed in a fire, witnessing serious workplace violence, or even working in a building when a major earthquake strikes. Stress-related reactions are normal in people and can be addressed with prompt action.

"Combat stress is a natural result of heavy mental/emotional work, when facing danger in tough conditions. Like physical fatigue and stress, handling combat stress depends on the level of your fitness/training. It can come on quickly or slowly, and it gets better with rest and replenishment."

Source: U.S. Army Office of the Surgeon General

Pertinent to Business Continuity Planning is how stress relates to your workforce. Critical incidents are traumatic events that create overwhelming stress in some people. The reaction may not appear for many days. Employees may have known someone who was seriously injured or even witnessed the accident. Symptoms include heightened tension, anxiety, disturbed sleep, and impaired concentration. If the employee's reaction interferes with their ability to work, they may need professional assistance.

Even after the emergency has passed, stress-related damage may linger for months. It is essential that confidential follow-up counseling be available to employees for up to 1 year after the event.

A good place to begin is to include a mental health counseling program along with your other company medical benefits. These programs assist employees with coping with the stresses of everyday living. Mental health counselors assist employees with a wide range of issues from divorce to handling teenagers to moral dilemmas. Mental wellness programs address the essential human concerns: social, emotional, occupational, physical, intellectual, and spiritual.

Another proactive step is to include stress management techniques in routine employee training. Helping employees cope with their daily stresses will reduce recovery time after injury or illness. It also strengthens their ability to cope with problems, reduce depression, and even to increase energy levels. Some companies operate in a high-pressure environment in their normal day-to-day activities. For these companies, routine mental health counseling can include stress management and stress relief training. This should also include training in ways to recognize stress in others and steps they could take to help them.

When drafting the services contract for stress and mental counseling, include a clause for on-site support in the event of a disaster. By adding this on-demand service, you have someone to call on short notice to assist in an emergency. Be sure you understand how that company reacts in wide-area disasters and where you are on the overall priority in the event that all their clients call at once.

In an emergency, there are three basic intervention techniques that can be used with your employees. The first is known as "defusing," which allows workers to release their pent-up feelings much like relaxing immediately after strenuous exercise. In this approach, employees meet at the end of the day in informal discussion groups. Topics in these groups range from what has occurred to stress management techniques. These meetings are short and last about an hour. This is best done no later than the day after the tragic event.

A more formal and focused discussion called a "debriefing" is a common way to address stress accumulated from a major event. This meeting may run for hours and allows people to explain their feelings and interpretation of the events. For many, this meeting will release the emotions that have been shoved aside in the rush to complete the recovery. It may also clear up misconceptions of what happened in the emergency or its immediate aftermath.

Person-to-person "crisis counseling" is the most time-consuming action for those most affected by the event. This should be made available to anyone who wants it but, based on how the debriefing or defusing sessions went, you may identify some people to refer to this program.

After the disaster strikes, everyone is focused on containing the damage, and so should you. However, the damage you are containing has nothing to do with the facility. After calling in your mental health service, walk around the disaster area and talk to the workers. Your containment action is to identify overstressed people whose judgment may be too impaired to safely assist with the immediate recovery. Dazed people are a potential danger to everyone, so gently escort them to emergency medical authorities. If this stress is not promptly addressed, the symptoms may linger for months. This will affect their ability to make critical decisions, rendering them of much less use as workers.

Employee coordination is a significant part of Human Resources contingency planning. As the recovery continues, the Human Resources specialist can refer to the employee skills matrix to suggest substitutes for recovery workers, allowing them to rest. Workers assigned to a rest period must not be allowed to continue working but must rest. This implies accommodations for a rest site.

Symbols and sensitivity are extremely vital to the surviving employees. Expressions of support for the families, organizing and attending memorials for the victims, and supporting trusts for the families are positive outlets for grief. Someone must organize these activities. Often the Human Resources department will help find sponsors within the departments and represent the company at all functions.

Labor Management Issues

A disaster will disrupt your employees' normal routine. While there will be plenty of work to do to get the business back on track, it will not be the same work done during normal times. What type of work employees will be expected to do and how they will be paid needs to be thought out before a disaster occurs.

What is the company policy for paying employees after a major disaster that prevents them from working? This is a very sensitive issue. On one hand, you have some hourly workers who need every paycheck on time to keep food on the table, and you have others with the financial resources to carry their family for several weeks until the paychecks begin flowing again. Continuity of income is a key family concern. Is it fair for a company to pay someone to sit at home? If you discharge your employees because recovery will take several months, then how much will it cost to hire and train new ones?

Some companies use an outside payroll service and some handle their paycheck generation internally. However you do it, consider cutting regular paychecks for all employees during the emergency. If using an outside concern, quickly arrange for regular paychecks. Hold all overtime claims until after the emergency is passed. If this will be too difficult, in the interim, consider paying everyone the same amount and reconcile the differences later.

Decisions like this are often complicated by legal requirements surrounding employment law. There is also the moral issue of abruptly discontinuing a family's potentially sole source of income. Things to consider:

1. Depending on your local laws, at the time at which you tell your employees that due to a disaster, they have no work until the damage has been repaired, did you just incur unemployment insurance liability? Is there a minimum notification period that must first be met?

2. If the people are not being paid, have their medical benefits, etc. just stopped? What are the local employment law issues involved with this?

3. If the people are not being paid, can they take vacation or sick leave to keep the money flowing? How will you handle the ones who immediately call in sick?

4. Your best or highly technical employees may be the first ones to jump ship if they think their family's cash flow is in jeopardy. How much does it cost to attract new talent to your company?

5. What is fair?

   ➤ How much should you pay the people who you do not need for the containment and recovery effort and who are sitting at home?

   ➤ How much should you pay the people working long hours on the disaster site assisting on the containment and recovery effort?

6. What should you do if you are paying the people to sit at home, and when you call them to come in and help with the cleanup, they refuse? What if they claim illness?

7. Is it easier to provide some sort of reward (bonus, extra vacation, promotions, etc.) for the people on the recovery site than to take away something from the employees temporarily sitting at home?

Containment and cleanup efforts can be very manpower intensive. As order returns to the emergency scene, there may be a need for general labor to help the emergency teams during the containment and the recovery. Rather than automatically call in outside temporary help, you can tap the people on your payroll who are sitting at home. Some additional issues to consider include:

1. How will you select people to come in to help with the clean-up and "extra hands" effort? (We will address building an employee skills matrix later in this chapter.)

2. How will you track ("clock in and clock out") people to the worksite to fairly account for their hours? This could be a clipboard, an honor system, or delegated to the supervisors to report daily.

3. If someone's house is swimming in 2 feet of swirling muddy water, is it fair to demand that they come in to work? What if this is a key person?

4. What if someone is physically able to help but refuses as the assigned job is beneath their dignity? (This is where your leadership skills will be tested!)

Outside Help

In an emergency, it can be very difficult to obtain high-quality technical help. Wide-area disasters can strain local technical talent pools. Usually, the first company to call for help will soak up everyone that is available. For example, in the event of a major hurricane, such as when hurricane Andrew struck south Florida in 1992, the area of devastation was so broad that all the available local technicians were fully occupied both with helping their companies and with saving their own homes. Even with the help of outside electrical line repair crews, it took over a month to fully restore electrical power.

Bringing in outside help is also fraught with perils. There is no time to obtain background checks, no time to carefully select the best people and to weed out the highly paid incompetents. These well-meaning people may have technical knowledge, but how much do they know specifically about your processes, equipment, and software systems? If you have used specific technical consultants in the past, they may be suitable—if they are available! Remember, you are in an all-out struggle to restore a minimal level of service to your facility. Every day your facility is hindered or inoperable, your competitors are becoming ever closer to your customers!

If you are a branch in a large company, you should be able to borrow the technical staff members from sister companies to begin emergency repairs. This avoids the problems of background checks and the high cost of consultants (since they are already employees). They may also be familiar with the company's terminology, priorities, and methods of approaching a problem. To tap this pool, you will need a telephone number at which they can be reached at any time.

To prepare for this, establish a mechanism to borrow personnel from other departments/divisions or branches/facilities within the company. Arrangements can be on a mutual exchange basis, depending on who needs what when. This will require additional funds for transportation, housing, and meals, but overall is much cheaper than hiring consultants.

Family Assistance

In a wide-area disaster, you have the additional problem of people worrying about their families and their property. This can be a major distraction to people working on the disaster site. Wide-area disasters might be earthquakes, hurricanes, or severe winter storms. Time spent helping your employees' families in a wide-area emergency can pay off with key workers staying focused on their jobs.

It is not unusual to have single parents among your key employees. In a wide-area disaster, their normal childcare arrangements may unravel and unless you assist in finding some arrangement, this key person may not be available. Another potential issue is if the disaster glances off of your facility but severely damages your employees' homes. What can be done?

To address these issues, temporary Human Resources policies can be implemented. These would include such things as:

➤ Flexible or reduced work hours so that childcare issues can be addressed.

➤ The establishment of a temporary day care facility for the children of recovery workers.

➤ Providing emergency shelter for employees' families, to include food and essential comfort items.

➤ Assisting employees with requesting help from relief services, such as the American Red Cross, Salvation Army, or government agencies.

➤ Stress counseling for families who may have lost their home or whose family members may have been injured during the disaster.

➤ Soliciting donations of goods or money from other company sites for the relief of the workers' families.

RISK ASSESSMENT

While we like to think that our employees are an asset, there are times when they can be a threat to the business. Stress can cause some individuals to act out violently, labor unions can go on strike, and key employees can be called away by government agencies in times of national emergencies.

Workplace Stress

Routine workplace stress affects different people in different ways. Some people take it in stride and leave it at the door when they go home. Others internalize their frustrations and slowly build a wall of resentment and distrust. Routine stress can be created by many things such as:

➤ An abusive management climate

➤ An unstable employment environment where people are (apparently) discharged for minor offenses

➤ Peer pressure that focuses on singling out co-workers for abuse

➤ In-fighting among managers

In extreme cases, workplace stress may manifest itself as a violent outburst by the employee against co-workers, critical machinery, or even themselves. Personnel managers must be on watch for stressful situations and implement stress abatement actions whenever the tension level rises too high. Personnel managers can casually monitor for excessive daily stress levels by regular employee meetings, walking around the facility chatting with workers, or even attending departmental staff meetings. All can serve to raise awareness of a problem area or person.

Some companies provide an outlet for overstressed workers with free and anonymous counseling services as an ongoing part of their workplace violence abatement programs.

Labor Stoppage

Few business situations evoke such strong emotions as a labor strike. Even the existence of a contingency plan for addressing such a thing makes people uneasy and fearful that the company is planning some vague negative action toward the workers. Given this perception, such plans are normally not kept in the master binders with the rest of the Business Continuity Plans. However, they must exist somewhere close at hand, be tested, and kept up to date.

Whatever the reasons for a strike, your employees will experience a wide range of emotions and reactions toward it. Always remember that when the dispute is settled, the strikers will again become your coworkers. Efforts must be made to eliminate the likelihood of long-lasting animosity by staying on top of the situation and not permitting events to escalate out of control. In this sense, the Human Resources department is "in the middle" watching both the strikers and the people crossing the picket line and dealing firmly with anyone who violates the rules.

The primary goal of a strike is to stop production as an economic lever to force a favorable agreement with the company's owners or managers. The Human Resources department will be deeply involved with those negotiations. These negotiations are beyond the scope of this chapter. What we have included here are those Human Resources actions useful for maintaining the flow of labor into the facility during a strike. From a Business Continuity standpoint, our goal is to maintain a flow of goods to your customers to meet their business needs. This outflow of finished goods also provides some cash flowing in to lessen the financial impact of the strike.

Depending on your local labor laws and agreements, a strike usually does not include management personnel. Employees classified as "Management" or supervisory can enter or leave the facility and either continue production at a reduced level, finish uncompleted goods in the facility, or ensure that production equipment is properly maintained. They should be prepared for long hours and very few days off.

However you use your management workers, you must be sure that prudent measures are taken to safeguard them whenever they come into contact with the strikers—usually when crossing the picket lines. Courts are inclined to grant large damage awards to victims of strike violence, but the party that pays this cash depends on how well the company has documented its mitigation steps. Will you be paying the court, or will it be the strikers?

To begin with, every person who enters the facility needs to be informed about the security situation before they come in contact with the picket line. This includes suppliers, contract employees, and management employees—everyone who will cross the picket line at your request. They should be fully aware of the security procedures and any special circumstances, such as threats of violence.

In all dealings with strikers, frequently refer to your legal counsel to ensure that your actions are in accordance with your company's legal rights. At the first instance of strikers engaging in disruptive behavior, obtain a court injunction against the union to restrain them from any illegal activity. This will put everyone on notice that their behavior is being monitored. By firmly addressing any violations of your company's rights, the potential for violence is decreased.

BEFORE THE STRIKE Before the strike begins, or immediately after the beginning of a wildcat strike, all management personnel should be thoroughly trained on the company's security policies, procedures, and activities that will be used during the strike. Do not assume that management will know your current policies or procedures. This is one of the mitigation actions to prevent problems before they occur. Document when this training occurred, an outline of the topics discussed, and who attended.

Preparations for a strike include:

➤ Ensure that all exterior lights are in good working order. Stockpile spare bulbs in the building in case existing lights are put out.

➤ Do not allow any hourly workers into the facility without specific company permission. Some workers may disagree with the strikers or may be essential to maintaining the facility's equipment.

➤ When a strike is imminent, gather supervisors and security personnel together to explain the importance of documenting any strike-related incidents. Provide preprinted forms to everyone to help ensure all the essential elements are captured. Everyone must have copies of these forms readily available.

➤ Remind your management team that they too will be held accountable for their conduct when crossing the picket line.

➤ Explain to everyone who may come in contact with a picket line as to their rights and the rights of the picketing workers.

➤ Change all external locks immediately before the strike.

➤ Establish a hotline to immediately report any incidents so prompt legal action can be taken.

➤ Establish an information telephone number where management personnel can call in to find out when and where they are needed.

➤ Establish a series of sites, usually shopping center parking lots, where anyone needing to cross the picket lines can meet and carpool into the facility.

➤ Verify that all company employee ID cards are current.

To reduce the chances of an incident, there should be as few vehicles as possible crossing the picket line. A Human Resources specialist should take the lead and form management employee carpools. When it is time to cross the picket line, assemble all the workers at a parking lot and pool them into as few company-owned vehicles as possible. Then all the vehicles can cross the picket line at once, both coming in and going out. Coordinate the crossing with security before it occurs.

Contractors must be informed and briefed as to the proper crossing of the picket line. Their company may not permit crossing the line, so you must check with each critical contractor before the onset of a strike. Truck drivers belonging to a union may refuse to cross a picket line. When using these companies, they must be notified to send out a supervisor or independent truck driver to move the truck across the line. Otherwise, you may see sorely needed incoming shipments turn away from your gate.

When negotiating service contracts, determine what their guidelines are for crossing a picket line. Often, they only require that the company send a vehicle to pick up their technicians and carry them across the line. Spell out your expectations as a clause in all your service contracts. At the first whiff of trouble, do not expect any further contractor support. It is considered your fight— not theirs.

RECORD KEEPING It is important that security guards maintain an ongoing record of illegal activities by strikers. This record will be invaluable if the company attempts to recover damages from the union at a later time. These records must include the time of the incident, the events leading up to it, and the incident itself. Review and collect these records daily.

One of the best ways to do this is by videotaping the entry gate any time that someone crosses a picket line. In this way, you can prove to the authorities who did what, and when. Although its primary intent is to deter violence by the picketing workers, it can also identify anyone crossing the picket line in a manner that may further inflame the situation.

Assign a photographer to all entrances with a video camera. Anonymity is a critical element of picket line violence. If you can strip that away, then most people will be reluctant to participate in an incident. A company employee who can identify incoming workers should accompany the security guard along with a trained photographer with a video camera (at each gate). Keep close tabs on who is manning the picket line, their attitude, and what they are doing (chatting, drinking alcohol, shouting, fighting, sleeping, etc.). Like anyone else, they will pass their time on the picket line in their own fashion. Immediately report problems noticed on the picket line (such as alcohol) as a written protest directly to the union president, who likely will not want a problem on the picket line either.

Establish a hotline to report any incidents so prompt legal action can be taken. The Human Resources department should assign someone to take these calls around the clock and to address them accordingly.

Collect all records daily and guard them closely. Things to record:

➤ The exact wording of picket signs must be recorded every hour, along with the number of pickets present and, if known, their names. Incidents can happen in an instant. After a violent incident, many of the people involved or witnesses may quickly disperse, making it difficult to determine who was present.

➤ Anytime anyone crosses the picket line. This can be people entering or exiting the facility as well as deliveries into the facility and finished goods leaving the facility.

➤ Any tampering with security arrangements around the company perimeter, such as cut fences, attempts to force open locks, and other signs of attempted sabotage.

FACILITY SECURITY During the time that labor negotiations are underway, we must safeguard the facility and all workers against violence or sabotage. The key component of this is a reliable security force to enforce the integrity of the facility's perimeter and ensure that anyone crossing the picket line can do so in safety. Success requires extensive planning and actively seeking to eliminate the opportunities for mischief by the strikers.

As the strike approaches, be on guard for major sabotage by outgoing employees. There are normally choke points about your facility where very expensive damage can be done with little effort. Post someone to watch over them as the strike deadline approaches and the workers file out. This minimizes the chance of a casual attack.

Anyone crossing a picket line for the benefit of your company becomes your responsibility to safeguard. They should call ahead and notify you when they will cross the picket line. Pass this on to your security staff, which should be present and monitoring the situation. They should park far enough away from the fence that objects cannot be tossed over onto their vehicles.

Everyone must be told of any violent incidents or threats. Employees, contract workers, everyone should make their own determination as to the safety of the situation. Also inform the police and fire department of every threat and incident. Remember, some companies will not allow their employees to cross a picket line out of fear of violence. Others will enter your facility if you will transport them both ways across the picket line.

Ensure that the local law enforcement authorities are informed about the strike as soon as it begins. It is important that they are aware that this is a potential flashpoint, and call them in whenever a confrontation is brewing. If they do not respond in a timely manner, then you must escalate the matter immediately to higher governmental authorities (county and then state).

All employees must show their employee ID card to security personnel when entering the facility. In this way you can track who is entering and leaving the facility. In a labor dispute, there is often additional security staff hired and they do not know even the top executives by sight. Ensure that all employees and contractors invited in during the dispute know they must show their company identity cards to gain entry.

On the other hand, there is no requirement for these people to show their identification to anyone on the picket line. This is a tactic by strikers to slow down picket line crossing, which may increase the likelihood of an incident. Management employees should avoid speaking to or provoking strikers on the picket line. Vehicles should proceed very slowly but resolutely across picket lines without touching any strikers. They have a right to picket and you have a right to cross the picket line.

NATIONAL GUARD AND MILITARY RESERVES As illustrated during the second Persian Gulf War, members of the National Guard and Reserves may be called upon for national service for extended periods of time. Their civilian jobs are protected by federal law during their absence. The Human Resources Manager should ensure that someone is cross-trained in their critical job skills (because deployments come on short notice). Your list should include their name and their unit (sometimes the news services announce a call-up before the individuals are notified).

Every year, National Guard and Reserve units perform at least 2 weeks of annual training. Although this is often done during the summer months, it can occur any time during the year. From time to time, Guard personnel may attend a formal training school for the 2 weeks in lieu of the unit's training. In either event, the individual will be absent for this time and cannot be forced to take vacation for this time period. Continuity plans should include cross-training someone to cover these absences.

A similar issue involves volunteer emergency services such as EMTs and firefighters. In a wide-area emergency, they may be called away for several days. An example might be a flood or an earthquake. Although they are volunteers, it may be negatively viewed by the employees and the community at large if you blocked their departure.

ACTION STEPS FOR YOUR PLAN

The two most important activities to cover in your plan are developing an employee skills matrix and communications. The skills matrix will track skills such as who knows CPR, who might be trained EMTs, etc. The employee skills matrix will allow you to apply the proper human resource at a particular problem at the right time. A well-designed communications plan will ensure that the right information is given to the right people at the right time.

Employee Skills Matrix

An employee skills matrix is a tool that compares the skill levels employees have attained for specific tasks or processes. From a Business Continuity perspective, this matrix can quickly identify who we can call on to stand in for a key person who is not available during an emergency. As a movie so succinctly put it a few years ago, "Who ya gonna call?" Much of this information is buried in the Human Resources department's personnel files and may have been included in resumes when the workers were hired. In a crisis, you need it at your fingertips.

An employee skills matrix can also be used to identify people from other departments who have an understanding of a business process or function. These people become excellent departmental plan testers as they know enough about an area to help test it but are somewhat distant from the plan's authors. Use Form 16-1, Skill Matrix by Job Process (see CD), to help you build a skills matrix for your organization.

Skills matrices are another area where Business Continuity Planning can overlap with other business areas for mutual advantage. The matrix developed for your Business Continuity Planning can be used to drive company training plans, management succession plans, identifying people for staffing new business initiatives, and a wide range of other uses. It is not unusual to uncover valuable employee skills not previously realized by company management.

When you are staffing your disaster containment and recovery teams, the matrix is a handy tool for identifying a specific individual to the proper group. Each team requires knowledgeable people but slightly different skill sets. The matrix can also identify people to write or review specific subplans.

BUILDING A MATRIX Skill matrices tend to be unique to an enterprise. They can also become quite long. To gauge the level of detail you want to use, model a matrix on a single department. This should reduce the likelihood that it will be too large (time consuming to complete) or too small (causing you to revisit people to fill in the gaps). Another caveat is when employees with skills in one department work in a different area of the company. This is common in departments such as Data Processing where an understanding of accounting makes it easier to support their programs. These cross-department skills are very important to note, but what was once a clean department by department report becomes somewhat entangled.

Assembling an employee skills matrix is a multistep job. The first step starts with a department's job descriptions. The department manager must ensure that there is a published job description for each position in their area and that these descriptions are up to date. The job description should generally describe the routine tasks that this person is expected to perform along with any specific (usually unique) duties required. As a side benefit, current job descriptions can provide the text when posting or drafting new job openings.

You can use the example skills matrix provided or follow along and build your own. It is recommended to use a spreadsheet program such as Microsoft Excel to build the matrix as it easily organizes information into rows and columns. The first step is to skip down a few lines (or "rows" in spreadsheet jargon) and begin entering the names of all employees in a department, from the manager at the top to the part-time clerk at the bottom. It is easier to build the matrix if the names are sequenced according to their work teams.

On the row above the names, we can enter column headings for the skills each of the people may have. The first headings should be for common skills expected of all employees, which may include safety issues, company process knowledge, or product knowledge. Each person will be assigned a score based on these skills. Each skill listed should encompass a process within the department. This is where you must determine how much is included in each category. As the matrix begins to fill in, expect that additional categories will be required. Categories are usually grouped by related subject matter. In an accounting department, you might group all the processes associated with accounts receivable with general ledger or accounts payable. Under these, subcategories might be collections, credit, reconciling purchase orders to materials receipt, etc.

After you have created a column heading, write a brief narrative of what you mean by that skill and any important subtasks it must include. Most people may claim mastery of a subject but, in reality, they mainly understand a subset of it. Few people know a process or subject completely from edge to edge. This narrative will be useful when debating what is included in a particular process. See Form 16-2, Skill Matrix by Technical Skill (see CD), for another example you can use.

RATING EMPLOYEES Consistently rating all employees can be a major challenge. Each evaluator will see things through the filter of their preferences and biases. Some people are by nature more modest about skills, some are overly boastful. If the workers feel this will be a tool for identifying future career advancement, then they will have an incentive to overstate their accomplishments.

The first step is to show the matrix to employees and ask them to rate themselves in each category. They should have a copy of the narrative that each skill is supposed to encompass so they can make their determination. They should understand that these ratings will not be used in a negative manner.

The second step is for the supervisor to rate the employees according to the same matrix while the employees are filling it in. The supervisor should not see the worker self-evaluation before filling in their opinion. They should make notes as to why someone was assigned a specific rating. This information will be very useful later. The scores entered by the employee and by the supervisor should be noted side by side on the matrix, maybe using a different color.

A meeting between the employee and their supervisor should provide individualized discussions to determine a final rating. This should not be a confrontational event since the supervisor may not always be aware of the extent of a team member's experience. Be sure to quiz each person for any outside hobbies, community services, or other skills that would be helpful to the Business Continuity effort. An example is someone that is a paramedic with the local volunteer fire department. Another example is someone serving in the Armed Forces Reserves or National Guard. Their military training may be pertinent.

Based on the final scores in each area, the manager can identify specific persons to provide backup support during an emergency or even when the primary person is ill. If there are few people skilled in a specific area, the matrix can be used to identify training opportunities. See Form 16-3 on the CD-ROM for a sample of Skill Matrix by Job Function.

ADDITIONAL SKILLS MATRIX BENEFITS A manager can use this completed matrix in many ways. One use is to develop a disaster management succession plan for filling key roles in a crisis. This plan identifies who will temporarily stand in for a key manager who has been killed or disabled. Succession plans are essential for Business Continuity but should not be used to identify "pre-determined" promotions. That removes the incentive for people within that organization to work hard because the next promotion is already locked in. Succession plans are also used to identify executives who should not travel together in the event of a transportation tragedy.

When conducting periodic performance reviews with your employees, include a review of the job descriptions. Any changes in responsibilities or expertise can be noted on the Employee Skills matrix and passed on to the training plan. Fairly applied, such recognition of skill improvement can become a powerful performance motivator.

Many managers have ambitions of advancing their careers. A completed and current employee skills matrix is a powerful tool to a new manager. It provides a quick snapshot of the competencies of the team as determined by the employees themselves. Company executives should insist on current matrices to aid them in moving around managers with a minimum of production impact.

A new matrix should be developed every year to identify improving skills. If the employee skills are not improving then you must question if the manager is developing the talent in the department or babysitting a bunch of losers. Compare the matrix from year to year to ensure employee expertise is improving.

In most companies, the Human Resources department provides all non-job-specific training. The Human Resources manager ensures essential training is conducted for incoming employees and ongoing training in departments. This should include safety training for the facility in general as well as a department specific explanation.

EMPLOYEE SKILLS MATRIX AND YOUR TRAINING PLAN A current employee skills matrix can turn a passive training program (tell me what you want) into a proactive asset (I see what you might need). It highlights areas where there are too few people trained to support a business function. Depending on its depth, it can also show which general training subjects should be offered, such as Microsoft Excel training, in-house developed classes on writing ad hoc SQL queries to the AS400, etc. A close look at the matrix may even identify some in-house instructors among your ranks!

Communications

Some companies have a designated spokesperson who will handle official communications or at least communications with the news media. If your company has one, then use this section to verify that all the essential tasks are covered by them. Branch offices will normally refer any important news media inquiries to their corporate headquarters spokesperson. Use this chapter to ensure that your company's spokesperson is ready in case a disaster arises.

If you are a small company, and these tasks are not covered, then they need to be included in the Human Resources plan. Consider carefully how you will address this. It is recommended that a few stock answers be written in advance as news releases for persistent reporters. These stock answers may buy you some time to gather your thoughts for a more comprehensive news release later.

WITH THE EMPLOYEES Sometimes in the heat of the emergency, executives are so focused on the problem at hand that they forget about the other people in the company. The Human Resources department can step forward and ensure that the other employees know the degree of the problem and the status of the recovery. After all, the health of the facility is the health of their job, so they are very much interested parties. Decisive actions here will minimize the rumors, which invariably are negative.

Communicating the same message to every person can be difficult. Often in a crisis the employees are dispersed around the facility and some of them may be at home (such as the off-shift teams). Communication can be one-way (announcements) or interactive (face-to-face). One-way communications is the fastest way to communicate. Unfortunately, the message received is open to interpretation.

Interactive communication provides for questions and comments by the recipients. This tells you if the message was well received, misunderstood, or not addressing their most pressing concerns. Interactive communications methods include:

➤ Addressing people directly in groups

➤ Using a voice mail box

Addressing people directly in groups is always the most personal way to communicate. It is also a good way to gauge the mood and temperament of the people by their response to your announcements and their questions. In this approach, your immediate answers to one person may alleviate the anxiety of many in the group.

A personal address moves the communications from the distant-front-office to a face-to-face meeting. This approach allows you to tailor the message to the audience so that they hear what is most pertinent to them as well as the overall situation. The problem with face-to-face meetings is that it may be hard for a large crowd to hear you and as you address different groups, your message may vary enough that each group will perceive it differently. The questions asked by later groups may include information that would have been helpful to earlier groups. Be sure to have someone recording every question raised and the answers provided. The entire list can be reviewed after the meetings and then republished to everyone.

Using a voicemail box that everyone can dial into ensures that everyone hears the same message in the same way. Of course, you can quickly see that voicemail does not provide any forum for questions or requests for clarifications. It is useful to provide a second telephone line with someone to answer questions or where they can leave a message. The answers to the most pertinent questions can be included in the next voicemail announcement. Also, if you have a lot of employees, the line may become jammed and very annoying to use.

In a wide-area disaster where the telephone service is disrupted or limited, employees should be encouraged to call between 10:00 P.M. and 6:00 A.M. to avoid peak telephone network traffic. Even in disasters where telephone lines are saturated, they are generally available in the late night hours.

WITH EMPLOYEES' FAMILIES People work to earn the wages needed to support their families. Therefore, it is understandable that their families may be anxious that a disaster at their place of work could have a serious impact on them.

A negative or worrisome attitude by the employees' families may have a negative impact on your workforce. This will increase the overall stress level of the workers.

Similar to the choices of how to communicate with the employees, you must consider how to best talk to the families. Always remember your audience. Meeting with the families in a mass venue will require a facility to shelter them during the presentation. Avoid use of industry jargon because some families may not completely understand your message.

One approach is to establish a family information line that is normally used to pass on company information. Using a voicemail box allows for a single message to everyone. When an emergency arises, everyone knows where to dial in to. Be aware that the news media may tap into these messages if they are not kept fully apprised of the situation.

WITH SURROUNDING RESIDENCES AND BUSINESSES When an emergency occurs, make a quick assessment of whether this event will impact anyone that works or resides near your facility. They must be immediately informed of anything that will harm them, such as a fire in a toxic chemical area that may spread fumes outside of the facility. If public safety officials are on the scene, consult with them first.

When in doubt, caution and assist your neighbors in their evacuation. Provide some place where they can go, such as a nearby hotel or public facility. You should also provide basic shelter for their pets, which may accompany them.

Your goals here are to avoid the likelihood of a lawsuit for exposing an innocent person to danger by neglecting to tell them. It will also help to build goodwill with the local government and your facility's neighbors. The people may not be pleased with the forced move at the time, but they will appreciate your consideration later.

WITH THE GENERAL PUBLIC The range of people interested in your disaster may be quite wide. If the emergency involved something newsworthy (as defined by the news media—not by us), then they may show up quite suddenly on your doorstep. What you say is always open to interpretation whether you like it or not, so it is best to provide them with a written statement concerning the incident. This statement should acknowledge the incident, state that the extent of damage is still being determined, and that as further information becomes available, it will be issued as a news release. Never express an opinion about the problem's causes or the extent of the damage. It is possible that your opinions stated to the news media will resurface later labeled as an official company announcement in some sort of legal proceedings.

Caution your employees working on the containment and recovery to not speculate to anyone as to the cause of the emergency or extent of the damage. Of course, they can speak freely with properly identified law enforcement personnel but should never take for granted the true identity of the person asking questions. If you cannot guide the news media away from your employees at the disaster site, then provide an escort knowledgeable in the problem and the recovery efforts so you at least know what was said by whom. The escort can quickly clear up any misunderstandings and guide the reporter to knowledgeable people.

On the other hand, the news media's coverage of your emergency is an opportunity to showcase your company's highly competent response. All emergencies have a large element of chaos. How well the chaos is handled will directly impact the perception of interested observers. Skillful handling of the media may lead to favorable stories on this event and issues in the future. If possible, keep the news media regularly informed of the progress made and consider making key executives available for interviews.

CONCLUSION

Mitigating the physical and emotional damage to your employees is just as important as protecting your physical assets. By demonstrating concern for your employees and their families, your recovery time can be dramatically shortened. Know how your employees can help you in an emergency, and how you can help them, as it is to everyone's benefit that the business recovers and gets back to normal as quickly as possible.

CHAPTER 17

BACKUPS
The Key to a Speedy Recovery

It would take battalions of angels to protect us
from our dreaded dangers, though in a long
lifetime few of the dangers come to anything.
—Author Unknown

INTRODUCTION

In most chapters of this book, we discuss ways to protect your data from external threats. But as no amount of protection is totally secure, in this chapter we discuss tools and techniques you can use to restore your data if they are damaged or lost in a disaster. Proper backups of critical data can mean the difference between surviving a disaster and letting a disaster put you out of business.

Backing up data onto some sort of secondary media is older than computing itself. Making copies of original data goes as far back as the written word. We've come a long way from the days when monks made hand copies of important works, but the idea is still the same—to share copies of the original data and to protect against the loss of the original.

In the computer era, live data are typically stored on media designed for fast update and retrieval. Backup data are typically stored on media that is designed for making inexpensive copies, with retrieval time being a secondary concern. Today, most live data are stored on magnetic disks, and backup data are usually stored on magnetic tape or optical disk.

Gartner Group Dataquest estimates that two of five companies that experience a disaster go out of business within 5 years.

PLANNING FOR DATA RECOVERY

Effective backups that completely protect critical data require thorough planning. You need to know what you have, where it's at, and how the data are used in the running of the business. You should also review the types of threats to your corporate data to ensure that backups will provide the maximum protection in the event of a disaster. Some items to consider include:

➤ Type of backups available for your environment.

➤ Backup scheduling.

➤ Select type of backup media.

➤ Ensure backups are made.

➤ Proper handling and storage.

➤ Testing/validating your backups.

➤ Recovery of files.

➤ Back up PCs and specialty equipment to network attached storage, such as robots, time clocks, security system.

➤ Control access to rooms where backups are created or stored.

When evaluating backup products, standardize on one or at most two backup products across all platforms within your organization. Standardizing on a backup product will:

➤ Reduce the amount of user training necessary.

➤ Allow for centralized monitoring and administration.

➤ Reduce the amount of time spent managing vendor relationships.

➤ Provide operational and financial economies of scale.

➤ Minimize variations.

You should also consider what your recovery needs will be in the event of a disaster. How quickly do you need to be back up and running? Different backup processes have different time to data performance characteristics.

Think about how your backup solution will be deployed throughout your organization. How will the backup media be handled? Can tape automation be used to reduce media handling issues? A combination of local and centralized servers and network bandwidth will also influence how a backup solution is deployed.

Document your procedures for backup operations and recovery. Ensure that everything needed to completely restore your systems is being backed up properly. Don't forget to include all major system elements such as operating system software, application software, database systems, hardware and operating system configurations, e-mail, custom applications, etc. Make sure that this document is updated each time a change is made to software or to your infrastructure.

The most important thing you can do to ensure the long-term success of a recovery strategy is to make sure that the backup process is integrated into your change control and application development processes. Changes to applications will many times require changes to the backup and recovery processes. Your information technology (IT) group, charged with ensuring the integrity of the backup and recovery processes, must work with the application development group to assess the impact of application changes to the disaster recovery plan.

Identifying Critical Data

The first step in developing a backup strategy is finding all the stores of data that are scattered throughout the organization. Critical company data can reside on servers, desktop PCs, laptop PCs, PDAs (personal digitized assistants), time clocks, telecommunications equipment, factory shop floor machines, fax machines, etc. Make sure to look beyond the standard "business computer" stores of data. Many devices used in organizations require data usually stored in specialized computers; make sure these data are backed up too. Use Form 17-1 (see CD) to help organize and prioritize your backup and recovery processes.

Of course most of your data require software to be usable. The types of software that you'll need to be able to restore include:

➤ **System Software.** This includes not just the operating systems but also partition information, directory structure, configuration files, hardware drivers, and service packs. Be on guard for slight differences in the restoration hardware that might cause hard-to-diagnose system errors.

➤ **Application Software.** Most organizations have a large number of purchased applications used to run the business; ERP (Enterprise Resource

Planning) systems, POS (Point of Sale) systems, accounting, shop floor, word processing software, etc. You must ensure that the versions restored are compatible with the backed-up data files.

➤ **Source Code for In-House-Developed Systems.** Many in-house-developed applications do not have well-developed installation procedures. Make sure it includes all of the files necessary for the application to run, such as Windows .dll files or configuration files.

Other items you may need to properly restore data and applications and to be operational include:

➤ Licenses and support agreements.

➤ Registration keys.

➤ User manuals.

➤ Insurance policies.

➤ Preprinted forms (checks, invoices).

Review with your legal counsel what data are legally required information for your organization. This might include things such as personnel records, union grievances, Occupational Safety and Health Administration (OSHA) compliance records, etc. Other important information you'll want to ensure that is backed up includes:

➤ Customer lists.

➤ Contracts.

➤ Product designs.

➤ E-mail directories.

➤ Account histories.

Key stores of corporate data are the desktop PCs scattered throughout your organization. It is important to work with the users of these PCs to ensure that these important data are being backed up properly. Use the desktop computer backup request Form 17-2 (see CD) to collect information from these users about what's important on their desktop system.

Once you have located your data, the next step is to determine what your restoration priorities are. You are not likely to be able to restore everything at once, so determine ahead of time the order and priority for restoring data. Create a classification scheme such as the one shown below and make sure all data backups are assigned a classification.

Code	Time to Data
AAA:	Immediate recovery
AA:	Up to 4 hours to recover
A:	Same-day recovery
B:	Up to 24 hours downtime
C:	24 to 72 hours recovery
D:	72 hours or greater

Backup Strategies

One decision you'll need to make is the type of backup method to use. There are three basic types of backup methods available to protect your important data:

1. **Full System Backup.** This method does a complete backup of all files and folders on your server. The positive result of this method is that all the files from your server are available in one place. Locating the latest version of any one file is easy. The negative result of this method is that a full system backup requires the most amount of time, and will usually require multiple tapes (or whatever backup media you are using.) If the files on the server do not change frequently, this method will also result in a large volume of data being stored unnecessarily on multiple tapes.

2. **Incremental Backup.** This method backs up only the data that have changed since the last backup. This method makes the most efficient use of the backup media, and the backup time required is relatively short. The downside to this method is that multiple tapes must be read if several files are to be restored. Each tape since the last full backup may have to be read to restore the desired files.

3. **Differential Backup.** This method starts with a full backup, and then subsequent backups only save files that have changed since the full backup. If a file is changed after a full backup is made, then that file will be saved each time a differential backup is made. This method is faster than doing

a full backup each time, but may be slower than an incremental backup. Fewer tapes are normally required, as the last full backup and the last differential backup are all that are required to restore any file.

Your data recovery requirements will probably cause you to use a combination of backup strategies. Periodic full backups will be required, and either incremental or differential backups made between full backups.

Determine Type of Media

The next step is to select the media and process you will use in backing up your data. There are numerous types of media available, such as magnetic tape and CD-ROM, as well as choices to be made about the actual process, such as manual versus automatic, and offline versus online. Factors to think about when making this decision include:

➤ How much data are there to back up?

➤ Is there downtime during which the data can be safely backed up?

➤ Where will the data be stored?

➤ How long must the data be stored?

➤ Are there legal requirements for storing the data?

➤ Are there databases to back up?

➤ Is there enough bandwidth to support network storage solutions?

➤ Does your database support online backup?

➤ Who will back up the data?

➤ How long will it take to retrieve the backup media?

➤ Who will restore the data?

➤ Where will the backup media be delivered?

➤ What kind of network environment do you have?

➤ Will the operating system or hardware environment change in the foreseeable future?

➤ What storage devices and media are already in place?

➤ Does the prospective backup software support your devices and existing software?

Three important factors to consider are Response Time Objective, Recovery Time Objective, and Recovery Point Objective. Response Time is the period immediately following the disaster in which you are able to restore the basic functions of the business process at some minimally acceptable level. Recovery Time is the time that is required to restore the business to a state which existed before the disaster occurred. Recovery Point addresses how much data you can afford to lose without a major impact on the continuation of the business. Consider each of these three factors when answering the backup strategy questions listed above to help you find the appropriate backup strategy for your business.

Traditional offline storage methods consist of processes using media such as magnetic tape and CD-ROM. The least effective backup process is to have each user backup their individual PC using floppies, CDs, Zip drives, or tapes. Relying on users to follow the proper backup procedures on a consistent basis is a sure recipe for failure. The next best option is to create storage on a file server on your local area network (LAN) for users to store their important files. The backup process is then performed by the IT professionals managing the network, and is therefore more likely to be done properly. The backup media will be handled properly, and successful restoration is much more likely. Periodic backups of files that are unique to each machine, such as configuration files, IE bookmarks, etc., can be done by the IT support personnel. Form 17-2 (see CD) is an example of a form your users can use to let their support people know what files they would like backed up.

While using tape for backups is an old technology, there are many reasons why it should still be an important part of your disaster recovery plan. Tape backups are especially good for these items.

1. **Data That Rarely Change.** A good example is application servers, which do not store data and are only changed when an application is updated. These servers only need to be backed up when an application changes and tape is an inexpensive way to store this information in case it needs to be restored.

2. **Meeting Regulatory Requirements.** For example, the Securities and Exchange Commission (SEC) and Federal Deposit Insurance Corporation (FDIC) require almost all financial institutions to keep tape backups of their systems. These requirements were created when tape was the pre-

ferred methodology for disaster recovery, but have not changed with the availability of newer technologies.

3. **Guarding Against Sabotage.** A tape backup stored securely off-site is less susceptible to tampering by disgruntled employees.

Use Form 17-3, Data Backup Checklist (see CD), to document your backup process.

With the proliferation of high-speed wide-area networks and reliable Internet connections, online storage methods are becoming increasingly popular. Backups can be made in a real-time fashion using a connection to a backup system on your local area network. The least expensive option is to use backup software that allows files and folders from one location to be copied to another system across the network, which then acts as the backup system. This type of software should allow you to not only specify the source and destination locations, but also to specify the frequency at which you want the copies to be made. The software should also allow for monitoring of important files for changes so that they can automatically be copied to the backup system.

One such product is SmartBackup from Onlime Media. They can be reached at www.onlimemedia.com.

Backups can also be made in a similar fashion using the Internet. This adds some additional security by having your data stored away from your production location. This option works well for companies that do not operate 24/7 and can leave their PCs on and connected to the Internet overnight. Techniques that use the Internet or another wide-area network can be implemented as remote journaling or electronic vaulting. Remote journaling saves transaction logs to a remote server, so that the data can be restored using the last full backup and the transaction logs sent since the last full backup. Electronic vaulting writes the actual data to a remote system. This system could be your recovery site, or a vendor that specializes in this service.

When looking at vendors for this service, some issues to look for are:

➤ The vendor should provide regular reports documenting what is being backed up.

➤ Review the restoration process requirements with the vendor to ensure that the data can be restored quickly enough to meet your time to data requirements.

➤ The data should be transmitted in an encrypted format to prevent others from being able to see the data. Ensure that the stored data are only available to authorized employees and that they are password protected.

➤ Will the vendor back up application software as well as the data?

➤ Review the vendor's disaster recovery plans to make sure they are protecting your stored data.

➤ Define the service-level agreement (SLA) with the vendor, being clear as to the vendor's responsibilities in the following areas:

◆ Backup data retention.

◆ Recovery speed.

◆ Recovery point objectives—how current will the restored data be?

Vendors in this market include Enveloc, Inc. (*www.enveloc.com*), Netspace (*www.netspace.info*), and FirstConnect (*www.firstconnect.net*).

Asynchronous backups write data to the backup machine at the same time as the data are being written to the live system; synchronous backups are written first to the backup, then after the write is confirmed the data are written to the live machine. Asynchronous backups are cheaper and can support many systems with a single backup device; synchronous backups are expensive and slower, but are more reliable. Additional information on online backup processes can be found in Chapter 11, Networks. Figure 17-1 is a list of data backup and recovery strategies, listing their strengths and weaknesses.

Don't forget about your mobile devices such as notebook PCs; according to a Display Search report, 29.3 million units shipped in 2003—representing a 17.5 percent increase over the preceding year.

Determine Schedule

Once you've determined what to back up and what to back it up on, the next step is to determine an appropriate backup schedule. Use Form 17-4 on the CD-ROM to help create and organize your backup schedule.

Protection, Detection, Correction Option	Strengths	Risks
RAID systems	RAID can often provide 100% protection against downtime.	• RAID systems can fall victim to high-risk threats, including power problems and human errors. • Two or more drives may fail at the same time, rendering your entire system unavailable.
Mirrored systems	Mirrored systems can provide adequate real-time backup of mission-critical data.	• Mirrored systems are exposed to many threats, ranging from incorrect system configuration to human error. • If the primary system is corrupted and then mirrored, your primary and mirrored systems are both corrupted.
Backup and restoration	By performing regular backups, data can be quickly restored, and business activities can be quickly resumed, after a data loss situation.	• Backups must be made completely and consistently if they are to be of any use. This is no easy task, considering that many networks operate 24 hours a day. • Tape backups can become corrupted or fall victim to human error. • Tape restoration retrieves data from the last backup, leaving a "gap" between old and new data. This "gap" necessitates data

FIGURE 17-1: Backup strategies.

Protection, Detection, Correction Option	Strengths	Risks
		re-entry or re-creation, adding to the costs in time and money of data loss.
Electronic vaulting	• Electronic vaulting can eliminate the hassle and error potential of manual and individual tape backups. • CD backups may present fewer opportunities for backup media corruption.	• Restoring from electronic vaults may still have a restoration "gap" between old and new data. • Depending on where the vault is located, and how quickly your data can be retrieved, you may face the expenses associated with additional downtime.
Anti-virus software	Anti-virus software, when used properly, can provide constant protection against virus corruption.	• Viruses are created at an astounding rate. This means that anti-virus software must be consistently updated to remain useful and effective. • An organization's anti-virus policies are not always followed or are not as good as they could be for proper protection. • Many companies lack anti-virus plans.
Disaster recovery/ business continuity plans	These plans can provide the necessary procedures to help an organization resume vital operations and return to normal business functions as	• Although they provide procedures on how to set up operations at a hot or cold site, disaster plans often fail to address data recovery concerns and options.

(continues)

Protection, Detection, Correction Option	Strengths	Risks
Disaster recovery/ business continuity plans *(continued)*	quickly as possible following a disaster situation.	• These plans emphasize major disasters, failing to address everyday incidents of data loss and data corruption. • People fail to update their disaster plans.
Commercial file recovery software	File recovery software can provide the necessary tools to recover lost files.	• In some cases, commercial software can provide a successful data recovery. However, there are instances when these utilities can aggravate an existing problem or fail to give the advanced tools needed for a complete data recovery. • Some commercial software products attempt to repair damage to a drive or volume before attempting to recover data. This can lead to additional data loss.
Data re-entry/ restoration	When files are lost or corrupted, data re-entry can be the easiest and most convenient way to resume normal business functions.	• Data re-entry is not always the most efficient recovery method, especially when the value of time, money, and the data is high. • With users manually re-creating lost data, the data re-entry process is especially vulnerable to human errors.

Protection, Detection, Correction Option	Strengths	Risks
Data protection experts (internal and external)	An internal or external "expert" can help recover lost or corrupted data.	Individuals make the mistake of attaching the "expert" label to anyone who knows more about computers than the individuals do. This means that data recovery operations may be left in the hands of someone unqualified to properly perform the job. Not only does this put data at risk, it may lead to additional data loss, downtime, and expenses for the company.
Data recovery services	• Data recovery service providers can successfully complete a full data recovery. • Data recovery service provides a fast turnaround time and quick restoration. • Data recovery restores your current data. • Data recovery services are cost effective.	• The capabilities of all data recovery companies are not the same. Because data recovery tools and techniques are typically developed "in-house," and because some tools and techniques are more powerful than others, some data recovery companies are better equipped to provide a total recovery. • In the event of a massive disk drive crash, even a professional data recovery company may be unable to retrieve lost data.

Source: The Data Recovery Solution, a White Paper by ONTRACK Data Recovery, Inc. ©1998 ONTRACK Data International, Inc.

Smaller operations tend to run their backups manually or rely on some-one to change the tapes each day. Manual processes are only as good as the people doing the work, and this is normally a job assigned to a low-ranking person in the organization. Automating your backup process makes the process much more reliable.

Based on research conducted with over 400 enterprises, Connected Corpo-ration estimates the average company-wide compliance with "manual" backup solutions to be approximately 8%.

Proper Storage and Handling

Proper storage of backup media is critical to ensure its availability when needed. Backup media should be stored off-site away from your computer sys-tems, to prevent them from being damaged in the same disaster that affects your systems. If your company has multiple locations, the cheapest method is to simply rotate backups between locations. Of course the locations must be far enough apart so that they are not affected by the same disaster.

Magnetic storage media requires every bit as much care as printed docu-ments. The useful life of a tape can be sharply reduced by improper storage or handling. Unlike paper, you cannot readily look at a tape and determine if it is still readable. Improper handling can result in a very fine tape being ren-dered unreadable.

Steps must be taken to ensure that no contaminant of any kind comes into contact with the recording media. Never touch the magnetic surface at any time. Therefore, magnetic media, whether reel tapes, cassettes, floppy disks, or whatever, should only be stored and used in a very clean environment. In these rooms, smoking, eating, and drinking must be prohibited. Ideally, an air filtration system will be employed to screen out airborne contaminants.

Magnetic media are susceptible to variations in temperature and humid-ity. If storage and operating temperatures vary more than 15 degrees F, allow time for the media to adjust to the different conditions. Allow 4 hours for every 15 degrees F of temperature difference. Strong sunlight will also damage mag-netic tape.

The components that make up magnetic tape will react with moisture and slowly begin a process of breaking down the chemical bonds. Carefully avoid water and moisture when tapes are exposed.

Before using a tape, inspect it for surface damage. Look for any debris on the tape (but never touch the media itself without lint-free gloves). If in doubt, discard the tape. Always return tapes promptly to their protective containers. Minimize how much tapes are handled. Ensure that any tapes being returned to service are first thoroughly bulk erased.

Magnetic tapes should never be dropped or treated roughly. When in storage, they should always be stored on end and never stored "flat" (with the reels parallel to the table). Magnetic tapes are susceptible to damage from magnetic fields. Never store tapes on or near machinery, in windowsills, or on top of electronic devices.

Another option is to use a commercial data storage facility. These facilities are specially designed to archive media and protect data from environmental threats.

Create Policies

The next step is to develop your official backup and recovery policy for the organization. The policy should address who owns the data, how to classify the data, how to prioritize the restoration of the data, and define the process for ensuring the backups are made. Use the sample policy in Form 17-5 (see CD) as a template to develop your backup and recovery policy.

TESTING VALIDATING YOUR BACKUPS

Testing the data restoration plan is critical. Do not wait until a disruption occurs to discover holes in the plan. Data recovery testing should include the following levels:

➤ Individual files.

➤ File directories.

➤ Business application data.

➤ Entire database.

➤ Operating system.

➤ Complete system recovery.

Testing is the only way to ensure that the data will be available in the event of a disaster. Your operations people need to practice various levels of restoration to ensure they'll be successful if a real recovery is necessary.

One option that is becoming available in some areas is the use of testing laboratories. These facilities allow you to test your data recovery plan using their hardware and operating system software. Many of these facilities were initially set up for testing application software on multiple platforms, and are now making their facilities available for testing data recovery plans. Using one of these facilities avoids the time and expense of duplicating hardware if your plan is to purchase new hardware immediately after a disaster. These facilities allow you to:

➤ Validate and troubleshoot your plan.

➤ Establish an accurate time frame for full recovery.

➤ Overcome potential failures in a noncritical situation.

➤ Accurately identify your specific hardware and software needs.

➤ Cross-train personnel to prepare for disaster recovery.

One such facility is the Platform Lab in Columbus, OH. They maintain an inventory of most hardware, operating systems, and database software, and are available on a day-rate basis for testing your recovery plan. They can be reached at www.platformlab.org.

Use the checklist in Form 17-6 (see CD) when reviewing your backup procedures.

CONCLUSION

While you can't eliminate all the threats to your critical data, you can be sure to have the data duplicated away from the disaster to prevent their loss. The most common way to do this is through the use of backups. The critical issues to consider in planning to back up your data are:

1. Identify critical data.

2. Determine the recovery time objective.

3. Develop a backup strategy.

4. Determine storage media.

5. Develop a backup schedule.

6. Create effective polices and procedures for backups.

7. Test, test, test.

CHAPTER 18

VIRUS CONTAINMENT
High Tech Pest Control

*I think computer viruses should count as life.
I think it says something about human nature
that the only form of life we have
created so far is purely destructive.
We've created life in our own image.*
—Stephen Hawking

INTRODUCTION

One of the biggest threats to the health of your computer systems are computer viruses. Like a vandal in the night, a computer virus can sneak into your systems and cause immense damage to applications and data. The products of some very bright people with a warped view of the world and too much time on their hands, computer viruses can in some cases steal your valuable data, and in most cases corrupt and destroy important corporate information. Like any other possible disaster, a well-thought-out process to protect your systems and to recover from an attack can prevent a virus attack from putting you out of business.

How important is this? Imagine the cost to recreate the vital data on a single PC. Imagine the nasty calls from your valued customers who received e-mails from a virus running on your computer! Imagine your corporate data splashed across the headlines. Or even more likely imagine that everyone discovers at once that their PC no longer works!

WHAT IS A COMPUTER VIRUS?

A computer virus is a specially designed program that can spread itself by infecting other files or the memory of a computer and then make copies of itself.

They are spread by users sharing media such as floppy disks and CDs, or can be spread through network connections and the Internet. Viruses normally infect executable programs, as the virus software must be executed before it can act. A virus can also infect the boot sector of hard drives or floppy disks, or can be imbedded in word processing and spreadsheet documents that contain macros, which are in themselves tiny programs. It is also possible for HTML documents containing JavaScript or ActiveX controls to spread viruses.

Viruses can be made to do anything that a software program can do. This includes formatting your hard drive, erasing data, copying data to another location, or sending an e-mail. What the virus actually does depends on the skill and intent of the person who designed the virus. Many viruses are designed to damage the infected systems, while others simply reproduce as rapidly as possible.

Some viruses are designed to read desirable information on the infected system (such as a password file) and send a copy to the author of the virus. This type of program is known as a "Trojan Horse," named after the famous hollow wooden horse that allowed the Greek soldiers entrance into the city of Troy, where they proceeded to unlock the city gates to allow in the rest of their army. A Trojan Horse program pretends to be another program, and silently performs some malicious act when the user runs it. The user never knows this is happening. Just like the Greek soldiers, a Trojan Horse program is usually used to allow other programs access to your computer. Like the citizens of Troy, by the time the attacked is detected, it is too late to stop it. And unlike Troy, you may not even know your passwords are floating around on the Internet.

In October 2000, Microsoft was the victim of a Trojan Horse virus. The Wall Street Journal reported that the virus allowed access to important source code for 12 days or so—with initial reports citing as long as 5 weeks—by installing a backdoor Trojan Horse on an employee's personal computer used to dial into the corporate network remotely. The backdoor, which was most likely installed through virus software, probably stole the remote user's passwords and e-mailed them back to the attacker, who was later able to log on to Microsoft's network as the authorized employee.

RISK ASSESSMENT

If your system communicates in any way with the outside word, it is vulnerable to infection. The first step is to identify all possible ways that a virus can enter your system. Potential problem areas include floppy and CD drives, Internet connections, mail gateways, and wireless network devices. It is critical to have a complete and up-to-date inventory of all these possible sources of virus infection. Once a virus has been detected, this inventory will be critical for containing the spread of the virus throughout your network. It may even be necessary to temporarily shut off access to the outside world to prevent the reinfection of your network while you clean up the mess and patch your defenses.

Most companies closely scan their incoming e-mail and pay close attention to attachments. However, if people use third-party e-mail services through their messaging service, it will bypass this security. Downloading files from the Internet can allow viruses into your PC.

The next step is to have a complete inventory of all mail, file, and Internet servers on your network, as an infected server will continue to infect any devices to which it is connected. In addition to performing a physical inventory, you should perform a port-scan to look for undocumented web servers that may have been installed without going through proper approval channels. Once all the servers have been located, make sure that all operating system security patches and anti-virus software updates have been applied to each one. Someone in the network administrative group should be assigned the responsibility of staying current with the endless barrage of virus alerts and operating system patches and updates.

BUILDING A VIRUS PROTECTION STRATEGY

A good protection plan consists of multiple layers of protection; each is designed to prevent the further spread of any viruses that reach your system. A typical network consists of the PCs used by most users, the servers to which they connect to share files and applications, and personal devices (usually personal digitized assistants, PDAs) that users can carry around with them. The servers are typically connected to the Internet and the outside world through an Internet gateway, and the PDAs are periodically connected to the user's PC to synchronize data. Figure 18-1 shows a typical network layout.

This layout suggests that four levels of protection are necessary to protect all your devices. Level 1 consists of your connection to the outside world through your Internet gateway. Level 2 includes your print, file, e-mail, and application servers. Level 3 consists of the standard desktop and notebook PCs that are connected to the various servers. The last layer, level 4, consists of devices that share data with the standard PCs such as Palm and Pocket PC devices. Each level should have the appropriate virus protection to attempt

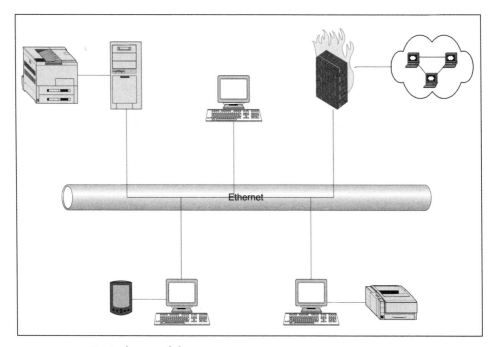

FIGURE 18-1: Typical network layout.

to stop an infection from moving to the next level. As you move from level 1 to level 4, the number of devices and amount of work necessary to clean up an infection can increase dramatically.

Before you begin assembling the company's anti-virus defenses, some groundwork must be accomplished.

1. Establish a written and published policy that no one is to load any software on their PCs. This includes software from home. This is also an antipiracy action.

2. Establish a written and published policy that no outsiders can plug into the network (which would defeat your Layer 1 protection). This includes contract employees, no matter how long they work there. Also, enforce this restriction on the radio frequency (RF) network.

3. Establish a written and published policy that data disks from vendors and anyone else outside of the organization must be checked for viruses before use.

4. Establish a written and published policy that all notebook PCs that ever leave the premises (traveling) must have up-to-date anti-virus software running on them.

5. Establish a written and published policy that no matter what the windows that pop up on a PC say, you never disable the anti-virus software to load or view anything. If you see such a window, leave it up and call tech support to clear it.

6. Ensure all your users are educated about what these policies are and why they exist.

LEVEL 1: Internet gateways. This is your first line of defense against viruses. Most organizations have only one or two gateways to the Internet for the entire company. This protection can be in the form of scanning software or rules-based policy enforcement. Scanning software allows you to check each file for viruses before allowing it to pass into your network. Rules-based policy enforcement allows you to create rules to block viruses, based on known content (e.g., I LOVE YOU in the subject line), even before the anti-virus manufacturers have released a signature. In addition, rules can be applied to look for old viruses that may have been reclassified as hoaxes. It is also important that your Internet gateway software or service report viruses found to demonstrate the value of the time and resources used here and to help track down the source of the virus.

LEVEL 2: Servers. Server-based virus protection not only protects the servers themselves from problems, but can also prevent devices connected to the server from using the server to spread a virus. Every server that stores e-mail messages or is used for storing files must have virus protection software installed and up to date. You should have both real-time protection to check each file as it comes in, and scheduled scanning to check the entire system periodically for a virus infection.

LEVEL 3: Desktop and notebook PCs. Desktop and laptop PCs represent the largest number of devices in most organizations. Many viruses come in to an organization through one of these devices, then infect the server, and then in turn infect other devices on the network. Anti-virus signatures need to be kept current, any real-time monitoring functions must be enabled, and scheduled scanning should take place frequently to make sure you are protected. Logon scripts can also be used to check that the virus protection is up to date before allowing the device to connect to the network. No computer should be allowed access to the network without ensuring that its antivirus software is up to date; this includes users accessing the network remotely.

Although many companies focus their efforts on the level 1 defenses, users can bypass them by loading files from unscreened sources such as from home, from a friend, downloaded from the Internet, etc. Therefore the added protection of desktop anti-virus software is needed in addition to the layer 1 and 2 software. Notebook PCs are purchased specifically for taking away from the desk and normally off the premises. They should *always* run current virus protection software.

LEVEL 4: PDA-type Devices. PDAs are relatively new to most organizations; the viruses and virus protection software are not as well developed as at the other levels. There are currently few viruses that infect PDAs, but the number is growing each day. If you have both Palm and Pocket PC devices, try to find virus protection software that will work on both to limit the number of software packages that must be supported.

Develop a Detection Plan

Once access points have been identified and your servers are inventoried and up to date, the next step is to develop your process for when a virus is detected. Policies and procedures must be developed to plan your response to a virus attack. The plan will include who will lead the virus response team, how the virus will be contained and eliminated, and how the postmortem will be conducted to prevent a repeat infection. An important part of the plan will address your use of independent security audits and ethical hacking to identify security and virus vulnerabilities in your systems.

Just as important as keeping your protection up to date is being able to detect a virus infection as quickly as possible. Symptoms vary widely depending on the nature of the virus, but common signs of a virus infection include:

➤ Strange e-mail messages sent to many recipients.

➤ Computers with reoccurring file corruption problems.

➤ Systems operating slower than normal.

➤ Strange errors that appear when starting applications.

➤ Web server logs that contain irregular or more than usual entries.

Communication between your support personnel is critical for the early detection of a virus infection. A single incident of a corrupted file or the single occurrence of a strange e-mail may by itself not raise any red flags, but repeated incidents reported in a short period of time may signal that a virus infection has occurred. Without sharing information about incidents that occur throughout your network, a virus infection will take considerably longer to detect. Someone within your network support group or help desk should be responsible for monitoring support incident trends that may signal that a virus has infected the network.

If your operations span several time zones, date- and time-sensitive viruses may be detected first in the most eastern operations of the firm. Use this variation in time zones to your advantage whenever possible, making sure those operations that detect a virus early inform the other operations about its occurrence. This may just give the rest of the company enough time to prevent the infection, or at least eradicate the infection if it has already occurred but has yet to do any damage.

Educate and Inform Users

It is important to establish when and how users will be informed when a virus infection is detected. The seriousness of a virus infection can range for the infection of a single PC up to the infection of the entire corporate network. Your communication plan should include predefined levels of infection severity and the communication network to be implemented at each level. Below is a suggested infection-level hierarchy:

➤ **Level 1 Infection.** The virus is contained to a single PC or small group of PCs and causes minimal or no damage. The virus uses an obscure vulnerability that affects a limited number of systems and is easily repaired.

➤ **Level 2 Infection.** The virus has infected a larger group of machines, including one or more servers. The damage caused is minimal but is a major annoyance. The virus takes advantage of an easily exploited vulnerability in either the desktop or server operating system.

➤ **Level 3 Infection.** This is a major infection, affecting a large number of machines. The vulnerability affects a large number of desktops and/or servers. May cause major damage to infected devices.

As the severity of the infection makes its way up the severity levels, the number of users to be notified must be increased appropriately. Decisions on actions to take to stop the spread of infection become more critical as the severity level increases; by the time the severity reaches level 3, you must disconnect all outside access to and from your networks while the infection is cleaned up and security vulnerabilities fixed.

Once an infection occurs, it is critical to gather as much information as possible concerning the symptoms and possible cure for the virus. A comprehensive and consistent approach to cleaning up the virus is important to ensure that it is completely and properly removed. Users should also be informed on a regular basis about the progress of your efforts to eradicate the virus and when their systems will again be available. As not everyone will have access to e-mail while a virus is being cleaned up, consider using the telephone to keep key users up to date on your progress. If your telephone system supports it, use a recorded message at a predetermined extension that users can call to get the latest information about the virus infection.

ACTION STEPS FOR YOUR PLAN

A major part of your plan must include procedures for containing a virus infection. Once a virus has been detected within the corporate network, the virus containment plan that you've developed must be put into action. The containment plan should include the following activities.

Immediate Action

The following steps must be taken immediately when a virus infection is suspected:

1. Notify the Network Manager. The Network Manager will summon any additional technical assistance required. A primary and secondary contact should be listed here.

2. Determine the scope of the "infection." An initial infection level should be assigned.

3. Notify the business recovery manager if the infection is a level 2 or higher.

4. Notify any other company sites if there is any chance that they might be infected.

Localized Virus Outbreak

A support technician responding to a report of a device problem normally is the first line of virus inspection. Information about each virus incident is reported using Form 18-1, Virus Incident Report, on the CD-ROM. Each support technician must follow the following procedures when a virus is detected.

This will assist in identifying the source to contain it and reduce the opportunity of reinfection.

1. **Identify the Virus.** Once a support technician has identified a virus, they must notify the Network Manager immediately. The virus detection software that found it usually reports the type of virus found. The type of virus found determines the solution to be applied.

2. **Contain the Contamination.** Once the virus has been identified, prompt action is necessary to keep the virus from spreading further. Ask the user the following questions:

   a. When did you first notice these symptoms?

   ➤ Have you recently brought in any programs from outside of those provided by the company?

   ➤ Who have you exchanged files with?

   ➤ What network directories have you used recently?

   ➤ Has anyone else been using your PC?

   b. Check all the other computers in this area for virus infection.

   c. Notify any departments with whom this person has recently exchanged files.

3. **Eliminate the Virus.**

   a. Make a copy of the infected device's directory structure to capture the date and time that files were last changed. The oldest infected file will give an idea of how long the virus has been there.

   b. Clean the virus from the infected device.

   ➤ Perform a power-on boot of the infected device using an anti-virus diskette or program.

   ➤ Monitor the device start-up for error messages.

   ➤ Note the name of any viruses found.

   c. Determine if any files have been destroyed. System files must be replaced or repaired for the device to return to service. Lost data files can be restored from the last data backup copy made. If the user "doesn't bother" with backups, maybe this will make them a believer in the future!

d. Check all the user's diskettes and other removable media. If they have more than 20, the user should be provided with a temporary copy of the virus software so they can check the media themselves.

e. Document each device found to be clean or to have a virus. Turn this list over to the Network Manager.

f. Ensure the users' storage areas on the servers are scanned.

g. If the user exchanges files with any personal devices, loan them a copy of the anti-virus software to scan their personal device and return it within 48 hours.

h. Submit the completed Virus Incident Form (Form 18-1; see CD) to the Network Manager immediately after completing the call.

i. Alert all Network Managers within the corporation about this virus and the user involved so they can determine if they need to check any of their users.

4. Determine the Source of the Virus.

a. In what programs did the virus software find the virus?

b. Ask the user when they first noticed the virus and what had they been using before that.

c. Print a directory structure of the infected device and note any software not purchased by the company and any files that were changed today.

General Virus Outbreak

If there is a widespread virus outbreak, then a company-wide task force is activated to coordinate the response, in addition to following the same steps as the local virus outbreak. The result of every major outbreak is a better understanding of this process. As the virus is attacked, keep good notes of who is doing what and when for a postmortem review. Use the forms in this chapter to provide for consistent data collection and to organize information for quick reference. The cost of clearing up a major outbreak may be covered under the company's Business Interruption insurance, so good records of the hours and any expendable material used is important.

1. Determine That This Is a Widespread Problem. Several virus reports from throughout a facility or department will signal that this is a widespread problem. Most viruses are confined to an individual device or to a local work group. If a virus infestation is suspected of being widespread, the Network Manager contacts the Disaster Recovery Manager and continues with the next steps.

2. **Determine How the Virus Is Being Spread.** This is critical to containing the virus. All servers must be scanned thoroughly to see if the bug is in the network management shared storage areas. Be sure to include all servers in the local vicinity.

3. **Ensure the Backup Media Is Clean.** Identify any data backups that may be infected. They must be scanned by anti-virus software before using.

Many viruses will attach themselves to a network process that is executed as users log onto the service. Anyone who logs onto the network after the central network software is infected will catch the virus. All others will be unaffected.

---

4. **Organize to Eradicate the Virus.** If your company has a large number of devices to check, it is critical to be well organized to minimize the amount of time it will take to check each device. To ensure that all units are checked only once and that none are missed, a Disaster Manager is appointed to coordinate the effort. The Disaster Manager performs the following tasks:

   a. Informs the proper business and data processing management about the problem, how many devices are infected, their location and potential damage. If necessary, the telephone system is used to broadcast messages explaining the situation.

   b. Provides the necessary people resources, to include purchasing of contractor overtime and approval of help desk overtime for this project. Contractor overtime must be coordinated through their home company management and may require an emergency purchase order.

   c. Determines when the technicians will fan out around the facility to address the virus. Each is assigned an area to cover to better maximize resources. Senior technicians are mixed with volunteers to provide quick answers to questions.

d. Coordinate a Post Mortem Review meeting on the second working day after the recovery (the first day after the incident will still be hectic). This is to ensure that the "lessons learned" are captured.

e. Keeps business management informed of the recovery's progress and of the end of the crisis.

f. Coordinates with company security personnel to have locked offices opened.

The Network Manager also plays a critical role in managing the eradication of the virus. This person manages the technical details of this project. The Network Manager's tasks include:

1. During the virus attack:

➤ Manages the people on the project and keeps everyone focused on the task at hand.

➤ Ensures all the technician anti-virus disks are ready to go with the new "token" to indicate that the device has been cleaned. This token is used by the network login process to determine if the device has been cleaned of infection. If the token does not exist on the device at login, the login attempt is refused. The token is an empty file with a specific name. The network logon software is altered to check for the presence of the file before permitting anyone back onto the network.

➤ Scans the servers to locate any infected files, cleans the network drives, and determines the strategy for eliminating the virus.

➤ Changes the network to require the new "token" at sign-in. Determines the proper time to turn this feature on (and prevent anyone else from logging in).

➤ Ensures all the information tracking forms are in place and sufficient copies are made. The technicians need "stay behind" sheets and forms for documenting which devices were unreachable. Good documentation is essential for a proper Post Mortem Analysis.

➤ Reports resources used (time and consumable resources) to Business Interruption Insurance as required.

➤ Gets copies of maps of all affected facilities. The maps will help to ensure that all areas are covered. Keep a master copy of the map at the help desk to indicate those areas already completed. Make copies of the maps for the technicians. The one PC that you miss may reinfect everyone!

➤ Conduct the Technician briefing for everyone who will be working on cleaning the devices. State their tasks clearly. Do not assume they understand what you want accomplished until you explain it to them.

➤ Ensure that all business critical devices are addressed early in the process. Use the help desk's Business Critical Device list and check them off as they are completed.

2. Ongoing tasks:

➤ Maintain the anti-virus plan.

➤ Document incidents, both large and small, to pinpoint areas of virus entry. Use the appropriate network software tools to track activity on the network that might signal the presence of a virus.

➤ Ensure the Anti-Virus Technician packets are ready to go at all times.

➤ Keep anti-virus software up to date, and one copy per kit.

➤ Maintain the network anti-virus software with periodic updates and check it regularly to ensure it functions properly.

➤ Obtain and keep updated maps of the facilities.

➤ Provide ongoing user education and general awareness of the dangers of viruses and forbid them from bringing outside programs and data disks into the facilities.

The help desk also plays a critical role in managing the eradication of the virus. The help desk is the key command and control point for the eradication of the virus and the recovery of the affected devices. The help desk is responsible for:

➤ The help desk technicians will stay at the help desk to coordinate activities, augmented by someone in Operations as required.

➤ The usual help desk traffic will still be coming in and the regular people are essential for this.

➤ If a telephone message system is available, the help desk keeps it updated with a project status message on the hour.

➤ Colors in areas on acetate-covered maps that are cleared of viruses to indicate overall progress.

➤ Maintains the master copy of Technicians working on the project (Form 18-2, Technician Tracking Form; see CD). Anyone joining the project or leaving it must call in to the help desk so that you know who is available.

➤ Maintains the master list of the Infected Devices found (Form 18-3, Infected Devices Form; see CD).

➤ When the project is completed or quits for the night, issues a recall message to all Technicians who have not checked in.

➤ At the end of project, collects from each Technician and consolidates into one report:

    a. Infected Devices (Form 18-3, Infected Devices Form; see CD).

    b. Devices that could not be checked (Form 18-4, Devices Not Checked Form; see CD).

The Technicians are the foot soldiers responsible for going to each device to be checked and cleaned of the virus. The following steps are necessary to support the Technicians in performing this function:

➤ Ask for volunteers from among the regular IT staff.

➤ Ask any contract technicians to stay overtime until the problem is resolved.

➤ Spread out your strong technicians among the volunteers so one will be close at hand to address any difficult technical issues that may arise. If multiple facilities are involved, make sure there is a least one Technician at each location at all times.

➤ Follow Technician instructions (Form 18-5, Technician Instructions Form; see CD).

➤ As required, call corporate security to open locked doors.

3. Creating the "token" file. After the virus has been removed from every device and server, the next step is to ensure any devices that may have been missed in the cleanup not be allowed to connect to the network. One method to do this is to modify the network login process to check for a "token" on the device attempting to make a connection. If the "token" is not there, we assume that the device has not been checked for viruses. The "token" is simply a file that a Technician places in the root directory of the device once it has been checked and pronounced clean. Keep track of the filename used; it must be changed to something else when the next attack occurs.

4. Brief and dispatch the virus cleanup crew. The Network Manager should assemble the Technicians being dispatched to clean up the infected devices and review the action network. The Network Manager should review:

a. What has happened and what is known about the virus.

b. Provide any information on how it happened.

c. Assemble a roster of who is available (Form 18-2, Technician Tracking Form; see CD), and for what hours. Be sure they note their pager or cell phone number on this list. This roster is the key personnel control tool:

➤ When the task is finished, we know who to call back in.

➤ If someone does not call in regularly, we can call them.

➤ Documentation of who was sent to where.

➤ Anyone who leaves early needs to call the help desk to check out of the list.

d. Ensure each person has a pager or some sure method for communicating with the help desk.

e. Pass out copies of the anti-virus software and written instructions of what to do at each device. Provide copies of notices for end users:

➤ Virus OK Notice Form (Form 18-6; see CD).

➤ Virus Alert Form (Form 18-7; see CD).

➤ Virus Warning Form (Form 18-8; see CD).

➤ Devices That Could Not Be Checked (Form 18-4; see CD).

➤ Infected Devices Form (Form 18-3; see CD).

f. Read and explain each item on the Technician Instructions (Form 18-5; see CD). Provide a copy to each person.

g. Priority is given to business critical devices.

h. Assign areas for people to work in. To some extent they can pick areas most familiar to them but concentrate on those areas where devices are the thickest, such as Accounting.

i. Keep in close contact with the help desk so that a Technician can be quickly sent to any problem spots. Some PCs' A: drive may not work so be ready to address these problems are they arise.

5. Next-day actions.

➤ Any device that could not be checked the previous day now cannot get onto the network. Bring in one or two of the Technicians 1 hour early the next day to handle the calls from users who are now "dead in the water."

➤ If you have multiple facilities, make sure you have at least one Technician at each facility to handle any problems.

➤ Ensure there are two qualified people at the help desk to handle calls from people whose devices could not be checked.

➤ Using the same volunteers as the day before, dispatch Technicians to visit all devices that could not be checked the night before.

➤ The Network Manager continues to monitor the situation, crossing off completed devices from the list of units skipped until the calls from users decrease. After lunch, all PCs still on the "skipped" list are logged and a Technician dispatched to fix them.

➤ Update management on the status of virus eradication and resources used. Include a breakdown of hours spent by straight time, overtime, and contractor overtime expense.

➤ Based on the patterns of infected devices found, attempt to determine how the infection originated and who brought it into the facility.

➤ Review how well the process went and fill out the Virus Review Report (Form 18-9; see CD).

CONCLUSION

As long as we connect our computers to the outside world, we will be at risk for a virus infection. While viruses can be difficult to prevent, they can be much more difficult to cure. Your best bet is to make sure you don't get infected in the first place. Some general tips to avoiding getting infected by a virus include:

1. Install virus protection software from any of the well-known virus protection software companies.

2. Keep your virus protection software updated, and make sure it is always on. New viruses are being developed every day.

3. Make sure your virus software starts automatically each time you start your computer, and that it checks for a virus before executing any program.

4. Scan every file before loading or opening any executable file, no matter where it came from. There have been many cases of commercially purchased software being infected.

5. Be suspicious of any executable file received from unknown sources as e-mail attachments. Even attachments received from known sources may be infected, and may in fact have been sent by the virus itself.

6. Disable any auto-run functions in your e-mail software; this includes JavaScript or any executable code.

7. Disable the automatic execution of macros in Word and Excel if you are not using macros.

8. Be very careful when accepting programs or other files during online chat sessions, as this is a common means of spreading viruses.

9. Perform regular system backups so that if a virus does erase or damage a file on your hard drive it can be replaced.

CHAPTER 19

HEALTH AND SAFETY
Keeping Everyone Healthy

Our health always seems much more valuable after we lose it.
—Author Unknown

INTRODUCTION

As stated previously, the goal of this book is to show you a step-by-step approach to analyzing your business situation and building written procedures for avoiding problems or reducing their damage should they occur. Issues that affect the health and safety of your employees and the surrounding community are becoming much more critical as the public becomes more concerned about the environment. This chapter will help you develop plans for protecting everyone from hazards in the workplace.

HEALTH AND SAFETY ISSUES

If you have 10 or more full-time equivalent employees, the Occupational Safety and Health Administration (OSHA) has mandated that you take certain steps to protect the health and welfare of your employees, including preventing foreseeable emergencies and responding to them.

The Environmental Protection Agency (EPA) also requires the development of plans to prevent damage to the environment resulting from business activities. These plans typically require the identification of engineering controls implemented to reduce the probability of an event such as a spill as well as administrative procedures and training for employees. They also require the development of a plan to reduce the impact once a problem arises. Figure 19-1 lists some of the more common emergency plans required by OSHA and the EPA that apply to many companies. This list is not complete for all federal, state, and local requirements. Furthermore, if protecting the business from disasters is important, don't wait for the government to require it.

A first step will be a review of the threshold requirements to each of these rules to see which ones are already required and start with these. (OSHA rules are cited for general industry; comparable Department of Labor rules may exist for construction, longshoring, mining, etc.) To do this, you need to make an inventory of your chemicals, wastes, processes, and confined spaces.

RISK ASSESSMENT

Chemical Hazards

If you are already filing a Tier II report to the EPA, you may have most of the information at your fingertips. If not, use the Material Safety Data Sheets (MSDS) for each chemical to determine if the product contains any of the specific chemicals listed in 1–4 in Figure 19-1. You should develop a data table that includes the product name or part number, chemical ingredients of concern, quantity used annually, quantity stored at one time, and the locations stored. From this list you will be able to determine if certain prevention or response plans may need to be developed.

One of the most fundamental questions you need to ask yourself is "Why do I have all these chemicals anyway?" The best control plan is to plan not to have the chemical. If this isn't feasible, then consider substituting it with a less-dangerous chemical or reducing the quantities stored on-site. Property protection insurers look to the size of the container as a measure of risk. Bigger containers mean bigger risks even if the same quantity of chemical is stored.

As an example, a chemical inventory conducted at your facility shows that you have a 1000-gallon gasoline tank and a 5000-gallon diesel fuel tank for your fleet of vehicles, a paint booth that uses 3800 gallons per month of paints containing no EPA-listed solvents, and seven drums per month of methyl ethyl ketone (MEK), which is used as a paint thinner and cleanup solvent. The cleanup solvent and scrap paint yield six drums per month (about 2500 lb) of liquid waste.

Based upon this information, you determine that EPA requires an SPCC (Spill Prevention Control and Countermeasures) plan and a Hazardous Waste

	Agency	Plan	Subject	Threshold	Citation
1	EPA	RCRA Contingency	Hazardous waste releases	> 1000 kg of hazardous waste per month	40 CFR.262.34
2	EPA	Spill Pevention Control and Countermeasures	Oil spills to water	> Gallons of petroleum products stored above ground or . . . complicated	40 CFR.112
3	EPA	Emergency Planning and Community Right to Know Act	Reporting of environmental releases and coordination with Local Emergency Planning Commission	> Reportable Quantities (RQs) for chemicals	40 CFR.301 - 303
4	EPA and OSHA	Risk Management Plan and Process Safety Mgt.	Certain listed chemicals that have potentially large off-site impacts	> RQ for listed chemicals see rules	40 CFR.68 and 29 CFR 1910.119
5	OSHA	Hazardous Waste Operations and Emergency Response (Hazwopper)	Emergency response – safety of response team	If have a hazwopper team	29 CFR 1910.120
6	OSHA	Emergency Action and Fire Prevention Plan	Fires, emergency notifications and evacuations	If > 10 employees	29 CFR 1910.38
7	OSHA	Confined space rescue	Rescue employees in a confined space	If > 10 employees & if have confined spaces entered by your employees	29 CFR.1910.146
8	OSHA	Vertical standards for specific chemicals	Emergency Plans involving the specific chemical	See individual rules	29 CFR 1910 various chapters

FIGURE 19-1: Federal emergency planning regulations.

Contingency Plan. In addition, you realize that an accidental release of 5000 pounds of MEK would need reporting to various local, state, and federal agencies.

Another kind of chemical release is one that you have control over; operational releases. Say you have a catastrophic failure to an air pollution control device that is required by your operating permits. Due to a lightning strike or fire, the only damage at the facility is this piece of equipment. Your ability to operate the business is unhindered except that you would be out of compliance with your environmental permits. Is this a disaster? You bet! Many air pollution control devices are built to order. Lead times may be months. Many permits are federally enforceable so that even the state does not have the authority to grant waivers. Your only course of action may be to shut down the process for several weeks until you shift production elsewhere or to operate in violation of the law unless you have a plan. It is critical to know your permit; some things to think about when getting your permit include:

1. Try to get flexible terms.

2. Know the malfunction laws.

3. Know the political landscape.

4. Know to whom you need to talk if there's a problem.

5. Know to whom you can switch production in an emergency, and have contracts ready.

6. Know what it takes to replace critical equipment.

7. Have business interruption insurance that specifically addresses the issue.

Employee Fatalities or Multiple Hospitalizations

In addition to the chemical plans, OSHA requires plans that protect people from hazards in the workplace. These include the response to fires, to chemical emergencies (Hazwopper), and to emergencies in confined spaces. All these plans require the same basic elements of identifying the hazards and developing plans to prevent or to mitigate the unwanted outcomes.

No matter whether or not you had identified regulatory requirements for emergency planning, you need to notify OSHA immediately when there has been an occupational or workplace-violence fatality or multiple hospitalizations in the workplace (29 CFR 1910.39). An investigation may begin within a few hours and may continue for weeks. Some manufacturing operations or pieces of machinery may be shut down until the investigation is completed.

A plan to protect employees and the business will include identification of those hazards, the development of engineering controls, administrative procedures, and employee/contractor training. Confined spaces, sources of energy that require energy control, protection, and lockout, fall hazards, machine guarding around presses, robots, shears, gears, etc. all result in numerous occupational hazards. Several of these hazard categories are required to have specific written control plans. A carefully developed plan may be just the tool to identify a hazard that must be identified and abated which otherwise may have killed a valued employee and shut down your business.

For example, you begin the development of a confined spaces entry plan. You inventory spaces that meet the OSHA definition for confined spaces and realize that pits under your presses, chemical storage tanks, a boiler, and the wastewater sewer line all meet the definition. The most likely entry scenarios are identified as well as the unusual. Perhaps the normal entry in the chemical storage tank is cleaning with water during which no hazardous vapors are generated. However, once every 10 years the tanks are lined with an epoxy coating that is applied by hand spraying. This liberates large quantities of potentially dangerous vapors. An employee is overcome. The attendant outside the tank rushes in to help and immediately succumbs to the same vapors. Two are now dead.

Many rescuers have died in confined spaces because they did not have a plan or failed to follow it. The unidentified, invisible, or odorless hazards that placed the first entrant in danger will do the same to the rescue team that is unprepared. For this reason, OSHA requires a written plan and training to the plan. OSHA prefers rescue from outside the space via a retractable lifeline. Whenever this option is feasible, it should be used. It requires identifying the spaces where it can be used, making equipment available, training employees how to use the equipment, etc.

Workplace violence and acts of terrorism are a more and more common form of disaster. Multiple shootings, letters containing anthrax, bomb threats, and more are occurring with greater frequency. The two most important elements of a security program are the creation of a physical barrier to unauthorized entry and a procedure to identify people as they enter the premises. After these two steps are achieved, then higher levels of security can be developed as specific risks are identified.

Off-Site Hazards

One result of the Risk Management Plan (RMP) regulation mentioned in item 4 of Figure 19-1 is that off-site consequences are considered and some information is publicly available. As a result, you can assess some chemical hazards that could occur off your property that may have disastrous effects upon your business. Although the federal government elected not to put detailed information on the Internet, you can quickly find out if an address of interest to you could be affected by a chemical accident at another facility. The most common scenarios are clouds of toxic chemicals or explosions with the ability to cause damage over a great distance. The EPA web page where this **Vulnerable Zone Indicator System (VZIS)** is located is *http://yosemite.epa. gov/oswer/ceppoweb.nsf/frmVZIS?OpenForm*. You can use the VZIS to determine whether the address may be in the vulnerable zone of a facility that submitted a Risk Management Plan (RMP). The RMP rule originally required the development of plans for propane storage. This part of the rule was later withdrawn; however, the off-site consequences of an exploding propane storage tank can be up to a mile.

Major transportation arteries should be considered a risk for hazardous material incidents with the potential of large-scale evacuations. Whether it is a tanker overturned on an icy interstate or a train derailment, when large quantities of chemicals are involved the emergency management authorities will not hesitate to order an evacuation of all downwind and at-risk areas.

For both the RMP scenarios and the transportation incidents, the plans that need to be developed by you are for a safe and orderly shutdown of your business in the event an evacuation is ordered. This plan may be the same you would use for a hurricane or any other incident requiring evacuation. The primary considerations during an evacuation are to protect the people evacuating, to protect anyone reentering the building by shutting down potentially dangerous equipment, and protecting your investments as time permits.

Another off-site incident can be the loss of potable water due to accidental or deliberate contamination of public water supplies or other problems that shut down a municipal water treatment works. How is water used in your facility? How much is used? What quality is required? The answers to these questions may cause you to consider placing contracts for water to be trucked in from another municipality in the event of an emergency. If the neighboring communities all receive water from the same body of water, you may consider having a contract with a company that can get their water from another source, such as a private well or a different lake or river.

Indoor Air Quality Problems

Indoor air quality problems have grown in recent years. The culprits are different but the results are similar. Something has invaded the building that makes it uninhabitable for people. We are not usually thinking about lead-based paint or asbestos insulation. These are knowable and containable when present. What we are focusing on here are those things that scare people because they can't see it or can't see all of it. People begin to complain of respiratory illnesses. They compare notes on everyone they know who has worked here and has cancer or emphysema or asthma. Pretty soon an attorney is involved. Sometimes the culprits can be found and controls installed in the heating and ventilation system to eliminate the problem—radon gas, formaldehyde from carpets and pressed wood, volatile chemicals from copier machines, office chemicals, industrial chemicals, vehicle exhausts, etc.

The newest problems are biological in nature and therefore are more difficult to control because these tiny organisms may remain unhidden and reproduce only to strike again. "Toxic mold" is the name given to many assorted molds and mildews and bacteria that grow on or in building structures. Biological attacks such as the anthrax spores in the Capitol offices are another example. Both can require extensive decontamination and may result in the abandonment of a building.

Indoor air quality concerns may be the result of outside factors such as the anthrax letters, pollution from a neighboring business, or the contractor who is patching the asphalt roof of your building where you didn't turn off the fresh air intake. Or, indoor air quality concerns may be the result of your building design, housekeeping, or processes. Although the causes are many, the symptoms and therefore the plans share many similarities. Generally we are worried about being exposed to something we breathe. Address issues quickly and with concern. Prevent. Investigate. Mitigate. Control it before it controls you.

MITIGATION

Dealing with environmental emergencies often means that some chemical has escaped its desired container or location. You must quickly determine how to stop the ongoing release, assuming some remains, and how to prevent the release from spreading and causing harm.

The EPA may require engineering controls for certain situations, for example, containment dikes that hold 110 percent of the capacity of the largest tank. However, many chemicals are legally stored outside of containment dikes. Other engineering controls include designating storage locations that are not susceptible to damage by forklifts and are placed away from floor drains.

Spill response equipment must be purchased and placed in strategic locations to effectively contain a chemical spill. Determine the types of response equipment required, whether you need to stop leaks in drums or tanks, slow the flow of chemicals across the floor, in a sewer, or down a creek, etc. Ensure spill control materials you select are appropriate for the chemicals you need to control. Some supplies are selective to petroleum products, others to aqueous products. Nonsparking brass tools are needed when responding to spills of materials that may ignite or explode. Acids or bases may react adversely with some metals or rubber.

Notifications to government agencies are required by various rules. Determine which rules require you to notify whom. Notification should be done as soon as it is practical. Definitely notifications should be within minutes if a spill is reaching a public waterway or is off the property or has the potential to harm the environment or people. In all cases, notifications should be made within the work shift when it occurred. The order of notification should be local, then state, then federal. This corresponds with their ability to mobilize in response to the incident.

Not all personal protective equipment (PPE) is created equal. Some may be effective in responding to one chemical or hazard and totally ineffective for another. Check the manufacturers' data for respirators, gloves, chemical-resistant clothing, etc. to determine the exact requirements for the potential hazards you might encounter.

According to OSHA, evacuation should be to a safe area of public access. Local fire codes will dictate how many exits are required from rooms and buildings based upon the occupancy, construction, and other hazards present. Exit routes need to be well marked, even in the event of a power outage. This can be accomplished with battery-powered backups on exit lighting, emergency standby generators, or glow-in-the-dark signage. Some of the problems encountered by OSHA or fire code inspectors are unmarked exits, exits blocked inside or outside, aisle ways blocked, and evacuation routes not up to date with changes to building layouts.

A roll call to account for people may be one of the more difficult tasks, especially for large facilities or those where people frequently come and go. However, as soon as possible after disasters that may have the potential for loss of human life (e.g., fire, tornado, explosion) you need to get a headcount.

If Joe isn't there, is it because he wasn't at work, he left for a doctor's appointment before the explosion, he is on the rescue team and stayed behind as directed, or he is among the casualties? The quicker this can be determined, the quicker the emergency scene will be brought under control and potential danger to other rescuers reduced. Employees need to know they should not leave the property after a disaster until they have been accounted for and dismissed. Employees who left or called in sick might be asked to call in to an emergency number. There have been cases where the missing were presumed casualties and rescue workers continued to search, only to find out the person was safe at home.

DEVELOPING A PLAN

As you first reviewed those categories that EPA and OSHA required you to review, you discovered the focus by the EPA is on off-site environmental impacts and the focus of OSHA is on employee impacts. You must decide for your operation where the business impacts intersect these regulatory categories. In some cases, the regulatory threshold will be sufficiently protective; if you do what is required by the rules, you may deem nothing else is required. Other times, you realize that the regulatory minimum is not enough and that the plan should include more than EPA or OSHA would require.

What can happen here? Tanks leak, containers rupture, incompatible chemicals are mixed, valves are left open, alarms fail, and containment systems leak. Or is the problem people related? The new worker, a new procedure, something changed and somebody was not informed. The contractor's employees couldn't read the warning signs or instructions, either because they could not read or were not fluent in English. These are some of the common scenarios you must consider when developing the plans identified above. What happens once a chemical release begins? Which way will it go? Will it cause an explosion, kill the fish in the creek, or upset the city wastewater treatment plant? Do the neighbors need to be evacuated? Who needs to be evacuated? Let's take a few of these in more detail.

Releases of chemicals can be in the form of solids, liquids, or gases. Gases will disperse the fastest so plans must take this into account. There will be no time to make decisions on the spot if the potential releases could cause explosions or if they are toxic. Evaluate the most likely fault scenarios and make the changes now that will reduce their likelihood. Develop engineering controls such as protective barriers. Create administrative procedures such as using only trained employees and sign-offs. Provide readily available leak detection equipment. Prominently display on the cover of the plan who to call immediately. Two special notes for gases: some gases are heavier than air and seek the lowest levels and may travel long distances at floor level unnoticed until finding a pit, basement, or other lower space. Those gases that are lighter than air rise and disperse. These require different placement for leak detection.

Releases of liquids are the next priority. Again, the characteristics of the specific materials will dictate the response actions. Liquids flow downhill: this means sumps, dikes, etc. can be an effective means to prevent the spread of a release and leak detection equipment can be placed in fewer places. Depending on the liquid, it may or may not evaporate quickly and result in both a gaseous and a liquid release.

Solids may not be thought of as a particularly hazardous physical state. Consider, however, that fine dusts created from grain, grinding operations, etc. can create explosive atmospheres. In addition, spills of solid materials may wash into a drain during a rain event and be quickly transported off the property.

ACTION STEPS FOR YOUR PLAN

Here are things you will need to write your plan. They are in no special order and, of course, you can tailor these items to meet the needs of your site.

1. Begin with your standard plan format. Keep in mind that regulatory requirements may drive the development of your plan to include many things beyond your standard format. Your audience includes the late-shift security staff but may also designate specific persons under the law who act as emergency coordinators or incident commanders who have the full support of management to do whatever it takes to bring the emergency under control. This person may be on-site or on-call depending upon the specific regulatory requirements and your individual circumstances.

2. You need the names of your primary and secondary support people who work at this site, plus the primary and secondary support people whom you can call on from another company site. You may make an arrangement with a professional emergency response team to send people during a disaster. In many cases, their arrival will be hours away so you may need some on-site ability to keep the problem from getting worse before they arrive.

3. Include the chemical maps previously discussed. Use a computer-assisted drafting- (CAD-) generated floor plan to indicate all the main

chemical storage, use, and waste locations on the property and storm and floor drains. Indicate the direction of flow in drains and for the surface around major chemical storage locations. Note the presence of lower levels where liquids or vapors could migrate.

4. Add in the emergency response equipment inventory list with the description for each item. Prepare a checklist of your monitoring, testing and alarm equipment, their location, and how to test them. You may need to preplace some supplies and equipment for use on short notice. Also, in your checklist, include detailed instructions on how to check the devices for use on the spot. Validate the checklist by using someone unfamiliar with it.

5. Identify the Personal Protective Equipment (PPE) required to respond to emergencies. Determine the sizes required for your response team, the quantities required, and the location(s) where they will be stored. Include PPE inventory status on a scheduled inspection. Some equipment may have a limited shelf life. Make sure to rotate supplies so they are effective when needed most.

6. Communication with media, employees, and especially government contacts is critical. If the emergency generated activity on police and fire scanners, then the local news crews can be expected to know of the situation and a phone call or visit on-site will likely come soon. Establish who will be the primary and secondary media contact. This should NOT be your emergency coordinator. You do not want your coordinator pulled away from their duties to answer questions to the media. It is best to have someone who is not a technical expert but rather someone who can handle themselves well in front of a camera or with a reporter. To that end, a response of "I don't know but I can find out" is better than a technical person speaking from the top of their head without preparation and providing information that is played up negatively by the media.

Be careful what you ask for from local governments. Some businesses have called local fire departments or other emergencies agencies for nonemergency assistance such as the use of large fans to exhaust smoke or vapors from a building only to have that department "take control" of the emergency once they are on the scene. Once on the scene, they have a primary job to protect the safety of people, the environment, and properties, not to reestablish your operations as fast as possible. What you thought was go-

ing to be 30 minutes of interruption while you cleared vapors from the building may turn into a 2- or 3-hour ordeal. Having your own equipment or obtaining a source other than the fire department to borrow equipment is the best way to avoid this problem.

After a Disaster

1. Follow up with an incident debriefing. Ask yourself many questions. What were the lessons learned? Could the incident have been prevented? Did the emergency detection and notification systems work? Did we follow the plan? Were the supplies available? Was anyone hurt? Did we have trouble finding out the properties of the chemicals involved? Ask the local emergency responders who were involved for their input as well. Maintain a copy of this report with the incident report. Regulatory agencies want to see that you have learned from the past and are taking precautions to make sure it doesn't happen again. If you fail to learn, history may repeat itself and it may even be worse the next time.

2. Follow up the reports to the regulatory agencies as required. Some of the federal and state laws require a written follow-up once a release has been reported.

3. Update the written emergency plans. Again, some of the federal regulations require plans to be updated following an event where the plan was determined to be inadequate. Usually the updates are expected within 6 months.

Testing

The plans need to be tested. Testing a plan provides the opportunity to learn what might go wrong. Tests don't have to be live drills, they can also be tabletop, "what if" scenarios that are scripted but require those responding to make decisions and consider their consequences. It also compresses time so that an 8-hour exercise may be reduced to just 2 or 3 hours.

Where possible, include your emergency service providers—the local HazMat response team, fire department, or contract service providers. Have someone play the role of the "Live at 6:00" TV news reporter.

Debrief and incorporate the suggestions into the plan where appropriate.

CONCLUSION

As environmental issues become a greater part of the public conscience, protecting the health and safety of your employees and the surrounding community becomes even more important. It is more than just "the right thing to do." A disaster in this area can not only harm employees or the environment, but can put you out of business for a long time if the disaster causes bad publicity and a lengthy investigation by the authorities. Proper planning can protect everyone's health.

CHAPTER 20

TERRORISM
The Wrath of Man

Terrorism: The systematic use of violence as a means
to intimidate or coerce societies or governments.
—WordNet ® 1.6, ©1997 Princeton University

INTRODUCTION

Terrorism has many definitions. In its simplest form, it is a violent action intended to inflict harm on some person or object with the intention of coercing someone in the future to act in a specific way. Terrorists function similarly to a publicity-hungry cinema actress. They will create any spectacle or perform any action to gain attention for their organization or cause.

The other chapters of this book assumed you had some personal knowledge of the nature of the risks your company faced, such as a fire, a power outage, or severe weather. The issues surrounding terrorism are somewhat foreign to many business people, so a brief history is provided. This may help you to better prepare a risk assessment and initiate mitigation actions to protect your employees and your company.

Some governments use terror as a coercive tool to manipulate their own populations. The French Revolution's "Reign of Terror" and Stalin's suppression of the Ukrainian farmers are classic examples. Other masters of this evil action include Hitler and Cambodia's Pol Pot. This is known as state terrorism. Recent exposure of mass graves in Iraq vividly demonstrates that the practice continues in some parts of the world. This type of terrorism generally remains within its own borders. You must be aware of such activities when exporting goods or traveling internationally to such a situation.

Terrorism can be against property as well as people. Some animal lovers have splashed blood on people wearing fur coats. Although somewhat violent, this action is intended to dramatize the killing of animals for their fur and not to permanently harm the fur wearer.

Terrorists seek to magnify their power through the news media. They strive to obtain maximum publicity from the meager means at their disposal. An attack on a "mom & pop" grocery store doesn't have the same impact as attacking the corporate headquarters of a multinational company. In fact, an attack on the store will swing public opinion against the attackers. Many people are apathetic if large companies are attacked, so terrorists focus efforts on them (and also this is where the money is).

Some terrorists look for visible targets where they can avoid detection before and after an attack such as international airports, large cities, major international events, resorts, and high-profile landmarks. Some terrorists are suicidal and committed to die during their attack, such as a suicide bomber. Others mix with the crowds before and after the attack.

The form of a terror attack depends on several factors: the means available, the political issues involved, and weaknesses in the target. The means available refers to the weapons the terror organization has at its disposal. Not everyone is familiar with handling explosives or is an accurate marksman. The political issues refer to what is bothering the person. If they personalize their issue by identifying it in a single individual, then the attack may be sharply focused on that person. Weakness in targets can be from how available they are to how easy it is to commit the crime. A clean getaway is not always a requirement, and an arrest may be one of the goals to further publicize the issue.

Terrorism can be broken down into two primary categories: "domestic" or "international." This distinction refers to the origin of the individuals or groups responsible for it.

Domestic terrorism involves groups or individuals whose terrorist activities are directed at the people of the United States or its government. Domestic terrorists are organized and exist within this country and do not receive any foreign direction or support.

International terrorism involves groups or individuals whose terrorist activities are foreign based. These groups exist outside of our country or are directed or supported by someone outside of our country.

Counter terrorism actions are proactive steps to deter a terrorist attack and to respond quickly. Counter terrorism actions include increased police patrols and fighter aircraft patrolling key cities. Other counter terrorism actions involve police monitoring of suspected terror groups to prevent or protect against an attack.

Antiterrorism steps are defensive in nature and reduce the vulnerability of people and property to terrorist acts. Antiterrorism involves mitigation action to reduce the likelihood of an attack or its damage.

A BRIEF HISTORY

Most terrorist organizations espouse some sort of social or political agenda as a justification for their actions. Terrorism is defined in the Code of Federal Regulations as "the unlawful use of force and violence against persons or property to intimidate or coerce a government, the civilian population, or any segment thereof, in furtherance of political or social objectives." The key elements to remember are violence, intimidation, and coercion.

In 1605, England was in the midst of sectarian strife between Protestant and Catholic. To further their cause, a group of Catholic supporters plotted to blow up the English Parliament as it sat in session. A co-conspirator, Guy Fawkes, managed to stockpile 36 barrels of gunpowder in the cellar of the Parliament building. When authorities were tipped off to the plot, the conspiracy was foiled. Using violence to advance or defend a religion? Bombing of government buildings? Does this sound familiar?

Assassination had long been a method of terrorism. The Guy Fawkes bomb plot against the English Parliament would easily meet our current definition of terrorism. Terrorist groups as we know them began to emerge in the late 19th century in Europe. One of the reasons has been recent changes in technology that have created powerful explosives and weapons that are small and easy to handle. Modern communications ensures new visibility for terrorist groups out of proportion to their actual size.

Some terrorist acts are just a cover for old-fashioned criminal activity such as kidnapping, bank robberies, etc. Jesse James, whose criminal career spanned 20 years, always tried to cast himself as the defender of the common man, all the while robbing and murdering.

The concept of terrorism is more acceptable in some cultures than it is in others. Depending on your point of view, one man's terrorist is another man's patriot. Western culture seems to favor the underdog. Hollywood movies love to show one person (the "common man") overcoming all odds to defeat the undefeatable. Depending on your political point of view, Robin Hood was a protector of the people or a common thief. The same goes for a terrorist. Are they a hero or a murderer?

To magnify the effect of their attack, terrorists depend on widespread public notice of their actions. World leaders are normally as well protected as they want to be. A nation's citizens see themselves as vulnerable to a terrorist action and could potentially apply pressure on their leaders to accommodate them. Playing to this public sentiment is the reason terrorists espouse some form of social or political platform.

One common goal of terrorism is to establish a fear in the population while showing the authorities as incapable of protecting everyone, everywhere, all of the time. The terrorists seek to goad law enforcement authorities into actions that may be viewed as repressive by the population to gain sympathizers or overt supporters for their cause. Their violent actions are combined with political announcements espousing selfless actions (food for the poor, freedom for jailed comrades, or any number of things). Terrorism always tries to cloak itself in some "just" cause, whether true or not. Terrorism sometimes attempts to excuse its indiscriminate violence as attacking those who benefit from whatever evil they are attacking. Fulfilling any demand leads to others because the demand is only a cover for the violence.

Terrorist attacks range from a single impulsive person to a large group and carefully planned actions. A common element is that they are all calculated to gain the greatest impact with minimal resources. We find them throughout history. Some countries have used terrorist threats to extort "protection" money (Barbary pirates), to sell their services (Ninja assassins), or even to intimidate their own population.

Terrorism is different from guerilla warfare. Terrorists attack the opponent's population because they lack the strength to attack their armed forces. Guerilla warfare includes some terrorist actions but is focused on military targets. The main difference between the two is the number of casualties among the general population. Terrorists work for maximum damage, and the guerrillas seeks to establish a "moral" status by minimizing them.

Whether you feel that terrorists are patriots or murderers, in terms of Business Continuity Planning, we don't care what they are. They represent a threat to the ongoing profitability of the business. The risk of a terrorist attack occurring must be assessed and a mitigation plan implemented.

RISK ASSESSMENT

Like any other part of your plan, you must make a risk assessment of the threat to your facilities and employees from terrorism. Based on this risk assessment, a mitigation plan can be assembled to protect your property and improve the safety of your employees. Unfortunately, the nature of terrorism is surprise and, in some instances, the attackers are more than a little mentally unbalanced, so even if you believe you have nothing to fear you should still perform a risk analysis.

On February 29, 1993, a bomb exploded in the parking garage of the World Trade Center in New York City, resulting in the death of five people and thousands of injuries. The crater was 200 by 100 feet and five stories deep.

The first thing to assess is the location of your facility. Begin your risk analysis with an examination of your location. Stand outside and look around. Are you near:

➤ A government building (some people have a grudge against the IRS, for example)?

➤ A landmark whose destruction might have symbolic significance, such as a war memorial, a natural feature, a major bridge, or a famous building?

➤ A defense supplier? An attack on them may close the roads surrounding them and therefore you!

The definition of what is "too near" is up to you. If one of these facilities were attacked nearby, how disruptive would it be to your business? At a minimum, the streets around the target would be blocked for rescue teams and then, later, investigations. If you are several city blocks away and there are many avenues of approach, you should be all right. If the potential target is next door, then there is a risk.

Your mitigation plan for your location is to:

➤ Identify ways to keep your business open if a nearby attack occurs. You may need to provide information on alternate access routes to suppliers or customers. In general, it would be difficult to move your location, but you can pay close attention to who your neighbors are and who may be considering relocating to your vicinity.

➤ Another mitigation action may be to provide some separation or barrier between your building and a close neighbor who may be a target. Concrete walls may slow down a fire or the blast of an explosion. Ensure vulnerable spaces within your facility (such as your computer room) are not located on the side of the building toward the potential target.

➤ If you are in a large building that also houses potential targets, consider relocating to another building. If you cannot relocate, can you move out your most sensitive operations?

What goods or services does your company provide? Sometimes seemingly innocent lines of business can attract violent protest. Sometimes peaceful protest can turn violent if demands go unfilled and the people involved feel threatened by something. What is the risk that the products or services provided by your company will make it a target?

"On September 9, 1980, the "Plowshares Eight" carried out the first of what have come to be known as plowshares actions. Eight peacemakers entered the General Electric plant in King of Prussia, PA, where the nose cones from the Mark 12-A nuclear warheads were manufactured. With hammers and blood they enacted the biblical prophecies of Isaiah (2:4) and Micah (4:3) to "beat swords into plowshares" by hammering on two of the nose cones and pouring blood on documents."

(*Source:* From a web site maintained by the organization "Swords into Plowshares" http://www.plowsharesactions.org/webpages/webintro2.htm).

Organizations that may be in danger include the following:

1. **Police or Military Suppliers.** Some people feel that suppliers of military goods are contributing to the violence between nations, while others are thankful for a strong defense industry. If you directly or indirectly supply goods to the military or even police departments, this may place you in the sights of a terrorist. In the previous example, a supplier of components for nuclear weapons could attract antiwar as well as environmental issues protesters.

2. **Controversial Businesses.** Some businesses can raise the emotions of people by the mention of their name. One of these controversial businesses is women's health clinics that perform abortions. Whatever your

opinion of this service, these facilities have over the years been the target of violent attacks. Is such a facility near you?

Animal rights groups have targeted fur coats as unethical and have publicly attacked people wearing them by splashing blood on the coat and the person wearing it. Other animal rights groups include those that believe that dolphins are killed and discarded during tuna fishing, those in opposition to some livestock farming practices, and on and on. Unless you are the first target, you can gain some insight into how controversial your business is to some group by regularly monitoring news broadcasts and your industry-specific media.

3. **Government Buildings.** The infamous attack on the Murrah Federal Building in Oklahoma City in 1995 was a violent protest against U.S. government policies. Whatever the reason, government offices will remain a target of violent protest in the future. Sometimes these buildings rent excess space to other companies. If you are in such a building, consider what the risks may be and how they might be mitigated.

Another potential source of terrorism is your employees. Some things to consider when evaluating the potential for terrorism include:

1. **Who Are Your Employees?** Even with a proper screening, employees can be a source of risk of domestic terrorism. Sometimes crime can be an act of opportunity and they are already inside your facility. It is important that all employees are screened before hiring and monitored for unusual behavior.

2. **Security for Your Employees.** An important counter terrorism is your facility's security. But all life (for most of us) is not within your company's four walls. People drive to and from work and around their community. Train your employees, and specifically your executives, to watch for suspicious behavior. Kidnapping is a high-profile crime that a terrorist can use for daily publicity.

An easy action is to vary your travel times. When traveling away from the facility, keep your itinerary vague, including departure and arrival times, flight number, etc. In smaller airports this may be more difficult.

When traveling away from your facility, there are some simple steps to take that will lessen the likelihood that you will be caught up in a terrorist attack.

1. **Avoid Crowds.** Crowds are easy to find; just look at an airport's luggage carrousel. People crowd around waiting for their bags. Instead of joining the crowd, select a point off to the side or where the crowd is the thinnest to watch for your bags. Crowds are easy to find at public venues such as sports events and other gatherings. In 1996, a bomb was placed near a sound stage during the Olympic Games in Atlanta. Keep on the lookout for people acting suspiciously. Other crowded places that have previously attracted terrorists include nightclubs and theaters.

2. **Dress to Blend in.** Do you look as if you belong there or are you obviously a traveler? Try to look unimportant and focused on where you are going.

3. **Avoid Unattended Parcels or Baggage.** The 1996 Atlanta bomb was in a knapsack. Although people sometimes carelessly discard parcels or even forget things, if you see a package and no one is around, alert the police. Never accept packages from strangers.

4. **If You Are Driving in a Strange City.** Consider hiring a local driver or security company to move you around.

5. **Always Be Alert and Aware of Your Surroundings.** The nature of terrorism suggests there will be little or no warning. Take a few moments to see where the emergency exits and staircases are and consider how you might exit a congested area quickly.

A terrorist attack can take several forms, depending on the technology available to the attacker, the nature of the political issue motivating the attack, and the points of weakness of the target. Therefore the goal is to identify and eliminate the points of weakness to protect your facility. Some items to consider include:

1. **Enforce Your Security Plan.** Most companies use security guards to ensure that only employees can enter. Sometimes this is as basic as a receptionist with a remote switch for opening the entrance door. Ensure that only properly identified personnel can enter the facility. Even if the front door is locked and well protected, often the receiving dock in the rear of the building is wide open! A chain is only as strong as its weakest link.

2. **Ensure Everyone Understands the Evacuation Procedures.** Depending on the circumstances, you may want to take shelter within the building (storm shelter) or evacuate outward. If there was a problem outside your building, it would not be a good idea for everyone to exit according to the

normal evacuation plan. It might be better to move them away from the walls in question or to direct everyone out a specific side of the building.

3. **Bomb Threats.** Your security plan should contain detailed instructions on what to do when a bomb threat is received. Try to get as much information from the caller as you can and *write it all down as it is said.* Notify the police and the facility management immediately.

Information on what to do when a threat is received should placed at all "public" inbound numbers such as switchboard, receptionist, help desk, or 800 numbers. Time should be set aside to train everyone how to fill out the form and the best way to react to a threat.

In most cases, the building should be promptly evacuated using your evacuation procedures.

➤ Ensure the people standing outside do not block access routes for emergency vehicles. Avoid standing in front of windows in case the bomb blows glass shards out onto the people.

➤ Avoid suspicious packages and keep everyone else away from them.

Sometimes, the use of bombs is a matter of how convenient your building is. Permitting parking immediately adjacent to your building could set the scene for a vehicle-transported bomb, as in the case of the 1995 Oklahoma City bomb. In the 1993 vehicle-transported bomb attack against the World Trade Center, the vehicle was parked in the lower-level parking garage.

To reduce the likelihood of an explosive-filled vehicle destroying your facility, do not allow anyone to park near the building. In the case of under-building parking garages, place strong steel bars across the door opening so that only passenger vehicles can enter (no trucks). Install large obstacles around the main entrance (often large cement planters holding trees) to reduce the likelihood that someone could drive straight into the building.

Install heavy curtains with weighted bottoms to cover windows. This will reduce the amount of inward flying glass from an explosion outside your building.

Some facilities and public buildings have removed trash cans from outside their structure. Trash cans are an easy place to dump a bomb disguised as a discarded box.

Your employees are an important line of defense in detecting terrorist activity. Educate your employees by doing the following:

1. **Explain the Importance of Your Facility's Security Program and Ask for Their Help.** You can't be everywhere but your employees are. Teach them what to look for. How would you describe a person acting suspiciously? What should they do if they see an unattended parcel? Do they keep their packages with them or properly stowed away? How much of this training your employees should have is based on your risk assessment of an attack. If you are a high-risk target, then they should be very involved. If the employees understand how the security process benefits them, they will be more inclined to actively support it.

2. **Report Suspicious Activity to Police.** Explain how to file a police report of suspicious activity. The police need the traditional facts of who, what, where, when, why, and how. Your security policies should provide guidelines on who should file police reports. The policy might require all observations to be confirmed by a second person before reporting. Your security policy might require that a security supervisor investigate before calling in law enforcement. Perhaps an incident report form would be helpful to gather the details.

3. **Report All Threats to Police.** The old saying is that barking dogs don't bite. However, a threat is not a time to gamble whether it was real or not. All threats should be reported immediately to the police. The police will also want to know how the threat was transmitted to you, when you received it, etc. You might add these fields to your incident report form.

The next step is to determine what the Homeland Security Threat Levels mean to you. Based on their intelligence sources, the Office of Homeland Security issues changes to their threat level (see end of this chapter). Given your assessment of the risks to your facility, what will this mean to your company? You may establish contingency plans based on elevated threat levels if your situation is risky. These might be to increase security patrols, temporarily close some operations, or to confine all freight pickups and deliveries to a few hours of the day.

You should also check your insurance coverage. Just exactly what sort of threats does your insurance cover? Are you covered against a terrorist attack? In the aftermath of the attack on September 11, 2002, some insurance companies invoked the war clause, which states that no losses are covered due to war. This statement was inadvertently supported by the government when they declared a "War on Terrorism."

Check with your insurance company to determine what is and what is not covered. In general, domestic terrorism is covered as a criminal action. However, international terrorism may not be covered. Now is the time to find out.

HOMELAND SECURITY ADVISORY SYSTEM

1. Low Condition (Green). This condition is declared when there is a low risk of terrorist attacks. Federal departments and agencies should consider the following general measures in addition to the agency-specific Protective Measures they develop and implement:

➤ Refining and exercising as appropriate preplanned Protective Measures.

➤ Ensuring personnel receive proper training on the Homeland Security Advisory System and specific preplanned department or agency Protective Measures.

➤ Institutionalizing a process to ensure that all facilities and regulated sectors are regularly assessed for vulnerabilities to terrorist attacks and that all reasonable measures are taken to mitigate these vulnerabilities.

2. Guarded Condition (Blue). This condition is declared when there is a general risk of terrorist attacks. In addition to the Protective Measures taken in the previous Threat Condition, federal departments and agencies should consider the following general measures in addition to the agency-specific Protective Measures that they will develop and implement:

➤ Checking communications with designated emergency response or command locations.

➤ Reviewing and updating emergency response procedures.

➤ Providing the public with any information that would strengthen its ability to act appropriately.

3. Elevated Condition (Yellow). An Elevated Condition is declared when there is a significant risk of terrorist attacks. In addition to the Protective Measures taken in the previous Threat Conditions, federal departments and agencies should consider the following general measures in addition to the Protective Measures that they will develop and implement:

➤ Increasing surveillance of critical locations.

➤ Coordinating emergency plans as appropriate with nearby jurisdictions.

➤ Assessing whether the precise characteristics of the threat require the further refinement of preplanned protective measures.

➤ Implementing, as appropriate, contingency and emergency response plans.

4. **High Condition (Orange).** A High Condition is declared when there is a high risk of terrorist attacks.

➤ Coordinating necessary security efforts with federal, state, and local law enforcement agencies or any National Guard or other appropriate armed forces organizations.

➤ Taking additional precautions at public events and possibly considering alternative venues or even cancellation.

➤ Preparing to execute contingency procedures, such as moving to an alternate site or dispersing their workforce.

➤ Restricting threatened facility access to essential personnel only.

5. **Severe Condition (Red).** A Severe Condition reflects a severe risk of terrorist attacks. Under most circumstances, the Protective Measures for a Severe Condition are not intended to be sustained for substantial periods of time.

➤ Increasing or redirecting personnel to address critical emergency needs.

➤ Assigning emergency response personnel and prepositioning and mobilizing specially trained teams or resources.

➤ Monitoring, redirecting, or constraining transportation systems.

➤ Closing public and government facilities.

Source: Department of Homeland Security *www.dhs.gov/dhspublic/*.

CONCLUSION

While terrorism is not a new threat, until recently the threat of terrorism was miniscule in the U.S. Recent political events have made this a threat that you need to consider when developing your disaster recovery plan. Even if you are unlikely to be a target, your neighbors might be. The world has become a scarier place, and you must be aware of your surroundings to keep safe.

HELPFUL WEB SITES FOR DISASTER RECOVERY

In addition to this book, there is a wide range of help available for building your disaster recovery plan. Help is available from local, state and federal governments, from emergency agencies, and from trade organizations. The resources listed below will give you a start in finding resources in your area.

Government

www.fema.gov
www.emergencymanagement.org/states
www.sba.gov/disaster

Industry Resources

www.drj.com
www.contingencyplanning.com
www.disasterrecoveryworld.com
www.drie.org
www.dr.org
www.acp-international.com

Restoration

www.bmscat.com
www.documentreprocessors.com
www.servpro.com

Human Resources

http://helping.apa.org/therapy/
    traumaticstress.html

www.redcross.org
www.psych.org

Recovery Space

www.fireproof.com
www.rentsys.com

Internet Backups

www.backvault.com
www.backup.com

Government Agencies

Federal Agencies

Federal Emergency Management
    Agency (FEMA)
National Headquarters
Tel: (202) 566-1600

➤ Region I, Kenneth L. Horak
    (MA, CT, ME, NH, RI, VT)
    Tel: (617) 223-9540 Fax: (617) 223-9519

➤ Region II, Joseph F. Picciano
(NY, NJ, Puerto Rico, Virgin Islands)
Tel: (212) 225-7209 Fax: (212) 225-7281

➤ Region III, Peter G. Cole
(PA, MD, DE, VA, WV, DC)
Tel: (215) 931-5608 Fax: (215) 931-5621

➤ Region IV, Mary Lynne Miller
(GA, AL, FL, KY, MS, NC, SC, TN)
Tel: (770) 220-5200 Fax: (770) 220-5230

➤ Region V, Janet M. Odeshoo
(IL, IN, MN, MI, OH, WI)
Tel: (312) 408-5501 Fax: (312) 408-5234

➤ Region VI, Gary E. Jones
(TX, AR, LA, NM, OK)
Tel: (940) 898-5104 Fax: (940) 898-5325

➤ Region VII, Arthur Freeman
(MO, IA, KS, NE)
Tel: (816) 283-7054 x7061
Fax: (816) 283-7582

➤ Region VIII, Douglas Gore
(CO, MT, ND, SD, UT, WY)
Tel: (303) 235-4800 x4812
Fax: (303) 235-4976

➤ Region IX, Karen Armes
(CA, AZ, HI, NV, Pacific Island Trust
Territories)
Tel: (415) 923-7100
Fax: (415) 923-7112

➤ Region X, Tamara Doherty
(AK, ID, OR, WA)
Tel: (425) 487-4604 Fax: (425) 487-4622

US GEOLOGICAL SURVEY NATL
EARTHQUAKE INFORMATION CENTER
Tel: (303) 273-8500
www.earthquake.usgs.gov

State Agencies

ALABAMA
State Of Alabama, EM
Lee Helms, Acting Asst Director
5898 County Road 41
Clanton, AL 35046-2160
Tel: (205) 280-2200 Fax: (205) 280-2410
E-mail: info@aema.state.al.us
www.aema.state.al.us/

ALASKA
State Of Alaska, Emergency Services
David Liebersbach, Director
PO Box 5750
Ft. Richardson, AK 99505-5750
Tel: (907) 428-7000 Fax: (907) 428-7009
E-mail: dave_liebersbach@ak-prepared.com
www.ak-prepared.com/

ARIZONA
State Of Arizona, EMA
Michael Austin, Director
5636 E. McDowell Road
Phoenix, AZ 85008
Tel: (602) 244-0504 Fax: (602) 231-6271
E-mail: austinm@dem.state.az.us
www.dem.state.az.us

ARKANSAS
State Of Arkansas, EMA
Bud Harper, Director
PO Box 758
Conway, AR 72033
Tel: (501) 730-9750 Fax: (501) 730-9754
E-mail: wharper@adem.state.ar.us
www.oes.state.ar.us/

CALIFORNIA
State Of California, OES
Dallas Jones, Director
2800 Meadowview Road
Sacramento, CA 95832
Tel: (916) 262-1816 Fax: (916) 262-1677
E-mail: dallas_jones@oes.ca.gov
www.oes.ca.gov

COLORADO
State Of Colorado, EMA
Tom Grier, Director
15075 S. Golden Rd.
Golden, CO 80401-3979
Tel: (303) 273-1622 Fax: (303) 273-1795
E-mail: tom.grier@state.co.us
www.state.co.us/gov_dir/loc_affairs_
dir/oem.htm

CONNECTICUT
State Of Connecticut, OEM
John Wiltse, Director
360 Broad Street
Hartford, CT 06105
Tel: (860) 566-3180 Fax: (860) 247-0664
E-mail: Jkahn.ctoem@juno.com
www.mil.state.ct.us/oem.htm

DELAWARE
State Of Delaware, EMA
John Mulhern, Director
165 Brick Store Landing
Myrna, DE 19977
Tel: (302) 659-3362 Fax: (302) 659-6855
E-mail: jmulhern@state.de.us
www.state.de.us/dema

FLORIDA
State Of Florida, EMA
Joseph Myers, Director
2555 Shumard Oak Blvd.
Tallahassee, FL 32399-2100
Tel: (850) 413-9886 Fax: (850) 488-1016
E-mail: myersj@dca.state.fl.us
www.floridadisaster.org

GEORGIA
State Of Georgia, EMA
Gary McConnell, Director
P.O. Box 18055
Atlanta, GA 30316-0055
Tel: (404) 635-7000 Fax: (404) 635-7205
E-mail: vbarfleft@gema.state.ga.us
www.State.Ga.US/GEMA/

HAWAII
State Of Hawaii EM
Edward Correa, Director
3949 Diamond Head Road
Honolulu, HI 96816-4495
Tel: (808) 733-4300 Fax: (808) 733-4238
www.scd.state.hi.us/

IDAHO
State Of Idaho, Disaster Services
John Cline, Director
4040 Gard St., Bldg. 600
Boise, ID 83705
Tel: (208) 334-3460 Fax: (208) 334-2322
E-mail: jcline@bds.state.id.us
www.state.id.us/bds/bds.html

ILLINOIS
State Of Illinois, EMA
Mike Chamness, Director
110 E. Adams St.
Springfield, IL 62701-1109
Tel: (217) 782-7860 Fax: (217) 782-2589
E-mail: mchamnes@iema.state.il.us
www.state.il.us/iema/

INDIANA
State Of Indiana, EMA
Patrick Ralston, Executive Director
302 West Washington, Room E208
Indianapolis, IN 46204
Tel: (317) 232-3986 Fax: (317) 232-3985
E-mail: pralston@sema.state.in.us
www.sema.state.in.us

IOWA
State Of Iowa, Disaster Services
Ellen Gordon, Director
Hoover State Office Bldg. Level A
Des Moines, IA 50319
Tel: (515) 281-3231 Fax: (515) 281-7539
E-mail: ellen.gordon@emd.state.ia.us
www.state.ia.us/government/dpd/emd/
    index.htm

KANSAS
State Of Kansas, EM
Gene Krase, Director
2800 SW Topeka Blvd
Topeka, KS 66611-1287
Tel: (913) 274-1409 Fax: (913) 274-1426
E-mail: Immarcum@gtop.wpo.state.ks.us
www.ink.org/public/kdem/

KENTUCKY
State Of Kentucky, EMD
Ronn Padgett, Executive Director
100 Minuteman Parkway
Frankfort, KY 40601-6168
Tel: (502) 607-1682 Fax: (502) 607-1251
E-mail: rpadgett@kydes.dma.state.ky.us
www.webserve.dmd.state.ky.us

LOUISIANA
State Of Louisiana, Emergency
    Preparedness
Michael Brown, Director
P.O. Box 44217
Baton Rouge, LA 70804-4217
Tel: (225) 342-1588 Fax: (225) 342-5471
E-mail: sburr@hotmail.com
www.loep.state.la.us

MAINE
State Of Maine, EMA
Arthur Cleaver, Director
72 State House Station
Augusta, ME 04333-0072
Tel: (207) 626-4503 Fax: (207) 626-4495
E-mail: art.w.cleavef@state.me.us
www.state.me.us/mema/memahome.htm

MARYLAND
State Of Maryland EMA
David McMillion, Director
5401 Rue St. Lo Drive
Reisterstown, MD 21136
Tel: (410) 517-3625 Fax: (410) 517-3610
E-mail: dmcmillion@mema.state.md.us
www.mema.state.md.us/

MASSACHUSETTS
State Of Massachusetts, EMA
Stephen McGrail
400 Worcester Road
Framingham, MA 01702-5399
Tel: (508) 820-2000 Fax: (508) 820-2030
E-mail: stephen.mcgrail@state.ma.us
www.magnet.state.ma.us/mema/
   homepage.htm

MICHIGAN
State Of Michigan, EMD
Captain Edward Buikema
4000 Collins Rd.
Lansing, MI 48909
Tel: (517) 333-5042 Fax: (517) 333-4987
E-mail: buikemae@state.mi.us
www.msp.state.mi.us/division/emd/
   emdweb1.htm

MINNESOTA
State Of Minnesota, EMA
Kevin Leuer, Director
444 Cedar Street Ste. 223
St. Paul, MN 55101-6223
Tel: (651) 296-0450 Fax: (651) 296-0459
E-mail: kevin.leuer@state.mn.us
www.dem.state.mn.us

MISSISSIPPI
State Of Mississippi, EMA
Robert Latham Jr., Director
P.O. Box 4501
Jackson, MS 39296-4501
Tel: (601) 352-9100 Fax: (601) 352-8314
E-mail: mema@sun1.its.state.ms.us
www.mema.state.ms.us

MISSOURI
State Of Missouri, EMA
Jerry Uhlmann, Director
PO Box 116
Jefferson City, MO 65102
Tel: (573) 526-9100 Fax: (573) 634-7966
E-mail: juhlmann@mail.state.mo.us
www.sema.state.mo.us/semapage.htm

MONTANA
State Of Montana, Disaster Services
John Prendergast
1100 N. Main, PO Box 4789
Helena, MT 59604-4789
Tel: (406) 841-3911 Fax: (406) 841-3965
Email: jigreene@state.mt.us
www.state.mt.us

NEBRASKA
State Of Nebraska, Civil Defense
Al Berndt, Director
1300 Military Rd.
Lincoln, NE 68508-1090
Tel: (402) 471-7410 Fax: (402) 471-7433
www.nebema.org

NEVADA
State Of Nevada, EMA
Frank Siracusa, Director
2525 S. Carson Street
Carson City, NV 89711
Tel: (775) 687-4240 Fax: (775) 687-6788
E-mail: fss@quik.com

NEW HAMPSHIRE
State Of New Hampshire, OEM
Woody Fogg, Director
107 Pleasant Street
Concord, NH 03301-3809
Tel: (603) 271-2231 Fax: (603) 225-7341
Email: Pennw@nhoem.state.nh.us
www.nhoem.state.nh.us/

NEW JERSEY
State Of New Jersey, OEM
Carson Dumbar, Director
NJ State Police, Box 7068
West Trenton, NJ 08628
Tel: (609) 538-6051 Fax: (609) 538-0345

NEW MEXICO
State Of New Mexico, EM
Ernesto Rodriguez, Director
P.O. Box 1628
Santa Fe, NM 87504-1628
Tel: (505) 476-9606 Fax: (505) 471-5922
E-mail: erodriguez@dps.state.nm.us
www.dps.nm.org/emc.htm

NEW YORK
State Of New York, EMA
Ed Jacoby, Director
1220 Washington Ave. Bldg. 22 Ste. 101
Albany, NY 12226-2251

Tel: (518) 457-2222 Fax: (518) 457-9995
E-mail: edward.jacoby@semo.state.ny.us
www.semo.state.ny.us

NORTH CAROLINA
State Of North Carolina, EMA
Eric Tolbert, Director
116 W. Jones Street
Raleigh, NC 27603-1335
Tel: (919) 733-3825 Fax: (919) 733-5406
E-mail: etolbert@ncem.org
www.ncem.org

NORTH DAKOTA
State Of North Dakota, EMA
Douglas Friez, Director
PO Box 5511
Bismarck, ND 58506
Tel: (701) 328-8100 Fax: (701) 328-8181
E-mail: dfriez@state.nd.us
www.state.nd.us/dem

OHIO
State Of Ohio, EMA
JR Thomas, Director
2855 West Dublin-Granville Rd.
Columbus, OH 43235-2206
Tel: (614) 469-9700 Fax: (614) 221-9594
E-mail: jwilliams@dps.state.oh.us
www.emafc.com

OKLAHOMA
State Of Oklahoma, EMA
Albert Ashwood, Director
PO Box 53365
Oklahoma City, OK 73152
Tel: (405) 521-2481 Fax: (405) 521-4053
E-mail: albert.ashwood@vem.state.ok.us
www.vem.state.ok.us

OREGON
State Of Oregon, EMA
Myra Thompson Lee, Director
595 Cottage St., SE
Salem, OR 97301
Tel: (503) 378-4124 Fax: (503) 588-1378
E-mail: mlee@oem.state.or.us
www.osp.state.or.us/oem

PENNSYLVANIA
State Of Pennsylvania, EMA
David Smith, Director
2605 Interstate Dr.
Harrisburg, PA 17110-9364

Tel: (717) 651-2001 Fax: (717) 651-2040
E-mail: davfmith@state.pa.us
www.pema.state.pa.us

RHODE ISLAND
State Of Rhode Island, EMA
Albert Scappaticci, Director
645 New London Ave.
Cranston, RI 02920
Tel: (401) 946-9996 Fax: (401) 944-1891
E-mail: CentracchioR@ri-arng.ngb
  .army.mil
www.state.ri.us/riema/riemaaa.html

SOUTH CAROLINA
State Of South Carolina, EMA
Stan McKinney, Director
1429 Senate Street
Columbia, SC 29201
Tel: (803) 734-8020 Fax: (803) 734-8062
E-mail: mckinney@strider.epd.state.sc.us
www.state.sc.us/epd/

SOUTH DAKOTA
State Of South Dakota, Emergency Services
John Berheim, Director
500 E. Capitol
Pierre, SD 57501
Tel: (605) 773-3231 Fax: (605) 773-3580
E-mail: myainfo@state.sd.us
www.state.sd.us/state/executive/military/
  military.html

TENNESSEE
State Of Tennessee, EMA
John White, Chief Operations
3041 Sidco
Nashville, TN 37204-1502
Tel: (615) 741-0001 Fax: (615) 242-9635
www.tnema.org

TEXAS
State Of Texas, EMA
Tom Millwee
5805 N. Lamar Blvd.
Austin, TX 78752
Tel: (512) 424-2430 Fax: (512) 424-2444
E-mail: tom.millwee@txdps.state.tx.us
www.txdps.state.tx.us/dem/

UTAH
State Of Utah, EMA
Scott Behunin, Director
State Office Bldg. Rm. 1110
Salt Lake City, UT 84114-1710

Tel: (801) 538-3400 Fax: (801) 538-3770
E-mail: frontdesk@dps.state.ut.us
www.dps.state.ut.us

VERMONT
State Of Vermont, EMA
Edward Von Turkovich, Director
103 S. Main Street
Waterbury, VT 05671-2101
Tel: (802) 244-8721 Fax: (802) 241-5556
E-mail: webmaster@dps.state.vt.us
www.dps.state.vt.us

VIRGINIA
State Of Virginia, Emergency Services
Michael Cline, State Coordinator
10501 Trade Court
Richmond, VA 23226
Tel: (804) 897-6504 Fax: (804) 897-6506
E-mail: mcline.des@state.va.us
www.state.va.us

WASHINGTON
State Of Washington, EMA
Glenn Woodbury, Director
P.O. Box 40955
Olympia, WA 98504-0955
Tel: (253) 512-7000 Fax: (253) 512-7207
www.wa.gov/mil/wsem/

WEST VIRGINIA
State Of West Virgina, OES
John Pack, Director
1900 Kanawha Blvd., Bldg 1, Room E-B80
Charleston, WV 25305
Tel: (304) 558-5380 Fax: (304) 344-4538
E-mail: jpack1@wzoes.state.wv.us
www.state.wv.us/wvoes

WISCONSIN
State Of Wisconsin, EMA
Edward Gleason, Director
2400 Wright St.
Madison, WI 53707-7865
Tel: (608) 242-3232 Fax: (608) 242-3247
E-mail: gleasone@dma.state.wi.us
www.dma.state.wi.us

WYOMING
State Of Wyoming, EMA
Robert Bezek, Director
5500 Bishop Blvd.
Cheyenne, WY 82009-3320
Tel: (307) 777-4900 Fax: (307) 635-6017
E-mail: wema@wy-arng.ngb.army.mil
http://132.133.10.9/

INDEX

ABOUT THE AUTHORS

MICHAEL WALLACE has 21 years of experience in the information systems and business consulting field. He began his career after graduation from Lima Technical College as a mainframe operator for Super Food Services, and then moved to a programming position at Reynolds+Reynolds.

He became a consultant after graduating magna cum laude from Wright State University with a Bachelor of Science degree in Management Science. He recently received his MBA from The Ohio State University. Mr. Wallace has been an application developer, system analyst, technical and business consultant, and recently assisted the State of Ohio in developing statewide IT policies.

Mr. Wallace is currently President of Q Consulting, an IT management and disaster recovery consulting firm. Q Consulting provides its clients with the thought leadership of years of accumulated experience and unparalleled experience in assisting companies with system strategies, policies and procedures, and system implementation through a proven methodology that provides effective and affordable solutions to our clients.

Mr. Wallace is a Microsoft Certified Professional, a past Vice President of the Columbus Computer Society, and has served on the board of directors of various computer organizations. He is presently a member of the Contingency Planners of Ohio and the Project Management Institute.

Mr. Wallace can be reached by e-mail at michaelw@qconsulting.biz.

LAWRENCE WEBBER has more than 25 years experience in the information services field. He began his career in the U.S. Marine Corps as a digital network repairman and then moved to a position as a COBOL programmer supporting the Marines' Logistics traffic management systems.

After his release from active service, he worked as a COBOL programmer on an IBM mainframe for Waddell & Reed in Kansas City before moving on to program factory support systems on a UNIVAC system at Temperature Industries. During his tenure at United Telecommunications in Kansas City, he rose to the position of Manager of the Information Centers, providing mainframe and personal computer support to four mainframe data centers and nine subsidiary telephone companies.

His next position was as Applications Manager at the law offices of Shook, Hardy & Bacon where he migrated a Data General professional services accounting system to a DEC cluster. He also migrated the 600+ person office from standalone IBM magnetic card machines to a PC LAN-based word processing network.

For the next 12 years, Mr. Webber held various systems engineering and data processing management positions with Navistar International Truck and Bus in Springfield, OH, where, among other achievements, he authored an extensive data systems Disaster Recovery plan for the 2-million-square-foot manufacturing facility. He is currently a Project Manager and Six Sigma Black Belt consultant.

Mr. Webber has an Associate in Science degree from Darton College in Albany, GA, in Data Processing, a Bachelor of Science degree in Business Administration and an MBA, both from Rockhurst University in Kansas City, MO, and an Associate in Science degree in Industrial Engineering from Sinclair Community College in Dayton, OH. He recently completed a Master of Project Management degree from West Carolina University.

Mr. Webber is a former Marine and retired from the U.S. Army Reserve as a First Sergeant in the Infantry. He is a certified Project Management Professional by the Project Management Institute, Certified in Production and Inventory Management by APICS, and is a Microsoft Certified Professional.

Mr. Webber can be reached by e-mail at lwebber@cfanet.com.